Organisational Change

PEARSON
Education

We work with leading authors to develop the strongest
educational materials in business and management,
bringing cutting-edge thinking and best learning practice
to a global market.

Under a range of well-known imprints, including
Financial Times Prentice Hall, we craft high quality print
and electronic publications which help readers to
understand and apply their content, whether studying
or at work.

To find out more about the complete range of our
publishing, please visit us on the World Wide Web at:
www.pearsoned.co.uk

Second Edition

Organisational Change

Barbara Senior

FT Prentice Hall
FINANCIAL TIMES

An imprint of **Pearson Education**
Harlow, England • London • New York • Boston • San Francisco • Toronto • Sydney • Singapore • Hong Kong
Tokyo • Seoul • Taipei • New Delhi • Cape Town • Madrid • Mexico City • Amsterdam • Munich • Paris • Milan

Pearson Education Limited
Edinburgh Gate
Harlow
Essex CM20 2JE
England

and Associated Companies throughout the world

Visit us on the World Wide Web at:
www.pearsoned.co.uk

First published 1997
Second edition published 2002

© Barbara Senior 2002

ISBN 0 273 65153 6

British Library Cataloguing-in-Publication Data
A catalogue record for this book can be obtained from the British Library.

10 9 8 7 6 5 4
08 07 06 05 04

Typeset by 63 in 10/13 pt Sabon
Printed and bound by Ashford Colour Press Ltd., Gosport

Contents

Part Three
Strategies for managing change

About this Book

Introduction

All people in all organisations are concerned and involved with change, whether of the small-scale variety, such as adopting an updated version of a computer program, or of the large-scale variety, such as a change of strategy with subsequent changes in structure and operations. Consequently, no study of organisational life is complete without complementary studies of the way change affects it and how that change can be managed. In a world of constantly fluctuating demand and supply, of changing customer needs as well as the wider concerns brought about by the legitimate expectations of employees, change is essential. The impetus for writing this book comes from the belief that organisations and change must live comfortably together or else they will perish. Its content derives from many years of experience in helping meet the learning needs of students of business and management with respect to the way people in organisations approach and deal with change and with managing and working with change in a variety of organisations.

The aim of this book

The overall aim of this book is to provide a discussion of change in relation to the complexities of organisational life. The text takes both a theoretical and practical approach to the issue of organisational change in seeking to meet both the academic and applied aims of most business and management courses.

More specifically this text aims to be:

- *Comprehensive* in its coverage of the significant ideas and issues associated with change at all levels of organisational activity from the strategic to the operational. Change is also examined in terms of its effects at the individual, group, organisational and societal levels.
- *Conceptual* in the way it explores and critiques theory and research with respect of organisations and change.
- *Practical* in its provision of descriptions and worked examples of different approaches to 'doing' change.
- *Challenging* through asking readers to undertake activities including responding to discussion questions. The text in each chapter is interspersed with activities intended to personalise ideas from the text and to reinforce learning. End of

chapter discussion questions, assignments and case examples ask for longer and more detailed responses.

● *Balanced* in its use of case studies and examples which are drawn from various types of organisations – public and private sector, small and large.

Who should use this book?

This book is intended for all who are interested in exploring, in some detail, issues associated with organisational change and how to deal with it. Specifically:

● *Undergraduate students* on business studies, modular or joint degrees should find it sufficiently structured to provide an understandable route through the subject.

● *MBA students* should find the blend of theory and practice appropriate to the academic and applied demands of their courses. Requirements to relate theory and research to their own situations should prove useful in their day-to-day organisational activities. The case examples and longer case study provide real-life instances of change.

● *Postgraduate students* on other specialist taught masters programmes should find sufficient practical examples in the text, and through the case examples and case study, to illustrate theory even if they have little practical experience of management and business themselves.

● *Students on professional courses* which include elements relating to the management of change.

● *Practising middle and senior managers* who wish to delve more deeply into theoretical discussions of change and its complexity in relation to organisational functioning. In addition, or alternatively, they could benefit from study of the various change models described in the book as they apply to different change situations.

Readers of the book will benefit if they have some prior knowledge of the subject area of organisational behaviour. However, the book is written so as to be understandable to those with no such prior knowledge.

Distinctive features

● *Clear structure.* The book is structured into three parts. The first part considers the nature of organisations operating in complex environments and responding to the 'winds of change'. It includes some detailed discussion of the causes of change. Theoretical perspectives are introduced with a discussion of the nature of change. Part One of the book acts as an introduction to Part Two which 'opens up' the organisation to expand on a number of issues which are crucial to an understanding of organisational change and how it happens. Finally, Part Three moves firmly into addressing the more practical considerations of

About the Author

Barbara Senior is Director of the Postgraduate Modular Scheme at University College Northampton, having previously worked for the College on the MBA programmes and as Leader of the MA Organisational Behaviour and Change Management. Before this, she was a Regional Manager for the Open College, Team Leader of the Work and Unemployment programme at the Open University and Senior Lecturer in Human Resource Management at Liverpool Polytechnic (now John Moores University). As Director of Highfield House Consultancy, she also provides a research and consultancy service to people and organisations who are working with change.

Leaving school at 16 years of age, she worked initially in administration in a large catering establishment and then in the gas industry before setting up a dressmaking and tailoring business. Meanwhile, she studied as a mature student with the Open University, gaining a first class honours degree in psychology and organisational systems studies. During this time, she also gained a master's degree in Organisational Psychology from Lancaster University. She is a Chartered Occupational Psychologist and Member of the Institute of Personnel and Development.

She is the author (with John Naylor) of two previous books on the subjects of work and unemployment. She has contributed a chapter titled 'Organisational change and development' to the book *Introduction to Work and Organizational Psychology*, edited by Nik Chmiel (Blackwell, 2000) and has published many articles and conference papers based on her research interests in the areas of team working and cross-cultural management. She lectures in the subject areas of organisational behaviour and change to MBA and other postgraduate students on management and business courses and has a particular interest in promoting creative thinking and innovation as part of this.

Acknowledgements

My very special thanks go to my husband, Gerry. I thank him for his tolerance of my many absences from family life, as well as his practical and moral support throughout the writing period. Proof-reading and checking of references are only two of his skills, as evidenced by his illustration for the book cover. He has shown great forbearance in listening to my ideas and my concerns. My two children, Jayne and David, have given good advice and kind words when needed.

A particular acknowledgement goes to UCN students who were asked to read the draft chapters as part of their studies and who gave me valuable comments, which helped to improve the final version. I am touched by their willingness to share their organisational experiences with me, some of which appear (in disguise) at various times in the book. My colleagues at UCN have shown great fortitude listening to my chattering when I needed someone to talk to. This book would not have happened without the encouragement of Jacqueline Senior (no relative!) and other members of staff at our publishers.

Finally, I have tried to be true to the large amount of research and work already accomplished in the subject area of organisational change. Every effort has been made to trace and acknowledge ownership of copyright.

Publisher's Acknowledgements

We are grateful to the following for permission to reproduce copyright material:

Illustration 1.4 from *Skills for All: Proposals for a National Skills Agenda*, Final Report of the National Skills Force, HMSO © Crown Copyright 2000; Figure 2.2 and Table 6.3 from 'Evolution is Revolution as Organizations Grow' by L. Greiner, *Harvard Business Review*, July–August, 1972, pp. 41 and 45, Copyright © 1972 by the Harvard Business School Publishing Corporation. All rights reserved; Table 3.1 from 'Fit, failure and the hall of fame', *California Management Review*, Vol. 26, No. 3 © 1984 by The Regents of the University of California; Figure 3.9 from 'The Effective Organisation: Forces and Forms' by H. Mintzberg, *MIT Sloan Management Review*, Winter, Vol. 32, Part 2. Copyright © 1991 by Massachusetts Institute of Technology. All rights reserved; Figure 4.2 from 'Measuring organizational cultures: a qualitative and quantitative study across twenty cases' by G. Hofstede, B. Neuijen, D.D. Ohayv and G. Sanders (1990), *Administrative Science Quarterly*, 35; Figure 4.6 from *Cultures and Organizations: Software of the Mind* by G. Hofstede (1991), McGraw Hill: Maidenhead; Figures 4.9, 4.10 and 4.11 from 'Matching corporate culture and business strategy' by H. Schwartz and S.M. Davis, *Organizational Dynamics*, Summer 1981, pp. 30–48, Copyright © 1981, Excerpta Medica Inc.; Figure 5.1 from 'Conflict and conflict management' in Dunnette, M.D. (ed.), *Handbook of Industrial and Organizational Psychology*, Chicago, Rand McNally; Illustration 5.9 from *Social Paradigms and Organisational Analysis* by G. Burrell and G. Morgan (1985), Heinemann Educational Publishers; Figure 6.1 from *Leadership Dilemmas: Grid Solutions* by R. Blake and A.A. McCanse (1991), Houston, Gulf Publishing. Copyright © 1991 by Robert R. Blake and the Estate of Jane S. Mouton; Figure 6.5 from *Beyond Rational Management: Mastering the Paradoxes and Competing Demands of High Performance* by R.E. Quinn (1988). Copyright © Jossey-Bass, a subsidiary of John Wiley & Sons, Inc.; Figure 6.6 from 'The Strategic Management of Corporate Change' in *Human Relations*, 45, (8), D. Dunphy and D. Stace, Copyright © Sage Publications Ltd, 1993; Figure 8.4, 'The Pugh Matrix', from Course P679 Planning and Managing Change, Block 4, Section 6, Copyright © The Open University.

We are grateful to the Financial Times Limited for permission to reprint the following material:

Article Look to the process for a better product, from FT Mastering Management, © *Financial Times*, 16 October, 2000; Extracts from FT Life on the net, © *Financial*

Times, 4 September, 2000; Extract from A key player in Sports Team, © *Financial Times*, 2 August, 2000; Extract from Many markets set for macroeconomic shock, © *Financial Times*, 18 October, 2000; Illustration 1.8 from Bigger role for governments will be in fashion next year. © *Financial Times*, 28 June, 1996; Illustration 1.9 from Consumer confidence ebbs, © *Financial Times*, 5 October, 2000; Illustration 2.1 from Novel to cut 900 jobs and restructure, © *Financial Times*, 7 September, 2000; Article Adaptability furnishes key to craftsmen's long survival, © *Financial Times*, 6 September, 2000; Article based on Lean regime for a fitter future, © *Financial Times*, 6 May, 1992; Case example from Ministers in talks with police chiefs, © *Financial Times*, 18 September, 2000; Case example from Culture clash may spark Schroders exodus, © *Financial Times*, 20 January, 2000; Illustration 5.7 from Chipping away at the glass ceiling, from the Times Higher, © *Financial Times*, 26 July, 1996; Illustration 5.13 from Flight to revival, © *Financial Times*, 22 March, 1996; Illustration 6.1 from World Bank chief's cry from the heart, © *Financial Times*, 29 March, 1996; Headline from Caste in Stone, © *Financial Times*, 10 April, 1997.

Whilst every effort has been made to trace the owners of copyright material, in a few cases this has proved impossible and we take this opportunity to offer our apologies to any copyright holders whose rights we may have unwittingly infringed.

PART ONE

The context and meaning of change

Change in organisations does not happen in a vacuum. If nothing happened to disturb organisational life, change would be very slow and, perhaps, merely accidental. However, many commentators on organisational life warn that the pace of change is accelerating and all organisations must be prepared to respond to, and even anticipate, change.

Part One of this book examines what is meant by organisational change and the reasons that it happens. Chapter 1 begins this process by proposing a model of organisation which recognises the fact that organisational life is influenced by many factors, mainly those originating outside the organisation. A metaphor of the 'winds of change' is used to show how organisational activities are the outcomes of historical developments as well as the results of the day-by-day vagaries of political, economic, technological and socio-cultural influences.

The second chapter of Part One investigates, in more detail, the nature of organisational change itself and introduces ways of working with it. Part One therefore sets the scene for the more detailed discussion of organisations and change in Part Two.

Chapter 1

Organisations and their changing environments

In this chapter, organisations are defined as systems comprising elements of formal organisational management and operations as well as elements of more informal aspects of organisational life. The organisational systems, themselves, are conceptualised as operating in three types of environments. These are the temporal, external and internal environments whose elements interact with each other to form the 'triggers' of change which are significant in bringing about organisational changes.

Objectives

To:

- *describe the general characteristics of organisations and their essential components*

- *say how different methods of wealth creation, viewed from a historical perspective, have influenced present-day organisational strategies and focus*

- *discuss the concept of organisations as systems operating in multi-dimensional environments and its implications for understanding the causes of organisational change*

- *recognise that change can be triggered from any number of directions: through historical influences, from the external environment and from within the organisation itself – the internal environment.*

● ● ● ● A view of organisations

It is sometimes difficult to track down a comprehensive definition of what is meant by 'an organisation'. Many books on management, decision making, even organisational design, do not give a straightforward definition of what organisation means. Some, however, have been attempted. The following are two of these:

> An organization is a social arrangement for achieving controlled performance in pursuit of collective goals.   (Huczynski and Buchanan, 2001, p. 7)

> Organization: a group of people brought together for the purpose of achieving certain objectives. As the basic unit of an organization is the role rather than the person in it the organization is maintained in existence, sometimes over a long period of time, despite many changes of members.   (Statt, 1991, p. 102)

Even though the second of these definitions appears more complex than the first, they both have the same theme – that of people interacting in order to achieve some defined purpose. However, as might be deduced, the interactions of people, as members of an organisation, need some kind of managing, that is there will be elements of co-ordination and control of these activities. In organisations of above ten or so people in size, this implies some kind of structuring of these people's activities which picks up the idea of organisational roles mentioned in Statt's definition. In addition, the activities of individual organisational members and their interactions with one another imply a process through which work gets done in order to achieve the organisation's purposes or goals. Above all, there is the requirement for decision taking about the processes (the means) by which the goals (the ends) are achieved. Illustration 1.1 encapsulates most of this but also

---

Illustration 1.1

The meaning of organisation

A typical working definition of an organization might say it is: (1) a social entity that (2) has a purpose, (3) has a boundary, so that some participants are considered inside while others are considered outside, and (4) patterns the activities of participants into a recognizable structure (Daft 1989). Although organizations are real in their consequences, both for their participants and for their environments, they are essentially abstractions. ... The hospital, the firm, or the school will have physical aspects to them, the buildings, the plant and equipment and the like, but to understand how organizations work we need to go further than this. The factory has something real and physical about it but this is not the organization; people are doing tasks to which there is a pattern, raw materials are taken in, converted, and distributed to markets; capital is provided by banks and other financial institutions; systems provide information for decision-making and co-ordination; people are talking about matters which do not necessarily appear to have anything to do with the job, some people remote from the physical plant, perhaps a continent away, are making decisions critical to our factory.

Source: Butler, R. (1991), *Designing Organizations. A Decision-Making Perspective* (London, Routledge, pp. 1–2).

adds the idea of a boundary which prescribes which people belong to the organisation and which do not.

The example of the factory given by Butler (1991) draws attention to the fact that organisations cut across geographical boundaries and, therefore, organisational boundaries are, in Butler's words, also 'abstractions'. Yet, the notion of an organisational boundary is very real in that it draws attention to the concept of an organisation's environment. By this is meant all those influences which may act to disturb organisational life but which are not considered directly as a part of it. The mention of capital provided by some kind of financial institution is a recognition that organisations are connected to wider systems which form part of the environment – such as those which supply finance and other resources, not least human resources.

This view of organisations draws on the concept of an organisation as a system of interacting subsystems and components set within wider systems and environments which provide inputs to the system and which receive its outputs.

This is shown in Figure 1.1 which identifies the main elements of most organisations and their functioning. These are grouped into two main subsystems – the formal and informal subsystems. Thus elements of the formal subsystem include the organisation's strategy, whether this is devised by a single person, as in the case

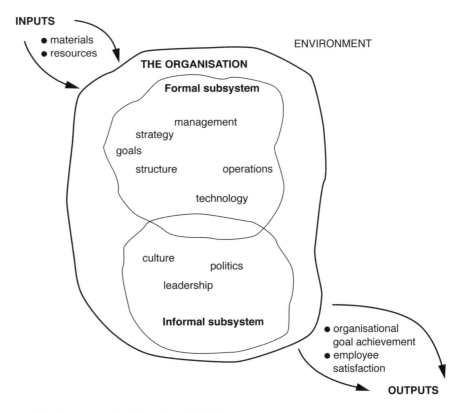

Figure 1.1 The organisation as a system

of a very small owner–manager company, or by the board of directors and top management group in a large multi-divisional organisation. Other components include the organisation's goals and the means of achieving these through operational activities such as the production of goods or provision of services. In addition, there is a service component which is that set of activities which help and facilitate the core operational activities to happen. Examples are the personnel departments, accounting and finance, information technology services and clerical and administrative support. Management, as the formal decision making and control element, is also evident in all organisations, whether this involves a few people or is spread throughout the organisation.

It is clear, from any examination of complex systems such as organisations, that some kind of structuring of activities is required if chaos is not to ensue. Thus the concept of organisational structure is central to that of organisational systems. However, over 20 years ago, Child (1973) drew attention to other more intangible elements of organisational life such as the political behaviour of organisational members. A more recent example is Nadler's (1988) inclusion of the informal organisation (patterns of communication, power and influence, values and norms) in his systems model of organisational behaviour. Stacey (2000) has coined the phrase 'shadow system' to describe these less predictable and more intangible aspects of organisational life. Thus, the idea of the 'informal subsystem' encapsulates the more hidden elements of organisational culture and politics and the rather less hidden element of leadership – including those who are led.

These relatively stable subsystems and elements of organisational functioning interact with each other in some kind of transformation process. This means taking inputs such as materials and other resources from the organisation's environment and transforming them into outputs which are received back into the environment by customers and clients. However, while these outputs can be thought of as the legitimate reason for the organisation's existence, an output that is relevant, in particular, to the informal subsystem is employees' behaviour and their satisfaction with their jobs. This is reinforced by Storey, Edwards and Sisson's (1997, p. 1) statement that: 'Given that technology and finance are increasingly internationally mobile and that innovations can be copied rapidly, it is the unique use of human resources, which is especially critical to long-term organisational success.'

However, the concept of organisational systems as open systems has not gone without criticism. As long ago as 1970, Silverman (1970) challenged the idea of organisations as systems, in that this notion rests on an assumption that defining an organisation's goals is uncontentious and that, within the organisation, there is consensus as to what an organisation's goals might be. A contrasting view of organisations, as being composed of individuals and groups with multiple different interests – who construe their actions in many different ways – came to the fore. Known as the 'social action' approach to understanding organisations, this became recognised as an alternative view to the idea of organisations as systems. More recently, with the development of the concepts of *modernism* and, particularly *postmodernism*, which are discussed further in Chapter 9, there is the assumption that the world is unpredictable and frequently chaotic in that change can occur in any direction at any time – witness the weekly pronouncements in the media of the latest Internet-based company to come into being and, nearly as frequently, their fading and in some cases their demise. Stacey's (2000) ideas on organisations as *complex* systems take the notion of unpredictability even further through emphasising the multitude of interactions in the individual (psychological), social, organisational and environmental domains and between any and all of them. He also stresses the difficulties or, as he sees them, impossibilities in trying to understand organisations and the people within them from the point of view of an objective outsider as some open systems theorists have done. Having said this, the concept of organisational systems as *open* systems is an important one. As already mentioned, all organisations receive inputs from their environments and provide outputs back into that environment. The boundaries of organisational systems are, therefore, permeable. This means that they are also significantly influenced in their strategies and activities by both historical and contemporary environmental demands, opportunities and constraints. The next section traces some historical trends which have influenced organisational strategies and processes through time. This tracing of history acts as a prelude to a consideration of the more immediate environment of organisations today and as they might present themselves in the future.

● ● ● ● The historical context for change

The forces which operate to bring about change in organisations can be thought of as winds which are many and varied – from small summer breezes which merely disturb a few papers to mighty howling gales which cause devastation to structures and operations causing consequent reorientation of purpose and rebuilding. Sometimes, however, the winds die down to give periods of relative calm, periods of relative organisational stability. Such a period was the agricultural age which Goodman (1995) maintains prevailed in the UK until the early 1700s. During this period, wealth was created in the context of an agriculturally based society influenced mainly by local markets (both customer and labour) and factors outside people's control such as the weather. During this time, people could fairly well predict the cycle of activities required to maintain life, even if that life might be at little more than subsistence level.

To maintain the meteorological metaphor, stronger winds of change blew to bring in the Industrial Revolution and the industrial age. Again, according to Goodman, this lasted until around 1945. It was characterised by a series of inventions and innovations which reduced the number of people needed to work the land and, in turn, provided the means of mass production of hitherto rarely obtainable artifacts; for organisations, supplying these in ever increasing numbers became the aim. To a large extent, demand and supply were predictable, enabling companies to structure their organisations along what Burns and Stalker (1966) described as mechanistic lines, that is as systems of strict hierarchical structures and firm means of control.

This situation prevailed for some time after the Second World War, with demand still coming mainly from the domestic market and organisations striving to fill the 'supply gap'. Thus, the most disturbing environmental influence on organisations of this time was the demand for products which outstripped supply. The (supposed) saying by Henry Ford that, 'You can have any colour of car so long as it is black', gives a flavour of the supply-led state of the market. Apart from any technical difficulties of producing different colours of car, Ford did not have to worry about customers' colour preferences: he could sell all that he made.

Figure 1.2 characterises organisations of this period as 'task oriented', with effort being put into increasing production through more effective and efficient production processes.

The push, during this period, for ever-increasing efficiency of production supported the continuing application of the earlier ideas of Taylor (1911) and scientific management allied to Fordism which was derived from Henry Ford's ideas on assembly-line production (see Wood, 1989). This was a period mainly of command and control, of bureaucratic structures and the belief that there was 'one best way' of structuring organisations for efficient production. However, as time passed, this favourable period for organisations began to wane as people became more discriminating in the goods and services they wished to buy and as technological advancements brought about increased productivity so that supply overtook demand. In addition, companies began, increasingly, to look abroad for additional markets.

At the same time, they faced more intensive competition from abroad for their own products and services. In the West, this development has been accompanied

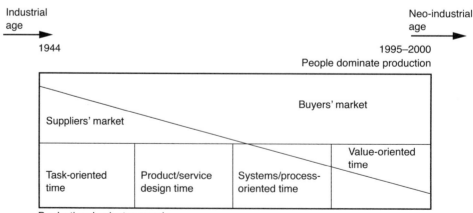

Figure 1.2 Market factors impacting on operations of Western organisations
Source: Goodman, M. (1995), *Creative Management* (Hemel Hempstead, Prentice Hall, p. 38).

by a shift in focus from manufacturing to service, whether this merely adds value to manufactured products or whether it is service in its own right; for instance financial services, help in selling houses, the services of doctors and solicitors or taking part in education and training. In the neo-industrial age of the advanced countries, the emphasis is moving towards adding value to goods and services – what Goodman calls the value-oriented time (*see* Illustration 1.2) as contrasted with the task-oriented, products/services-oriented and systems-oriented times of the past and current periods. Table 1.1 lists the organisational responses, in terms of marketing, production and people, to the different time periods.

Illustration 1.2

Value-oriented time

Customers

As competition becomes more severe and markets oversupplied, organisations must find products and services which are differentiated not only by purpose and form but by the 'added value' which attaches to them. This means identifying potential customer expectations and then exceeding them. In other words, organisations must constantly increase customers' perceived value for money.

As the life-cycle of a product shortens, organisations must be under constant pressure to introduce new product offerings. This implies a continuing striving for innovation in terms of both products and the services associated with them. Innovation is, however, not only associated with the product itself but also with ways of supplying and marketing it. What may differentiate one product offering from another is not the product itself but the innovative production techniques, quality and relationship marketing – skills which are difficult for the competition to copy.

Production

About the production processes of the future, Goodman (1995, p. 49) says:

On the supply side, production will continue to get leaner and more responsive to customer demand. Lean production appears to do the impossible. It delivers the great product variety once associated with craft production at costs that are often less than those associated with mass production.

Furthermore these benefits are provided together with products of high quality by sophisticated networking processes.

Human brainpower

The economies of the West can no longer rely on mass production processes. Ideas and brainpower have become an increasingly important component of modern product and service packages. It is through people's intelligence and creative thinking that organisations will improve competitiveness. Information technology and information systems are of more importance than the mass production systems which gave competitive advantage in the past. People in organisations will become their most important asset as it is only people who have the brainpower to focus on identifying and solving complex problems. To quote Goodman (1995, pp. 49–50):

The successful product packages of the future will result from the exposure of creativity to complex, curvilinear, messy, fuzzy logic-type problems. As demand grows for such value packages, so individuals will respond by having ingenious ideas. This will challenge organisations, with their liking for structure and order, as intensive creativity usually arises out of chaos and disorder conditions. ... Thus, old mind-sets and rule books will have to give way to new organisational patterns that continuously encourage individuals to have ideas.

Table 1.1 Key organisational responses in the United Kingdom 1994–1995

Key organisational responses	Task-oriented time	Product/service design time	Systems/process-oriented time	Value-oriented time
Marketing	Seller's market Focus on increasing sales	Development of market segments Positioning and targeting Niche marketing	Strategic marketing Increasing importance of single customer focus	Relationship marketing Value-added marketing
Production	Supplying volume Reducing costs	Automation Work study	Statistical process control Quality/service chain Just in time	Lean systems Information management Autonomous units Improving response times Networking
People	Compliance Work study Problems caused by growth and functionalisms	Manpower planning Human resources management Team working	Quality (systems) Kaizen Problem solving	Task/project-focused teams Cross-functional teams Information management Proliferation of messy problems

Source: Goodman, M. (1995), *Creative Management* (Hemel Hempstead, Prentice Hall, p. 40).

Change throughout the ages is encapsulated in the comments of Jones, Palmer, Osterweil and Whitehead (1996) when they say:

> As we approach the 21st century the pace and scale of the change demanded of organisations and those who work within them are enormous. Global competition and the advent of the information age, where knowledge is the key resource, have thrown the world of work into disarray. Just as we had to shed the processes, skills and systems of the agricultural era to meet the demands of the industrial era, so we are now having to shed ways of working honed for the industrial era to take advantage of the opportunities offered by the information age. ... Organisations are attempting to recreate themselves and move from the traditional structure to a dynamic new model where people can contribute their creativity, energy and foresight in return for being nurtured, developed and enthused.

Jones *et al.* are probably realistic as they predict these developments for Western advanced societies. However, it must be remembered that not all parts of the world are at this stage of development in terms of the move from agriculture to industry to services. Table 1.2 illustrates the numbers of people working in the agricultural, industrial and services sectors of the economy in China compared to Russia which is, itself, way behind Western countries in the proportion of its economic activity devoted to services. China is still predominantly an agricultural society, particularly when compared to the United Kingdom where only 3.5 per

Table 1.2 Russia and China: very different countries

Sectoral structure of employment (% of total)	Russia 1990	Russia 1994	China 1978	China 1994
Industry	42	38	15	18
Agriculture	13	15	71	58
Services	45	47	14	25
Total	100	100	100	100
Employment in the state sector	90	44	19	18

Source: Walker, T. (1996), 'China leads the pack – so far', *Financial Times*, 28 June, p. 4

cent of people work in the primary and utilities sector – which includes workers in the gas, electric and water industries as well as agriculture (Department for Education and Employment, 2000a, 2000b). Yet the article in the *Financial Times* (Walker, 1996) from which the statistics given in Table 1.2 are taken, indicates that China is quickly moving towards an industry and services dominated period.

More recently, Kazim, Williamson and McNulty (2000) reinforce this view with the title of their *Financial Times* article 'Foreign investors desert south-east Asia for China'. This later article gives statistics that show the situation for both countries for foreign direct investment in the early 1990s is now entirely reversed, with Asia receiving 61 per cent against China's 18 per cent in the 1990s compared to Asia now down to 17 per cent against China's rise to 61 per cent. Russia is taking rather more time to begin to change its economy as an editorial comment in the *Financial Times* (October, 2000) demonstrates. Even so, the winds of change are blowing strongly for countries such as Russia and China. Their progress through the agricultural, industrial and services periods will be swift in comparison with the time it took the more advanced Western countries to reach the same stage.

Activity 1.1   *Consider how you would describe an organisation with which you are familiar in terms of its wealth-creating capacity. For instance, try answering the following questions:*

- *With which sector of the economy (agricultural, manufacturing, services) are its outputs mainly associated?*
- *What type of market does it have? Use the categories given in Table 1.1 as a guide.*
- *Does it supply domestic or foreign markets – or both?*
- *Is it into volume production, automation of products/services or group/autonomous unit production?*
- *Does it practise just-in-time (JIT) delivery with an emphasis on quality service?*
- *What type of people does it employ – unskilled, skilled, professional?*
- *Are people easily attracted to work in the organisation?*
- *How much autonomy do employees have with regard to the work they choose to do and the way they do it?*
- *Is decision taking devolved to the lowest level possible or kept within the hands of top management?*

● ● ● ● An uncertain future

Some responses to Activity 1.1 may give a sense of an organisation operating in a fairly predictable environment, with a sense of security for the future – that is, where the winds of change are moderate and fairly constant. Other responses may suggest a sense of uncertainty about markets, demand, the ability to attract the type of labour required and whether employment will increase or decrease – an environment where the winds of change come in short unpredictable gusts. If creativity and innovation, working in teams to solve complex problems are indicative of the organisation analysed in Activity 1.1, it has quite likely already moved into value-oriented time.

Most people asked about organisational life today agree that it is becoming ever more uncertain as the pace of change quickens and the future becomes more unpredictable. This is echoed by academics and business people alike. For instance, looking ahead to the future, Drucker, writing in 1988, maintained that 20 years hence (i.e. about the year 2008) organisations would be almost wholly information based and that they would resemble more a symphony orchestra than the command and control, managed structures prevalent in the last decade (*see* Illustration 1.3).

With this as one example of the way organisations might change in the future, Drucker predicted the demise of middle management and the rise of organisations staffed almost exclusively with high-grade, specialist staff. The view that middle management will no longer be required is debatable and would certainly not be subscribed to by everyone (e.g. Eccles, 1996). However, for the UK, the projected growth in the numbers of professionals and knowledge-based workers and the decrease in numbers of lower skilled workers is supported by the latest figures and trends, published by the Department of Education and Employment (2000a) using the Institute for Employment Research's statistics (*see* Illustration 1.4).

Illustration 1.3

Organisations as symphony orchestras

Writing about the way that information technology is transforming business enterprises, Drucker says:

> A large symphony orchestra is even more instructive, since for some works there may be a few hundred musicians on stage playing together. According to organization theory then, there should be several group vice president conductors and perhaps a half-dozen division VP conductors. But that's not how it works. There is only the conductor-CEO – and every one of the musicians plays directly to that person without an intermediary. And each is a high-grade specialist, indeed an artist.

Source: Drucker, P. F. (1988), 'The coming of the new organization', *Harvard Business Review*, January–February, p. 48.

Illustration 1.4

Higher-level occupations growing fastest ...

Over the past 30 years, millions of new jobs have been created in managerial, professional and associate professional occupations (the share of these occupations having increased from 28 per cent of the workforce in 1981 to 36 per cent in 1998). The number of jobs classified as elementary and operative has fallen from 30 per cent of total employment in 1981 to 23 per cent in 1998. These trends are expected to continue (as the bar chart shows), though the rate of change is uncertain, and the forecasts we have commissioned suggest that by 2009, 40 per cent of jobs will fall into the managerial, professional and associate professional categories, with only 21 per cent in elementary and operative jobs, and 12 per cent in elementary jobs alone.

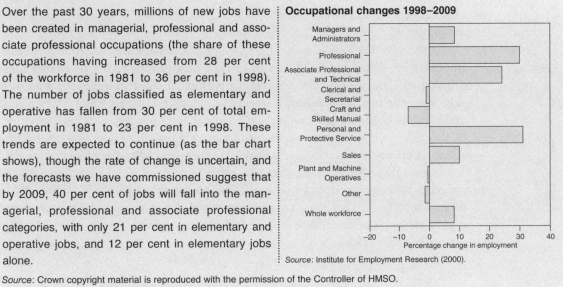

Occupational changes 1998–2009

Source: Institute for Employment Research (2000).

Source: Crown copyright material is reproduced with the permission of the Controller of HMSO.

Since the industrialisation of production, the more recent rise of ever more service industries and the information technology explosion, the pace of change in the environment in which organisations operate has quickened to such an extent that, nearly ten years ago, writers such as Clarke (1994, p. 1) were maintaining that: 'The last decade has brought with it a time of totally unprecedented change. In every direction businesses are in turmoil, from computing to financial services, from telecommunications to health care. Change is an accelerating constant.' This view was broadly confirmed by Dawson (1994, pp. 1–2) in his discussion of a 'new bias for organizational action', by which he means the need for managers to be leaders of change or else, in an increasingly competitive environment, their organizations will cease to exist.

The somewhat dramatic tone of these pronouncements appears to be supported, more recently, by two American academics turned consultants, Nadler and Tushman (1999, p. 45) who say: 'Poised on the eve of the next century, we are witnessing a profound transformation in the very nature of our business organisations. Historic forces have converged to fundamentally reshape the scope, strategies, and structures of large, multi-business enterprises.' At a less macro level of analysis, an article by Merope Mills in *The Guardian* (2000) refers to Graeme Leach, chief economist at the Institute of Directors, who claims that: 'By 2020, the nine-to-five rat race will be extinct and present levels of self-employment, commuting and technology use, as well as age and sex gaps, will have changed beyond recognition.' According to the article, Leach anticipates that: 'In 20 years time,

20–25% of the workforce will be temporary workers and many more will be flexible, that 25% of people will no longer work in a traditional office and the 50% will work from home in some form.' Continuing to use the 'winds of change' metaphor, the expectation is of damaging gale force winds bringing the need for rebuilding which takes the opportunity to incorporate new ideas and ways of doing things.

Whether all this will come to pass is arguable. Predicting the future is always fraught with difficulties. For instance, Furnham (2000) refers to Mannermann (1998, p. 427) who sees future studies as part art and part science and who notes: 'The future is full of surprises, uncertainty, trends and trend breaks, irrationality and rationality, and it is changing and escaping from our hands as time goes by. It is also the result of actions made by innumerable more or less powerful forces.' What seems uncontestable, is that the organisational world is changing at a fast rate – even if the direction of change is not always predictable. Consequently, it is crucial that organisational managers and decision makers are aware of, and understand, more about the environmental winds which are blowing to disturb organisational life; in other words to be able to analyse the factors which trigger organisational change.

● ● ● ● Organisations today – environmental triggers of change

---

Activity 1.2   *List (ideally by brainstorming) as many factors as possible which you think could affect what an organisation produces or sells, the markets for its goods or services, the methods of organising the way work gets done or the attitudes and performance of its members. Keep your list for later use.*

Figure 1.1 depicts an organisation as a system receiving inputs from its environment and releasing outputs back into it. The previous section discussed how social and technological changes have, in the past, impacted on the products and services offered by organisations and the way they operate. A number of writers have been mentioned, who predict ever more 'turbulent' (Emery and Trist, 1967) environments – ever more stormy winds.

The view of organisations existing as systems of interrelated elements operating in multi-dimensional environments has a number of supporters. The work of Checkland (1972), for instance, is well known for the development of the soft systems model – an approach designed specifically for analysing and designing change in what Checkland terms 'human activity systems', most frequently, organisational systems. Nadler (1988) has proposed a systems model applied to organisational behaviour and other authors such as Stacey (2000) use systems concepts in their discussion of organisations and change. Most writers on organisations stress the importance of the nature of the environment for organisational management and decision making. The following lists some of the elements of an organisation's environment which might have emerged from completing Activity 1.2:

- an organisation's markets (clients or customers)
- suppliers
- governmental and regulatory bodies
- trade union organisations
- competitors
- financial institutions
- labour supply
- levels of unemployment
- economic climate
- technological advances
- computing and information systems developments
- the growth of E-commerce and use of the Internet.

An organisation's environment will also include broader influences such as the internationalisation of trade, the prevailing political ideology, attitudes to trade unions, changes from public to private ownership or vice versa, demographic changes and changes in family structure and differences between the rich and the poor. Thus, Nadler and Tushman (1988, p. 152) summarise the environment as: 'All factors, including institutions, groups, individuals, events and so on, that are outside the organization being analyzed, but that have a potential impact on that organization.' The remainder of this section considers, more closely, examples of these and draws attention to the way changes in one or more elements of the organisational environment are likely to trigger consequent changes in some or all the ways an organisation and its constituent components operate.

The impact of PETS

Some analysts have found it useful to group different environmental factors into categories under the mnemonics PEST (Johnson and Scholes, 1999) and STEP (Goodman, 1995), both of which refer to the Political, Economic, Technological and Socio-cultural factors which influence organisations, their strategies, structures and means of operating, including their human resource practices. The mnemonic PETS could as easily be used. In addition, it is a useful metaphor to distinguish different aspects of the organisational environment and their specific relationship to organisations as triggers of change. Figure 1.3 illustrates the PETS factors which exist as part of an organisation's environment. All, at some time, will impact upon an organisation's formal and informal subsystems and their components as well as which products or services it offers and in which markets.

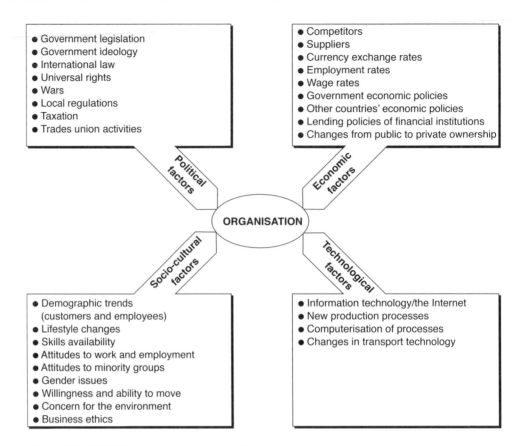

Political factors:
- Government legislation
- Government ideology
- International law
- Universal rights
- Wars
- Local regulations
- Taxation
- Trades union activities

Economic factors:
- Competitors
- Suppliers
- Currency exchange rates
- Employment rates
- Wage rates
- Government economic policies
- Other countries' economic policies
- Lending policies of financial institutions
- Changes from public to private ownership

Socio-cultural factors:
- Demographic trends (customers and employees)
- Lifestyle changes
- Skills availability
- Attitudes to work and employment
- Attitudes to minority groups
- Gender issues
- Willingness and ability to move
- Concern for the environment
- Business ethics

Technological factors:
- Information technology/the Internet
- New production processes
- Computerisation of processes
- Changes in transport technology

ORGANISATION

Figure 1.3 PETS factors and organisational change

Triggers for change from the technological environment

Examples of triggers for change emanating from changes in technology are many and varied. Illustration 1.5 uses the metaphor of a cat's behaviour to give an example of how changes in the technological environment, which were ignored as triggers for change, caused devastation to a once proud industry.

An article by Roy Westbrook, in the 16 October 2000 *Financial Times* 'Mastering Management' series has the sub-heading 'Production techniques have revolutionised product manufacturing'. Westbrook describes the way that, through devising very speedy production machine changes, customised 'one-off' products can be made using automated processes previously used only for mass production. An example of linking processes to information technology is in the increasing use of robots to perform human tasks. Westbrook gives statistics for what he calls 'robot density' (the number of robots for every 10,000 people employed). In 1998 the robot density for the UK was 19, that for the USA was 42 and for Japan 277. The relative differences in the use of robots between countries might be a function of the different spread of industries among them. However, Illustration 1.6 shows that the opportunity to use robots in increasing numbers is

Illustration 1.5

A clever cat

Picture the scene of a group of birds pecking away trying to find worms, with some confidence in the safety of numbers, heads down busying themselves about their own immediate purpose. A young cat, using relatively new skills, might easily pounce to catch one or more birds. Being inexperienced, the cat has only limited success. So the birds re-form and continue as if uninterrupted. Meanwhile, the cat goes away and practises and gets some more experience of hunting and returns to mount a much more skilful attack with far more resulting damage.

This analogy sheds light on the case of the British motorcycle industry when faced with Japanese competition. Early Japanese motorcycle models made few inroads into the traditional British motorcycle markets and, heads down, confident in a product and a process which had always been successful, the industry ignored the threat of the Japanese. However, like the older, wiser cat, the Japanese returned, pounced and dealt wounding blows from which the British motorcycle industry has never recovered. Thus, the British motorcycle industry paid the price for not changing in the face of developing technologies which allowed its competitors to forge ahead.

Illustration 1.6

Robots or people

Both cost and quality benefits are offered by robotics and the latter is critical in electronics. Certain areas of a semiconductor plant need to be 1000 times cleaner than a hospital operating theatre, so some tasks are carried out by robots in a vacuum. In disk drive assembly, the work is easier for robots than people. Matsushita Kotobuki Electronics (MKE) make Quantum's disk drives at an automated facility where 400 people and 150 robots produce 50,000 units a day. Quantum's main competitor is Seagate, which makes a similar number in Singapore and Taiwan, with few robots and 25,000 people.

Source: Westbrook, R. (2000), 'Look to the process for a better product', *Financial Times Mastering Management*, 16 October, pp. 6–7.

a matter of choice. If the choice to increase the use of robots is taken, this will inevitably have an impact on employment rates and the organisation of work for those far fewer workers retained in the new operations environment.

An extremely important and far-reaching influence on organisations in almost everything they do, is the increasing power of Internet-based communications. Consider the following quotations:

The internet has the ability to create the 'intelligent patient', someone able to talk on more equal terms with their doctor. This frightens much of the profession, although more enlightened doctors welcome a more balanced relationship with their patients.

(*FT Life on the net*, 4 September 2000, p. 1)

The internet bank that never sleeps is winning many converts. The premium savings rates and cheap loans seem too good to miss – until, that is, the system crashes and there is no one to shout at.
(*FT Life on the net*, 5 September 2000, p. 1)

There is no tombstone for Mary Ann Lucking, but 150 years after she died I found her on the web. This kind of discovery makes online genealogy exciting, but you should also be ready to rifle through musty papers in damp municipal buildings.
(*FT Life on the net*, 8 September 2000, p. 1)

Digitisation allows creators of music, television and film to store their work on computer files and transmit them to customers over the internet. But Christmas shoppers be warned. Innovation is so fast that this year's gadgets could be obsolete by Twelfth Night.
(*FT Life on the net*, 11 September 2000, p. 1)

A morbid set of Cassandra dotcoms has emerged, gloating about business-to-customer start-ups headed for liquidation not liquidity. The irony of this gloom is that online retailing is growing exponentially, as consumers lose their fear of buying over the internet.
(*FT Life on the net*, 13 September 2000, p. 1)

A boom in internet shopping could mean an end to your weekly battle through crowded supermarkets.
(Jessica McCallin, 'From mousemat to doormat', *The Guardian*, 23 September, p. 28)

Your airline will know you are gridlocked on the M25 thanks to the positioning system in your internet-enabled mobile phone. No need to panic. It will automatically book you on to a later flight, while e-mailing the details to your office and your spouse.
(*FT Life on the net*, 14 September 2000, p. 1)

The internet is a creative tool for learning. It is not about doing what we have always done in the classroom. It is not about replacing books or televisions or teachers or even parents. And it is not just about delivering knowledge. It is about adding to a child's most basic equipment.
(*FT Life on the net*, 15 September 2000, p. 1)

From club websites to event intranets, from stadium ticketing systems to computational fluid dynamics, and from virtual advertising to interactive television, the applications of information technology in modern-day sport seem almost limitless.
(Patrick Haverson, 'A key player in the sports team', *Financial Times*, 2 August 2000, p. 10)

Economists expect B2B (business to business) marketplaces to affect business practices, and in the process radically transform the process of innovation and productivity growth.
(Andrew Fisher, 'Many markets set for macroeconomic shock',
Financial Times, 18 October 2000, p. V)

A glance through these quotations illustrates how the increasing ability to communicate through the Internet is influencing significantly: banking, medicine, education, retailing, travel, entertainment and the capacity to trace family members, friends and others who died in the near and distant past. (Incidentally, to illustrate further the point, the full discussions associated with the *Financial Times* quotations are available on the web at www.ft.com/lifeonthenet.) However, as parts of some of these quotations show, Internet use is not always without problems and organisations who wish to reach markets, customers and clients need to remain alert to the fact that not everyone has access to computers or the new generation of Internet-linkable mobile phones – or has the ability and motivation to use them.

This remains an important consideration, particularly for those working and using education and health services, as Applebee, Clayton, Pascoe and Bruce (2000) in their study of Australian academic use of the Internet show and as Howcroft and Mitev (2000) in their study of the UK's National Health Service NHSnet show. In the UK, however, a Department for Education and Employment (2000b) document entitled 'Opportunity for all: skills for the new economy' says: 'Annual admissions of UK students to computer studies courses in our universities rose four-fold in the ten years to 1998, reaching over 16,500. ... *UK on-line computer skills training*, launched in May, offers ICT employability training for up to 50,000 unemployed people at a cost of £25m' (p. 19).

Looking to the East, Dan Roberts writing in the *Financial Times* (2000, p. 1) says: 'China now buys more mobile telecoms equipment from multinational suppliers than any market outside the US. These suppliers are investing at breakneck speed to meet the demand.' A third example, picked almost at random, is the 'high-tech eruption in Etna valley' (*see* Betts, 2000, p. 22) a location in Sicily where a high-tech resurrection is occurring in what the author calls 'this rambling poor city under Europe's biggest active volcano, long a stereotype of Italy's desperate and depressed deep south'.

The rapid rise and fall of what have become known as 'dot.com' Internet companies does not appear to have diminished the enthusiasm for the Web among European executives. The number and range of companies, new and existing, who are devising innovative ways of harnessing the Internet to their purposes is too great to detail here. A publication which gives much of this information including a frequently updated 'E-index' of pc, Internet and mobile phone penetration and access is 'Connectis' which bills itself as 'Europe's e-business magazine'. (Information on the English version can be found at www.ft.com/connectis.)

The explosive nature of the spread of Internet use and the opportunities brought about by advances in information technology generally, clearly impacts not only on organisations and those who work in them, but also on other parts of the organisational environment. As employees use E-mail and the Internet much more frequently through their workplace connections, employers have become increasingly anxious to monitor activity which is not work related. This has caught the attention of the UK trade unions to the effect that it was debated at the 2000 annual Trades Union Congress. Government legislation regarding the degree to which employers have investigatory powers of this nature is causing concern along with the degree to which these might impinge on employees' human rights in the light of the incorporation into law, in October 2000, of the European Union human rights convention. Without employer monitoring, managers may have little sense of how much time an employee is spending on non-work related E-mails and Internet surfing and staff may be subject to sexual harassment through receiving unsolicited pornographic material. With surveillance, a climate of distrust can be created.

The discussion so far illustrates the power of increased opportunities for technological communications to influence organisational life. It is instructive to look also at other triggers for change which, at various times, emanate from the PETS environment.

Triggers for change from the political environment

Returning to the PETS metaphor, an example of far-reaching changes as a result of a change of political leaders is given in Illustration 1.7. A change of government is analogous to the advent of a new lion king in a pride of lions in that the behaviour of government leaders is not far removed from that of the new lion king such is the force with which they seek to expunge previous ideologies and their effects.

The story of the new lion king may be stretching a point in assuming lions as PETS. However, just as the new lion king 'cleansed' the pride of lions of the old king's genes and thus caused a change in the characteristics and behaviour of the new generation of lions, so will a change in political ideology bring requirements for new behaviours in organisations because of the changed constraints and opportunities within which they must operate. In addition, not only do changes in the political environment influence organisations directly, they also interact with changes in the economic environment – for instance, the government-inspired privatisation of previously publicly owned institutions (e.g. in the UK, electricity, gas, the railways), or the co-operation of different countries to form economic trading blocs (e.g. the European Community or the ASEAN-4 Group). As Illustration 1.8 shows, changes coming from one sector of the environment are compounded by their interaction with influencing factors from other sectors of the environment – a clear demonstration that environmental triggers for change rarely act as single influences.

Illustration 1.7

A new lion king

A single lion will typically head a group of lionesses with their young, just as a prime minister will head a reigning government and parliament. When the lion grows old, he is prey to the attacks of younger lions looking to take over the 'harem' in the same way that a long-serving prime minister is prey to being usurped by those who want to take over power. If the younger lion is successful in driving the old one out, the younger lion will then proceed to kill all the existing young cubs in order to destroy the old lion's gene pool and introduce his own.

In such a way do new prime ministers and their governments act. For the old lion's gene pool, substitute the ideology of the old government and for the new lion's gene pool substitute the new government's ideology. The result is that the new government denounces and downgrades all that the previous government achieved; what was good then is no longer celebrated now. Within a short time, in the same way that the new lion's genes are established in the new generation of young lions, the acts of the new government become the only ones which matter.

Illustration 1.8

Bigger role for governments will be in fashion next year

FT

The revitalisation of the state to make the long-term development of the global economy more effective is the main theme of next year's World Bank development report. A draft outline of the report indicates a shift in thinking at the World Bank over the role of government in economic policy making.

The document says that 'an effective – not a larger – state is needed to create the institutional infrastructure for markets to flourish'.

The World Bank believes that 'the great (and false) debate between state and market for now seems to be over. Fiscal crises, the inflexibility of planning and the problems of public enterprises have shown the limits of the state'.

But it adds: 'the key objective is to show that the state and market are institutionally intertwined' and one must not dominate the other. ... A significant role

for the state in the 21st century will be in providing a framework under which the trade-off between market-based growth and escalating environmental problems are resolved. ...

It [the report] calls for 'good governments' which it says concerns 'creating an environment for the positive interplay between state, private and civil society institutions'. ...

'Competition for investment and jobs accelerates the shift towards better government discipline and business orientation.'

The report intends to look at how the state's interaction with the market and its own citizens can 'best be improved to achieve more sustainable economic development'. This – it believes – can be achieved through greater decentralisation, delegation and participation, 'bringing the state closer to the people'.

Source: Taylor, R. (1996), 'Bigger role for governments will be in fashion next year', *Financial Times*, 28 June, p. 4.

Perhaps the most important role for governments is the bringing of economic prosperity to their countries. However, they also act as law makers at more micro levels. The socialist government of the UK at the time of writing is proposing to enact a law that will make the hunting of foxes with dogs illegal. Arguments range for and against this. Interested rural communities argue that, not only will a long-standing tradition be outlawed and that people's rights to follow these pursuits be violated, but large numbers of jobs will be lost as a result – exacerbating further what they see as the impoverishment of those who live and work in rural areas. Those who argue for it say this practice is barbaric in a modern civilised society and that the number of jobs lost will be very small. What has come to be known as the Countryside Alliance, which brings together different interest groups from the rural areas, has become a forceful lobby on the government, not only regarding the hunting with dogs issue, but also regarding issues about lack of public transport, the decline in farming incomes and cost of fuel for private vehicle use, which is said to affect rural populations more severely than urban ones. The action the government could (or not, as the case might be) take on fox hunting, as well as actions concerning matters such as lack of public transport and the decline of farming, could have far-reaching effects on businesses operating in rural areas and those who work within them.

September 2000 saw French and British workers from the transport and oil industries, supported by farmers, taking action to protest at the price of fuel, saying that this affected negatively their ability to compete with similar organisations from other countries. However, reductions in the price of petrol and diesel would reduce both governments' tax revenues which would, presumably, have knock-on effects on their abilities to make money available for other purposes and industries such as education and health, thus affecting the organisations operating within these and the people working within them. If the governments acted to reduce the tax rates on fuel, and thus the price of it, this would clearly impact on the cost of travelling, not only for business purposes, but also for domestic and leisure purposes, which might in turn change people's lifestyles. Illustration 1.9 demonstrates the complexity of issues arising from what some might regard as a straightforward protest about the price of oil. The earlier description and the situation described in Illustration 1.9 demonstrate the multiplicity of cause and effect of actions by government, which, in turn, influence factors within the economic environment and which impact on different business and public sectors and the attitudes and behaviour of people within and outside them.

Illustration 1.9

French consumer confidence ebbs   FT

France's consumer confidence index slumped to its lowest level for more than a year in September according to the National Statistics Institute Insee.

In the survey of household opinion published yesterday, the indices of confidence fell a full ten points on the previous sample taken in July – no survey was taken in August.

This sudden reversal of consumer sentiment reflected the sharp change in the overall politico-economic climate in France following the end of the summer holidays and the impact of higher oil prices against the backdrop of the weak euro.

The most negative element in the survey emerged in attitudes towards the cost of living, especially in the future. However, there was also a decline in the number of households who said they were planning big purchases. This was accompanied by a belief that purchasing power was being eroded.

Government officials yesterday sought to play down the significance of the survey, arguing that September was a month in which public morale was seriously affected by oil price protests not just in France but across Europe.

In parallel the popularity of the Jospin government, which had been very constant over three years, suddenly plummeted in September because of its handling of the oil price rises.

Source: Graham, R. (2000), 'French consumer confidence ebbs', *Financial Times*, 5 October, p. 5.

Activity 1.3   *Look back at Figure 1.3 and your answer to Activity 1.2.*

How many of the PETS factors, listed by you and in Figure 1.3, 'appear' in the account of the UK government's role in relation to fox hunting with dogs, the actions of the Countryside Alliance and the issues raised by the results of the French survey of household opinion described in Illustration 1.9?

What do your conclusions tell you about the interconnections between the various aspects of the PETS environment?

Having read Illustration 1.9 and completed Activity 1.3, it is interesting to note that trade unions supported the protest in France while the one in the UK was not trade union led or supported. It is also interesting to note that the French government 'gave in' very soon to most of the demands for cheaper fuel by French protesters, while the UK government waited for some months until the planned annual pre-budget statement to announce a moderate easing of tax levied on petrol to reduce petrol prices, but still not as much as the protesters wanted. The protests in France appeared to take place within the recognised democratic process that involves government, trade unions, and employers. In the UK the trades unions and government felt that the protests were outside what they regarded as the democratic processes of the country and the recognised way of bringing about change. In both countries the issues of the governments losing popularity and, consequently, votes are also part of a hidden agenda in terms of their actions.

Triggers for change from the socio-cultural environment

As government policies, laws and actions affect organisations and people's everyday lives, so do the attitudes and expectations of people towards work, in the context of other aspects of their lives. All the factors listed as socio-cultural in Figure 1.3 influence the way organisations are set up, run and managed as well as their capacity to attract people to work within them.

Examples of how changes in the socio-cultural environment influence people's attitudes to work, and trigger other changes elsewhere, are:

● Social expectations for continuous increases in the standard of living which must, however, be set against fewer opportunities for permanent secure employment.
● Demographic changes causing 'gluts' or shortages in the numbers of young people coming into the labour market.
● Changes in family structures where men as well as, or instead of, women may wish to stay home to look after children.
● Demographic changes influencing the numbers of people in different age groups and therefore the numbers of people of working age compared to those of retirement age.

An article in the *Financial Times* (20 September 1996), by Kate Bevan, comments on the increase in the numbers of single men and women living alone (from 933,000 in 1971 to 1,705,000 in 1991 projected to 3,154,000 in 2011) in addition to the increase in single widowed people (from 1.6 million in 1971 to a projected 2.5 million in 2011) in the context of the changing role of housing associations which currently provide social housing for more than 900,000 tenants. The Housing Act of 1988 requires housing associations to seek funds from the private sector to replace partially funds which were hitherto provided through government. The ability to raise money in this way has meant that, as well as providing social housing, associations have moved into provision of accommodation for other groups such as medical staff (on behalf of health authorities) and students, thus encompassing profit and not-for-profit activities.

This widening of their scope also extends beyond the provision of housing (for which they were originally set up) to provision of community facilities such as meals on wheels and community alarm systems. However, a statement at the end of the article shows how the changes they have made in response to a change in the law and their funding base is beginning to distort their fundamental purpose of care and support of people who could be termed 'disadvantaged'.

Scase (2000), looking into the future, confirms the growth of single person households and an increase, in particular, of women living alone. He suggests also that in the next ten years in Britain, the population will age with no increase, and possibly a decline, in population coupled with a trend towards earlier retirement. These trends will have implications for the way advertising is oriented – towards the leisure and entertainment industries and from younger to what he calls 'time-rich, cash-rich, middle age consumers'. In addition, the rising costs of care for increased numbers of over 75s will drive developments in information computer technology in health care and welfare functions. Scase also comments that the increase in single person households will require the building of increased numbers of new homes (designed specifically for single person living), encourage the rejuvenation of inner city, urban areas and influence the development of interactive communication technologies including video surveillance systems against crime.

At least one implication of all this for many organisations is the requirement to increase investment in the creativity of their workers and systems to encourage innovation. This in turn has implications for the way organisations are structured (with hierarchical structures less evident) and for more flexible ways of working, frequently co-operating across organisations while still retaining a competitive edge – issues which are dealt with in more detail in Chapter 3 in particular and in many of the other chapters in this book.

This example illustrates how housing associations are being significantly affected, not only by democratic changes, but also by a combination of legislative, economic and other socio-cultural changes in the environment.

Activity 1.4   *Take the list you made as a result of carrying out Activity 1.2 and categorise each factor identified there according to whether you consider it to stem from the political, economic, technological or socio-cultural sectors of the environment.*

Triggers for change from the economic environment

Carrying out Activity 1.3 may show that some factors can be categorised in more than one way. This is not unusual and simply illustrates the fact that aspects of the organisational environment are interrelated and operate in a complex way to trigger change within organisations. However, because organisations operate in the main to make money or, in the case of public sector organisations (e.g. hospitals, schools, some railway systems) operate within budgets, some of their more serious concerns are with triggers for change in the economic environment.

This includes a concern for competitors and other issues, such as exchange rates, corporation tax, wage rates and skills availability, which determine their ability to compete (or, in the case of many publicly owned organisations, operate within budgets).

The European Union (EU) tends to be promoted as an *economic* union and, as such, its policies and requirements impinge on organisations in all its constituent countries. At the time of writing, in the context of the UK having recently agreed to a minimum wage for its own citizens, some other countries are suggesting that the EU should set a common minimum wage for workers in all its constituent countries. Examples such as this illustrate how organisations do not operate in their own clearly defined competitive environment. The capacity to compete is the result of a myriad different forces, which come from a range of different directions. What is more, at some times in an organisation's life, it will seek merely to survive, at other times to reduce profits in order to invest and at other times to push strongly for high profits in order to satisfy shareholders. Some organisations will, for a limited time, run at a loss or over budget – calculating that better times are in the future.

What is clear is that there is no one rationale for the way in which organisations react or interact with triggers for change coming from the PETS environment and perhaps constraints coming from their own histories and the influences of their temporal environments. External and internal politics play a part in decisions to change and in what way. While rational decision making may seem attractive, and many persuade themselves that this is what they are involved in, personal circumstances, attitudes and emotions also come into play. In addition, not only do triggers for change come from organisations' PETS environment, there are also forces for change operating within organisations themselves – and these also need to be managed. A number of writers (e.g. Huczynski and Buchanan, 2001; Johnson and Scholes, 1999; Paton and McCalman, 2000; Stewart, 1991) are in agreement in identifying these as internal triggers or sources of change. Consequently, organisations must cope with not only a plethora of external forces for change, but also internal forces for change.

Internal triggers for change

Drawing on the views of writers such as those just listed, the following is an indicative list of what might be categorised as internal triggers for change:

- an organisation becoming unionised or de-unionised
- a new chief executive or other senior manager
- a revision of the administrative structures
- the redesign of a group of jobs
- the redesign of a factory or office layout
- the purchase of new IT equipment
- a new marketing strategy
- a cut in overtime working

- staff redundancies
- strengthening of specific departments such as research and development.

A glance through this list will show that almost all can be conceptualised as changes in response to influences external to the organisation. It is, therefore, difficult in reality to separate completely internal from external triggers for change. Many writers suggest that changes in structure and ways of working should be aligned to changes in strategy which, in its turn, should be aligned to changes in the political, economic, technological and socio-economic environments. This argument is taken up in more detail in Chapter 3. Meanwhile, as the next section shows, there are other ways of categorising organisational environments which are more focused on organisations and change.

● ● ● ● Organisational responses to change

Thus far the discussion suggests that organisations operate in at least three types of environment, which together make up the total 'operating environment' (Sadler, 1989, p. 174) of an organisation. The first consists of the historical developments bringing changes over time. These range from those activities which are mainly industry focused to those which rely more on knowledge and brainpower – what Handy (1994) calls 'focused intelligence', that is the ability to acquire and apply knowledge and know how. This can be summarised as *temporal environment*. This is an environment which influences organisations in at least two ways. The first is in a general way, through the cycles of industry-based innovation which move organisations through major series of developments such as are shown in Figure 1.2. The second is in a more specific way through the life-cycle of the organisation itself. This includes its particular history built up from its founder days through periods of expansion and decline, all of which is instrumental in helping to explain an organisation's 'idiosyncrasies' of strategy and structure, culture, politics and leadership style.

The second type of environment is the external environment which includes the political (including legal), economic, technological and socio-cultural environment as well as those factors which are pushing for globalisation and an increasing concern with the physical environment (the PETS environment). The third environment is the organisation's internal environment which, to some extent, consists of those organisational changes which are the first-line responses to changes in the external and temporal environments. Figure 1.4 is a stylised depiction of the concept of organisations as systems operating in multidimensional environments, with all that this means for organisations and change. However, this way of conceptualising the organisational environment to some extent misses its dynamic nature and the degree of *strength* of the winds which are blowing for change.

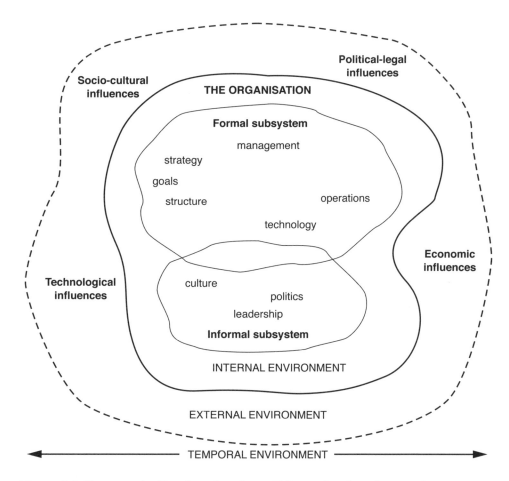

Figure 1.4 The organisational system in multidimensional environments

Environmental turbulence

The dynamics of any organisation's environment have also been described in terms of the degree of environmental turbulence. Ansoff and McDonnell (1990) state that a firm's performance is optimised when its aggressiveness and responsiveness match its environment. They propose five levels of environmental turbulence:

● *Level 1*: *Predictable.* A repetitive environment characterised by stability of markets; where the challenges repeat themselves; change is slower than the organisation's ability to respond; the future is expected to be the same as the past.

● *Level 2*: *Forecastable by extrapolation.* Complexity increases but managers can still extrapolate from the past and forecast the future with confidence.

● *Level 3*: *Predictable threats and opportunities.* Complexity increases further when the organisation's ability to respond becomes more problematic; however, the future can still be predicted with some degree of confidence.

● *Level 4*: *Partially predictable opportunities*. Turbulence increases with the addition of global and socio-political changes. The future is only partly predictable.
● *Level 5*: *Unpredictable surprises*. Turbulence increases further with unexpected events and situations occurring more quickly than the organisation can respond.

These levels can be compared to three different kinds of change situations proposed by Stacey (1996), namely: closed change, contained change and open-ended change – a description of which can be found in Illustration 1.10.

Illustration 1.10

Closed, contained and open-ended change

Closed change

When we look back at the history of an organisation, there are some sequences of events that we can clearly recount in a manner commanding the widespread agreement of the members involved. We are able to say what happened, why it happened, and what the consequences are. We are also able to explain in a widely accepted way how such a sequence of events and actions will continue to affect the future course of the business. We will call this a closed change situation.

Such closed change would normally apply to the continuing operation of an existing business. For example, consider a business that supplies pop records and tapes to the teenage market. Managers in that business are able to say with some precision how the number of customers in what market has changed over the past and furthermore how it will change for the next fifteen years or so. Those customers already exist. The managers can establish fairly clear-cut relationships between the number of customers and the number of records and tapes they have bought and will buy.

Contained change

Other sequences of events and actions flowing from the past are less clear-cut. Here we find that we are able to say only what probably happened, why it probably happened, and what its probable consequences were. The impact of such a sequence of events upon the future course of the business has similarly to be qualified by probability statements.

For example, the supplier of records and tapes will find it harder to explain why particular kinds of records and tapes sold better than others. That supplier will find it somewhat difficult to forecast what kinds of tapes and records will sell better in the future; but market research, lifestyle studies and statistical projections will enable reasonably helpful forecasts for at least the short term.

Open-ended change

There are yet other sequences of events and actions arising from the past and continuing to impact on the future where explanations do not command anything like widespread acceptance by those involved.

The company supplying records and tapes may have decided in the past to diversify into video film distribution, by acquiring another company already in that business. That acquisition may then become unprofitable and the managers involved could well subscribe to conflicting explanations of why this is so. Some may claim that the market for video films is too competitive. Others that the diversification was a wrong move because it meant operating in a different market with which they were not familiar. Others may say that it is due to a temporary decline in demand and that the market will pick up in the future. Yet others may ascribe it to poor management of the acquisition, or to a failure to integrate it properly into the business, or to a clash of cultures between the two businesses. What that team of managers does next to deal with low profitability obviously depends upon the explanation of past failure they subscribe to.

Source: Stacey, R. D. (1996), *Strategic Management and Organisational Dynamics*, 2nd edn (London, Pitman, pp. 23–4).

Both Ansoff and McDonnell's levels of environmental turbulence and Stacey's closed, contained and open-ended kinds of change situation can also be related to Stacey's (1996, p. 26) concepts of 'close to certainty' and 'far from certainty'. Thus, close to certainty describes a situation where organisational members face closed and contained change or, in Ansoff and McDonnell's terms, when the environment resembles levels 1 to 3. As the degree of environmental turbulence moves from level 4 to level 5 or, in Stacey's terms, to a situation of open-ended change, organisations can be said to be far from certainty. These changing situations have significant implications for the actions of managers as they attempt to choose appropriate strategies to deal with them.

Activity 1.5 offers the opportunity to carry out a simple environmental assessment of one or more organisations. Activity 1.5 is challenging and you will almost certainly say you need further information. However, organisations always exist in situations of imperfect knowledge and managers have to do their best in the circumstances. A start may be made by (simply?) identifying whether the forces for change are strong, moderate or weak. Strebel (1996) describes a strong change force as one causing a substantial decline or a substantial improvement in performance. He identifies a moderate force for change as one causing only a minor impact on performance while a weak one is one whose nature and direction are difficult to discern.

Activity 1.5   *Think about organisations with which you are familiar – three would be a good number. Carry out a simple environmental assessment for each organisation. To help this, consider the following:*

- *the PETS factors and the organisations' internal environments*
- *whether past historical developments (either in societal terms or organisational terms) have an influence on the organisations' strategies and operations.*

Using Ansoff and McDonnell's framework, make a judgement about the level of environmental turbulence prevailing for each organisation.

Match these levels to Stacey's types of change situations.

Identify the similarities and differences in the three organisations' environments.

What lessons can you draw about the probability of each organisation responding to future environmental triggers for change?

The strength of the forces for change can be related to the degree of turbulence in the environment: the stronger the force the more probable it is that the environment is moving to Ansoff and McDonnell's level 5. What this implies is that the ability to plan and manage change becomes ever more difficult as the forces and levels of turbulence increase. This is related to, but complicated further by, the different types of change that can be experienced by organisations.

● ● ● ● Conclusions

Organisations operate in multiple environments (temporal, external and internal). It is not difficult, therefore, to speculate on the effects that the many interacting influences referred to in this chapter can have on organisational life. The key task for organisations is to work with and try to manage these – in Schein's (1988, p. 94) words, organisations have continually to achieve 'external adaption and internal integration'. In addition, they need to be 'quick on their feet' to anticipate, where possible, opportunities and threats and react with knowledge to the 'unpredictable surprises' that Ansoff and McDonnell (1990) speak of. The purpose and focus of efforts to do so are, essentially, what managing organisational change is all about. This means understanding more fully how the formal aspects of organisational life respond to pressures from the internal, external and temporal environments – that is how change is leveraged through strategy, structure and operational processes. In addition, it means understanding the more informal processes such as power, politics and conflict, culture and leadership.

This chapter has commented on the winds of change as they blow variably and, to a degree, unpredictably. Having set the organisational environmental 'scene' in this chapter, Chapter 2 looks in more detail at the impact of these winds of change upon organisations with a more detailed examination of the nature of change itself.

Discussion questions and assignments

1 To what extent do you think the open systems concept is helpful in understanding how organisational change might happen?

2 Give examples of environmental forces for change which are likely to affect, significantly, the way organisations operate in ten years' time. Justify your choices.

3 Carry out an 'environmental scan' of an organisation which you know well. The following steps should help as well as access to large sheets of paper!

(a) Using the PETS framework, the results from Activities 1.2 and 1.3, and the suggestions in Figure 1.3, list those factors which you consider could affect the future performance of the organisation and/or the way it operates. Concentrate on those factors which are external to the organisation.

(b) Take this list and indicate where there are linkages between some factors and others. Doing this diagrammatically, using lines and arrows, helps. You could use a plus sign to show where the effects combine to reinforce each other and a minus sign to indicate where one factor might help negate another.

(c) Mark with a star those factors which are critically important to the organisation. Consider whether these originate mostly in the political–legal, economic, technological or socio-cultural parts of the PETS environment. Are they also linked to the general movement of organisations into value-oriented time?

(d) Finally, list the starred factors and rank them according to the volatility of the external environment. Consider whether this volatility provides an opportunity or a threat to the organisation and its future performance.

Through carrying out this process you may have realised how much you know about the organisation's environment but also how much you do not know! The outcome of this activity may be, therefore, not only an increased understanding of the environmental forces facing the organisation, but also a realisation that environmental scanning requires continuous vigilance and collection of information which must then be used creatively to help predict necessary changes within the organisation itself.

Case example

Shell may face fresh pressure over Nigerian oil discovery

FT

Shell, the Anglo-Dutch oil group which has come under international pressure to withdraw from Nigeria, is believed to have made a big oil discovery off the coast of the west African country. If the find is confirmed, it could rekindle international criticism of Shell's role in Nigeria under military rule. The company is the largest foreign oil producer in the country, accounting for about half the total output.

The company said yesterday it was conducting production tests at a well in the Bonga One exploration area in deep water off Nigeria. Shell said it was too early to assess the potential of the well. But oil industry observers in Lagos, Nigeria's commercial capital, say the company's operations at the site suggest that it has made a major discovery.

A Shell spokesman in Lagos said: 'We are doing reservoir tests now, and it can take several months to determine the size of the discovery. This is a whole new drilling environment, not like the [continental] shelf where the oil is being produced.'

Most of the company's Nigerian fields are onshore in the Niger delta, close to poor communities where resentment at the lack of local benefit from the oil industry has led to direct confrontation with Shell and other operators. This resulted in clashes with the Ogoni movement led by the late Ken Saro-Wiwa who

was executed last November after being convicted of the murder of rival Ogoni chiefs. The executions brought international criticism of Shell.

Shell has resisted demands that it withdraw from Nigeria, and it recently confirmed that it is to go ahead with a multi-billion dollar natural gas project in the country. But the problems associated with on-shore production have caused Shell and other large oil companies operating in Nigeria to look offshore for future developments. The deep water exploration blocks are seen as vital to the future of Shell and the oil industry as a whole in Nigeria.

In recent years, Shell has failed to replace its annual production with new discoveries. Its exploration division has been drawn to Nigeria because the geology of the deep water areas is similar to that of the US Gulf of Mexico, where a series of finds have been made by Shell recently.

Bonga One is the third well drilled in the new deep water blocks since international oil groups signed production-sharing contracts with the Nigerian government in 1993. The blocks are operated by Snepco, a different Shell subsidiary to the operator which is already producing nearly 1m barrels of oil a day, about half Nigeria's output.

Source: Robert Corzine in London and Paul Adams in Lagos, *Financial Times*, 8 March 1996, p. 1

▶

Case example *continued*

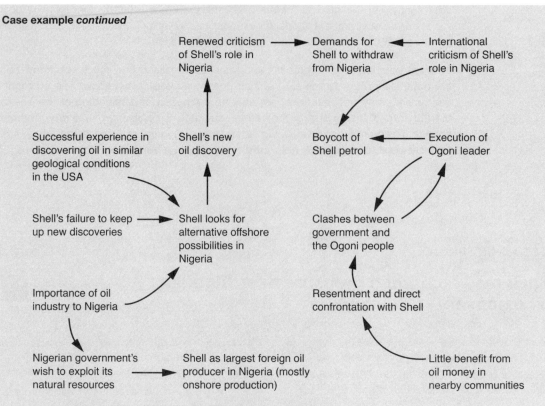

The multiple causes of the situation faced by Shell

Case exercise: Analysing the causes of change

Situations of change, such as the ones just described, draw attention to the complexity of the change environment. However, it is not sufficient merely to *identify* these triggers for change. Analysing the relationships between them – in other words, their systemic nature – is even more important. The multiple-cause diagram in the case example is an attempt to do this.

Multiple-cause diagrams such as this have the power to capture the complex dynamics of change situations. They help bring about a deeper understanding of how interventions in one variable can have far-reaching effects in other parts of the situation. They act, therefore, not only in a descriptive mode, but also as an analytical tool for understanding and managing change.

1 Write a brief account of how different elements of the temporal and PETS environments interact to influence the situation described in the case.

2 Consider how you could use multiple-cause diagrams to 'picture' the multiple and interacting causes which bring pressure for change in your own organisation or one you know well.

References

Applebee, A., Clayton, P., Pascoe, C. and Bruce, H. (2000), 'Australian academic use of the Internet: implications for university adminstrators', *Internet Research: Electronic Networking Applications and Policy*, Vol. 5, No. 2, 141–149. http://www.emerald-library.com

Ansoff, I. H. and McDonnell, E. J. (1990), *Implanting Strategic Management*, Englewood Cliffs, NJ, Prentice Hall.

Betts, P. (2000), 'A high-tech eruption in Etna valley', *Financial Times*, 17 October.

Bevan, K. (1996), 'The challenge of coping with change', *Financial Times*, 20 September.

Burns, T. and Stalker, G. M. (1966), *The Management of Innovation*, London, Tavistock.

Butler, R. (1991), *Designing Organizations. A Decision-Making Perspective*, London, Routledge, pp. 1–2.

Checkland, P. B. (1972), 'Towards a system-based methodology for real-world problem solving', *Journal of Systems Engineering*, Vol. 3, No. 2.

Child, J. (1973), 'Organization: a choice for man', in Child, J. (ed.), *Man and Organization*, London, George Allen & Unwin.

Clarke, L. (1994), *The Essence of Change*, Hemel Hempstead, Prentice Hall, p. 1.

Daft, R. L. (1989), *Organization Theory and Design* (2nd edn), St. Paul, MN, West Publishing Co.

Dawson, P. (1994), *Organizational Change. A Processual Approach*, London, PCP, pp. 1–2.

Department of Education and Employment (2000a), *Skills for All: Proposals for a National Skills Agenda*, Crown Copyright.

Department of Education and Employment (2000b) *Opportunity for All: Skills for the new economy. Initial Response to the National Skills Force Final Report from the Secretary of State for Education and Employment*, Crown Copyright.

Drucker, P. F. (1988), 'The coming of the new organization', *Harvard Business Review*, January–February, pp. 45–53.

Eccles, T. (1996), 'Management power and strategic change', *Financial Times*, 12 July.

Emery, F. E. and Trist, E. L. (1967), 'The next 30 years: concepts, methods and anticipations', *Human Relations*, p. 20.

Financial Times (2000), Editorial comment, *Financial Times*, 11 October.

Fisher, A. (2000), 'Many markets set for macroeconomic shock', *Financial Times*, 18 October, p. V.

FT Life on the net (2000), *Financial Times*, 4 September, p. 1. www.ft.com/lifeonthenet

FT Life on the net (2000), *Financial Times*, 5 September, p. 1. www.ft.com/lifeonthenet

FT Life on the net (2000), *Financial Times*, 8 September, p. 1. www.ft.com/lifeonthenet

FT Life on the net (2000), *Financial Times*, 11 September, p. 1. www.ft.com/lifeonthenet

FT Life on the net (2000), *Financial Times*, 13 September, p. 1. www.ft.com/lifeonthenet

FT Life on the net (2000), *Financial Times*, 14 September, p. 1. www.ft.com/lifeonthenet

FT Life on the net (2000), *Financial Times*, 15 September, p. 1. www.ft.com/lifeonthenet

Furnham, A. (2000), 'Work in 2020 prognostications about the world of work 20 years into the millennium', *Journal of Managerial Psychology*, Vol. 15, No. 3, pp. 242–54.

Graham, R. (2000), 'French consumer confidence ebbs', *Financial Times*, 5 October.

Goodman, M. (1995), *Creative Management*, Hemel Hempstead, Prentice Hall.

Handy, C. (1994), *The Empty Raincoat*, London, Hutchinson.

Haverson, P. (2000), 'A key player in the sports team', *Financial Times*, 2 August, p. 10.

Howcroft, D. and Mitev, N. (2000), 'An empirical study of Internet usage and difficulties among medical practice management in the UK', *Internet Research: Electronic Networking Applications and Policy*, Vol. 10, No. 2, pp. 170–81. http://www.emerald-library.com

Huczynski, A. and Buchanan, D. (2001) *Organizational Behaviour* (4th edn), Hemel Hempstead, Prentice Hall.

Johnson, G. and Scholes, K. (1999), *Exploring Corporate Strategy. Text and Cases* (5th edn), Hemel Hempstead, Prentice Hall.

Jones, P., Palmer, J., Osterweil, C. and Whitehead, D. (1996), *Delivering Exceptional Performance: Aligning the Potential of Organisations, Teams and Individuals*, London, Pitman.

Kazim, A., Williamson, H. and McNulty, S. (2000), 'Foreign investors desert south-east Asia for China', *Financial Times*, 13 October.

McCallin, J. (2000), 'From mousemat to doormat', *The Guardian*, 23 September.

Mannermann, M. (1998), 'Politics and science = futures studies', *American Behavioral Scientist*, Vol. 42, pp. 427–35.

Mills, M. (2000), 'Coming to a screen near you: By 2020 the workplace will have changed beyond recognition. Now, where have you heard that before? Merope Mills on the soothsayers and the sceptics', Office Hours, *The Guardian*, 18 September.

Nadler, D. A. (1988), 'Concepts for the management of organizational change', in Tushman, M. L. and Moore, W. L. (eds), *Readings in the Management of Innovation*, New York, Ballinger Publishing Company, pp. 718–32.

Nadler, D. A. and Tushman, M. L. (1988), 'A model for diagnosing organizational behavior', in Tushman, M. L. and Moore, W. L. (eds), *Readings in the Management of Innovation*, New York, Ballinger Publishing Company, pp. 148–63.

Nadler, D. A. and Tushman, M. L. (1999), 'The organization of the future: strategic imperatives and core competencies for the 21st century', *Organizational Dynamics*, Vol. 28, No. 1, pp. 71–80.

Paton, R. A. and McCalman, J. (2000), *Change Management: Guide to Effective Implementation* (2nd edn), London, PCP.

Roberts, D. (2000), 'A dragon with plenty of good connections', *FT Telecoms, Financial Times*, 20 September.

Sadler, P. (1989), 'Management development', in Sisson, K. (ed.), *Personnel Management in Britain* (2nd edn), Oxford, Blackwell, p. 174.

Scase, R. (1999), *Britain towards 2010: The Changing Business Environment*, Office of Science and Technology, Department of Trade and Industry, Crown Copyright.

Schein, E. H. (1988), 'Coming to a new awareness of organisational culture', *Sloan Management Review*, Vol. 25, No. 1, p. 94.

Silverman, D. (1970), *The Theory of Organisations*, London, Heinemann Educational Books.

Stacey, R. D. (1996), *Strategic Management and Organisational Dynamics* (2nd edn), London, Pitman.

Stacey, R. K. (2000), *Strategic Management and Organisational Dynamics. The Challenge of Complexity* (3rd edn), Harlow, Financial Times/Prentice Hall.

Statt, D. A. (1991), *The Concise Dictionary of Management*, London, Routledge, p. 102.

Stewart, J. (1991), *Managing Change Through Training and Development*, London, Kogan Page, pp. 118–20.

Storey, J., Edwards, P. and Sisson, K. (1997), *Managers in the Making: Careers, Development and Control in Corporate Britain and Japan*, London, Sage.

Strebel, P. (1996), 'Choosing the right path', *Mastering Management*, Part 14, *Financial Times*.

Taylor, F. W. (1911), *Principles of Scientific Management*, New York, Harper & Row.

Taylor, R. (1996), 'Bigger role for governments will be in fashion next year', *Financial Times*, 28 June, p. 4.

Walker, T. (1996), 'China leads the pack – so far', *Financial Times*, 28 June, p. 4.

Westbrook, R. (2000), 'Look to the process for a better product', *Financial Times Mastering Management*, 16 October.

Wood, S. (1989), 'The transformation of work?' in Wood, S. (ed.), *The Transformation of Work*, London, Unwin Hyman, Chapter 1.

Chapter 2

The nature of organisational change

This chapter introduces the idea that organisational change has many faces, that is that there are many different types of change. A basic distinction is made between convergent types of change and transformational change which is organisation wide and is characterised by radical shifts in strategy, mission and values as well as associated changes of structures and systems. Attention is drawn, also, to the idea that some change *emerges* while at other times change can be *planned*. The chapter concludes with an examination of the different change situations which organisations experience and provides an appreciation of their relationship to the way change might be designed and implemented – thus looking forward to the chapters in Part Three of the book, where different methodologies for designing and implementing change are discussed in more detail.

Objectives

To:

- *emphasise the complex nature of organisational change*

- *describe and discuss the multidimensional nature of organisational change*

- *analyse change situations in order to choose appropriate methods of managing and implementing change*

- *recognise that there are limitations to the 'common-sense' approach to managing change because of cultural, political and leadership influences.*

● ● ● ● The changing faces of change

Consider the statements in Illustration 2.1.

Illustration 2.1

Changing organisations

Xenos, a world leader in the development and implementation of software solutions that transform documents and data into e-content, today announced a restructuring of its organisation. The changes will help fast-track new product development, enhance customer support and enable the forging of new strategic alliances to fuel the company's future growth. Key elements of the restructure include: the consolidation of the company's product development; the merger of implementation services and pre-sales activities; a new customer support operation; the establishment of a new global marketing organisation, and the streamlining of finance, human resources and administration departments. The restructure involves a reduction in staff of 12 per cent across the organisation globally and one-time costs of approximately $1 million.

(M2 Communications Ltd, Wednesday 30 August 2000)

Novell to cut 900 jobs and restructure

Novell, a leading software company, yesterday announced a restructuring of its operations that included cutting 900 jobs, or 16 per cent of its workforce. The job losses had been expected as the company focused on e-business applications and moved beyond its core network operating system business.

(Tom Foremski, *Financial Times*, Thursday 7 September 2000, p. 7)

Moving forward, our single business managing the group's own licensed assets will be focused on cost cutting and greater efficiency. The group's other core businesses – customer sales, contract asset management and business process outsourcing – will be focused on growth, controlling costs and being genuinely profitable. Across them all, we will embrace the benefits of eBusiness – investing in ideas and pushing new boundaries, a very different and exciting approach from anything the group has done before. Business as usual is not an option for us. There are opportunities to seize. We will reorganise the group, effective from October 2000, and make progress on the firm base of the group's two cores skills, and we will play to our strengths in our initiatives to exploit the opportunities of competition and eBusiness.

(John Roberts, Chief Executive, *The United Utilities Shareholders' Review*, 2000, p. 1)

Adaptability furnishes key to craftsmen's long survival

As an example of the changing face of industrial Britain, High Wycombe in Buckinghamshire is hard to beat. ... Due to intense competition from furniture makers in lower-cost countries, High Wycombe's companies in this field have dwindled to about 20. But the survivors ... are far from downbeat. (For instance) Peter Head, managing director, says the company (Hands of Wycombe) has had to introduce new designs to keep up with the competition. It makes up-market office furniture – including 'pods' which combine a desk, chair and computer workstation and are directed towards the needs of high-technology businesses. These can sell for thousands of pounds.

(Peter Marsh, *Financial Times*, Wednesday 6 September 2000, p. 32)

Illustration 2.1 *continued*

A good year for 'patient protection' laws
Mark 1996 as the year of the managed-care customer. Mandated 48-hour maternity stays, bans on gag clauses imposed on physicians by HMOs, and other 'patient protection' measures sailed through state legislatures this year, each passing in at least 16 states. Portions of the Patient Protection Act, drafted by the American Medical Association, passed in at least 20 states. It was considered in another 15. ... The flurry of incremental reforms caught the managed-care industry off guard, said Joy Johnson Wilson, director of the health committee at the Denver-based National Conference of State Legislatures. She predicted managed-care organisations will change their practices to head off further legislation in 1997.

(*Modern Healthcare*, 28 October 1996, p. 22.)

All the statements in Illustration 2.1 identify actual or predicted organisational change. However, a cursory reading of these statements indicates that change in one organisation is not the same as change in another. For instance, at Xenos, it seems that there is very little which is left untouched in the changes that are planned. Change is proposed right across the organisation including a significant reduction in the number of staff. The article from which this extract is taken indicates that all these changes are a result of a change in Xenos' strategy which is, in turn, a reaction to the changing commercial, technological and economic environment in which the company operates.

Novell's restructuring is reported to be costing $40m–$50m but it expects to set $25m of savings against this. The report on Novell again indicates that the changes are large scale and are in response to changes in market demand for the software products supplied by Novell. By contrast, while United Utilities' Chief Executive's statement in the annual report indicates that 'business as usual is not an option', he goes on to say that, in seeking to deliver growth (while at the same time delivering cost reductions) the intention is to do it in a way that aligns with the group's core skills, that is not doing 'things we do not understand'. Consequently, United Utilities gives the impression that, while changes must occur in response to government regulatory requirements and the increasing possibilities of E-commerce, some parts of the group's businesses, while striving for growth, will do this using what they know rather than venturing into unknown territory.

It is arguable whether the term 'adaptability' should be applied to the changes being made at United Utilities. This is, however, an appropriate term to describe how the fourth organisation mentioned – Hands of Wycombe – has responded to changing demands for its product. Continuing to serve a market which they know well, they have, even so, had to keep up with the changing demands for their products brought about by changing requirements resulting from the advent of computer-based office systems. The final example of change features the many ways in which new legislation impacts on, in this case, part of health services in the USA. However, as the article implies, the changes required from this particular group of care providers would seem to be well within their capabilities without radical restructuring or wholesale reorganisation.

Strebel (1996a, p. 5), in an article which originally appeared in the *Financial Times*, says 'Change may be a constant but it is not always the same' and this is well exemplified by the examples just given. Building on this notion, what follows in this chapter is a discussion of a number of frameworks for categorising change and why it is necessary to do so if organisational change is to be successful. The discussion starts with a broad generalisation of the concept of change.

Varieties of change

A starting point for considering the nature of organisational change is Grundy's (1993) three 'varieties of change' as shown in Figure 2.1. As a background to proposing these, Grundy states that many managers perceive change as a homogeneous concept, while others describe change as being primarily the enemy of stability. However, he maintains that it is possible to differentiate a number of characteristic types of change.

The first of these he defines as 'smooth incremental change'. Smooth incremental change is change which evolves slowly in a systematic and predictable way. Grundy maintains that this type of change is mainly reminiscent of the UK situation from the 1950s to early 1970s, but that this situation would be relatively exceptional in the 1990s and the future. It is important to note that, in Figure 2.1, the vertical axis represents *rate* of change, not *amount* of change. Thus, smooth incremental change does involve an amount of change but this happens at a constant rate.

The second variety of change Grundy terms 'bumpy incremental change'. This is characterised by periods of relative tranquillity punctuated by acceleration in the pace of change. He likens the 'bumps' to 'the movement of continental land

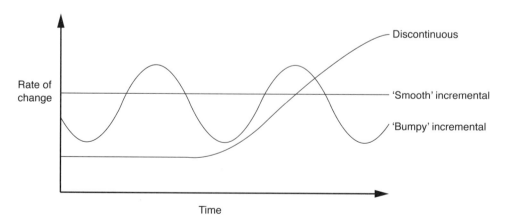

Figure 2.1 Major types of change

Source: Grundy, T. (1993), *Implementing Strategic Change* (London, Kogan Page, p. 25).

masses where the "fault" enables periodic readjustment to occur without cataclysmic effect' (p. 24). He says that the triggers for this type of change are likely to include those from both the environment in which organisations operate as well as internal changes such as those instigated to improve efficiency and ways of working. An example given is the periodic reorganisations that organisations go through. One way of categorising both types of incremental change is to see them as change which is associated more with the *means* by which organisations achieve their goals, rather than as a change in the goals themselves. The last two examples of change described earlier (at Hands of Wycombe and in the managed-care sector of American health care generally) could be posed as instances of this type of change.

Grundy's third variety of change is 'discontinuous change', which he defines as 'change which is marked by rapid shifts in either strategy, structure or culture, or in all three' (p. 26). An example given is that of the privatisation of previously publicly owned utilities, for instance electricity generation and distribution. Another example is what Strebel (1996b) calls a 'divergent breakpoint', that is, change which results from the discovery of a new business opportunity and he instances the first Apple computer, the arrival of the Macintosh and, most recently, the new chips and software. The opportunities offered by the development of the Internet and being able to access this, not only through computers, but also through television sets and mobile telephones, are most likely to lead to forms of discontinuous change in many organisations. The change involving strategy, structure (and almost certainly culture and the relative influence held by different individuals and groups) being undertaken by Xenos is a good example of discontinuous change. However, not all instances of discontinuous change are linked to technological innovations. Health scares rendering some food products unsaleable can have cataclysmic effects throughout an industry. Thus, discontinuous change can be likened to change in response to the higher levels of environmental turbulence detailed by Ansoff and McDonnell, which were described in Chapter 1.

Organisational convergence and upheaval

Grundy's three types of change are somewhat simplistic and appear to be based on observation rather than investigation and research. This is not the case with a framework for describing change proposed by Tushman, Newman and Romanelli (1988) – even though it is similar to that of Grundy in some respects. On the basis of an examination of numerous organisational studies and case histories, these writers propose a model of organisational life which consists of 'periods of incremental change, or convergence, punctuated by discontinuous changes' (p. 707).

They suggest there are two types of converging change: fine-tuning and incremental adaptations. Both these types of change have the common aim of maintaining the fit between organisational strategy, structure and processes. However, whereas fine-tuning is aimed at doing better what is already done well, incremental adaptation involves small changes in response to minor shifts in the environment in which organisations operate – what the authors popularly call the 'ten-percent change'.

Both fine-tuning and incremental adjustments to environmental shifts allow organisations to perform more effectively and optimise the consistencies between strategy, structure, people and processes. Yet, Tushman *et al.* show how, as organisations grow, become more successful and develop internal forces for stability, these same forces eventually produce resistance when, for whatever reason, an organisation's strategy must change. Thus at times of major change in an organisation's environment, incremental adjustment will not bring about the major changes in strategy, structure, people and processes which might be required. At times such as these, Tushman *et al.* maintain that most organisations will be required to undergo discontinuous or frame-breaking change. Thus, in any organisation's life-cycle, periods of relative tranquillity will be punctuated with (probably shorter) periods of frame-breaking change.

Illustration 2.2 summarises the definition of frame-breaking change advanced by Tushman *et al.*

An example of frame-breaking change springing from changes in the legal and political conditions under which British Rail had previously operated (an example of what Tushman *et al.* categorise as 'industry discontinuities') can be found in the privatisation, around 1997, of British Rail, in particular the splitting of the management of the rail infrastructure (the track, stations, timetabling, signalling etc.) from the running of the trains. However, this is not the first frame-breaking change that has happened to British Rail since its nationalisation in 1962.

In 1984, British Rail was restructured from a monolithic entity into three passenger product sectors – Inter-City (long-distance passenger services), London and South East (London commuter services) and provincial services (the necessary, but basically unremunerative services). This restructuring left freight and parcel services as a separate business. For the first time since nationalisation, the organisation was asked by government to produce a corporate business plan.

A second fundamental reorganisation took place in 1992 entitled 'Organising for Quality'. This included transferring the responsibilities of the six geographically based regions entirely to a business management structure based on the type of rail service provided (Thomas, 1992). This prevailed until 1993 when the government passed another act which sought to 'provide and encourage the injection of private sector involvement, expertise and discipline into the provision of public services' (Smith, 1993, pp. 12–13). The effects of this act resulted in the transfer of passenger services to private sector management by franchising arrangements.

At the time of writing, the franchises have come up for renewal with harsher criteria being put upon those bidding for them in the light of serious problems with some existing operators in achieving targets for trains running to time and without cancellations.

The changes British Rail has gone through, as a result of the 1993 Act, fit the definition of revolutionary change advanced by Tushman *et al.*, that is changes of

Illustration 2.2

On frame-breaking change

The need for discontinuous change springs from one or a combination of the following:

- Industry discontinuities – sharp changes in the legal, political or technological conditions which shift the basis of competition. These could include: deregulation, substitute product technologies, substitute process technologies, the emergence of industry standards or dominant designs, major economic changes (e.g. oil crises), legal shifts (e.g. patent protection, trade/regulator barriers).
- Product/life-cycle shifts – changes in strategy from the emergence of a product to its establishment in the market, the effects of international competition.
- Internal company dynamics – the implications of size for new management design, new management style as inventor–entrepreneurs give way to the need for more steady state management, revised corporate portfolio strategy which can sharply alter the role and resources assigned to business units or functional areas.

The scope of frame-breaking change includes discontinuous change throughout the organisation. Frame-breaking change is usually implemented rapidly. Frame-breaking changes are revolutionary changes of the system as opposed to incremental changes in the system. Frame-breaking change usually involves the following features:

- Reformed mission and core values – new definition of company mission.
- Altered power and status – reflecting shifts in the bases of competition and resource allocation.
- Reorganisation – new strategy requires a modification in structure, systems and procedures, change of organisation form.
- Revised interaction patterns – new procedures, work flows, communication networks, decision-making patterns.
- New executives – usually from outside the organisation.

Frame-breaking change is revolutionary in that the shifts reshape the entire nature of the organisation. It requires discontinuous shifts in strategy, structure, people and processes concurrently. Reasons for the rapid, simultaneous implementation of frame-breaking change include:

- Synergy – the need for all pieces of the organisation to pull together.
- Pockets of resistance – have a chance to grow and develop when frame-breaking change is implemented slowly.
- Pent-up need for change – when constraints are relaxed, change is in fashion.
- Riskiness and uncertainty – the longer the implementation period, the greater the period of uncertainty and instability.

Source: Based on Tushman, M. L., Newman, W. H. and Romanelli, E. (1988), 'Convergence and upheaval: managing the unsteady pace of organizational evolution', in Tushman, M. L. and Moore, W. L. (eds) (1988), *Readings in the Management of Innovation* (New York, Ballinger Publishing Company, pp. 712–13).

the system. They also meet their requirement that frame-breaking change should be rapid, by which they mean implementation in something like an 18–24-month period. It is interesting to note, though, that although different periods in the life to date of the UK railway system could be said to equate to periods of frame-breaking change, taking a long-term view, the history of the system could be said to conform to the model of organisational life given by Tushman *et al.* earlier, that is, 'periods of … convergence, punctuated by discontinuous changes'. Tushman *et al.* say: 'Our research strongly suggests that the convergence/upheaval pattern occurs within departments … at the business-unit level … and at the corporate level of analysis' (p. 708). This suggests that frame-breaking change is not restricted to the strategic level of organisations, as the work of two Australian researchers shows.

Fine-tuning to corporate transformation

Grundy (1993) does not claim any particular status for his typology of change; he states specifically that it is not an empirically tested model. The power of the Tushman *et al.* typology is its claim to be based on research and investigation. This is also the case with the typology put forward by Australian academics Dunphy and Stace (1993). What is more, they claim the status of a model when their typology of change, on the one hand, is combined with a typology of styles of change management, on the other. The full Dunphy and Stace model is discussed further in Chapter 6. What is interesting here is the four descriptions which represent their scale of change. Illustration 2.3 reproduces these descriptions.

A simple correspondence between Grundy's and Dunphy and Stace's categorisations of change is not possible. However, it is reasonable to suggest that Dunphy and Stace's scale types 1 and 2 are typical of Grundy's concept of smooth incremental change, while their scale types 3 and 4 are reminiscent of Grundy's bumpy incremental and discontinuous types of change respectively. The benefit of the Dunphy and Stace model, though, is in the detailed descriptions of each scale type and its testing with the executives, managers and supervisors of 13 Australian organisations from the service sector. Interestingly, organisations operating scale 1 and 2 type changes were in the minority, leading the researchers to conclude that modular and corporate transformations had become the norm rather than the exception.

However, care must be taken with conclusions such as this based on a small sample of 13 organisations from one sector of industry only. For instance, Abrahamson (2000) in an article entitled 'Change WITHOUT pain' challenges the need for organisations to rush headlong to change as fast as they can, following each change with another one as the first seems not to work. What he recommends is a process of 'painless tinkering with existing business practices and alternating a few bigger changes with a lot of incremental ones', which seems very much like Grundy's bumpy incremental change with quite long periods of incremental change between the bumps.

Having said this, Dunphy and Stace are not on their own in suggesting the types of change they do. For instance, there is a great deal of correspondence between the typology of Tushman *et al.* and that of Dunphy and Stace. It is fairly clear that Dunphy and Stace found the same two types of change as are grouped by Tushman *et al.* under the concept of converging change. Both sets of researchers use identical names – 'fine-tuning' and 'incremental adjustment'. Where Dunphy and Stace go beyond Tushman *et al.* is in, apparently, splitting what Tushman *et al.* termed 'frame-breaking' change into two types – 'modular transformation' and 'corporate transformation'. This is a useful development in detailing more

Illustration 2.3

Defining the scale of change

Scale Type 1: Fine tuning

Organizational change which is an ongoing process characterized by fine tuning of the 'fit' or match between the organization's strategy, structure, people, and processes. Such effort is typically manifested at departmental/divisional levels and deals with one or more of the following:

- Refining policies, methods, and procedures.
- Creating specialist units and linking mechanisms to permit increased volume and increased attention to unit quality and cost.
- Developing personnel especially suited to the present strategy (improved training and development; tailoring award systems to match strategic thrusts).
- Fostering individual and group commitment to the company mission and the excellence of one's own department.
- Promoting confidence in the accepted norms, beliefs, and myths.
- Clarifying established roles (with their associated authorities and posers), and the mechanisms for allocating resources.

Scale Type 2: Incremental adjustment

Organizational change which is characterized by incremental adjustments to the changing environment. Such change involves distinct modifications (but not radical change) to corporate business strategies, structures, and management processes, for example:

- Expanding sales territory.
- Shifting the emphasis among products.
- Improved production process technology.
- Articulating a modified statement of mission to employees.

- Adjustments to organizational structures within or across divisional boundaries to achieve better links in product/service delivery.

Scale Type 3: Modular transformation

Organizational change which is characterized by major realignment of one or more departments/divisions. The process of radical change is focused on these subparts rather than on the organization as a whole, for example:

- Major restructuring of particular department/divisions.
- Changes in key executives and managerial appointments in these areas.
- Work and productivity studies resulting in significantly reduced or increased workforce numbers.
- Reformed departmental/divisional goals.
- Introduction of significantly new process technologies affecting key departments or divisions.

Scale Type 4: Corporate transformation

Organizational change which is corporation-wide, characterized by radical shifts in business strategy, and revolutionary changes throughout the whole organization involving many of the following features:

- Reformed organizational mission and core values.
- Altered power and status affecting the distribution of power in the organization.
- Reorganization – major changes in structures, systems, and procedures across the organization.
- Revised interaction patterns – new procedures, work flows, communication networks, and decision-making patterns across the organization.
- New executives in key managerial positions from outside the organization.

Source: Dunphy, D. and Stace, D. (1993), 'The strategic management of corporate change', *Human Relations*, Vol. 45, No. 8, pp. 917–18.

clearly the different levels at which frame-breaking change can take place. It still recognises the implications of these types of change for goals and purposes, but identifies the fact that these may have different meanings at the departmental/divisional level than at the corporate/organisational level.

Activity 2.1   *Look again at Dunphy and Stace's scale types of change (see Illustration 2.3). Position an organisation with which you are familiar on the following scale:*

Fine tuning	Incremental adjustment	Modular transformation	Corporate transformation

◄──►

Tushman et al. (1988) say: 'The most effective firms take advantage of relatively long convergent periods. These periods of incremental change build on and take advantage of organization inertia. Frame-breaking change is quite dysfunctional if the organization is successful and the environment is stable. If, however, the organization is performing poorly and/or if the environment changes substantially, frame-breaking change is the only way to realign the organization with its competitive environment' (pp. 713–14).

Form a view as to whether the type of change now being experienced by your organisation fits the environment in which it is currently operating and which is likely to prevail in the foreseeable future.

The types of change discussed earlier are helpful for a number of reasons which are discussed later in this chapter. However, they indicate little about the way change comes about, other than to say it occurs, generally, in response to changes in the organisational environment. Writers about types of change such as those identified above assume, perhaps, that change can be *planned*. However, as the next section shows, this is not always the case.

Planned and emergent change

Fine-tuning and incremental change are features of all organisational life and, while they can be planned, are frequently associated with change as it *emerges*. The idea of emergent change has been linked by Wilson (1992) with the concept of organisations as open systems. Writers such as McAleer (1982), Checkland (1972), von Bertanlanfy (1971) and Kast and Rosenzweig (1970) have produced detailed discussions of the concept of a system which includes organisational systems. Briefly, these discussions include the idea of organisations striving to maintain a state of equilibrium where the forces for change are balanced by the forces for stability. Therefore, organisations viewed as systems will always strive to restore equilibrium whenever they are disturbed. According to this view, the organisational system is constantly sensing its environment in order continuously to adjust to maintain its purpose and optimum state.

It could be speculated that, in an ideal world, organisational sensing of the environment would be so effective as to render frame-breaking change unnecessary. If organisations responded continuously to the need for change, they would have no need for the periodic upheavals which sometimes seem inevitable. In other words, through their assessing continuously the environments in which they operate, change should emerge almost 'naturally'.

However, writers such as Tushman *et al.* (1988) and Johnson (1987, 1988) describe a phenomenon whereby managers and other organisational personnel become so comfortable with 'how we work here' and 'what we hold important here' that they also become impervious to warning signs of impending difficulties from the environment. According to Tushman *et al.*, this is the effect of what they call the 'double-edged sword' of converging periods of change. Thus, the habits, patterns of behaviour, finding out the best way to do things and commitment to values which have been built up during periods of converging change can contribute significantly to the success of the organisation. However, the organisational history built up during this period can also be counterproductive in restricting the vigilance needed towards the environment and may become a source of resistance to the need for more radical forms of change.

Johnson (1988, p. 44) refers to the organisational 'paradigm' to describe the core set of beliefs and assumptions held commonly by the managers of an organisation. He says:

> This set of beliefs, which evolves over time, might embrace assumptions about the nature of the organisational environment, the managerial style in the organisation, the nature of its leaders, and the operational routines seen as important to ensure the success of the organisation.

The fact that the paradigm is held relatively commonly, is taken for granted and is not, therefore, seen as problematical means that signals from the environment are filtered through it. These signals are only made sense of in terms of what Johnson (1988, p. 44) calls 'the way we do things around here'. Therefore, when signals for change come from the environment, he says:

> [Their] relevance is determined, not by the competitive activity, but by the constructs of the paradigm [and] in these circumstances it is likely that, over time, the phenomenon of 'strategic drift' will occur: that is gradually, probably imperceptibly, the strategy of the organisation will become less and less in tune with the environment in which the organisation exists.   (Johnson, 1988, p. 44)

As the process of strategic drift continues, an organisation's strategy, structure and processes gradually move further away from a path which would take account of the triggers for change coming from the environment. It is at these points that more frame-breaking or revolutionary change becomes necessary to realign the organisation's purposes and operations with environmental imperatives.

From the discussion so far, it is clear that the process of strategic drift forces organisations into a more conscious deliberate *planning* of change. However, the distinction between emergent and planned change is not clear-cut. Criticisms of the idea that change can be planned logically and systematically have been made by Wilson (1992). He argues that planned change is a management concept which relies heavily on a single view of the way change ought to be done. This view assumes that the environment is known and, therefore, that a logical process of environmental analysis can be harnessed in the service of planning any change.

Wilson says this view emphasises the role of human agency, that is, that chief executives and managers are able to invoke the changes they feel are necessary and that this process is not problematic. His argument is that this view does not take account of the context in which change must take place; for instance, the cultural and political components which influence most, if not all, implementations of any planned change.

Quinn (1980) has also criticised the idea of planned change as something which is deliberately and carefully thought through and then implemented. His research into the decision-making processes of a number of organisations demonstrated that most strategic decisions are made in spite of formal planning systems rather than because of them. As reinforcement of this idea, Stacey (2000, p. 92) summarises the key points made by Quinn as follows:

1 Effective managers do not manage strategically in a piecemeal manner. They have a clear view of what they want to achieve, where they are trying to take the business. The destination is thus intended.

2 But the route to that destination, the strategy itself, is not intended from the start in any comprehensive way. Effective managers know that the environment they have to operate in is uncertain and ambiguous. They therefore sustain flexibility by holding open the method of reaching the goal.

3 The strategy itself then emerges from the interaction between different groupings of people in the organisation, different groupings with different amounts of power, different requirements for and access to information, different time spans and parochial interest. These different pressures are orchestrated by senior managers. The top is always reassessing, integrating and organising.

4 The strategy emerges or evolves in small incremental, opportunistic steps. But such evolution is not piecemeal or haphazard because of the agreed purpose and the role of top management in reassessing what is happening. It is this that provides the logic in the incremental action.

5 The result is an organisation that is feeling its way to a known goal, opportunistically learning as it goes.

Quinn terms this process 'logical incrementalism' in that it is based in a certain logic of thinking but is incremental in its ability to change in the light of new information and the results of ongoing action. Opportunism plays an important part in this process (*see* Illustration 2.4).

● ● ● ● Predictable change

In some respects, change could be viewed as neither wholly emergent nor planned. As cycles of growth and activity are an essential part of living, so the concept of an organisational life-cycle (Greiner, 1972; Kimberley and Miles, 1980) has been used to describe the stages through which organisations go as they grow and develop. Figure 2.2 illustrates these in terms of the size and maturity of organisations.

Illustration 2.4

Proactively managing incrementalism in the development of corporate strategies

Quinn (1979) makes the following statement to illustrate how executives proactively manage incrementalism in the development of corporate strategies.

Typically you start with general concerns, vaguely felt. Next you roll an issue around in your mind till you think you have a conclusion that makes sense for the company. You then go out and sort of post the idea without being too wedded to its details. You then start hearing the arguments pro and con, and some very good refinements of the idea usually emerge. Then you pull the idea in and put some resources together to study it so it can be put forward as more of a formal presentation. You wait for 'stimuli occurrences' or 'crises', and launch pieces of the idea to help in these situations. But they lead toward your ultimate aim. You know where you want to get. You'd like to get there in six months. But it may take three years, or you may not get there. And when you do get there, you don't know whether it was originally your own idea – or somebody else had reached the same conclusion before you and just got you on board for it. You never know. The president would follow the same basic process, but he could drive it much faster than an executive lower in the organization.

Source: Quinn, J. B. (1979), 'Xerox Corporation (B)', copyrighted case, Amos Tuck School of Business Administration, Dartmouth College, Hanover, NH.

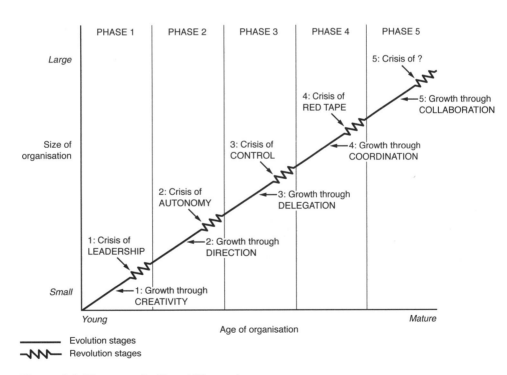

Figure 2.2 The organisational life-cycle

Source: Reprinted by permission of *Harvard Business Review*. Greiner, L. E. (1972), 'Evolution and revolution as organizations grow', July–August, p. 41. Copyright © 1972 by the President and Fellows of Harvard College. All rights reserved.

Greiner maintains that, as organisations grow in size and mature, their activities go through five phases, each of which is associated with a different growth period in an organisation's life. In addition, as each growth period moves into the next, the organisation goes through a shorter-lived crisis period. These are, respectively, the evolution and revolution stages shown in Figure 2.2. Illustration 2.5 is a brief description of a typical life-cycle pattern which is complemented by Clarke's (1994) useful categorisation of the characteristics and crisis points associated with each phase of growth (*see* Table 2.1).

Illustration 2.5

A typical life-cycle pattern

1. The entrepreneurial stage

In this first (often entrepreneurial) stage, the first task to be achieved is to provide a service or manufacture product. Survival is the key strategy. Organisational culture is fashioned by the founders of the organisation. It may be a brand-new organisation or a new subsidiary or part of an established, larger organisation. Success brings growth and the need to recruit more staff. Staff need managing, and the question of future organisational strategy becomes more complex. The alternatives are to limit growth and remain small (but risk being unable to sustain competition) or to grow and recruit professional managers.

2. The collective stage

The organisation begins to take 'shape'. Departments and functions begin to be defined and the division of labour is the dominant theme. The professional managers recruited tend to be strong leaders who share the same vision as the founders. Further growth brings the need for management control and delegation. The organisation has begun to establish its position; internal tasks are allocated and who has responsibility and autonomy to carry them out become pre-eminent.

3. The formalisation stage

Systems of communication and control become more formal. There is a need to differentiate between the tasks of management – to make strategic decisions and to implement policy – and those of lower-level managers, who are expected to carry out and oversee operational decisions. Bureaucratisation occurs as systems of co-ordination and control emerge, including salary structures, reward and incentive schemes, levels in the hierarchy, reporting relationships and formalised areas of discretion and autonomy for lower-level managers. The organisation continues to grow, but burdened by the process of bureaucratisation the need for the structure to be 'freed up' becomes pressing.

4. The elaboration stage

This is the stage of strategic change. The organisation may have reached a plateau in its growth curve and may even show the first stages of decline in performance. Managers used to handling bureaucratic structures and processes usually have to learn new skills to achieve change, such as team work, self-assessment and problem confrontation. This stage may also include the rapid turnover and replacement of senior managers.

Source: Based on Greiner, L. (1972), 'Evolution and revolution as organizations grow', *Harvard Business Review*, July–August.

Activity 2.2   *Consider an organisation you know well.*

Using the descriptions in Illustration 2.5 and Table 2.1, position the organisation on the Greiner graph in Figure 2.2

Table 2.1 Characteristics of Greiner's phases of growth

	Phase 1 Creativity	Phase 2 Direction	Phase 3 Delegation	Phase 4 Co-ordination	Phase 5 Collaboration
Structure	● Informal	● Functional ● Centralised ● Hierarchical ● Top down	● Decentralised ● Bottom up	● Staff functions ● Strategic business units (SBUs) ● Decentralised ● Units merged into product groups	● Matrix-type structure
Systems	● Immediate response to customer feedback	● Standards ● Cost centres ● Budget ● Salary systems	● Profit centres ● Bonuses ● Management by exception	● Formal planning procedures ● Investment centres ● Tight expenditure controls	● Simplified and integrated information systems
Styles/people	● Individualistic ● Creative ● Entrepreneurial ● Ownership	● Strong directive	● Full delegation of autonomy	● Watchdog	● Team oriented ● Interpersonal skills at a premium ● Innovative ● Educational bias
Strengths	● Fun ● Market response	● Efficient	● High management motivation	● More efficient allocation of corporate and local resources	● Greater spontaneity ● Flexible and behavioural approach
Crisis point	● Crisis of leadership	● Crisis of autonomy	● Crisis of control	● Crisis of red tape	?
Weaknesses	● Founder often temperamentally unsuited to managing ● Boss overload	● Unsuited to diversity ● Cumbersome ● Hierarchical ● Doesn't grow people	● Top managers lose control as freedom breeds parochial attitudes	● Bureaucratic divisions between line/staff, headquarters/field, etc.	● Psychological saturation

Source: Clarke, L. (1994), *The Essence of Change* (Hemel Hempstead, Prentice Hall, p. 12).

The Greiner model is useful for identifying an organisation's situation, thus providing warning of the next crisis point it may have to face. It therefore helps in the planning of necessary change. It also assists managers and other organisational personnel to realise that change is, to some extent, inevitable; organisations must of necessity change as they grow and mature. It therefore helps legitimise the need for change and may be useful in discussions to bring about a reduction in resistance to change. However, while it may be possible to predict the next crisis point (through application of the concept of the organisational life-cycle), more needs to be done to develop ways of bringing about the necessary changes from one stage to another. It therefore becomes necessary to have some models and techniques for diagnosing the type of change situation prevailing at any one time in order to determine what kind of change approach to take.

● ● ● ● Diagnosing change situations

> Those who pretend that the same kind of change medicine can be applied no matter
> what the context are either naive or charlatans.   (Strebel, 1996a, p. 5)

Strebel begins an article entitled 'Choosing the right path' with these words. He
goes on to say, 'Thus, change leaders cannot afford the risk of blindly applying a
standard change recipe and hoping it will work. Successful change takes place on
a path that is appropriate to the right situation' (p. 5). Pettigrew and Whipp
(1993, p. 108), reporting on their study of a range of UK companies across four
industry sectors, said: 'One of the central characteristics of the firms under study,
therefore, is that the management of strategic and operational change for competitive success is an uncertain and emergent process.'

Being able to diagnose change situations is, therefore, important if organisations
are going to have any chance of responding to and managing change successfully.
However, diagnosing any organisational situation is not an exact science. There
are, though, some tools and techniques which can help. For instance, the Greiner
model of the organisational life-cycle is useful for drawing attention to periods
when organisational change is likely to be needed. In addition, there are a number
of techniques for strategic planning (e.g. stakeholder, SWOT and PETS analyses),
the application of which can lead to consciously planned change. In particular, an
analysis of an organisation's strengths and weaknesses and the opportunities and
threats (SWOT) presented by changes in its environments can increase awareness
of the need for continuous incremental type change and, hopefully, avoid the
process of strategic drift already discussed. Using multiple-cause diagrams assists a
greater understanding of the interactions between the many different and often
simultaneous causes of change.

There are, however, a number of other methods which can be used for anticipating when change is imminent and for deciding an appropriate approach to use for
its management and implementation.

Looking for breakpoints

The discussion thus far has focused on the requirement to scan the organisational
environment for signals which could trigger change within organisations. To help
with this, Strebel (1996b) has suggested a model of *industry* behaviour. This
model is similar to that of Greiner in the concept of a cycle of behaviour. However,
while Greiner links his model mainly to changes in the structure and management
of organisations, Strebel links his model more to an organisation's competitive
environment (*see* Figure 2.3). He uses the concept of the 'evolutionary cycle of
competitive behaviour' to introduce the idea of 'breakpoints', that is those times
when organisations must change their strategies in response to changes in competitors' behaviour.

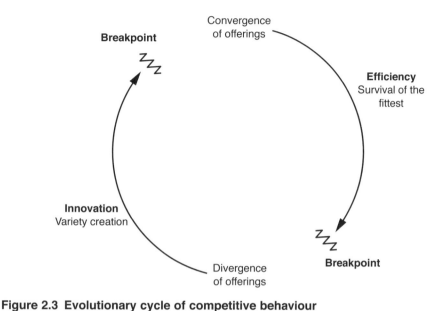

Figure 2.3 Evolutionary cycle of competitive behaviour

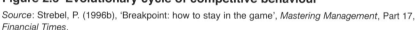

Source: Strebel, P. (1996b), 'Breakpoint: how to stay in the game', *Mastering Management*, Part 17, *Financial Times*.

The cycle of competitive behaviour involves two main phases. One is the innovation phase when someone discovers a new business opportunity, whatever its source. This triggers a breakpoint to introduce a phase in the evolutionary cycle which causes a *divergence* in competitors' behaviour as they attempt to exploit the new opportunity with innovative new offerings. Strebel (1996b) says this phase corresponds to variety creation in the evolutionary cycle and gives examples of the first Apple computer, the arrival of the Macintosh and, most recently, the new chips and software, all of which triggered breakpoints. He goes on (p. 13) to say:

> Divergent competitive behaviour aimed at enhancing the value of offerings continues until it becomes impossible to differentiate offerings because value innovation has run its course and imitation of the competitors' best features has taken over. As the offerings converge and the returns to value innovation decline, someone sees the advantage of trying to reduce delivered cost. Competitors converge on total quality management, continual improvement, and re-engineering or restructuring of the business system in an attempt to cut costs and maintain market share.

This brings about the other of the two phases – that of *convergence*. During this phase, the least efficient leave the scene and only the fittest survive. This is a phase of cost cutting and consolidation until the returns from cost reduction decline and people see the advantage of looking for a new business opportunity – bringing a new breakpoint with the cycle starting all over again. In summary Strebel (1996b, p. 5) says:

The competitive cycle suggests that there are two basic types of breakpoint:

- Divergent Breakpoints associated with sharply increasing variety in the competitive offerings, resulting in more value for the customer.
- Convergent Breakpoints associated with sharp improvements in the systems and processes used to deliver the offerings, resulting in lower delivered cost.

It should be noted that although the competitive cycle repeats itself, the industry continues to evolve and Strebel presents this in diagram form with respect to the computer industry (*see* Figure 2.4).

The vertical axis in Figure 2.4 represents the innovation–variety creation phase of the cycle of competitive behaviour; the horizontal axis represents the efficiency–survival phase. The vertical arrows denote periods of innovation (following divergence breakpoint) while the horizontal arrows denote periods of efficiency seeking and cost cutting (following convergence breakpoint). Strebel stresses that the diagram is not to scale. However, he says that, over time, industries move up the diagonal with increasing customer value and lower delivered cost. Clearly, some industries (e.g. those based on commodities) offer less opportunity for innovation and customer-value creation. Others (e.g. clothing and fashion) offer fewer opportunities for cost reduction. They evolve mainly through innovation in the direction of customer value.

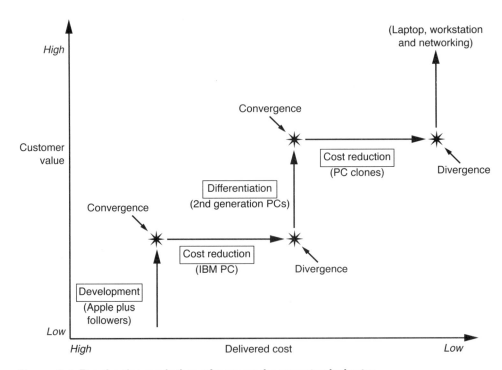

Figure 2.4 Breakpoint evolution of personal computer industry

Source: Strebel, P. (1996b), 'Breakpoint: how to stay in the game', *Mastering Management*, Part 17, *Financial Times*.

Strebel's model is very useful in explaining the external environment in which organisations operate, in particular the economic and technological aspects. What is as useful is his advice on how to detect patterns in the environment that indicate a breakpoint might be imminent. Illustration 2.6 details this advice.

It is clear there are a number of issues associated with the identification of breakpoints. First, organisations need to have both formal and informal systems attuned to searching for indicators from the environment. The formal systems will probably include those involved with: environmental scanning, benchmarking and data collection and interpretation. In addition, the way in which organisations are structured must help, rather than hinder, these activities.

As important are the more informal aspects of organisations, such as open attitudes on the part of managers and personnel, a degree of co-operation rather than destructive competition between divisions and departments, and a culture supportive of innovation and change. Part Two of the book discusses these factors and others in more detail. Before moving on to these, the final section of this chapter describes another way of assessing both the impact and the magnitude of

---

Illustration 2.6

Looking for breakpoints, with leading indicators

The timing of breakpoints is impossible to predict because they might be triggered by many different factors and because they require both a latent market and a supplier with the right business system. However, with an understanding of an industry's evolution it is possible to look for patterns indicating that a breakpoint may be imminent. Specifically, the competitive cycle can be used to look for leading indicators of a potential breakpoint.

The tendency of the competitive cycle to oscillate between divergence (variety creation) on the one hand and convergence (survival of the fittest) provides the framework.

Convergence is usually easier to anticipate, because it is built on an offering that already exists. Typical indicators are contained in the following list. When several of these are in place, all that is needed is a player, or event, to trigger the breakpoint:

- Competitors: Convergence is visible in increasingly similar products, service and image.
- Customers: The differentiation between offerings looks increasingly artificial to customers and the segmentation in the market starts breaking down.

- Distributors: The bargaining power in the industry often shifts downstream to distributors who play competitors off against each other.
- Suppliers: They cannot provide a source of competitive advantage because everyone knows how to use their inputs.

Divergence is more difficult to anticipate because it is based on a new offering that does not yet exist. However, if the following are in place, the industry is ready for a new offering that breaks with the past.

- Customers: An increasingly saturated market is accompanied by declining growth rates and restless customers.
- New entrants: Restless customers are attracting new entrants.
- Competitors: Declining returns may force them to experiment with new offerings or look elsewhere for profits.
- Suppliers: New resources and, especially, new technology are frequently the source of a divergent breakpoint.
- Distributors: They lag behind because they have to adapt to the new offering.

Source: Strebel, P. (1996), 'Breakpoint: how to stay in the game', *Mastering Management*, Part 17, *Financial Times*, p. 14.

impending change as an essential tool in determining the most appropriate methodology for carrying out the change management process. However, rather than diagnosing change by scanning the organisation's competitive environment (as Strebel recommends), this approach characterises organisational problems (and therefore the need for change) in terms of their complexity, variability, people involvement and how much consensus there is on what constitutes the problem and what might bring a solution.

Hard (difficult) and soft (messy) problems

The discussion so far shows how situations forcing change vary in complexity and seriousness. Thus, a minor upset in some part of an organisation's environment (most likely to be the internal environment) can bring about small-scale, incremental change. Other disturbances (more likely to come from the external environment) will have a much more wide-ranging impact on an organisation's strategy, structure and processes.

In the preceding section, reference was made to Strebel's advice on identifying industry breakpoints. Sometimes, however, the signals arriving on managers' desks are not as clearly categorised as Strebel implies, neither can they always be separated easily into those concerned with competitors, customers, suppliers and distributors. These signals are frequently confused and diffuse and it is not easy to see clearly just what type of situation prevails – the only thing managers perceive are 'problems'. These problems may vary in complexity and seriousness, ranging from minor upsets to major catastrophes, from temporary hitches to gnawing 'tangles'. McCalman and Paton (1992) use the terms 'hard' and 'soft' to describe, respectively, these two types of problems. Alternatively, the Open University (1985) uses the terms 'difficulties' and 'messes', the latter term based on Ackoff's (1993) article entitled 'The art and science of mess management'.

Illustration 2.7 demonstrates some differences between difficulties and messes and shows how difficulties are simply more limited sorts of problems while messes are larger and much more taxing for those who want some kind of change to 'solve' the problem. However, messes are not just bigger problems, they are *qualitatively* different from difficulties.

In distinguishing between these two types of problem, the Open University authors use the concepts of 'hard complexity' as characteristic of difficulties and 'soft complexity' as characteristic of messes. In beginning an explanation of these they say:

> Complexity is not just a matter of there being many different factors and interactions to bear in mind, of uncertainty concerning some of them, of a multitude of combinations and permutations of possible decisions and events to allow for, evaluate and select. It is not only a computational matter – such as operational researchers deal with. Complexity is also generated by the very different constructions that can be placed on those factors, decisions and events.
>
> (Open University, 1985, p. 18)

Illustration 2.7

Difficulties and messes

Difficulties **are bounded in that they:**

- Tend to be smaller scale.
- Are less serious in their implications.
- Can be considered in relative isolation from their organisational context.
- Have clear priorities as to what might need to be done.
- Generally have quantifiable objectives and performance indicators.
- Have a systems/technical orientation.
- Generally involve relatively few people.
- Have facts which are known and which can contribute to the solution.
- Have agreement by the people involved on what constitutes the problem.
- Tend to have solutions of which the type at least is known.
- Have known time scales.
- Are 'bounded' in that they can be considered separately from the wider organisational context and have minimal interactions with the environment.

Messes **are unbounded in that they:**

- Tend to be larger scale.
- Have serious and worrying implications for all concerned.
- Are an interrelated complex of problems which cannot be separated from their context.
- Have many people of different persuasions and attitudes involved in the problem.
- Have subjective and at best semi-quantifiable objectives.
- Have an absence of knowledge of factors and uncertainty as to what need be known.
- Have little agreement on what constitutes the problem let alone what might be possible solutions.
- Have usually been around for some time and will not be solved quickly, if at all; bringing about an improvement may be all that can be hoped for.
- Have fuzzy time scales.
- Are 'unbounded' in that they spread throughout the organisation and, sometimes, beyond.

The consequence of these different interpretations of complexity is to describe hard complexity as characteristic of those problems which lend themselves to quantification and an optimal solution – an example is working out the best timetables for workers on production lines to achieve the most output. Soft complexity, by way of contrast, is indicative of situations where the description of events is ambiguous and there is a 'tantalising multiplicity of different interpretations and reconstructions' (Open University, 1985, p. 18) which can be put upon a problem, let alone its possible solution.

The introduction of new working practices is an example of a messy problem involving soft complexity. For instance, not everyone will agree there is a problem and a need for new working practices. Some will interpret this action as a wish to reduce numbers of staff. Others may see it as an attempt to split up possibly troublesome groups. Yet others may even view this optimistically in terms of getting extra experience and, perhaps, new responsibilities. Management is likely to think it a 'good thing' while any trade union will want to know what is in it for the other employees. What is more, if the changes have implications for pay and status, the possible 'losers' will see the world very differently from the possible 'winners'.

Activity 2.3 1 *Note three difficulties you have faced at work or in similar situations elsewhere.*

2 *Note two (if possible three) messes you have ever faced or been involved in.*

3 *Using Illustration 2.7, list the ways in which the difficulties differ from the messes. What might this tell you about ways of dealing with them?*

The change spectrum

Asking a number of questions about a change situation may help to identify whether it is likely to involve hard or soft complexity and whether it can, therefore, be seen to be more of a difficulty or more of a mess. Using the terms 'hard' and 'soft' to distinguish these two types of problem, McCalman and Paton (1992) have devised what they call the 'TROPICS' test to help locate a change situation on a continuum from hard to soft. Illustration 2.8 presents the TROPICS factors as dimensions on which a change situation can be positioned, according to whether it is further towards the hard or soft end of each factor.

The TROPICS test, as with any analysis of problems according to the lists in Illustration 2.7 and Illustration 2.8, can only be a guide to the nature of the problem. What is important is to have undertaken exercises such as these in order to understand more clearly the type of change situation faced, in order to guide the design, planning and implementation of any change. This is because problem

---

Illustration 2.8

The tropics factors

Hard		*Soft*
Time scales clearly defined/ short to medium term		Time scales ill-defined/ medium to long term
Resources needed for the change clearly identified		Resources needed for the change uncertain
Objectives clearly stated and could be quantified		Change objectives subjective and ambiguous
Perceptions of the problem and its possible solution shared by all		No consensus on what constitutes the problem/ conflicts of interest
Interest in the problem is limited and defined		Interest in the problem is widespread and ill-defined
Control is maintained by the managing group		Control is shared with people outside the managing group
Source of the problem originates from within the organisation		The source of the problem originates from outside the organisation

solving and managing subsequent change is not simply an intellectual problem. As situations move away from being difficulties and towards what has been termed a mess, they encompass not only issues which can be addressed through the application of intellect, but also issues which have emotional and social dimensions which require different kinds of approaches for their solution. Simplistically, these approaches can be categorised as hard and soft and there are a number of models of change which, in broad terms, attach to these different approaches. These are considered further and in much more detail in Part Three of the book when the issues of 'doing' change are addressed.

Activity 2.4   *Take each example you thought of in answer to Activity 2.3 and apply the TROPICS test to it. To do this, put a cross on each line according to whether your example is nearer to one end or the other of the factor. When you have done this for all factors for each example, make a judgement as to whether your example is, overall, a hard or soft problem/change situation.*

Did the TROPICS test confirm or refute your judgement of what is a difficulty and what is a mess in terms of your answer to Activity 2.3?

Conclusions

Organisational change can be conceptualised in simple terms as Grundy's three types of change show. However, the nature of organisational change is much more complex than this, as other typologies of change demonstrate. Not only are there different types of change, which manifest themselves in different organisations, change also appears differently at different levels of an organisation and in its various functions. The discussion in this chapter has demonstrated the multi-dimensional nature of organisational change.

However, change does not happen in a vacuum and should not always be un-expected, as illustrated by Greiner's description of the life-cycles that organisations go through as they are born and develop. As a complement to models such as Greiner's, which consider change at the organisational level, Strebel's model of change at the industry level is useful in looking to the wider environment for triggers for change. This model, together with the TROPICS test can be used to analyse situations where change is considered desirable in order to understand which approach might be adopted in order to bring it about. Chapter 1 examined the different environments in which organisational life takes place and how changes in an organisation's environment can trigger changes in the organisation itself. This chapter discussed the nature of organisational change. Table 2.2 summarises the similarities and congruences between the theories and research discussed in these chapters. Finally, these two chapters, which form Part One of the book, set the scene for the more detailed discussion of issues of change in Part Two and approaches to implementing change in Part Three.

Table 2.2 Environmental conditions and types of change

Environmental forces for change			Types of change			
Ansoff and McDonnell (1990)	Strebel (1996a)	Stacey (2000)	Tushman *et al.* (1988)	Dunphy and Stace (1993)	Grundy (1993)	Stacey (2000)
Predictable	Weak	Close to certainty	Converging (fine-tuning)	Fine-tuning	Smooth incremental	Closed
Forecastable by extrapolation	Moderate	Close to certainty	Converging (incremental)	Incremental adjustment		Contained
Predictable threats and opportunities				Modular transformation	Bumpy incremental	
Partially predictable opportunities	Strong			Corporate transformation		
Unpredictable surprises		Far from certainty	Discontinuous or frame breaking		Discontinuous	Open ended

Discussion questions and assignments

1 Discuss the proposition that: 'All change can be categorised as either incremental or radical.' Use examples from your own experience to support points made.

2 To what extent are Dunphy and Stace's four types of change helpful in working with 'real-life' change in organisations? Illustrate your answer with examples from organisations you know well.

3 Discuss Quinn's (1979) contention that change occurs through a process of 'logical incrementalism'. Give examples to support your argument.

4 To what extent do organisational messes get treated as if they were difficulties? What are the organisational consequences of this? Does it matter how change situations are classified?

Case example

Inertia and the death of the suit: 1960s Leeds offers a useful case study

FT

A much-debated topic in business strategy is corporate inertia – the inability of companies that dominate their markets to shift direction when consumer tastes change or when new technology comes along.

Two well known examples are the sluggish response of General Motors to Japanese competition in small cars and International Business Machines' failure to break out of the mainframe mentality when the personal computer revolution was gathering pace. The managers are blamed for short-sightedness or com-

placency – but can any lessons be learnt from their experience? What stopped them adjusting more quickly?

Some light is shed on these questions by a new study of a British industry that had extraordinary success from the 1920s to the 1960s but then went into decline – and, unlike GM and IBM, did not recover.

At the start of the period the Leeds men's clothing industry, led by Montague Burton, evolved a strategy that precisely matched the growing demand for reasonable quality, low-priced men's suits. This demand, as

Case example *continued*

Katrina Honeyman explains in a lively and well researched book, emerged in the late 19th century as economic and fashion changes reduced the difference between the quality of garments worn by different social groups.

By the 1920s, the democratisation of men's clothing was complete: the working man was able to dress like a gentleman. That he could afford to do so was due to manufacturing and marketing innovations made by Burton and the other Leeds firms. Their idea was to apply mass-production principles to a non-uniform product: the made-to-measure suit. Customers were measured in manufacturer-owned retail shops and their orders were transmitted to large, well-equipped factories in which work was organised along 'Fordist' lines. At its peak Burton's Hudson Road factory employed 10,000 people, turning out 50,000 suits a week.

Control over manufacturing and retailing was crucial. So, too, were close links with property companies to finance the acquisition of shops. The Leeds-based firms were also able to draw on an array of local resources and skills. Like Silicon Valley, this Yorkshire city became a dynamic cluster of mutually reinforcing industrial and commercial activities.

The initial impetus had come from an influx of Jewish tailors, fleeing persecution in eastern Europe in the second half of the 19th century: Montague Burton arrived in England from Lithuania in 1900. Starting with small workshops, the more enterprising gradually expanded their operations, taking advantage of cheap female labour to perform unskilled work.

The business began to lose momentum in the 1960s. Men's clothing became more casual, fragmenting the market and undermining the 'style monotony' of the inter-war years. The multiple tailors, Ms Honeyman writes, were 'catastrophically slow' to respond to the demand for non-matching trousers and jackets. This coincided with a rise in imports from low-cost suppliers in the Far East and continental Europe.

One possible response was to move upmarket and a few Leeds manufacturers did so – principally those that had been operating on a smaller scale. But Burton and the other big multiples had huge factories geared to the home market and they could not easily diversify. Most of them eventually abandoned manufacturing and became pure retailers.

Ms Honeyman blames management ineptitude. (In Burton's case the problem was made worse by the failure of the founder, who died in 1952, to provide for an orderly management succession.) But she also criticises the industry for relying for too long on a low-skill, labour-intensive manufacturing strategy, investing almost nothing in training.

There was, she suggests, a conspiracy between employers and the male-dominated National Union of Tailors and Garment Workers, which preserved the privileged position of male cutting-room workers at the expense of female machinists who constituted three-quarters of the labour force. It was not until the 1970 strike that female workers made their voices heard and by that time the industry was in decline.

Would more of the industry have survived if employers had taken training more seriously? The rise of the multiple tailors was based on a set of inter-related skills and business practices. To have changed part of the formula would not have been enough: a 'reinvention' of the industry was necessary.

What happened to the multiple tailors in the 1960s and 1970s falls into the category of disruptive change, which forces companies to rethink every dimension of their business. In such cases the wise course may be to abandon the old formula as soon as it becomes clear that the game is up, and do something different.

Sources: *Well Suited, a History of the Leeds Clothing Industry*, Katrina Honeyman, Oxford, OUP.
Geoffrey Owen, *Financial Times*, 7 November, 2000
Geoffrey Owen is senior fellow at the Institute of Management, London School of Economics.

Case exercise: Change that did not work

1 What lessons can be learned about this change failure?

2 Could Montague Burton and other companies like it have done something different?

3 Is it simply the case that some organisations which are part of changing industries are doomed to fail? Could the large clothing companies have predicted what might happen?

▶

Case example *continued*

There are at least two other articles, which can be found on the globalarchive.ft.com/ globalarchive Website.

The first is published in the *FT* (20 October 2000) and is entitled 'INSIDE TRACK: Farewell to the business suit: INTERNATIONAL BUSINESS MACHINES: IBM's staid image has been replaced by a message in interactive coloured lights'.

The other, which is from the *FT Weekend Magazine* (14 October 2000) is entitled 'Leeds' ambition to be capital city of the north forms the backdrop of the new TV legal drama, *North Square*'.

References

Abrahamson, E. (2000), 'Change WITHOUT pain', *Harvard Business Review*, Vol. 78, Issue 4, July–August, pp. 75–80.

Ackoff, R. L. (1993), 'The art and science of mess management', in Mabey, C. and Mayon-White, B. (eds), *Managing Change* (2nd edn), London, PCP.

Ansoff, I. H. and McDonnell, E. J. (1990), *Implanting Strategic Management*, Englewood Cliffs, NJ, Prentice Hall.

Checkland, P. B. (1972), 'Towards a systems based methodology for real world problem solving', *Journal of Systems Engineering*, Vol. 3, No. 2.

Clarke, L. (1994), *The Essence of Change*, Hemel Hempstead, Prentice Hall.

Corzine, R. and Adams, P. (1996), 'Shell may face fresh pressure over Nigerian oil discovery', *Financial Times*, 8 March, p. 1.

Dawson, P. (1994), *Organizational Change. A Processual Approach*, London, PCP.

Dunphy, D. and Stace, D. (1993), 'The strategic management of corporate change', *Human Relations*, Vol. 46, No. 8, pp. 905–20.

Foremski, T. (2000), 'Novell to cut 900 jobs and restructure', *Financial Times*, 7 September, p. 32.

Greiner, L. (1972), 'Evolution and revolution as organizations grow', *Harvard Business Review*, July–August.

Grundy, T. (1993), *Managing Strategic Change*, London, Kogan Page, pp. 24–6.

Johnson, G. (1987), *Strategic Change and the Management Process*, Oxford, Blackwell.

Johnson, G. (1988), 'Processes of managing strategic change', *Management Research News*, Vol. 11, No. 4/5, pp. 43–6. This article can also be found in, Mabey, C. and Mayon-White, B. (eds), *Managing Change* (2nd edn), London, PCP.

Kast, F. E. and Rosenzweig, J. E. (1970), *Organization and Management: A Systems Approach*, New York, McGraw-Hill.

Kehoe, L. and Taylor, P. (1996), 'The online challenge flavers', *Financial Times*, 14 March, p. 23.

Kimberley, J. R. and Miles, R. H. (1980), *The Organizational Life-cycle*, San Francisco, Jossey-Bass.

McAleer, W. E. (1982), 'Systems: a concept for business and management', *Journal of Applied Systems Analysis*, Vol. 9, pp. 99–129.

McCalman, J. and Paton, R. A. (1992), *Change Management. A Guide to Effective Implementation*, London, PCP.

Marsh, P. (2000), 'Adaptability furnishes key to craftsmen's long survival', *Financial Times*, 6 September, p. 7.

Modern Healthcare (1996), A good year for 'patient protection' laws, *Modern Healthcare*, 28 October, p. 22.

M2 Communications Ltd (2000) Xenos restructures to fuel future growth: Organisational changes will benefit new product development, customer support and future alliance strategy. Wednesday 30 August. http://ebb.onesource.com

Open University (1985), Block 1, 'Managing and messy problems', Course T244, *Managing in Organizations*, Milton Keynes, Open University.

Pettigrew, A. and Whipp, R. (1993), *Managing Change for Competitive Success*, Oxford, Blackwell.

Quinn, J. B. (1979), 'Xerox Corporation (B)', copyrighted case, Amos Tuck School of Business Administration, Dartmouth College, Hanover, NH.

Quinn, J. B. (1980), 'Managing strategic change', *Sloan Management Review*, Summer, pp. 3–20.

Roberts, J. (2000), 'Business as usual', *United Utilities Shareholders' Annual Review*, Warrington, United Utilities plc, p. 1.

Smith, D. (1993), *The History of British Rail*, Department of Transport, London, Cloister Press, pp. 12–13.

Stacey, R. (2000), *Strategic Management and Organisational Dynamics, The Challenge of Complexity* (3rd edn), London, Financial Times/Prentice Hall.

Strebel, P. (1996a), 'Choosing the right path', *Mastering Management*, Part 14, *Financial Times*.

Strebel, P. (1996b), 'Breakpoint: how to stay in the game', *Mastering Management*, Part 17, *Financial Times*.

Thomas, C. (1992), *A History of the Rail Network*, London, British Railways Board, pp. 4–5.

Tushman, M. L., Newman, W. H. and Romanelli, E. (1988), 'Convergence and upheaval: managing the unsteady pace of organizational evolution', in Tushman, M. L. and Moore, W. L. (eds), *Readings in the Management of Innovation*, New York, Ballinger Publishing Company.

von Bertanlanfy, L. (1971), *General Systems Theory*, Harmondsworth, Penguin.

Wilson, D. C. (1992), *A Strategy of Change*, New York, Routledge.

Selfridges, a study of change Part 1

A house of brands

Wandering around the fourth floor of Selfridges store in Oxford Street, London (the fifth and highest floor is the beauty salon), you pass a counter selling soaps, cut to order, which is next to a stand where you can have a shoulder and neck massage. This, in turn, is next to a department selling bed linen, designed by Ralph Lauren. The fourth floor floats above the third floor – one of two floors selling women's wear – with designer names such as Escada, Yves St Laurent, Cacharel, lingerie by La Perla, the latest Missoni swimwear and elegant cashmere by Pringle and TSE. A lot of money could be spent here!

Around all this, notices appear about 'Rock and Shop', an event in aid of the Terrence Higgins Trust, which involves artists coming to perform in the store. There is a notice about a book signing by Ian Hislop. You are surrounded by more designer names like Versace, Vivienne Westward, Clements Ribero, Boyd and Prada. You can choose between one to four eating places on each floor, including the lower ground floor – there are 18 eating and drinking places in total. These range from coffee bars to an oyster and champagne bar; there is a sushi bar where little dishes of food pass by you on a moving counter. Formal restaurants contrast with a stand up quick sandwich bar.

On the first floor, the men's clothing department (more designer names like Helmut Lang, Paul Smith, Yohji Yamamoto, DriesVan Noten) is positioned next to the children's department. Should you encourage your child to take a ride on the large rocking horse or play with the huge counting frame or sit on a cuddly ladybird or play with a robot, while you decide which children's clothes to buy from the large array to cover any occasion?

Meanwhile, on the ground floor, there are separates which might appeal to younger customers, lots and lots of lipsticks, accessories, jewellery, men's underwear (e.g. Calvin Klein shorts), wines and spirits, scarves and bags – a long queue of women, managed by a security guard, waiting to be let into (a few at a time) the newly opened Louis Vuitton handbag concession. You can also sip an espresso, read a newspaper (bought in the store) and get your briefcase repaired. Not forgetting that looking good yourself is allied to living in a looking good home. The lower ground floor offers pots and glasses of every colour, shape and size along with kitchenware, aprons, oven gloves, trouser presses, washing machines, luggage, music, spectacles and a travel department.

This is just a flavour of what Selfridges chief executive Vittorio Radice calls a 'House of Brands'. However, the image of Selfridges has changed throughout time.

Selfridges' history

Gordon Selfridge, the founder of the store, was born in Wisconsin in the USA in 1858. While working for 'the marble palace of retailing', Marshall Fields in Chicago, he introduced the idea of the annual sale, lit the store windows at night and is credited with coining the phrase 'only X shopping days to Christmas'. However, he felt frustrated when all of his plans were not realised and decided to open up his own store, choosing England because he did not want to compete with Marshall Fields.

The £400,000 store – the site alone is now valued at £324m – caused a hubbub when it opened, with its own library, post office, American soda fountain and a Silence Room, where a sign read, 'Ladies will refrain from conversation'! Madame Barry of Bond Street was the very first customer, paying 1s 4d for a handkerchief. Gordon Selfridge continued to innovate introducing such things as credit, in-store exhibitions of the latest scientific discoveries leading to the world's first television sales department and even a department selling aeroplanes following Amy Johnson's epic flight to Australia.

Gordon Selfridge took the group public in 1921. However, the austerity of the 1930s depression years followed by the Second World War proved to be lean times, with the store endeavouring to carry out 'business as usual'. Two years after the war ended, in 1947, Gordon Selfridge died in his sleep with little to show, in terms of his own fortunes, for his earlier successes. In 1951, Selfridges' old adversary, Lord Woolton, Chairman of Lewis's department stores, bought the store for £3.4m. In 1965, Charles Clore, the man behind Sears retailing empire, took control of both Selfridges and Lewis's. In April 1997 Selfridges' demerger from Sears was announced and the store returned to its original name of Selfridges & Co. Subsequently, after 33 years as part of Sears group, Selfridges was demerged and made its stock market debut, as Selfridges & Co., in July 1998.

The years 1965 to 1996

Selfridges continued to trade under the umbrella of Sears with customers loyal to a store which their mothers and grandmothers had shopped at. The tradition of Selfridges as a store which could supply almost anything was maintained. However, by the early 1990s, sales had started to decline. According to Judith Waddell, Human Resources Director, the image and culture of Selfridges was more that of a shop – albeit a very large corner shop – than a huge multi-purpose department store with currently 3000 employees, some one million individual stock items, 70 million customers a year and 54,000 square metres (540,000 square feet) of shopping area (one million square feet for the whole site which includes a hotel and underground carpark). Separate sections for haberdashery, hats, shoes, leisurewear and formal wear did not, according to Vittorio Radice, make sense in the context of designers spending many years putting together an overall image which includes dress or suit, shoes, hat, blouse, shirt etc. – that is when every designer markets the entire look, head to toe.

According to Peter Williams, the Finance Director, talking about the current expansion into other cities: 'Ten years ago, people would have looked at this place and said: "What do you mean, you want to bring this to Birmingham? Forget it! This is a boring department store – don't bother".' He goes on to say that, in the early 1990s, when he went to meetings at which Selfridges were trying to persuade the directors of Sears to provide money for refurbishing the store, they would say: 'Should we put all this money in because department stores are dinosaurs of the retail industry?' At this time, Selfridges was seen as the poor relation to Harrods and John Lewis. It could not attract the top brands and Sears were resisting spending money on it. Even so, in early 1992 refurbishment of the east end of the store was carried out. This led to such good results in terms of increased sales that a master plan for refurbishing the whole of the store was devised.

All change at Selfridges

The strategic vision

The success of the changes to the east end of the store's internal environment led to plans to change the store as a whole in terms of its physical look and layout and its products. Around the same time, decisions were made to examine the possibilities of opening additional city-based stores outside London but still in the UK. The possibilities of leveraging the brand through opening stores based in cities outside London were explored. In March 1996 Vittorio Radice was brought in from Habitat to run the company, bringing with him both multi-site experience and a clear vision of the future of brand-focused retailing. Subsequently, in March 1996, Vittorio Radice left Habitat to become, first, Managing Director and then, after the demerger from Sears, Chief Executive of Selfridges.

On the belief that if changes were not made Selfridges would eventually close and die, one of the first things Vittorio Radice did was to look again at Gordon Selfridge's vision when he started the London store. He wanted to bring back Gordon Selfridge's idea of shopping as entertainment and fun. He believes that most purchases are based on impulse, that department store shopping meets wants rather than needs and has set out to make buying a very enjoyable experience with offerings of all that is fashionable and desirable. To this end, he masterminded the £90 million investment by Sears on improving both the outside and inside look of the store as well as the customer focus and the products sold. To some extent Selfridges was going back to its roots while, at the same time, going forward with a sense of rejuvenation and the message that Selfridges must reflect the 'Spirit of the City'.

Inheriting an old but, essentially, beautiful building, the intention was to create a brand new store with improved vertical and horizontal circulation, a modernised infrastructure and release the 'power of the brand'. For instance, during an interview with the Chief Executive in his large, but not lavish, office, he picked up a handful of fashion and home magazines pointing out that every magazine was not talking about private labels (e.g. St Michael from Marks & Spencer) but about brands. One of the aims of the changes was to move Selfridges' market position nearer to that of Harrods and Harvey Nichols, stores located in up-market Knightsbridge. However, Selfridges' location on Oxford Street, the busiest street in London, was seen as an advantage emphasising the concept of accessibility within the metropolis. The intention was to attract younger customers while retaining most, if not all, the prevailing customer base of 33 per cent under 29 years of age, 37 per cent between 30 and 49 years and 30 per cent over 50 years of age.

What Selfridges does *not* intend to do, at least for the present, is to sell its products over the Internet. It is a believer in E-commerce with regard to BtoB (business to business) and is exploring the possibilities of linking its 3000 or so suppliers through the Internet. However, the belief is that customers likely to patronise Selfridges want the Selfridges experience through visiting the store. The Directors believe that they are unlikely to buy designer clothes, tableware, luggage and the latest children's toy through sitting at a computer.

Case exercise: Selfridges (part 1)

1 Using the Internet and other souces, as well as the information given in the Case Study, summarise the elements in Selfridges' temporal and external environments in terms of the influence they had on what Vittorio Radice perceived to be the need for the changes at Selfridges.

2 What type of change do you think Selfridges was pursuing? In terms of the concepts and ideas put forward, particularly in Chapter 2, justify your views.

3 How far do you think the changes made are appropriate in relation to the environments in which Selfridges was operating?

The second part of the Selfridges story can be found at the end of Part Two of the book.

PART TWO

Organisations for change

Everything exists in the context of a wider environment. This is true for entities such as organisations. The idea of organisations as systems operating in a wider environment was developed in Part One of the book, where there was some discussion of the environmental triggers for change and their potential for influencing organisational policy and practices. However, organisations are not simply the hapless recipients of the winds of change blowing from this external environment. They, in turn, form an environment – the internal environment – for the activities which take place within them. Thus, the strategy an organisation pursues and the way in which it is structured will be significant for its capacity to respond to and initiate change.

Strategy and structure can be thought of as the more formal, overt aspects of an organisation's functioning. As important, however, are the more informal, covert aspects of organisational life such as organisational culture (set in the context of its national culture), organisational politics and issues of power, co-operation and conflict, as well as the way the organisation is led.

Part Two of the book extends the discussion in Part One, to investigate the internal life of the organisation in terms of its relations with the external environment and the opportunities and constraints for change. The four chapters in Part Two reflect this focus and, with the discussion from Part One, prepare the ground for the more practically oriented material on the designing and implementing of change to be presented in Part Three.

Chapter 3 is oriented to the more formal structural aspects of organisational life while Chapters 4 and 5 concentrate on the more informal contexts of organisational culture and politics and their significance for the success or otherwise of any change process. The final chapter discusses the role of leadership in the change process as a lead into Part Three of the book, which is oriented towards the more practical issues of designing and implementing change.

Chapter 3

Organisational structure and change

This chapter discusses the characteristics of different types of organisational structures and provides details of the advantages and disadvantages of each in relation to organisational performance and the ability of organisations to introduce and implement change. More recent examples of network and 'virtual' organisational forms are examined as having the potential to respond more quickly to changes in organisations' internal and external environments. Factors such as an organisation's strategy, its size and the technology used are examined as to the degree of influence they may have on choice of structure. There is recognition that there is still ample 'room' for managers to exercise personal choice in these matters.

Objectives

To:

- *define what is meant by organisational structure and the organisational forms through which it manifests itself*

- *discuss the relationship between an organisation's strategy and its structure*

- *evaluate the contingency relationships between organisational structure, size, technology and the external environment*

- *assess the extent to which different types of organisational structure and form can cope with and adapt to a variety of change processes.*

● ● ● ● The meaning of organisation structure

The introduction to this part of the book states that everything exists in a wider environment. This is true for entities such as organisations, as discussed in Part One of the book. However, organisations as systems are, in particular, *social* systems. They are social because, in most organisations, to get work done requires the grouping of individuals and the activities they do into some type of divisions or sections. Thus, in order to achieve its goals and objectives, an organisation needs to have some way of dividing work up so that it can be allocated to members of the organisation for its execution. In other words, the work and the people who will manage and do it must be structured if chaos is not to ensue. The allocation of responsibilities, the grouping of workers' activities and the co-ordination and control of these, are all basic elements of what is called an organisation's structure which is in essence the social structuring of people and processes. Wilson and Rosenfeld (1990, p. 215) offer the following definition of organisation structure:

> The established pattern of relationships between the component parts of an organization, outlining both communication, control and authority patterns. Structure distinguishes the parts of an organization and delineates the relationship between them.

Bartol and Martin (1994, p. 283) include the additional element of 'designed by management' in their definition of structure, which is:

> The formal pattern of interactions and coordination designed by management to link the tasks of individuals and groups in achieving organizational goals.

Activity 3.1 *What other elements do Bartol and Martin give in their definition of organisation structure which do not appear in Wilson and Rosenfeld's definition?*

These two definitions taken together give a sense of the objectives which any structure must serve (meeting the goals of the organisation) as well as the process through which these objectives can be met (the effective and efficient ordering of activities and delineation of the relationships between them). Note, however, the emphasis in Bartol and Martin's definition on individuals *and* groups. In addition, the word 'formal' in Bartol and Martin's definition draws attention to the fact that organisational structures are typically created by management for specific purposes. From one perspective, therefore, an organisation's structure could be regarded as the official definition of the way that particular organisation functions. However, organisational life is never as neat as this. Organisational structures are not 'objective' in the sense that they can be understood by reference simply to some organisation chart or description of formal power and status relationships between individuals and groups.

Organisations also have what has become known as 'informal' structures which are not designed by management but are the outcome of friendship and interest groupings as well as those which serve political purposes, sometimes not related to the organisation's goals. These issues are not ignored in this chapter but arise in more detail in the discussions of organisational cultures, power and politics and the leadership of change associated with the other chapters in this part of the book.

The dimensions of structure

Organisation structure can vary along a number of dimensions. An early, but influential, piece of research by Pugh, Hickson, Hinings and Turner (1969) identified the following six primary dimensions of organisation structure:

- *Specialisation*: the number of different specialist roles in an organisation and their distribution.
- *Standardisation*: the number of regularly occurring procedures which are supported by bureaucratic procedures of invariable rules and processes.
- *Formalisation*: the number of written rules, procedures, instructions and communications.
- *Centralisation*: where authority lies in the hierarchy to make decisions that have an impact for the whole organisation.
- *Configuration*: the width and the height of the role structure, i.e. the 'shape' of the organisation, how many layers there are and the number of people who, typically, report to any one person.
- *Traditionalism*: how many procedures are 'understood' rather than having to be written down, how commonly accepted is the notion of 'the way things are done around this organisation'.

As a result of the research done to confirm these dimensions, Pugh *et al.* established four underlying dimensions which they described as:

- *Structuring of activities*: the extent to which there is formal regulation of employee behaviour through the processes of specialisation, standardisation and formalisation.
- *Concentration of authority*: the extent to which decision making is centralised at the top of the organisation or at some other headquarters.
- *Line control of workflow*: the extent to which control of the work is exercised directly by line management rather than through more impersonal procedures.
- *Support component*: the relative size of the administrative and other non-workflow personnel performing activities auxiliary to the main workflow.

In another large study, Child (1988) found general confirmation of the dimensions established by Pugh *et al.* and made some additions of his own. These were:

- the way sections, departments, divisions and other units are grouped together
- systems for communication, the integration of effort and participation
- systems for motivating employees, for instance, performance appraisal and reward.

It is clear from this that structure, applied to organisations, is a multi-dimensional concept and the assumption is that organisations can be structured in many different ways according to where they might be placed on any of the dimensions mentioned. Thus, in theory, there could be a limitless number of different combinations of these variables. However, most people would agree that some categorising of organisation structures is possible. What is more, there is some evidence to show that some types of structures are more appropriate to some types of organisational situations than others. This is discussed later in the chapter. First, it is necessary to understand the broad range of structures that are possible.

Models of structure

Bureaucratic structure

One of the best known forms or organisation structure is the bureaucratic form. Morgan (1989) states that the term bureaucracy was coined in the eighteenth century by the French economist Vincent de Gournay. However, it was the German sociologist Max Weber, in the early twentieth century, who defined and expanded its meaning and indeed maintained that it was the only effective way to organise work. An account of Henderson and Parsons's (1947) translation of Weber's writing on 'Legitimate authority and bureaucracy' can be found in Pugh (1990). This identifies three ideas which are central to the concept of bureaucracy. These are:

● the idea of rational legal authority
● the idea of 'office'
● the idea of 'impersonal order'.

There are a number of fundamental elements to these ideas. These are:

● a continuous organisation of official functions bound by rules
● a specified sphere of competence, i.e. differentiation of function
● the organisation of offices (i.e. positions) follows the principle of hierarchy
● the separation of members of the administrative staff from ownership of production or administration
● no appropriation of his/her official position by the incumbent
● administrative acts, decisions and rules are formulated and recorded in writing, even in cases where oral discussion is the rule or is even mandatory.

Illustration 3.1 summarises the characteristics of the pure form of bureaucratic structure.

The endurance of the bureaucratic form of organisation structure is evident in many organisations. In particular, it typified, until recently, most if not all large public sector UK organisations. For instance, McHugh and Bennett's (1999, p. 81)

Illustration 3.1

Bureaucracy

Weber specified several characteristics of his ideal organization structure. The four major ones are the following:

- Specialisation and division of labour. Work is finely divided between well defined and highly specialised jobs or roles.
- Hierarchical arrangement of positions. Roles are hierarchically arranged with a single chain of command from the top of the organisation to the bottom.
- A system of impersonal rules. The incumbents of roles (or positions) carry out their duties impersonally in accordance with clearly defined rules.

- Impersonal relationships. Co-ordination of activities relies heavily on the use of rules, procedures and written records and on the decision of the lowest common superior to the people concerned.

Other characteristics of a bureaucracy identified by Weber are: the selection of officials solely on the basis of technical qualifications; appointment not election; remuneration by fixed salaries with a right to pensions; only under certain conditions can the employing authority terminate an employment; the employee can leave at any time; a system of promotion according to seniority or achievement or both.

Source: Based on Weber, M. (1947), *The Theory of Social and Economic Organisation*, Free Press, translated and edited by Henderson, A. M. and Parsons, T., in Pugh, D. (1990), *Organization Theory. Selected Readings*, Penguin. (German original published in 1924.)

---

account of an attempt to bring about change in a large public sector agency describes organisations such as the one they studied in the following way:

> A rigid bureaucratic maze typified structural formation within many such organisations with the majority of members having narrowly defined and highly specialised jobs, and being protected from making decisions through their constant deference to authority and reference to their rule books.

The difficulties expressed by McHugh and Bennett regarding the significant problems foreseen in changing such a structure could well support Weber who was convinced of the case for the prevalence and endurance of the bureaucratic form. For instance, he says (Pugh, 1990, p. 12):

> It would be sheer illusion to think for a moment that continuous administrative work can be carried out in any field except by the means of officials working in offices. ... For bureaucratic administration is, other things being equal, always, from a formal, technical point of view, the most rational type. For the needs of mass administration today, it is completely indispensable.

Illustration 3.2 is a brief description of a construction company called the Beautiful Buildings Company (known as the BB Company). The organisation chart illustrates its current bureaucratic structure. The BB Company will be used in later parts of the chapter to illustrate other types of organisational structures, when it will be seen that Weber's commitment to the bureaucratic form is not shared by everyone.

Illustration 3.2

The Beautiful Buildings Company

The Beautiful Buildings Company (known as the BB Company) is a construction company involved in the design and building of a variety of different types of building.

For instance, it prides itself on having won contracts to build a new civic hall in one of the world's leading cities. It is known for its imaginative designs and the construction of a range of factory and other industrial type buildings. Just over 12 months ago, it took over a smaller building company specialising in home building for middle to higher-income families. It would like to develop further into the area of commercial office buildings.

During the past 20 years, the company has grown from operating solely in the UK to securing contracts in Australia and North America and has footholds in a number of mainland European countries.

The BB Company is headed by Gillian Lambeth, the daughter of the previous owner. There are a number of directors reporting to Gillian who are each in charge of one of the company's main functions. Marcos Davidson, the Marketing Director, has been the person most involved in promoting the company's activities outside the UK.

Currently the company is structured on typical bureaucratic lines as illustrated in the simplified chart shown here.

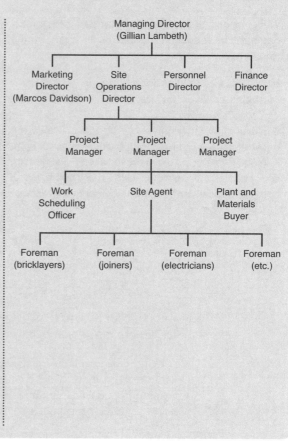

Activity 3.2   *If you are currently working in an organisation, draw an organisation chart for it. Otherwise, draw one for an organisation with which you are familiar.*

After you have produced your own chart, try to obtain any official chart or description of the organisation.

Compare your version with the official version.

To what extent would you regard your organisation's structure as reminiscent of a bureaucratic one? How much of a match is there between either of these versions and the BB Company's bureaucratic structure? To what extent does the organisation of work conform to Weber's bureaucratic principles?

How far do you think an organisation, structured as a bureaucracy, can adapt to strong 'winds of change' blowing from its environment?

An examination of readers' responses to Activity 3.2 shows them to be many and varied. Of particular interest are the differences between individuals' perceptions of their organisations' structures and (where they exist) the formal statements of these provided by senior management. This is not surprising, according to Jackson and Carter (2000), who offer a strong argument for the view that structure, although just as necessary for organisations as for (say) buildings, is not, in the case of organisations, something *concrete* and *objective*, but essentially *abstract*. Adopting what they term 'a poststructuralism' approach to explaining structure, they maintain (in contradiction to Weber) that there is no obvious and *natural* way of ordering the management of organisational activities. What is more, they maintain that what one person perceives or experiences as (say) an authoritarian, oppressive structure, another person perceives as a structure which is democratic and which treats everyone fairly according to the rules.

It is certainly the latter of these two views of bureaucracies which was part of Weber's thinking. The bureaucratic form of organisation, as conceived by Weber, was intended to imply neutrality and fairness in the way people in organisations were treated. However, the term *bureaucratic* has, more recently, taken on negative connotations with notions of undesirable and burdensome rules and regulations, too much 'paperwork' and overweening means of control. The phrase 'too much bureaucracy' is often heard, particularly in large public sector organisations, such as the one studied by McHugh and Bennett. Their study illustrates graphically the difficulties faced by such organisations in instituting change (*see* the case example at the end of Chapter 6). However, bureaucratic forms of structure are in themselves varied and, as such, can have different effects on those working in them.

Tall and flat bureaucracies

Figures 3.1 and 3.2 illustrate the difference between tall and flat structures. Figure 3.1 is of interest in demonstrating how widening the span of control (the number of people reporting to any one superior) reduces the number of levels in the structure, while retaining all the staff. Figure 3.2, contrariwise, shows how flattening the structure through doubling the span of control can 'save' 780 managers, that is 57 per cent of the number of management positions while retaining the number of lower level positions. Knowing this, however, does not reveal how many levels an organisation should have (how vertically differentiated it should be) or what the span of control (horizontal differentiation) should be at each level.

One rule of thumb is, that the more similar are the jobs to be done by individuals at any one level (the standardisation of jobs), the more people a manager can co-ordinate and control. Managing many people doing very different kinds of jobs occupies a manager's attention far more than when all are doing the same. Butler (1991) says that as task ambiguity increases (the extent to which the task is ill-defined) there is an increase in the number of problems which a manager has to solve and these add to managerial overload. Another rule of thumb is that the

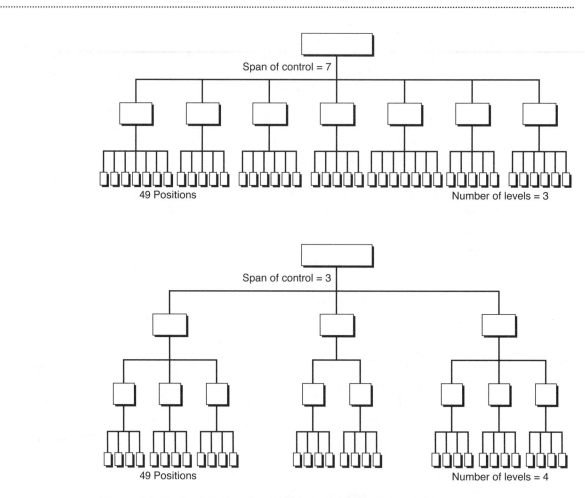

Span of control = 7

49 Positions

Number of levels = 3

Span of control = 3

49 Positions

Number of levels = 4

Figure 3.1 Flattening the structure but retaining the people

Source: Mullins, L. J. (1999), *Management and Organisational Behaviour*, 5th edn (London, Financial Times/Prentice Hall, p. 535).

more decentralised the decision making is and, therefore, the fewer decisions which have to be made by the manager (and it is difficult to tell this from simply looking at an organisation chart), the broader the span of control. Where most decisions have to be made by managers, then the larger the number being managed (the greater the span of control) the more overloaded is the manager. Mullins (1999) mentions other factors which affect the span of control such as the physical location or geographical spread of subordinates, the abilities of subordinate staff and the ability and personal qualities of the manager concerned.

With regard to the number of levels in the structure of the organisation (often referred to as the 'scalar chain' or 'chain of command'), Drucker (1989) suggests that these should be as few as possible. Too many levels bring difficulties in understanding of objectives and communicating both up and down the hierarchy. The current desire in many organisations for flatter structures follows this principle.

Members at each level

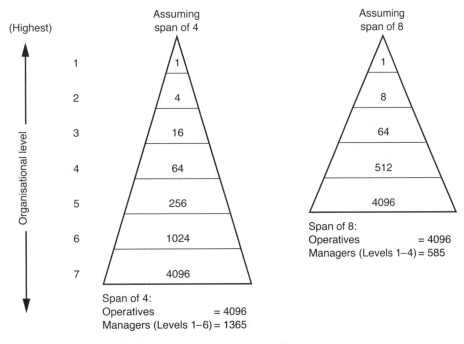

Figure 3.2 **Flattening the structure to 'save' people**

Source: Robbins, S. P. (2001), *Organizational Behavior*, 9th edn (Englewood Cliffs, NJ, Prentice Hall, p. 419).

However, a more precise method of calculating the number of levels for an organisation has been devised by Jaques (1990). He claimed to have identified time-span boundaries which can be drawn around an individual's role.

Jaques used the term 'the time-span of discretion' to refer to the target completion time of the most complex tasks which make up any job role. He makes clear that this target completion time is not always made explicit, but is inevitably always there – otherwise the carrying out of the task could not be planned. For example, someone labouring on one of the BB Company's building sites will see (or others will see) the results of his or her work in a very short time from carrying it out. For instance, the results of mixing concrete (a typical task for a building labourer), well or otherwise, will show within a few hours and certainly within days. By the same token, the results of the work that Gillian Lambeth, head of the BB Company, does – such as devising strategy for the next five years or formulating policy regarding moves into additional areas – will not show up as successful or otherwise for many years. Thus, Gillian Lambeth might have a time span of discretion of five years or more while the labourer will have a time span of discretion of no more than the time it takes to check whether the concrete mix is right or not.

Illustration 3.3 shows how different time spans are mapped to different levels (stratum in Jaques's terms) in the organisational hierarchy. Of note is the geometric

Illustration 3.3

Elliot Jaques and the time span of discretion

This regularity – and it has so far appeared constantly in over 100 studies – points to the existence of a structure underlying bureaucratic organisation, a sub-structure in depth, composed of managerial strata with consistent boundaries measured in time span as illustrated.

The data suggest that this apparently general depth structure of bureaucratic stratification is universally applicable and that it gives a formula for the design of bureaucratic organisation. The formula is easily applied. Measure the level of work in time span of any role, managerial or not, and that time span will give the stratum in which that role should be placed. For example, if the time span is 18 months, that makes it a Str-3 role; or 9 months, a Str-2 role.

If the role is a managerial role, not only can the stratum of the role be ascertained, but also how many strata of organisation there should requisitely be, including shop or office floor Str-1 roles if any. Measure the level of work in time span of the top role of the bureaucratic hierarchy – say, chief executive of the hierarchy, or departmental head of a department within the hierarchy – and that time span will give the stratum in which the role will fall and therefore the number of organisational strata

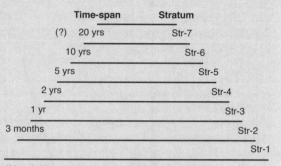

(*Note*: Later work by Jaques and Clement (1994) gives an additional stratum level 8, of 50 years time-span.)

required below that role. For example, if the role has a time span of 3 years, it makes the bureaucracy a Str-4 institution and calls for four levels of work organisation including the top role and the shop or office floor if the work roles go down to that level. If the bottom work role, however, is above the 3-month time span – say, for example, 6 months, as may be the case in some types of professional institution – then the institution will require only three levels of work organisation, namely, Str-4, an intermediate Str-3 and the bottom professional Str-2.

Source: Jaques, E. (1990), 'The stratified depth-structure of bureaucracy', in Pugh, D. S. (ed.), *Organization Theory* (London, Penguin, pp. 23–4).

Note: The chapter by Jaques from which this is taken and which is reproduced in Pugh (1990) comes from Jaques, E. (1976), *A General Theory of Bureaucracy* (Oxford, Heinemann).

progression of the time-span differences compared to the arithmetic progression of the bureaucratic levels, a pattern which Jaques says became observable after very many investigations of his theory. He claims this progression has its basis in the operation of a fundamental psychological process. If this is the case, it suggests a certain 'naturalness' in the way the time-span theory operates. Jaques's theory is, however, of more than academic interest. He claims it can be used in a practical sense to design the number of levels for any organisation. The latter part of Illustration 3.3 gives the details of how this can be done.

The way in which an organisation is configured, that is, the 'shape' of the organisation in terms of its height and width, is one consideration for those who are charged with formally designing its structure. However, managers in different organisations choose different ways of defining 'specialisation' of tasks. Thus, the division of tasks horizontally across the organisation can be done in a number of different ways.

Horizontal differentiation – the departmentalisation of work

The decision on which way to departmentalise frequently relies on the characteristics of the work to be done, the size of the organisation, the physical location(s) of its activities and the need to maintain a balance between high-level strategic decision making and lower-level operational imperatives. There are also issues as to who has the power to decide and the consequences for gain or loss of power and influence, given one type of structure against another. Some people argue for departmentalisation by function, others argue for departmentalisation by product, by customer or by geographical location. Each method of structuring has its advantages and disadvantages, which may not be the same, of course, for some employees compared to others. In the main, the comments on the advantages and disadvantages of each type, as given in the following, represent a management, 'organisational' view. Activity 3.3 (on page 84) addresses the issue of advantages and disadvantages from other people's points of view.

Departmentalisation by function

This is one of the most frequently found ways of structuring, particularly in the stages of an organisation's development when the early entrepreneurial phase is giving way to a more settled phase of sustained growth guided by able and directive leaders, the phase Greiner (1972) calls the 'growth through direction' phase (*see* Figure 2.2 in Chapter 2). The US 'large integrated corporations' resulting from the Industrial Revolution of the late nineteenth century and into the 1990s, referred to by Cohen and Agrawal (2000) (*see* Chapter 1) were almost certainly structured on these lines.

Cohen and Agrawal mention manufacturing, distribution and retail which conform to today's frequently found functions, including: finance, production (whether goods or services), marketing/sales, distribution and personnel/human resource management. Some types of organisations such as hospitals will have medical services, housekeeping and ancillary services as well as finance and perhaps research and development. Depending on the culture of the hospital, customer care might be important. Retailers will have buying and selling departments, customer care and finance. Any of these types of organisation could also have personnel or human resource management departments which might include training and health and safety. The organisation chart of the BB Company in Illustration 3.2 shows the BB Company restructured along functional lines. This is a simplified example of a functional structure – only the operations department is developed below level 3.

Illustration 3.4

Advantages and disadvantages of functional structures

Advantages

Departmentalisation by function has advantages in its logical mirroring of the basic functions of business. Each function has its high-level representative to guard its interests. Tight control is possible at the top. It encourages the development of specialist skills and expertise and provides a career structure within the function. Training can be organised relatively easily along specialist lines. In organisations where technical skill gives competitive advantage, the functional structure can enhance this.

Disadvantages

The advantages of a functional structure to small and medium-sized organisations become disadvantages as organisations grow and diversify products or services or locate in geographically distant places. There can be delays as one function waits for another to complete its work and co-ordination of activities across functions can be difficult. Functionalism sometimes encourages narrowness of viewpoint and works against the development of innovation, which requires co-operation from a number of sources. Functional structures limit the opportunity for the development of general managers.

Associated with departmentalisation by function is the degree of specialisation of departments. The example of the operations function of the BB Company shows it splitting up into separate projects, each managed by a different project manager. Each project includes sections dealing with work scheduling, site management and plant and materials procurement. All the different specialist building crafts (joinery, bricklaying, roofing, electrical works, heating/plumbing etc.) are found at the lower levels of the hierarchy.

A functional structure serves organisations well as they move from what Greiner (1972) termed the 'growth by creativity' stage in a company's development to the 'growth by direction' stage (*see* Figure 2.2 in Chapter 2). However, as they grow and diversify in customer and product markets – as Nestlé did in the early 1990s (*see* Illustration 3.5 later in the chapter) – they pass through what Greiner calls a 'crisis of autonomy'. This is characterised by demands for greater autonomy on the part of lower-level managers who frequently possess greater knowledge about markets and operations than do top management. Situations likely to arise are those in which each different class of product experiences a different level of turbulence in its environment. This may, therefore, signal that the time has come to departmentalise by product rather than by function. Illustration 3.4 lists advantages and disadvantages of functional structures.

Departmentalisation by product or service

It is not difficult to imagine the problems that the BB Company might have, given a functional structure. Its current and hoped-for activities cross at least four product areas (public buildings, industrial buildings, houses/homes, office and other commercial-type accommodation). Each of these product areas is governed by different sets of customer expectations, research and design problems and

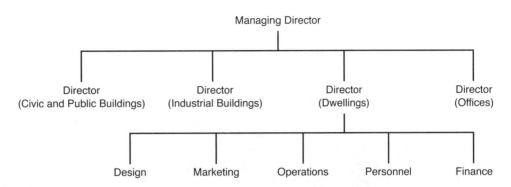

Figure 3.3　The BB Company – departmentalisation by product

building regulations. Each is prey to different political, economic, technological and socio-cultural influences.

Departmentalising by product might then be a sensible move for the BB Company. Figure 3.3 shows a product-based structural grouping for the BB Company.

For the BB Company, the division of work into groupings based on its four main categories of building projects enables staff with expertise in a particular area to share it with others working on the same products. The people working in each department have collective responsibility for the business processes and cycles of activity for that department's products. Departmentalisation by product or service becomes more effective as an organisation grows and begins to diversify its activities into a number of differentiated product/service areas. This was, apparently, the reason for Nestlé's restructuring which took place in the early 1990s (*see* Illustration 3.5).

Illustration 3.5

Structural transformation at Nestlé

During the 1980s, the Swiss food giant Nestlé operated a 1600-person head office controlling operations in over 100 countries. By the start of the 1990s, Nestlé undertook to reorganise to make it slimmer, faster and more innovative.

Its head office and some of its national companies were originally organised on the basis of strong functional departments. Such specialists previously held tight control over decisions in these areas in the operating companies. Seven new strategic business units (SBUs) were formed to cover Nestlé's main product markets. One SBU had a worldwide strategic, as opposed to operational, responsibility for product-management decisions in the main functional areas like production and finance. Two hundred head office jobs were cut. Regional management units were given more control over the companies in the regions than they previously had and the principle of 'business asymmetry' was employed, meaning that SBUs can be organised differently depending upon their particular needs as dictated by market conditions and production technologies.

Nestlé's changes were not new to the business world and had been adopted by their competitors long before.

Source: Based on Lorenz, C. (1992) 'Lean regime for a fitter future', *Financial Times*, 6 May, p. 16.

Illustration 3.6

Advantages and disadvantages of departmentalisation by product

Advantages

Departmentalisation by product or service has advantages of maximising the use of employees' skills and specialised knowledge. Staff are able to specialise more than with a strict functional structure. For instance, building designers may specialise in factory design or design for homes. Sales people in particular can concentrate on developing expertise in just one range of products. There is more opportunity for innovative ideas for new or modified products to flourish. Product differentiation facilitates the use of specialised capital (money and equipment). Product divisions can be made cost centres, and maybe profit centres, in their own right thus making them responsible for budgets and sales. Differentiation by product makes it easier to concentrate on different classes of customer, particularly when different products coincide with different customer groupings. Where a product division has its own set of business functions, these can be co-ordinated towards the product's markets. Finally, this type of structure offers good opportunities for the training of general managers.

Disadvantages

There can be overlap of functions from one product division to another, that is, duplication of central service and other staff activities. Overall administration costs tend to be higher than in pure functional structures. Where business functions are not wholly devolved, product-based divisions are 'top sliced' to provide resources for more centralised functions. This can be felt by product line managers as burdensome overheads, which detract from their overall profits. Top management may have more difficulty in controlling what happens at the product divisional level. Co-ordinating policy and practice across product areas can be complex.

Nestlé clearly saw advantages in restructuring on a product combined with a location basis. As might be expected, however, there are disadvantages as well as advantages in structuring on a product/service basis as Illustration 3.6 shows.

It appears, from looking at the BB Company's product-based structure and the freedom for the Nestlé's SBUs to organise differently, that once a pure functional structure has been rejected, functionalism could still have a place. This will be either in centralised functions before product departmentalisation takes place, or within product/service divisions. However, increased use of computer programmes and communications networks, such as intranets as well as the Internet, are shifting the balance of importance of some 'departments' against others.

Departmentalisation by location

The description of the BB Company indicates that its operations span more than one country, although it might be stretching a point to say it is becoming multinational. However, the company might be advised to structure on the basis of its being located in different geographical places in order to develop further its operations outside the UK (*see* Figure 3.4).

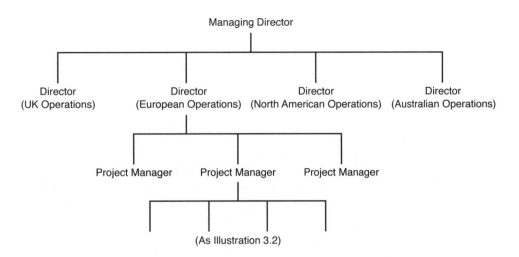

Figure 3.4 The BB Company structured on a geographical basis

Departmentalisation by location is common where organisations operate over a wide geographical area, whether this involves a number of different countries, areas within the same country or very widespread sites. It is attractive to large organisations whose activities are physically dispersed. Thus, managers may be put in charge of geographical regions, each of which is further differentiated on a functional or product/service basis. Although not shown in Figure 3.4, further differentiation of product or function could occur at the next level down. Contrariwise, some territorial differentiation might occur within other structure types. For example, in hotels, housekeeping staff may be allocated to particular floors and bar staff to particular bars. Some government organisations (e.g. the postal service), which operate on a national basis, structure themselves geographically. This enables them to offer a similar service across the nation but, where necessary, modify this service to suit more localised geographical requirements. For instance, different monopolistic companies supply water to different areas of the UK. Unlike the post office, however, which sets common costs of postage across the UK, the water companies operate a differential pricing structure according to the geographical location of their customers, the rateable value of properties to be charged and whether a water meter is installed or not. Illustration 3.7 identifies the advantages for this form of structure but also its disadvantages.

An overall advantage of differentiation by any means other than purely by function is that it offers the opportunity for variations in structure to occur in different parts of the organisation. For instance, a geographically based structure can be differentiated on the basis of product, or indeed customer, at other levels. Similarly, a product-based structure could incorporate aspects of differentiation by geography and/or customer.

Illustration 3.7

Advantages and disadvantages of departmentalisation by geographic area or territory

Advantages

Departmentalisation by geographic area/territory offers the advantage of being close to conditions in a division's locality and can clearly offer the opportunity to co-ordinate activities in a region. The employment of locally based staff means that travelling time is reduced. Local staff are more likely to know the conditions prevailing in a region. The establishment of manufacturing or service operations in the region reduces transportation costs. In some cases, labour costs may be lower in one region than another and it may, therefore, be advantageous for organisations to set up a division in that region. Structures based on geography provide good training grounds for general managers.

Disadvantages

The more geographically differentiated the structure, the more the requirement for management and administration. For example, with a head office in Belgium and regional divisions in Hong Kong and San Francisco, it would be difficult to give personnel services wholly from the centre. Each location would need to develop its own personnel functions, not least because of different employment laws prevailing across the different locations. This duplication of services can be costly. Control from top management can be a problem, particularly where headquarters is very far from some regions. In some regions, it may be difficult to recruit the skills required. This may be for reasons of culture or that the local population has not had the level of general education deemed sufficient for the purposes of the work they would have to do.

Activity 3.3 *Consider the three different ways of horizontally structuring organisations as already discussed.*

From your own experience and that of others known to you, what advantages and disadvantages are there, in each of these types, for the following groups of workers?

- *Professional 'experts' who specialise in a narrow field of work (e.g. nurses working in operating theatres; writers of distance learning materials concerned with the training of staff in personnel departments).*
- *Unskilled workers on factory assembly lines.*
- *Marketing managers.*
- *Call centre advisory staff, located in one place, but taking calls from anywhere in the world.*

How similar/different are the advantages and disadvantages for one group of workers compared to another? How far do your findings demonstrate the argument that different individuals and groups will perceive the 'same' organisational structures in different ways?

A summary of the discussion in this chapter to date is that, despite Weber's arguments for the strict functionally based, bureaucratic form, there are many complex and different ways of structuring organisations, each of which has its advantages and disadvantages, which might be very different for one group of employees to another. For instance, those at the top of organisations generally experience 'structure' of whatever form rather differently from those at lower levels. In functionally structured organisations, marketing departments frequently operate to different rules and time scales to production departments. Employees working in the East Asian division of an organisation are likely to experience organisational life differently to those working in the American division.

However, the examples of the BB Company have all shown a similar adherence to the principles of hierarchy and a single chain of command. This goes against the view of Morgan (1989) who maintains that most hierarchically structured organisations are being reshaped in response to the changing demands and challenges of the world around them. He says some of these changes are marginal but others are more radical and result in significant transformations in organisational form. This category of new organisational form can be loosely termed a *network* structure of which the matrix or grid organisation is a forerunner.

Matrix organisation

The essence of a matrix structure is that a set of departments or divisions is superimposed, horizontally, across a traditional hierarchically organised structure. Thus the structure is (normally) functionally designed in terms of its vertical axis, but designed on some other principle (product, customer, region) in terms of its horizontal axis. There are, therefore, two chains of command, one vertical and one horizontal, which operate at the same time.

Figure 3.5 shows a hypothetical matrix structure for an advertising agency. In this case, the heads of marketing, finance, personnel, research and development form the vertical lines of reporting while the different customer bases represent the divisions which operate horizontally across the structure.

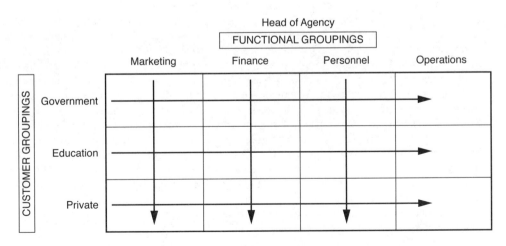

Figure 3.5 Matrix structure for an advertising agency

According to Greiner (1972), organisations move to a matrix form of structure through a 'crisis of red tape' brought about as they mature in the 'co-ordination' phase of the organisational life-cycle (*see* Figure 2.4, Chapter 2). Thus, staff begin to resist the control systems which centralised managers impose on decentralised product/customer or geographical groupings. He says this is particularly the case as organisations become too large and complex to be managed through formal programmes and bureaucratic paper systems. A move to a matrix structure emphasises interpersonal collaboration in an attempt to overcome the red tape crisis.

Drawing on Davis and Lawrence's (1977) work, Bartol and Martin (1994) maintain that organisations which ultimately adopt a matrix structure usually go through four identifiable stages. These are:

Stage 1 is a *traditional structure*, usually a functional structure, which follows the unity-of-command principle.

Stage 2 is a *temporary overlay*, in which managerial integrator positions are created to take charge of particular projects (e.g. project managers), oversee product launches (e.g. product managers), or handle some other issue of finite duration that involves co-ordination across functional departments. These managers often lead or work with temporary interdepartmental teams created to address the issue.

Stage 3 is a *permanent overlay* in which the managerial integrators operate on a permanent basis (e.g. a brand manager coordinates issues related to a brand on an ongoing basis), often through permanent interdepartmental teams.

Stage 4 is a *mature matrix*, in which matrix bosses have equal power.

(Bartol and Martin, 1994, pp. 321–2)

Illustration 3.8

Advantages and disadvantages of matrix structures

Advantages

With a matrix organisational design, decisions can be decentralised to the functional and divisional/project-level managers. This facilitates speed of operation and decision making. There is increased flexibility in being able to form and re-form cross-functional teams according to business priorities. These teams can monitor their own localised business environments and move quickly to adapt to changes in them. Staff belonging to particular functional departments have the opportunity of working with staff from other functional departments, yet maintain their alliance and information-sharing with their own professional grouping. Through allocating functional staff to one or more projects on a permanent or semi-permanent basis, loyalties to the projects are built. Matrix structures allow for flexible use of human resources and the efficient use of support systems.

Disadvantages

Matrix structures are complex and, because they add a layer of project managers, can be administratively expensive. There can be confusion over who is ultimately responsible for staff and project outcomes, particularly if things go wrong. The dual arrangement and need for enhanced communications between the 'arms' of the matrix can increase the potential for conflict, particularly between the functional and project managers. Staff may have to juggle their time between different projects or divisions and project managers may make competing demands on staff, who work across more than one team. The emphasis on group decision making could increase the time to respond to change.

Matrix structures rely heavily on teamwork for their success, with managers need-ing high-level behavioural and people management skills. The focus is on solving problems through team action. In a mature matrix structure, team members are managed simultaneously by two different managers – one is their functional line manager and the other the team or project leader. This type of organisational arrangement, therefore, requires a culture of co-operation, with supporting train-ing programmes to help staff develop their teamworking and conflict-resolution skills. Illustration 3.8 summarises the advantages and disadvantages of matrix structures.

Activity 3.4	*Koontz and Weihrich (1990) say that matrix-type organisations occur frequently in construction, aerospace, marketing and management consulting firms in which professionals work together on a project.*
	Figure 3.5 shows a matrix structure for an advertising agency, which is an example of the last of the instances just mentioned. The BB Company, as a building construction company, is an example of the first of Koontz and Weihrich's examples.
	Using any general knowledge you may have of the building industry to embellish the description of the BB Company, design a matrix structure for the way the organisation, as a whole, might operate. Then design a matrix structure for a division or department which dealt only with the building of homes.
	Compare your results with those of anyone else who can be persuaded to do this. Argue the pros and cons for any differences.

Wilson and Rosenfeld (1991) say it is usually not worth investing in a matrix structure unless the tasks to be performed are complex, unpredictable and highly interdependent. While many organisations continue to operate in stable pre-dictable environments, many others are required to innovate in the face of environmental turbulence. The matrix form of organisation, which emphasised working in teams, will help in this objective. However, some organisations have gone beyond a matrix structure to devise structures which Morgan (1989) calls 'loosely coupled networks', but which can be (more generally) called 'network organisations' (Snow, Miles and Coleman, 1992).

Network organisations

The process through which organisations go as they reshape themselves from being rigidly structured bureaucracies to what might be termed 'loosely coupled or organic networks' has been set out by Morgan (1989). Figure 3.6 is a pictorial representation of the transition from the rigid bureaucracy to the loosely coupled organic network.

The discussion so far has already set out the characteristics of models 1 to 4 in Figure 3.6, that is, the three bureaucratic types and the matrix organisation. Of

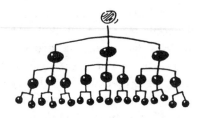

Model 1: The Rigid Bureaucracy

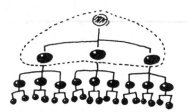

Model 2: The Bureaucracy with a senior 'management' team

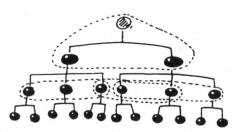

Model 3: The Bureaucracy with Project Teams and Task Forces

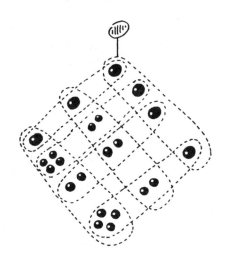

Model 4: The Matrix Organization

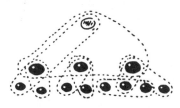

Model 5: The Project Organization

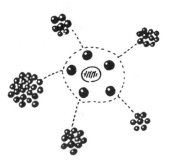

Model 6: The Loosely-coupled Organic Network

Figure 3.6 From bureaucracies to matrix, project and network organisations

Source: Reprinted by permission of Sage Publications, Inc. Morgan. G. (1989), *Creative Organization Theory. A Resource Book* (London, Sage, p. 66). Copyright © 1989 by Sage.

interest here is what Morgan calls the 'project organisation' and the 'loosely coupled organic network'.

According to Morgan, the project organisation carries out most of its activities through project teams. Although there are, notionally, still functional departments, they are there only to play a supporting role. The main work of the organisation is done wholly through the work of teams which rely for their success on being 'dynamic, innovative, powerful and exciting' and to which senior management tries to give free rein within what has been defined as the strategic direction of the organisation. Morgan summarises the nature of the project organisation in the following way.

> The organisation is much more like a network of interaction than a bureaucratic structure. The teams are powerful, exciting, and dynamic entities. Co-ordination is informal. There is frequent cross-fertilisation of ideas, and a regular exchange of information, especially between team leaders and the senior management group. Much effort is devoted to creating shared appreciations and understandings of the nature and identity of the organisation and its mission, but always within a context that encourages a learning-oriented approach. The organisation is constantly trying to find and create the new initiatives, ideas, systems, and processes that will contribute to its success.
>
> (Morgan, 1989, p. 67)

The project organisation has overlapping characteristics with what Mintzberg (1983, p. 262) calls 'The Adhocracy'. The adhocracy, as its name suggests, is an *ad hoc* group of people (mainly professionals) who are brought together for a single purpose associated with a particular project. The team may be together for a few months or, in rarer cases, for several years. Once the project is complete or moves into a different stage of its life, the team will disband. An example is that of a group of professionals coming together to make a film. Adhocracies are characterised by having few formal rules and regulations or standardised routines – in terms of the dimensions of structure advanced by Pugh *et al.* (1969), they are low on standardisation and formalisation. The shape of the organisation is flat, but with horizontal differentiation generally high because adhocracies are staffed mainly by professionals, each with his/her own specialism.

The project organisation usually employs its own staff. The adhocracy may also do this but may additionally have staff who, for the time the adhocracy exists, work on a contract basis. This contrasts with Morgan's (1989) description of the loosely coupled organic network. In terms of a continuum of organisational forms, this type of network organisation might be said to be at the end furthest from the rigid bureaucracy. The loosely coupled organic network describes a form of structure which, rather than employing large numbers of people directly, operates in a subcontracting mode. The small number of permanent staff set the strategic direction and provide the necessary operational support to sustain the network. However, while project teams and adhocracies have limited lives, the loosely coupled network can be a permanent structure. Figure 3.7 depicts three types of network.

Internal networks

According to Snow *et al.* (1992, p. 11), the internal network 'typically arises to capture entrepreneurial and market benefits without having the company engage in much outsourcing'. Hinterhuber and Levin (1994), by way of contrast, depict

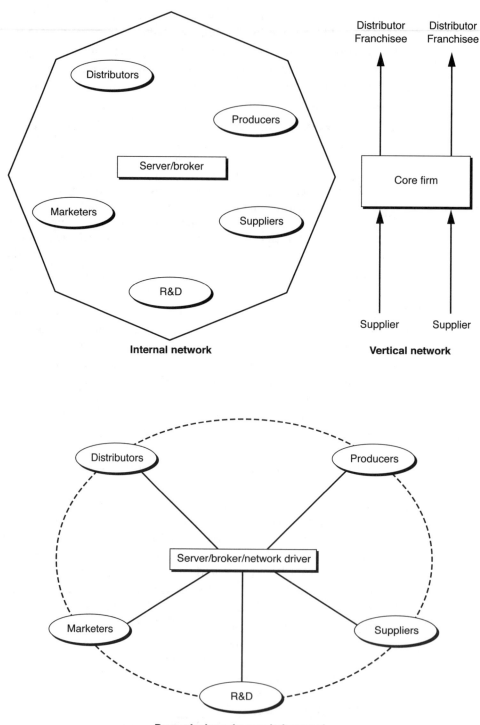

Figure 3.7 Common types of network

internal networks as collections of profit centres or semi-independent strategic business units.

Internal networks are typical of situations where an organisation owns most or all of the assets associated with its business. However, it has usually created 'businesses within the business' which, although still owned by the organisation as a whole, operate independently in terms of the discipline of the market. The argument is that, if they are subject to market forces, they will constantly seek innovations that improve performance. What is interesting is that these quasi-independent units are encouraged to sell their output to buyers outside the organisation to which they belong.

A typical example would be the training and development unit which, on the one hand, 'sells' its services to its parent organisation and, on the other hand, seeks to sell its services to other organisations. The internal network is not dissimilar to Morgan's description of a project organisation.

Vertical networks

A second network type is the vertical network (Hinterhuber and Levin, 1994). This is typical of the situation where the assets are owned by several firms, but are dedicated to a particular business. This is similar to what Snow *et al.* call a 'stable' network which consists of 'a set of vendors ... nestled around a large "core" firm, either providing inputs to the firm or distributing its outputs' (Snow *et al.*, 1992, p. 13). Thus, the core organisation spreads asset ownership and risk across a number of other independent organisations and, additionally, gains the benefits of dependability of supply and/or distribution. The distributors can be franchisees. Toyota in Japan could be perceived as the core firm within a stable network of organisations. Clegg (1990), referring to Cusamano (1985), notes that Toyota has some 220 primary subcontractors of which 80 per cent had plants within the production complex surrounding Toyota in Toyota City. Handy's (1989, p. 110) description of what he terms the 'federal organisation' is reminiscent of the Toyota example. He says:

> [Federalism] allows individuals to work in organisation villages with the advantages of big city facilities. Organisational cities no longer work unless they are broken down into villages. In their big city mode they cannot cope with the variety needed in their products, their processes, and their people. On the other hand, the villages on their own have not the resources nor the imagination to grow. Some villages, of course, will be content to survive happy in their niche, but global markets need global products and large confederations to make them or do them.

Dynamic, loosely coupled networks

For Snow *et al.* (1992), the dynamic network organisation is the one which has 'pushed the network form to the apparent limit of its capabilities' (p. 14). This form operates with a lead firm (sometimes called the 'server', 'broker' or 'network driver') which identifies and assembles assets which are owned by other companies. The lead firm may, itself, provide a core skill such as manufacturing or design. However, in some cases the lead firm may merely act as broker. The dynamic network is probably the form which is nearest to Morgan's loosely coupled organic network.

Illustration 3.9 describes TFW Images, a communications and image design organisation where the lead firm provides the core skill of design and 'brokers' other activities such as photography and illustration, printing, translations into other languages, and marketing.

If TFW Images also chose to outsource the design and writing process and the invoicing of clients and collection of payments, it would be as far along the network continuum as is apparently possible.

However, whether dynamic networks operate in a partial or pure broker capacity, they are unlikely to function effectively without good and effective

---

Illustration 3.9

TFW Images

TFW Images was formed in 1989 by two ex-employees of IBM who became the managing director and creative director of the company. They were very soon joined by a sales director with experience from a range of companies, mainly manufacturing. The main business of TFW Images is communications in its widest sense. Examples of its activities are: designing corporate brochures which might include annual reports as well as advertising material, designing and organising conferences and all the material that goes with them and creating company logos and other symbols of corporate identity.

TFW Images' main client was, and still is, IBM. In fact, the rise of the company coincided with the large-scale changes which IBM went through as it refocused its efforts away from the mainframe computer market towards that of the personal computer market. As technology began to replace people, TFW Images was able to take advantage of the willingness of companies like IBM to outsource some of their design requirements.

From a high point of directly employing 17 people (two of whom were in Paris), TFW Images now has seven direct employees. Of the original three directors, one remains, the creative director, although he does not currently carry a particular title.

In a volatile market – there are other competitors and the fortunes of IBM are less certain nowadays – one reason for the company's success is its ability to maintain a flexible structure which can be tailored to the demands of the market. Essentially, TFW Images is an organisation which 'brokers' services from other organisations to bring its products to the market. Thus, rather than employing printers, photographers, illustrators, market researchers and additional writers and designers directly, it closely associates with other companies and independent consultants who offer these services. The use of sophisticated computer systems facilitates the transfer of the part-finished products from one part of the network to another, wherever it might be in the world.

Most recently, TFW Images has joined in partnership with Omni-Graphics, a well-established design company operating mainly in the publishing and arts spheres of activity. Examples of Omni-Graphics' activities are: the design of calendars, brochures for and layout of art galleries and the design of news magazines.

Given the equality of skills and size of the two organisations, the benefits of the partnership will come from their complementary activities (TFW Images is business oriented while Omni-Graphics is arts oriented) and the financial advantages which will flow from this. The management of the two partner organisations will remain separate and both will keep their own names. Thus, to any client, nothing will have changed. Yet, conceptually and financially, a new overarching organisation has been 'virtually' created.

communications between their 'parts'. This is what is likely to distinguish dynamic or loosely coupled organic networks from the more 'in-house' internal and stable networks. For instance, TFW Images could not operate without fast and effective information technology links to the other organisations with which it associates. The power of the computer allied to telecommunication links enables TFW Images' design team to send its output anywhere in the world to be modified or added to by other writers and illustrators, to be marketed appropriately and, where appropriate, printed or manufactured to the specification for the finished product. Except for its relatively permanent status, the company might be likened to what some are now calling the 'virtual organisation', particularly given its current situation of joining together in partnership with Omni-Graphics.

The virtual organisation

The concept of the virtual organisation can be allied to that of the network organisation. The virtual organisation (Davidow and Malone, 1992, referred to in Luthans, 1995) comes from the idea of 'virtual memory' rather than 'virtual reality' – virtual memory being a way of making a computer's memory capacity appear greater than it is. Simply put:

> The virtual organisation is a temporary network of companies that come together quickly to exploit fast-changing opportunities. Different from traditional mergers and acquisitions, the partners in the virtual organisation share costs, skills, and access to international markets. Each partner contributes to the virtual organisation what it is best at.
>
> (Luthans, 1995, p. 487)

Illustration 3.10 summarises the key attributes of the virtual organisation.

Illustration 3.10

Key attributes of the virtual organisation

- **Technology.** Informational networks will help far-flung companies and entrepreneurs link up and work together from start to finish. The partnerships will be based on electronic contracts to keep the lawyers away and speed the linkups.
- **Opportunism.** Partnerships will be less permanent, less formal and more opportunistic. Companies will band together to meet all specific market opportunities and, more often than not, fall apart once the need evaporates.
- **No borders.** This new organisational model redefines the traditional boundaries of the company. More co-operation among competitors, suppliers and customers makes it harder to determine where one company ends and another begins.
- **Trust.** These relationships make companies far more reliant on each other and require far more trust than ever before. They'll share a sense of 'co-destiny', meaning that the fate of each partner is dependent on the other.
- **Excellence.** Because each partner brings its 'core competencies' to the effort, it may be possible to create a 'best-of-everything' organisation. Every function and process could be world class – something that no single company could achieve.

Source: Business Week, 'The virtual corporation', *Business Week*, 8 February 1993, pp. 98–102.

It seems clear from Illustration 3.10 that network (particularly dynamic network) and virtual organisations are suited to organisational environments which are themselves dynamic. The emphasis in these forms of organisation is on horizontal rather than vertical structuring and the concept of partnership rather than command and control. However, organisations structured on these principles have implications for employment and the reward expectations of employees, whether full time, part time, contract or in other kinds of relationships with the organisation. Network and virtual organisations are only able to offer stable secure employment to a few, from whom they expect commitment and loyalty. The idea of the ultra-flexible firm is attractive for the owners and core staff, but can bring a sense of being used to those who are employed on a short-term contract basis, particularly if these people are employed in temporary, perhaps part-time, less skilled, lower-paid jobs. Lack of commitment may not be restricted to the lower paid. More highly paid consultants and contractors will give service as long as it suits them, but may desert as soon as something more attractive comes along.

Luthans (1995) uses the term 'horizontal organisations' to cover the more recent matrix and network type of organisational design. He maintains that, in these organisations, teams are used to manage everything, with team performance, rather than individual performance, being rewarded. Yet, team working does not always come naturally to people; they frequently require training for this form of working. The emphasis on empowerment and more democratic ways of working, which comes with these 'modern organisation designs' (Luthans, 1995, p. 458), does not happen without planned human resource development. What is more, the move away from classical ways of organising may not suit every organisational situation. The main issue for organisations is not whether one form of structure is any better than another. It is whether the structure currently adopted is one which is able to facilitate the achievement of the organisation's purpose and respond to the need for organisational change in the particular environmental circumstances prevailing for particular organisations.

● ● ● ● Influences on structure

Choosing how to structure is not straightforward. The way an organisation is structured is closely linked to many factors as Figure 3.8 shows.

One of the most important links is the relationship between organisational strategy and organisational structure – as an organisation changes its strategy to respond to political, economic, technological or socio-cultural changes in its external environment, so should its structure change to maintain the strategy–structure relationship. However, apart from technological advances from outside the organisation, which may force changes in production methods or in the way that services are delivered, the organisation's own use of technology, particularly information technology, will affect the way in which it is structured. The earlier

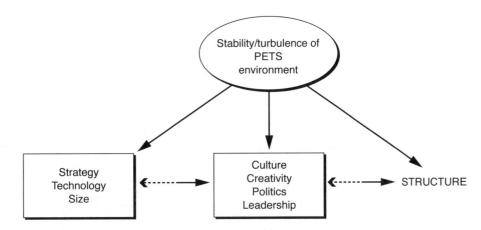

Figure 3.8 The determinants of organisational structure

discussion shows also how organisational structure is likely to change as organisational size increases.

What is less tangible is the role that organisational culture and politics have on decisions to structure one way rather than another. That is why, in Figure 3.8, these two factors are shown as mediating variables rather than as direct influences. There is nothing set, however, in the way all these variables should be regarded. Figure 3.8 is offered as a helpful descriptive device for summarising the factors which influence organisational forms rather than as a tried and tested model of how they work in practice. Even so, there is a body of literature which is of help in deciding which organisational structure is most appropriate to which set of circumstances. Before moving to this, it is salutary to stop and think why 'good' or appropriate organisational structure is so important to the efficient and effective operation of organisations.

The consequences of deficient organisational structures

An example of the consequences, for the organisational functioning of a deficient organisational structure, is a list produced by Child (1988) (*see* Illustration 3.11). What is interesting about this list is that some of the main 'dysfunctions' listed (e.g. 'Motivation and morale may be depressed') could be regarded as having little to do with structure. Yet, as the other points make clear, structural deficiencies could very well be major contributing causes.

Activity 3.5   *Consider your own organisation, or one you know well, or, if the organisation is large, a particular section of it. Do any of the five proposed consequences of structural deficiencies listed in Illustration 3.11 apply to the prevailing situation?*

If the answer is yes to any of the points, what does this imply for the way the organisation is structured? What changes could be made? Justify your conclusions by reference to the discussions of different structural forms discussed.

Illustration 3.11

Consequences of deficient organisational structures

There are a number of problems which so often mark the struggling organisation and which even at the best of times are dangers that have to be looked for. Child suggests the following list which he says structural deficiencies will exacerbate.

1. *Motivation and morale may be depressed because*:
   (a) Decisions appear to be inconsistent and arbitrary in the absence of standardised rules.
   (b) People perceive that they have little responsibility, opportunity for achievement and recognition of their worth because there is insufficient delegation of decision making. This may be connected with narrow spans of control.
   (c) There is a lack of clarity as to what is expected of people and how their performance is assessed. This could be due to inadequate job definition.
   (d) People are subject to competing pressures from different parts of the organisation due to absence of clearly defined priorities, decision rules or work programmes.
   (e) People are overloaded because their support systems are not adequate. Supervisors, for instance, have to leave the job to chase up materials, parts and tools as there is no adequate system for communicating forthcoming requirements to stores and tool room.

2. *Decision making may be delayed and lacking in quality because*:
   (a) Necessary information is not transmitted on time to the appropriate people. This may be due to an over-extended hierarchy.
   (b) Decision makers are too segmented into separate units and there is inadequate provision to co-ordinate them.
   (c) Decision makers are overloaded due to insufficient delegation on their part.
   (d) There are no adequate procedures for evaluating the results of similar decisions made in the past.

3. *There may be conflict and a lack of co-ordination because*:
   (a) There are conflicting goals which have not been structured into a single set of objectives and priorities. People are acting at cross-purposes. They may, for example, be put under pressure to follow departmental priorities at the expense of product or project goals.
   (b) People are working out of step with each other because they are not brought together into teams or because mechanisms for liaison have not been laid down.
   (c) The people who are actually carrying out operational work and who are in touch with changing contingencies are not permitted to participate in the planning of the work. There is therefore a breakdown between planning and operations.

4. *An organisation may not respond innovatively to changing circumstances because*:
   (a) It has not established specialised jobs concerned with forecasting and scanning the environment.
   (b) There is a failure to ensure that innovation and planning of change are mainstream activities backed up by top management through appropriate procedures to provide them with adequate priority, programming and resources.
   (c) There is inadequate co-ordination between the part of an organisation identifying changing market needs and the research area working on possible technological solutions.

5. *Costs may be rising rapidly, particularly in the administrative area, because*:
   (a) The organisation has a long hierarchy with a high ratio of 'chiefs' to 'Indians'.
   (b) There is an excess of procedure and paperwork distracting people's attention away from productive work and requiring additional staff personnel to administer.
   (c) Some or all of the other organisation problems are present.

Source: Child (1988) *Organizations: A Guide to Problems and Practice* (London, Paul Chapman).

A well-structured organisation (i.e. one which is functioning effectively and efficiently) can be compared to a healthy human being. For instance, a healthy human being will have a fully functioning brain which controls what the body does; the nervous system carries messages from the brain to all parts of the body. The body, in turn, has a skeletal structure which, if damaged, will severely hamper its movements and the ability to respond to the brain's messages. Without the skeleton the body will collapse. Blood is needed to feed the brain and other parts of the body. Muscles help strengthen the skeleton and the whole body in order to help it operate more efficiently. Thus, all components are required to ensure a fully operating, effective organism. However, the skeletal structure is that part of the person which supports the rest. It is not sufficient to ensure effective functioning of the person, but it is a necessary precondition upon which the other parts depend.

In such a way does an organisation work. The analogy here is that the brain is the organisation's strategy, the skeleton the structure, the blood supply the financial resources, the nervous system and the muscles, the people and the technology and information systems. So, however intelligent the *strategic* 'brain' and developed the nervous system and the muscles (the people, technology and information systems) without an appropriate structure – the 'skeleton' – to provide the basic support, the organisation will, at the least wobble and even, possibly, collapse. Conversely, without a strategy (a brain) to direct it, the structure (the skeleton) will become misaligned to its purpose. The first contingency factor to be considered is, therefore, the relationship between strategy and structure.

The strategy–structure 'fit'

As always when considering concepts associated with the behaviour of people, there is rarely one accepted and clear definition. According to Burnes (1996) this is also true of any attempt to define strategy and strategic management. It is not the purpose here to rehearse all the arguments for one definition against another. For the purpose of this discussion, the definition given by Johnson and Scholes (1999, p. 10) will suffice for a start. They say:

> Strategy is the *direction* and *scope* of an organisation over the *long term*: which achieves *advantage* for the organisation through its configuration of *resources* within a changing *environment*, to meet the needs of *markets* and to fulfill *stakeholder* expectations.

The term stakeholder is taken to represent anyone who has an interest in the organisation which is affected by the policies and practices of that organisation. This includes not only shareholders, suppliers, financiers and customers – that is, interested parties outside the organisation – but also employees.

To accompany this definition, Johnson and Scholes list seven characteristics which they say are associated with the words 'strategy' and 'strategic decisions'. Essentially this list elaborates the notion that strategy and strategic decisions encompass all the organisation's activities; that they are concerned with the organisation's internal and external environments; that they are influenced by the values and beliefs of those who have power in the organisation; and that they affect the long-term direction of the organisation.

Mintzberg, Quinn and James (1988), in asking the question, 'Is strategy a process or the outcome of a process?' draw attention to the issue of whether strategy should be regarded as being amenable to rational planning or whether it is the emergent result of a social and political process. Mintzberg's (1994) own view is that effective strategies are a mixture of both deliberate and emergent strategies. It is clear that, sometimes, strategy can be thought about and planned prior to the process of its implementation. The organisational changes that follow will be incremental or more radical, depending on the nature of the process of implementing the strategy. Such changes most frequently involve changes in the organisation's structure, because it is the structure that must provide the framework within which the strategic process must operate to achieve the organisation's objectives. According to Robbins (2001) structure should follow strategy, a statement which confirms Miles and Snow's (1984a, p. 10) statement that:

> It is becoming increasingly evident that a simple though profound core concept is at the heart of many organisation and management research findings as well as many of the proposed remedies for industrial and organisational renewal. The concept is that of fit among an organisation's strategy, structure, and management processes.

The implications of this are that different types of strategy can be identified and consideration given to the most appropriate structure for each type. A number of scholars and researchers have discussed this proposition. The first to be considered is Chandler (1962).

Chandler's strategy–structure thesis

Chandler's strategy–structure thesis has been summarised by Miles and Snow (1984b). This summary shows that Chandler developed his thesis from an extensive study of nearly 100 large US companies, whose history he traced from around the mid-1800s. What Chandler found was that owner-managed companies were predominant during the 1800s. These organisations usually started simply with a single product line and a structure where the owner–manager took all major decisions as well as attempting to monitor the activities of the employees. Miles and Snow refer to this type of organisation as having an 'agency' structure, given that key subordinates would act as agents of the owner–manager to ensure his/her wishes. The term agent was used to imply that these subordinates did not occupy specialised functional roles as might be found in today's organisations.

As companies grew, they became more complex and were then more likely to employ professional managers who began the process of dividing the organisation into different functional areas. The appearance of the functional organisation (around the turn of the century) enabled some growth to occur, particularly through acquiring suppliers, to ensure guaranteed inputs, and through market penetration. The strategy of these organisations was to supply a limited number of standardised products, with the aim of supplying a national rather than a purely regional market. The structure of these functional organisations provided the means of standardised production on a high-volume basis to a limited number of markets. This structure proved cost effective and delivered profits accordingly. The disadvantages of this type of structure were, first, that it did not allow ease of movement into new products and markets and, second, it produced specialists rather than generalists, with few managers able to look at the overall picture of the company activities and its prospects. In Miles and Snow's (1984b, p. 40) words:

> Each succeeding product or market innovation became increasingly difficult to adminis-
> ter within the confines of the specialised functional structure. It was against this back-
> drop – the desire to diversify thwarted by administrative complexity – that the search for
> another organisational form began.

This new form turned out to be the divisional structure, which, according to Chandler, appeared simultaneously in four pioneering firms during the 1920s and 1930s: General Motors, Du Pont, Standard Oil of New Jersey and Sears, Roebuck. The divisional structure could take the form of departmentalisation by product or region. However, whatever the basis of this move to horizontal differ-entiation, each division was most likely to become its own cost and profit centre, which was seen as essential if control was to be maintained and growth encour-aged. What is more, each division would be able to develop its own strategy in line with its products, markets and (if organised into geographical divisions) its cultural environment. These different strategies might well produce their own types of structure.

According to Miles and Snow (1984b), during the 1960s and 1970s two com-peting strategies were pushing companies into a new form of structure. These strategies were, first, the pressure for functionally structured organisations to improve their capacity for product development – which sometimes resulted in project groupings being added to the basic structure. The second strategy was the pressure for organisations structured into product-differentiated divisions to take advantage of cost savings by centralising some functions such as manufacturing which would, for instance, allow economies of scale. These two apparently com-peting strategies came together in the form of the organisation which has been dis-cussed above as the matrix form. Table 3.1 illustrates the evolution of these organ-isational forms, together with their associated mechanisms and means of control. It includes the dynamic network structure already described and which, at the time of writing (1984) and in the later paper by Snow *et al.* (1992), was held to be the structure for the year 2000 onwards.

Table 3.1 Evolution of organisational forms

	Product/market strategy	*Organisation structure*	*Core activating and control mechanisms*
1800	Single product or service Local/regional markets	Agency	Personal direction and control
1850	Limited, standardised product or service line Regional/national markets	Functional	Centre plan and budgets
1900	Diversified, changing product or service line National/ international markets	Divisional	Corporate policies and division profit centres
1950	Standard and innovative products or services Stable and changing markets	Matrix	Temporary teams and lateral allocation devices such as internal markets, joint planning systems, etc.
2000	Product or service design Global, changing markets	Dynamic network	Broker-assembled temporary structures with shared information systems as basis for trust and co-ordination

Source: Based on Miles, R. E. and Snow, C. C. (1984a), 'Fit, failure and the hall of fame', *California Management*.

Miles and Snow's strategic types

Miles and Snow (1984b) have developed a categorisation of business strategies which can also be likened to Chandler's typology, as Miles and Snow themselves discuss. Illustration 3.12 describes Miles and Snow's three basic types of strategic behaviour, together with a fourth strategy which is really not a strategy at all in that organisations described as 'reactors' might be said to have no clear strategy of their own.

Miles and Snow liken their strategy types to Chandler's historical discussion of strategy and structure, saying that today's organisations are the products of their ancestors. For instance, they associate *Defenders* with the organisations which were typical of the period before the 1920s, that is, those with limited product/ service lines, functional structures and centralised planning and control systems focused on cost efficiency.

Prospectors are likened to the divisionalised organisations of the 1920s and 1930s which proliferated in the 1950s. They seek to develop diversified products and structure themselves into product groups organised into decentralised operating divisions. *Analysers* are said to have the characteristics of the most recent of Chandler's organisation forms. Thus, small Analysers 'are alert to diversification opportunities but tend to limit their expansion activities to those that can be handled by the present production technology and organisation structure (typically functional)' (Miles and Snow, 1984b, p. 41). Of large Analysers, Miles and Snow (*ibid*.) say:

Illustration 3.12

Miles and Snow's typology of strategic behaviour

On the basis of their research and observations of many hundreds of companies in a wide range of industries, Miles and Snow claim to have identified four types of strategic behaviour with associated organisational characteristics. The types are as follows:

- **Defenders** have narrow and relatively stable product-market domains. As a result of this, they seldom need to make major adjustments in their technology, structure or methods of operation. They focus on improving the efficiency of their existing operations. Defenders' characteristics include a limited product line; single, capital-intensive technology; a functional structure; and skills in production efficiency, process engineering and cost control.
- **Prospectors** continually search for product and market opportunities and regularly experiment with potential responses to emerging environmental trends. They are often the creators of change and uncertainty to which their competitors must respond. Because of this, they are usually not completely efficient. Prospectors' characteristics include a diverse product line; multiple technologies; a product or geographically divisionalised

structure; and skills in product research and development, market research and development engineering.

- **Analysers** operate in two types of product-market domains – one relatively stable, the other changing. In their stable areas, these organisations operate routinely and efficiently through use of formalised structures and processes. In their more innovative areas, key managers watch their competitors closely for new ideas and then they rapidly adopt those that appear to be the most promising. Analysers' characteristics include a limited basic product line; search for a small number of related product and/or market opportunities; cost-efficient technology for stable products and project technologies for new products; mixed (frequently matrix) structure; and skills in production efficiency, process engineering and marketing.
- **Reactors** are those organisations in which strategy–environment inconsistency exists or in which strategy, structure, and process are poorly aligned. There is some evidence that, in highly regulated industries, Reactors perform less well than the other three types.

Source: Based on Miles, R. E. and Snow, C. C. (1984b), 'Designing strategic human resource systems', *Organisational Dynamics*, Vol. 13, Part 8, pp. 37–8.

Larger Analysers create semiautonomous divisions to handle major diversification efforts but tend to do so only when those products and markets are viewed as relatively stable and manageable. Typically, large Analysers use matrix structures to handle market and product innovations until these can be incorporated into the established production system.

Mintzberg's forces and forms

A more recent paper by Mintzberg (1991) offers the concepts 'forces' and 'forms' which can be loosely translated as strategy and structure, although Mintzberg himself uses these terms sparingly. However, his descriptions of the forces which drive organisations to adopt particular forms are similar to the strategies which Chandler, and Miles and Snow, identify. Figure 3.9 illustrates the seven forces, each of which is associated with a particular form.

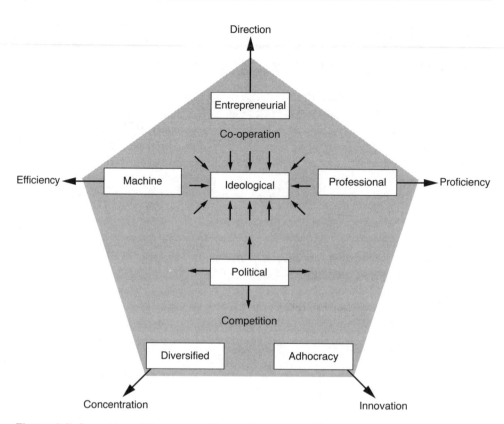

Figure 3.9 A system of forces and forms in organisations

Source: Mintzberg, H. (1991), 'The effective organization forces and forms', *Sloan Management Review*, Winter 1991, Vol. 32, Part 2, p. 55.

The seven forces which drive the organisation can be described briefly as follows:

- The force for *direction*, which can be likened to having a 'strategic vision'. This gives a sense of where the organisation must go as an integrated entity.
- The force for *efficiency*, which balances the costs and benefits – the lower the ratio of costs to benefits the higher the efficiency. The force for efficiency tends to encourage standardisation and formalisation, focusing on rationalisation and restructuring for economy.
- The force for *proficiency*, that is for carrying out tasks with high levels of knowledge and skills.
- The force for *concentration*, which means the opportunity for particular units to concentrate their efforts on serving particular markets. This is necessary in organisations that are diversified in structure.
- The force for *innovation*, which encourages the search for new products or services or for different ways of delivering them. The force for innovation encourages adaptation and learning.
- The forces for *co-operation* and *competition* are the forces which Mintzberg calls 'catalytic'. Co-operation describes the pulling together of ideology, that is,

the culture of norms, beliefs and values that 'knit a disparate set of people into a harmonious, cooperative entity' (Mintzberg, 1991, p. 55). Competition describes the pulling apart of politics in the sense of politics as the non-legitimate, technically not sanctioned organisational behaviour.

Mintzberg uses the term 'configuration' to describe the situation when any one of these forces drives an organisation to its corresponding form – as evidenced by the boxed areas in Figure 3.9 and which are described in Illustration 3.13.

According to Mintzberg, the *entrepreneurial* form tends to dominate when the forces for direction are paramount. This tends to be in start-up and turnaround situations and in small, owner-managed organisations. The *machine* form tends to appear when the forces for efficiency become paramount, for instance, in situations of mass production and mass service organisations. Mintzberg gives examples of hospitals, accounting practices and engineering offices to illustrate the *professional* form of organisation which results from the force for proficiency. The drive here is for perfecting existing skills and knowledge rather than inventing new ones. This is different from the force for innovation which pushes organisations into an *adhocracy* form, which is characterised by independent project teams with fluid structures. Finally, the *diversified* form arises as a result of the force for an organisation to concentrate on more than one distinct product or market. Each division will have a different structure and enjoy considerable autonomy from the small central headquarters.

Mintzberg calls the fit between the forces and forms that organisations take 'configuration': 'My basic point about configuration is simple: when the form fits, the organisation may be well advised to wear it, at least for a time' (Mintzberg,

---

Illustration 3.13

Mintzberg's organisational forms

- **Entrepreneurial form** – tends to be low in formalisation and standardisation, but high in centralisation with authority located in a single person.
- **Machine form** – high formalisation and standardisation, centralised authority vested in rules and regulations, functional departments.
- **Professional form** – high in complexity and formalisation, but low in centralisation; allows the employment of trained specialist staff for the core work of the organisation.
- **The adhocracy form** – very low in standardisation and formalisation, little hierarchy, much use of project teams which may well be temporary.
- **Diversified form** – a combination of functions and products, with products dominating; they can be of matrix form or organised as divisions on the basis of products/markets.

These five forms are based on descriptions given by Mintzberg in his 1979 and 1983 books. In his 1991 paper, on which much of this section is based, he added the *ideological* and *political* forms, giving as examples the Israeli kibbutz and a conflictual regulatory agency respectively. However, he says these two forms are not common and restricts his discussion to the five forms described here.

1991, p. 58). This argument supports those of Chandler and Miles and Snow that organisational structure should align itself with organisational strategy. The implications of this are that, as an organisation's strategy changes, so must its structure if tensions, contradictions and, eventually, crises are not to ensue. However, strategy is not the only factor upon which structure is contingent.

The influence of size on structure

One of the outcomes of the large research projects carried out by Pugh and his associates (1969), mentioned earlier in this chapter, was that size of organisation (measured by numbers employed) is positively correlated with overall role specialisation and formalisation (measured by the amount of paperwork procedures and usage). However, as Pugh (1973) points out, there are organisations whose size suggests particular structural configurations, but which confound the predictions. Even so, he suggests that the degree of constraint on organisational form imposed by variables such as size and technology is substantial, possibly accounting for some 50 per cent of the variability.

The work of Pugh and his associates does not have much to say about the relationship between organisational size, structure *and* economic performance. However, Child (1988) did carry out a study of the effects of size on organisational performance. His findings were that, for large organisations, the more bureaucratically structured they were, the better they performed. Smaller organisations performed better if they were less bureaucratically structured. The significant size appeared to be around 2000 employees. Thus, in organisations below this size, performance is assumed to be better in those which have little formal structure whereas in organisations with more than 2000 employees the association between more bureaucracy and superior performance was greater.

Both Pugh's and Child's research was done some time ago and might be assumed to precede the prevalence of the more 'modern' types of structure such as the matrix or the network. Thus the use of number of employees as a measure of size might not be as useful a measure for organisations with either of these types of structure. In highly divisionalised organisations, the size of the divisions is more likely to influence structure than is the size of the organisation as a whole. In network structures, it is perhaps not size in its relation to structure which is significant in determining performance, but the type of relationship existing between core and other parts of the network and between permanent and temporary or contract staff.

Illustration 3.14 is an account of the way one division of a medium sized multinational organisation was able to change radically its structure independently of the structure of other divisions in the organisation – with good results. What must be noted about this change, however, is the very careful way it was planned with the total involvement of the workers, foremen, managers and trade union in its implementation.

Illustration 3.14

From hierarchy to self-managed teams

In 1994, a factory of some 200 employees, which was part of a division of an American organisation manufacturing ceramics, took a deliberate decision to move from a hierarchically structured organisation to one based on self-managed teams. The factory, based in Scotland, was one of 74 manufacturing plants employing a total of 8500 people in 21 countries. As the company started operating new plants, employees were often sent for training or retraining to the Scottish factory, which, by that time, was the oldest in the company. However, the management realised that the factory's status as a 'master plant' could not be taken for granted. In the words of the operations manager: 'Here we are, a successful company in the west of Scotland. But the head office is in Brussels and we have no customers nearer than the north of England and no raw materials near by.' Having no natural advantages other than themselves, the concern was that, if they were not seen as being as good as the rest they would 'wither on the vine'.

Consequently, a change programme was put into place under the banner of what is known as the business excellence model developed by the European Foundation for Quality Management (EFQM). The programme centred on the introduction of self-managed teams. Elements of the programme included the institution of new work practices for which all staff received training. All facilitators gained NVQs at level 3 with all 185 shop floor workers gaining at NVQ level 1. Every employee had an individual development plan linked to team targets, which in turn linked to wider business objectives. The factory's time clock was removed to symbolise management's trust in the workforce. People no longer had to clock in. Consultations and negotiations with trade union representatives overcame their initial resistance, particularly in the context of no loss of jobs.

Over the period 1994 to 1997, the differential pay rates for different production jobs were replaced by a single wage structure and complete labour flexibility across jobs and departments. At an average age of 51, the plant's foremen underwent an extensive development programme designed to equip them for their new roles as facilitators rather than supervisors.

Indicators of the success of the new structure came from the results of employee opinion surveys. These indicated significantly increased levels of overall satisfaction and satisfaction with quality and productivity, company image, employee involvement and career development. Satisfaction with health and safety 'a dismal 53 per cent in 1993' went up to 90 per cent. At the time of this account (1999), all aspects of the business – including HR, purchasing, accounts and senior management – were self-managing teams. However, the ultimate measure of success comes from the company's results. The Scottish plant's turnover rose from £37 million in 1993 to £55 million in 1998 – a result which the company attributes to the competitive edge gained from empowering the employees and giving them responsibility for quality. Cost savings amount to £500,000 a year. Most significantly, the company's market share has grown.

Source: Based on Arkin, A. (1999), 'Peak practice', *People Management*, 11 November, pp. 57–9.

Activity 3.6 *Refer back to Chapter 1 and the discussion of external and internal environmental triggers for change. Drawing on your own speculations and intuition, as well as what you can glean from the account, write down where you think the triggers for change were coming from for the organisation in Illustration 3.14. How might some triggers have interacted with others?*

If your organisation (or your particular part of it) is structured into self-managing teams, what, if any, are the issues which cause most concern? What benefits are there for managers and others?

If your situation is one of individualised working or managed teams, what benefits and problems could you envisage in moving to a structure of self-managed teams?

The influence of changing technology

Two major studies are usually referred to in any discussion of the relationship of technology to organisational structure. These are, first, the work of Woodward (1965) and, second, the work of Perrow (1967).

Woodward studied 100 manufacturing firms in the south-east of England to investigate the relationship between organisational performance and elements of organisational structure such as unity of command and span of control. The companies were divided into three categories according to their methods of production, that is, the type of technology used: unit or small batch production; large batch and mass production; and process production.

Woodward found that there was a definite relationship between the types of technology used and aspects of organisational structure – in particular, the number of levels of management authority and the span of control of first-line supervisors. In addition, she concluded that the effectiveness of organisations was related to the 'fit' between technology and structure. In her words, 'not only was the system of production an important variable in the determination of organisational structure, but also that one particular form of organisation was most appropriate to each system of production' (p. 69). For instance, firms falling within the large-batch/mass-production category were more likely to be successful if they had adopted a more mechanistic type of structure (e.g. similar to Mintzberg's machine form). Firms falling into either of the other two categories were more likely to be successful if they adopted a more organic structure (e.g. more flexible, de-centralised with low standardisation and formalisation).

One criticism of Woodward's study is that it was done using only manufacturing organisations and, therefore, defined technology in a particular kind of way. The work of Perrow (1967) defined technology in a more general way which was more concerned with knowledge technology (that is, with both the ends and the means of achieving an output) than production technology. He suggested that technology could be viewed as a combination of two variables. The first of these he called 'task variability' and the second 'problem analysability'. Thus, a task which is highly routine would be low in task variability and vice versa; in other words, variability refers to the number of exceptional or unpredictable cases which have to be dealt with. Problem analysability refers to the extent to which problems are clearly defined and can be solved by using recognised routines and procedures, in other words, whether a task is clearly defined or whether it is ambiguous in terms of the task itself and how it might be completed. Where task completion requires innovative thinking, it is likely to be low on problem analysability.

Perrow used these two dimensions to construct a two-by-two matrix which provided a continuum of technology ranging from the routine to the non-routine as shown in Figure 3.10. The cells in the matrix represent four types of technology: routine, engineering, craft and non-routine.

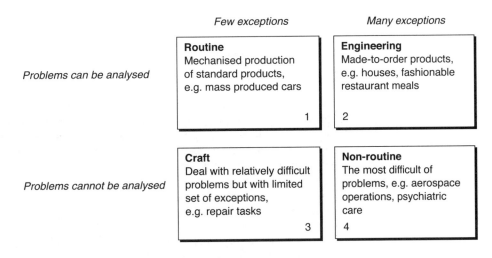

Figure 3.10 Perrow's technology classification
Source: Based on summaries by Robbins (1993) and Mullins (1999).

In line with Woodward, Perrow argued that each type of technology would produce the best organisational performance if linked to an appropriate structure. Consequently, technologies such as are described in cell 1 are most likely to fit well with mechanistic structures. Cell 2 technologies require mechanistic structures but with aspects of organic organisational forms. It is proposed that cell 4 technologies link most closely to much 'looser' organic structures (perhaps of the matrix, project or network type) while cell 3 technologies require mainly organic structures with aspects of mechanistic bureaucracies.

Butler (1991, p. 100) says that, 'in complex organisations technologies cannot be operated by individuals acting singly', which leads to his discussion of Thompson's (1967) identification of an additional dimension of technology interdependence. According to Butler, interdependence applies to the ways that work activities flow from one unit, group or department to another. Thompson suggests three types of technological interdependence: pooled, sequential and reciprocal (*see* Illustration 3.15).

It is not difficult to speculate on the different organisational structures, which would support one form of technological interdependence rather than another. Butler (1991) uses the concept of decision-making capacity to differentiate between those situations where the capacity for decision making would need to be large and others where it would need to be small. Situations where mediating technology prevailed would be examples of the former and those of intensive technology examples of the latter. Long-linked technology would require something in between. Thus, intensive technologies are likely to require more horizontal linkages throughout the organisation, with mediating and long-linked technologies requiring more vertical integration.

From this discussion, in particular of the work of Woodward, Perrow and Thompson, it appears that there is a link between organisation structure and

---

Illustration 3.15

Technological interdependence

Pooled interdependence

This is the lowest degree of interdependence, which occurs when units operate independently but their individual efforts are still significant for the overall success of the organisation. There is no flow of products or services between the different units, but they are all dependent on a central headquarters for resources and are responsible to it for outputs. Thompson calls this form of interdependence a mediating technology. An example would be a bank, which mediates resources between lenders and borrowers.

Sequential interdependence

This involves a higher degree of interdependence between units in that one unit must complete its work before another takes over. Sequential interdependence is typified by the traditional assembly line type of production. Thompson called this type of technological interdependence long-linked technology.

Reciprocal interdependence

This is the most complex situation, with the highest degree of interdependence among units. For example, one unit's inputs to another are reciprocated by that unit's outputs becoming inputs to the first unit. This is further complicated where a network of units operate in this way. Examples might be the work of a hospital in looking after patients or a university in educating students. Thompson called this form of technological interdependence intensive technology.

---

technology, and the hypothesis that organisational structure is contingent upon type of technology predominating in organisations is upheld. Robbins (2001) summarises the evidence for this. He divides the evidence up in terms of its relationship to different aspects of structure. Thus, he finds that technologies involving more routine work are moderately associated with structures that are highly differentiated both horizontally and vertically and vice versa. As regards formalisation of processes and procedures, the more routine the technology the more formalised the structure. However, although routine technologies might be related to centralisation of decision making, where highly developed formalised rules and regulations exist, decision making might be devolved but in line with the requirements of the formalised documentation.

While Robbins's summary is useful, it tends to assume a single technology for a single organisation. Although this might be true, there are many cases where large organisations in particular have multiple technologies. Butler (1991, p. 110) asks the question: 'From an organisational design viewpoint what basis is there for deciding about the hierarchical priority to be given to particular units?' Drawing on Thompson's (1967) findings, he suggests that intensive technologies, as the most costly to operate, should first of all be identified and units organised around these. The implication is that these units would be structured into more organic forms than those based on mediating and long-linked technologies. However, where there are a number of units using intensive technologies, these, in turn, would need to be linked together through some form of sequential or pooled interdependence. Thus, for the multi-divisional organisation, there may be a variety of technologies and associated structures in the divisions, with each division linked to the central hub of the organisation through pooled interdependence.

Woodward's, Perrow's and Thompson's research was done some time ago, before the widespread increase in the use of more advanced communications technologies including those using intranets and the Internet. For instance, many manufacturing organisations now work much more closely with suppliers and distributors – with either or both linking directly into the information systems of the manufacturers. In this way, suppliers, for instance, know just when additional components are required and where. Of the 'old' systems, Ody (2000, p.1) says: 'The supply chain used to be simple, serial and linear, with raw materials moving slowly through manufacturing production and onward via the distribution system to retailers and end-consumers' – in other words like Woodward's mass production or Thompson's long-linked technology. She goes on to say: 'Today, talk is of "supply networks", "parallel chains", "enhanced concurrent activities", and "synchronised models", with information technology set to cut both inventory and lead times throughout the pipeline still further' – a mixture of pooled, sequential and reciprocal interdependence, with perhaps more of the first two than the third. In this kind of scenario, the need for people to carry out the tasks of integrating one process with another reduces the numbers of staff employed, but demands more of those who are left.

This would appear to be somewhat in line with what has become known as 'business process reengineering'. BPR, as it has become known, concentrates on reorganising the core processes of an organisation to eliminate those which do not contribute directly to what can be defined as an organisation's 'core competencies'. BPR requires management to reorganise around horizontal processes including the institution of cross-functional and self-managed teams. Hammer and Champy (1993), the academics who coined the term 'reengineering' emphasise the need for radical, all-encompassing change (frame-breaking or discontinuous change – *see* Chapter 2) which is driven from the top of the organisation – a process which in itself is contentious given the amount of resistance it is likely to cause. (This issue is debated further in Chapter 6.)

Not everyone has been convinced of the benefits of BPR, the implementation of which has resulted in reductions in people employed – especially middle managers. In some instances, working on the reengineered processes is very much like working on a complex production line. The team philosophy appears liberating but the work processes are still regimented and are carried out in regulated form. How far BPR can be applied to organisational processes as complex as, say, looking after elderly people in residential homes or educating children is uncertain. How far BPR can be applied in organisations where processes are not standardised and where creativity and innovation are the means of survival is also uncertain. It seems hard to imagine in organisations where the goals are not constant and where the boundaries are 'fuzzy' and diffuse.

Robbins (2001) talks of the 'boundaryless' organisation where both internal and external boundaries are eliminated. He refers to Lucas Jr's (1996) use of the term 'the T-form (or technology-based) organisation'. The removal of internal vertical boundaries flattens the hierarchy with status and rank minimised. This type of organisation uses cross-hierarchical teams, which are used to co-ordinating their own work. The removal of external barriers against suppliers has been mentioned already. With regard to customers, the increasing use of what Hollinger (2000) refers to as e-tailing, makes the buying of goods from a wide range of producers and retailers much easier for those linked up to the Internet. In the UK, even the post offices have entered this field through offering home shoppers the opportunity to collect goods bought over the Internet at post offices. At the time of this account (October 2000), the intention is to trial this service at 1000 post offices spurred on by internal research predicting that the number of on-line shoppers will reach 6 million by January 2001, doubling the 1999 figure (*see* Grande, 2000, p. 6).

The breaking down of organisational barriers extends also to the home/work boundary. Lyons (2000, p. 60) says: 'For many people, the division between work and life is becoming blurred … people now live and work in the post-farm, post-factory setting. They travel, they work at home. They even work while they travel – in hotels, planes, cyber cafes, and at "touch down spaces".' This division is becoming blurred mainly because of the ability of workers to maintain contact with their offices and organisations through the use of E-mail and mobile phones, which can also be used to send and accept E-mails and other telecommunications. Cooper (2000, p. 32) remarks: 'The future of employment seems to lie either in small and medium-sized businesses or in outsourced and portfolio working for virtual organisations.' This type of working is only made possible by the increased accessibility and use of telecommunications.

Not everyone, however, is convinced of the conclusions of a survey of 1500 workers and 150 companies by the Institute of Directors which claims that, by 2020, the nine-to-five rat race will be extinct and present levels of self-employment, commuting and technology use will have changed beyond all recognition. According to Mills (2000, p. 2) in her reporting of comments made by Graeme Leach, Chief Economist of the UK Institute of Directors:

> The labour market of 2000 is far more traditional than perceived. It is not dominated by part-time employment, flexible working, home-working, teleworking or portfolio workers. But by 2010, I think that's all going to be different. There's going to be a huge sea-change in the labour market.

Mills quotes other people such as the director of the Helen Hamlyn Research Centre who support this view on the basis of an ageing population and the relative shortage of young workers who, it is said, will demand more family-friendly policies. According to Mills, Clare Lees, an associate director of the Henley

Centre, which forecasts work trends, is not convinced by the homeworking habit when she comments: 'Right now, only 1% of the working population are formally contracted home workers – its hardly a mass market.' By contrast with the work-to-home proponents, Lees highlights the home-to-work trend, where lengthening working hours encourage people to do home shopping and Internet surfing at the office, which is seen by employers as a treat, which if not condoned, would mean low retention of staff.

In spite of the arguments for and against homeworking, *flexible working* is certainly part of the present-day organisational world. The consequences for management, of the many different forms of working and the ways tasks are organised, are complex. In many cases, organisations must operate different structures in different parts of their operations. There are, as yet, unknown ways that more sophisticated and complex management, operational and information technologies could be used to change the way work is done and how it is managed. The virtual organisation is a reality made possible by developments in information technology. Woodward, Perrow and Thompson concentrated on the links between operational technologies and organisational structures with varied implications for the dimensions of structure identified by Pugh *et al.*, discussed at the beginning of this chapter. In the world of virtuality, managing staff and operations 'at a (real and virtual) distance' could well increase the need for centralised decision making and/or formalisation in terms of written rules, procedures, instructions and communications. It is clear that, along with size, technology, in its broadest sense, must take its place as one of the determinants of organisational structure – changes in technology quite frequently lead to changes in structure. In addition, the fact that organisations operate in environments external to them means that these also will influence the form they take.

The influence of the external environment

Environmental stability and turbulence

The nature and components of any organisation's external environment have been discussed in previous chapters. The use of the PETS mnemonic drew attention to the political, economic, technological and socio-cultural components of the external environment. Ansoff and McDonnell's (1990) categorisation of levels of environmental turbulence was used to warn about the need for organisations to maintain a state of appropriate responsiveness to changes from one level to another (*see* Chapter 1). A conclusion from these discussions is that an organisation's structure will be affected by its external environment because of environmental uncertainty.

One of the best-known studies on the effects of the environment on organisational structure is that of Burns and Stalker (1961). In studying some 20 British industrial organisations, these researchers concluded that organisations had different structures depending on whether they operated in more stable environments which changed little over time or in more dynamic, changeable environments which were unpredictable in their instability. They claim to have identified two main types of structure – mechanistic structures which they maintain were more suited to the more stable unchanging environments and organic structures which were more suited to the unpredictable, more dynamic environments. Mechanistic structures conform to Morgan's models 1 and 2, shown in Figure 3.6 (rigid bureaucracies and bureaucracies with a senior management team) and Mintzberg's 'machine' form of organisation (*see* Illustration 3.12). Organic structures resemble Morgan's models 4, 5 and 6 and Mintzberg's 'adhocracy' and 'diversified' forms of organisation. Illustration 3.16 describes the way Burns and Stalker perceived organic structures.

Lawrence and Lorsch (1967) went further than Burns and Stalker in suggesting that different departments within organisations face different environments and that, in successful organisations, each department would structure itself in line

---

Illustration 3.16

Organic structures

The organic form is appropriate to changing conditions, which give rise constantly to fresh problems and unforeseen requirements for action which cannot be broken down or distributed automatically arising from the functional roles defined within a hierarchic structure. It is characterised by:

(a) The contributive nature of special knowledge and experience to the common task of the concern.

(b) The 'realistic' nature of the individual task, which is seen as set by the total situation of the concern.

(c) The adjustment and continual re-definition of individual tasks through interaction with others.

(d) The shedding of 'responsibility' as a limited field of rights, obligations and methods. (Problems may not be posted upwards, downwards or sideways as being someone else's responsibility.)

(e) The spread of commitment to the concern beyond any technical definition.

(f) A network structure of control, authority, and communication. The sanctions which apply to the individual's conduct in his working role derive more from presumed community of interest with the rest of the working organisation in the survival and growth of the firm and less from a contractual relationship between himself and a non-personal corporation, represented for him by an immediate superior.

(g) Omniscience no longer imputed to the head of the concern; knowledge about the technical or commercial nature of the task may be located anywhere in the network; this location becoming an ad hoc centre of control authority and communication.

(h) A lateral rather than a vertical direction of communication through the organisation, communication between people of different rank, also, resembling consultation rather than command.

(i) A content of communication which consists of information and advice rather than instructions and decisions.

(j) Commitment to the concern's tasks and to the 'technological ethos' of material progress and expansion is more highly valued than loyalty and obedience.

(k) Importance and prestige attach to affiliations and expertise valid in the industrial and technical and commercial milieux external to the firm.

Source: Burns, T. and Stalker, G. M. (1961), 'Mechanistic and organic systems', in *Management of Innovation* (London, Tavistock, p. 120).

with its specific sub-environment. Thus in organisations operating in fairly stable environments, there would be less need for departments to be differentiated one from another. However, to ensure success, those organisations operating in highly uncertain environments would need to differentiate those departments most exposed to the environment (e.g. research and development) from those which were less exposed (e.g. production). In addition, where differentiation of departments was required, an organisation would need to ensure appropriate integrating mechanisms between departments to avoid the negative effects of different structures and operating procedures for different departments. This was confirmed by the results of their research which showed that the successful organisations, in the three industries they studied, were the ones which had a high degree of integration between departments.

Robbins (2001) also addresses the issue of environments specific to different parts of organisations. Drawing on other research (*see* Robbins, p. 432), he suggests that environments can be characterised in terms of three key dimensions. The first is the *capacity* of the environment, which refers to the degree to which it can support growth. The second is the degree of *stability* in the environment; stable environments are low in volatility whereas unstable environments are characterised by a high degree of unpredictable change. The third is environmental *complexity*, that is the degree of homogeneity or heterogeneity among environmental elements. Given this three-dimensional definition of environment, Robbins concludes that the scarcer the capacity and the greater the degree of instability and complexity, the more organic a structure should be; the more abundant, stable and simple the environment, the more mechanistic a structure should be.

Socio-cultural influences

The discussion so far has concentrated on what can be termed 'macro' influences on organisational structure. Size of organisations, as they grow or shrink, the effects of changing technologies and the degree of turbulence which in general reflects changes in the political and economic environments. Conclusions can be drawn that increasing size pushes organisations towards increasingly bureaucratic structures, which Robbins (2001, p. 434) concludes is still the most efficient way to organise large-scale activities. By the same token, the desire of employees for more flexible ways of organising their home/leisure/work relationships, coupled with the opportunities for self-employment and/or virtual forms of working may force organisational structures into forms which are as yet little understood.

Regardless of the size of organisations and type of technology used, the use of more flexible working patterns and ways of structuring the work appears to be increasing. An interesting issue, however, is whether this trend is a result of initiatives taken by employers for the sole benefit of business or in response to the changing expectations of those who they wish to employ. For instance,

Cooper (2000, p. 32), an academic specialising in research concerned with stress, says:

> The future of employment seems to lie either in small and medium-sized businesses or in outsourced and portfolio working for virtual organisations. Since the industrial revolution, managerial and professional workers have not experienced high levels of job insecurity, so will people be able to cope with permanent job insecurity without the security of organisational structure?

By way of contrast, Bevan (2000, p. 20), in an article entitled: 'Flexible designs on domestic harmony', reports on a UK government initiative which pays for advice to employers on implementing a better work/life balance. Examples of employees who have benefited from more flexible work arrangements, imply few difficulties as they choose arrangements to suit their particular home and life circumstances. The benefits to employers and businesses seem to outweigh the disadvantages.

It is difficult to know whether most people would prefer not to work on production lines, doing repetitive work, supermarket checkouts or as labourers in the winter on building sites if they had the choice of interesting work which they could arrange to suit their personal circumstances. Work serves many purposes besides being a source of earnings. According to Robbins (2001, p. 435), however: 'While more people today are undoubtedly turned off by overly specialised jobs than were their parents and grandparents, it would be naïve to ignore the reality that there is still a segment of the workforce that prefers the routine and repetitiveness of highly specialised jobs.' Not everyone is suited to working in highly organic or loosely structured networks, let alone working in virtual reality.

People choose organisations as much as organisations choose people. Those working in organisations are more likely to remain in organisations whose structures, with their particular degrees of centralisation, formalisation, specialisation and traditionalism, suit their individual and group preferences and needs. Designing organisational structures, which satisfy the needs of those working in and associated with them is not straightforward. Indeed, designing organisational structures for change, while at the same time ensuring that the needs of the market and of employees are met, is as much an art as a science.

● ● ● ● Organisational structure and change

The discussion in this chapter has led to the conclusion that there are many influences on the way an organisation might structure for successful performance and to cope with change. What is apparent is that there is no one best way to design organisational structures or any particular form which will guarantee successful performance. Depending on factors such as strategy, size, technology used, the degree of predictability of the environment and the expectations and lifestyle of employees, an organisation could well be successful and respond to the need for change whether it was structured along strict bureaucratic, mechanistic lines or as one of the newer network forms.

Care must be taken, however, not to assume that these contingency relationships are straightforward and that, provided the 'formula' is learned and applied, success will result. Robbins (1993, p. 528), drawing on the work of Child (1972) and Pugh (1973), states that: 'Strategy, size, technology and environment – even when combined – can at best explain only fifty percent of the variability in structure.' In addition, the idea that there is a one-way causal relationship between an organisation's environment and its structure is open to question.

Organisations are not only influenced by their environments, they may, in turn, be able, themselves, to influence certain parts of their environments. For instance, the political environment can be influenced through lobbying, customers in the economic environment influenced through advertising and people's expectations of employment influenced by the way groups of organisations design jobs. The existence of monopoly conditions clearly helps organisations modify their environments. In times of high unemployment, the introduction of technology which significantly changes working practices will be easier.

If organisations are able, to some extent, to manipulate their environments to suit their strategies and structures, this will enable them to preserve existing structures and operational arrangements. The pressure to do this is evident from Mullins's (1999, p. 570) statement that: 'Developing organisations cannot, without difficulty, change their formal structure at too frequent an interval. There must be a significant change in contingency factors before an organisation will respond.' This implies a considerable time lag between situational change and changes in structure. Therefore, even if changes in strategy, size, technology and environmental factors do build forces for changes in organisational structure, there are other factors which may accelerate or, more likely, impede this process.

One of these factors is associated with the concept of 'strategic choice' (Child, 1972) and draws attention to the power of senior managers to choose which criteria they will use in assessing what organisational changes should take place. Managers who may lose power and/or position are unlikely to choose those alternatives which, from a logical–rational point of view, maximise the organisation's interest. Robbins (1993, p. 528) summarises this view of structure as the 'power–control' explanation of organisational structure, that is, 'an organisation's structure is the result of a power struggle by internal constituencies who are seeking to further their interests'. Thus, given the discretion available to management, rather than changes in organisational structure being logically planned and implemented, what results will be a structure which 'emerges' to satisfy not only the imperatives of the internal and external environments, but the personalities and power needs of dominant stakeholders.

Organisational politics and the issue of power balance are not the only factors influencing structural change in organisations. Neither does the mere process of changing an organisation's structure necessarily bring about permanent change in management strategy, style of operating and other employees' attitudes and behaviours. The pervasiveness of organisational and national cultures can be strong enough to work against change. Thus the mechanisms for managing any kind of organisational change must take account of what French and Bell (1990) call the informal, 'covert' aspects of organisational life such as people's values and feelings, the informal, as opposed to formal, groupings and the norms of behaviours which become part of any organisation but which are rarely 'spelt out'. Johnson (1990) puts emphasis on the role of symbols, rituals, stories and myths as being important parts of an organisation's culture. He says that organisational change cannot be brought about simply by changing strategy and structure. The organisational culture has a significant and maybe even dominant role to play if anything more than incremental change is to happen. This is the subject of the next chapter.

Conclusions

Organisational structure can be likened to the skeleton of the organisation supporting the implementation of strategic decision making and operational processes. This chapter has focused on issues associated with the strategy, size, technology, environment and structure 'fit'. Structural change is seen to be influenced by changes in these situational factors. A number of different organisational forms have been described and the appropriateness of them to different situations in which organisations find themselves discussed. Of particular interest, in environments which push for organisational change, are the newer project and network forms of organisation. The significant development of communications technologies has increased the possibilities for virtual working in what can be called virtual organisations.

However, it is not feasible to think that organisations can constantly restructure as their environments move and change. Chapter 1 showed how organisations are, to some extent, a product of their history. In addition, organisations have existing structures, workforces, who are used to working in them, existing cultures, current businesses to sustain and, in many cases, trades unions to satisfy. Redesigning an organisation's structure has to be carefully planned with change taking place as current business performance has to be sustained. This implies a mixture of incremental and transformational change.

Having said all this, focusing on the formal aspects of organisational life, such as structure, can furnish only part of the explanation of why and how organisations choose to change and, if they do so, what form that change might take.

The next two chapters, therefore, extend this discussion further by addressing the more informal, 'covert' aspects of organisational life; that is, the prevailing values, attitudes and beliefs about what should be done and how – the culture which is part of, and surrounds, organisations – and the politics which are equally important in any examination of organisations and change.

Discussion questions and assignments

1   Starting from scratch underplays the fact that significant redesign has to be planned and implemented in a real-life context that won't go away. Hospitals re-engineering projects run into the problems of physician power. Government projects are often stifled by a context where people can't see the need for fundamental change. In manufacturing and service organisations, plans to implement a new way of doing business are often undermined by the thinking and mindsets of the old way. These realities have to be actively managed and changed if new initiatives are to succeed.

(Morgan, 1994)

To what extent do these or similar issues apply to your own organisation or one you know well? Anticipating what has still to be discussed in the chapters to come, put forward ideas for how managers and other relevant people might address them.

2   *'In spite of the talk about network and virtual organisations, most organisations conform to more traditional structure types.'* Discuss in relation to your own organisation and others you know well as well as any information you can gain from articles, the media and the Internet.

Case example

Ministers in talks on police reforms

FT

Home Office ministers and police chiefs are discussing radical changes to the police force, some of which are likely to be incorporated in the Labour party's election manifesto. The discussions focus on the service's organisational weaknesses, which ministers fear are undermining efforts to convince the electorate the government is tackling crime successfully. Senior officers are strongly resisting being drawn into party politics. However, they accept that in the run-up to an election, ministers are anxious to draft proposals for change that have at least their tacit support. Significantly, some of the more radical proposals are emanating from future police chiefs – middle-ranking officers being trained to commander level – although they are gaining support in the Association of Chief Police Officers. Proposals entitled 'agenda for change' were agreed internally by senior officers following a meeting at the police training college in Bramshill on September 6. They include a review of all conditions and allowances to produce more flexible working and to improve the quality of service delivery. According to existing regulations, off-duty officers required at short notice to deal with emergencies, as well as working officers dispatched to extra or alternative duties, receive considerable overtime payments.

In addition to changing working practices, ministers and senior officers are considering the introduction of a pilot scheme involving a two-tier police force, with some community policing tasks being carried out by uniformed security staff recruited from outside the police service. The government accepts that police numbers are too low to provide the visible patrols in some neighbourhoods that make communities feel safe. The discussions in Whitehall are also focusing on the need for police forces to make better use of new technology. One internal police document notes that within the 43 English and Welsh constabularies, 'IT infrastructure is still poor, with lack of national collaboration and co-ordination'.

Areas of tension between the government and police include what one internal police document described as a 'conflict between central and locally set priorities'. There is also criticism of 'over-supervision and inspection fatigue.'

Source: Jimmy Burns, Social Affairs Correspondent, *Financial Times*, 18 September, 2000

▶

Case exercise: Questions

1 To what extent do you agree that the proposed changes are 'radical'? Justify your conclusions by reference to the discussions in Chapter 2.

2 Attempt to match the proposals for a 'two-tier' police service and the increased use of IT to one (or a mixture) of the organisational forms discussed in this chapter. Justify your conclusions.

3 What effects might the proposed move to more flexible working have on the perception of 'over supervision and inspection fatigue'?

References

Ansoff, I. H. and McDonnell, E. J. (1990), *Implanting Strategic Management*, Englewood Cliffs, NJ, Prentice Hall.

Arkin, A. (1999) 'Peak practice', *People Management*, 11 November, pp. 57–9.

Bartol, K. M. and Martin, D. C. (1994), *Management* (2nd edn), Maidenhead, McGraw-Hill.

Bevan, S. (2000) 'Flexible designs on domestic harmony', *Financial Times*, October 5, p. 5.

Burnes, B. (1996), *Managing Change. A Strategic Approach to Organisational Dynamics*, London, Pitman.

Burns, J. (2000) 'Ministers in talks on police reform', *Financial Times*, September 17.

Burns, T. and Stalker, G. M. (1961), *The Management of Innovation*, London, Tavistock.

Business Week (1993), 'The virtual corporation', *Business Week*, 8 February, pp. 98–102.

Butler, R. (1991), *Designing Organizations: A Decision Making Perspective*, London, Routledge.

Chandler, A. D., Jr (1962), *Strategy and Structure: Chapters in the History of the Industrial Enterprise*, Cambridge, MA, MIT Press.

Child, J. (1972), 'Organization structure, environment and performance: the role of strategic choice', *Sociology*, January, pp. 1–22.

Child, J. (1988), *Organizations: A Guide to Problems and Practice* (2nd edn), London, Paul Chapman.

Clegg, S. R. (1990), *Modern Organizations: Organisation Studies in the Postmodern World*, London, Sage.

Cohen, M. and Agrawal, V. (2000) 'All change in the second supply chain revolution', in Mastering Management, *Financial Times*, October 2, pp. 8–10.

Cooper, C. (2000) 'Rolling with it', *People Management*, 28 September, pp. 32–4.

Cusamano, M. (1985), *The Japanese Automobile Industry: Technology and Management at Nissan and Toyota*, Cambridge, MA, Harvard Industry Press.

Davidow, W. H. and Malone, M. S. (1992), *The Virtual Corporation*, New York, Harper Business.

Davis, S. M. and Lawrence, P. R. (1977), *Matrix*, Reading, MA, Addison-Wesley.

Drucker, P. F. (1989), *The Practice of Management*, Oxford, Heinemann Professional.

French, W. L. and Bell, C. H., Jr (1990), *Organization Development. Behavioral Science Interventions for Organization Improvement* (4th edn), Englewood Cliffs, NJ, Prentice Hall.

Grande, C. (2000) Post offices to hold goods for e-shoppers, *Financial Times*, October 30, p. 6.

Greiner, L. (1972), 'Evolution and revolution as organizations grow', *Harvard Business Review*, July–August.

Hammer, M. and Champy, J. (1993) *Reengineering the Corporation: A Manifesto for Business Revolution*, New York, Harper Business.

Handy, C. B. (1989), *The Age of Unreason*, London, Business Books.

Hinterhuber, H. H. and Levin, B. M. (1994), 'Strategic networks – the organization of the future', *Long Range Planning*, Vol. 27, No. 3, pp. 43–53.

Hollinger, P. (2000), Festive internet rush may surprise retailers, *Financial Times*, October 30, p. 6.

Jackson, N. and Carter, P. (2000), *Rethinking Organisational Behaviour*, Harlow, Financial Times/Prentice Hall/Pearson Education.

Jaques, E. (1990), 'The stratified depth-structure of bureaucracy', Chapter 2 in Pugh, D. S. (ed.), *Organization Theory*, London, Penguin.

Jaques, E. and Clement, S. D. (1994), *Executive Leadership*, Oxford, Blackwell.

Johnson, G. (1990), 'Managing strategic action; the role

of symbolic action', *British Journal of Management*, Vol. 1, pp. 183–200.

Johnson, G. and Scholes, K. (1999), *Exploring Corporate Strategy. Texts and Cases* (5th edn), Hemel Hempstead, Prentice Hall.

Koontz, H. and Weihrich, H. (eds) (1990), *Essentials of Management*, New York, McGraw-Hill, pp. 155–72.

Lawrence, P. R. and Lorsch, J. W. (1967), *Organization and Environment: Managing Differentiation and Integration*, Boston, Harvard Business School.

Lorenz, C. (1992), Lean regime for a fitter future, *Financial Times*, 6 May, p.16.

Lucas, H. C. Jr (1996), *The T-Form Organization: Using Technology to Design Organizations for the 21st Century*, San Francisco, Jossey-Bass.

Luthans, F. (1995), *Organizational Behavior* (7th edn), New York, McGraw-Hill.

Lyons, L. (2000), 'Management is dead', *People Management*, 26 October, pp. 60–4.

McHugh, M. and Bennett, H. (1999) 'Introducing teamwork within a bureaucratic maze', *The Leadership and Organization Development Journal*, Vol. 20, No. 2, pp. 81–93.

Miles, R. E. and Snow, C. C. (1984a), 'Fit, failure and the hall of fame', *California Management Review*, Vol. 26, No. 3, pp. 10–28.

Miles, R. E. and Snow, C. C. (1984b), 'Designing strategic human resource systems', *Organisational Dynamics*, Vol. 13, Part 8, pp. 36–52.

Mills, M. (2000) 'Coming to a screen near you ...', *in Office Hours, The Guardian*, September 18, p. 2.

Mintzberg, H. (1979), *The Structuring of Organizations*, Englewood Cliffs, NJ, Prentice Hall.

Mintzberg, H. (1983), *Structure in Fives: Designing Effective Organizations*, Englewood Cliffs, NJ, Prentice Hall.

Mintzberg, H. (1991), 'The effective organization forces and forms', *Sloan Management Review*, Winter, Vol. 32, Part 2, pp. 54–67.

Mintzberg, H. (1994), 'Rethinking strategic planning. Part I: pitfalls and fallacies', *Long Range Planning*, Vol. 27, No. 3, pp. 12–21.

Mintzberg, H., Quinn, J. B. and James, R. M. (1988), *The Strategy Process: Concepts, Contexts and Cases*, London, Prentice Hall.

Morgan, G. (1989), *Creative Organization Theory. A Resource Book*, London, Sage.

Morgan, G. (1994) 'Quantum leaps ... step by step', *The Globe and Mail Canada's National Newspaper*, 28 June. Also available at http://www.imaginiz.com/leaps.html

Mullins, L. (1999), *Management and Organisational Behaviour* (5th edn), London, Pitman.

Ody, P. (2000) Working towards a total, visible network, *Financial Times Survey Supply Chain Management*, October 25, p. 1.

Perrow, C. (1967), *Organizational Analysis: A Sociological View*, London, Tavistock.

Pugh, D. S. (1973), 'The measurement of organisation structures: does context determine form?' *Organisational Dynamics*, Spring, 1973, pp. 19–34. Also in Pugh, D. S. (ed.) (1990), *Organization Theory. Selected Readings*, London, Penguin.

Pugh, D. (1990), *Organization Theory. Selected Readings*, London, Penguin.

Pugh, D. S., Hickson, D. J., Hinings, C. R. and Turner, C. (1969), 'Dimensions of organization structure', *Administrative Science Quarterly*, Vol. 17, pp. 163–76.

Robbins, S. P. (1993), *Organizational Behavior*, Englewood Cliffs, NJ, Prentice Hall.

Robbins, S. P. (2001), *Organizational Behavior* (9th edn), Englewood Cliffs, NJ, Prentice Hall.

Simon, H. A. (1960), *The New Science of Management Decision*, New York, Harper.

Snow, C. C., Miles, R. E. and Coleman, H. J., Jr (1992) 'Managing 21st century network organizations', *Organizational Dynamics*, Winter, pp. 5–19.

Thompson, J. D. (1967), *Organizations in Action*, New York, McGraw-Hill.

Weber, M. (1947), *The Theory of Social and Economic Organisation*, Free Press, translated and edited by Henderson, A. M. and Parsons, T., in Pugh, D. S. (1990), *Organization Theory. Selected Readings*, London, Penguin. (German original published in 1924.)

Wilson, D. C. and Rosenfeld, R. H. (1990), *Managing Organizations, Text, Readings and Cases*, Maidenhead, McGraw-Hill.

Wilson, D. C. and Rosenfeld, R. H. (1991), *Managing Organizations, Text, Readings and Cases: Instructors Resource Book*, Maidenhead, McGraw-Hill.

Woodward, J. (1965), *Industrial Organization: Theory and Practice*, London, Oxford University Press.

Chapter 4

Cultures for change

This chapter complements Chapter 2. In contrast to the emphasis in that chapter on the formal aspects of organisational functioning, this chapter begins the process of addressing the informal aspects of organisational functioning with an exploration of the concept of culture as it influences organisational life and organisational change processes. The meaning of culture at both the organisational and national levels is discussed and different models and typologies are compared. Methods for diagnosing and identifying organisational culture are discussed together with the different sources from which organisational culture derives. The links between organisational strategy, structure and culture are explored in order to understand the issues associated with and possibilities for changing organisational culture. The chapter ends with a discussion of the feasibility of changing an organisation's culture according to the strategy and context prevailing at the time. Much of what is said in this chapter relates to issues of organisational politics and power discussed in Chapter 5 and approaches to designing and implementing change in Chapters 7 and 8, but Chapter 8 in particular.

Objectives

To:

- *recognise the importance of the informal organisation and its role in relation to organisations and change*

- *explain the meaning of culture in the context of a range of perspectives offered by researchers in the field*

- *compare and contrast different cultural models and typologies*

- *diagnose organisational culture as the first step in the process of culture change*

● *identify the sources, including those of the wider society, from which an organisation derives its culture in order to understand how culture pervades all aspects of organisational life*

● *examine different cultures in terms of their capacity to help or hinder organisational change*

● *investigate degrees of strategy–culture compatibility and their implications for large-scale strategic change.*

The informal organisation

It is clear from the discussion in the previous chapters that organisations are composed of formal elements such as structure, strategy and technology. In addition, there is, apparently, little that is contentious in describing their size, whether this is measured by number of employees or by one or more financial indicators. The goals of an organisation and its financial resources might also be regarded as fairly understood and explicit elements of organisational life. As explained previously, these aspects of organisational functioning can be termed the formal organisation. Thus, the determination of an organisation's goals, its strategy and structure, the technology it will use and its need for financial resources can, legitimately, be associated with logical thinking and rational methods of decision making. In addition, because these more formal organisational features can be reasonably understood by most people, they are, in the main, susceptible to the process of *planned* change (*see* Chapter 2).

However, as the comments at the end of Chapter 2 showed, organisational life is not nearly as neat and tidy as this implies. This has been well expressed by French and Bell (1990) in their use of the concept of the informal organisation and the metaphor of the 'organisational iceberg'. Figure 4.1 illustrates this idea pictorially.

The iceberg metaphor can be used to depict two contrasting aspects of organisational life. The first is that part of the iceberg which is visible above the water and which is composed of the more easy-to-see and formal aspects of an organisation. The second is the hidden part of the iceberg which is composed of the more covert aspects of organisational life. These include, for instance, the values, beliefs and attitudes held by management and other employees, the emergent informal groupings which occur in every organisation, the norms of behaviour which direct how things are done but which are rarely talked about and the politics of organisational life which are mainly hidden but which, for all that, are a powerful driver of decisions and actions.

It is significant that the metaphor of an iceberg not only points to the overt and covert aspects of organisations, but draws attention to the proposition that the informal systems, as well as being hidden, are the greater part of the organisational

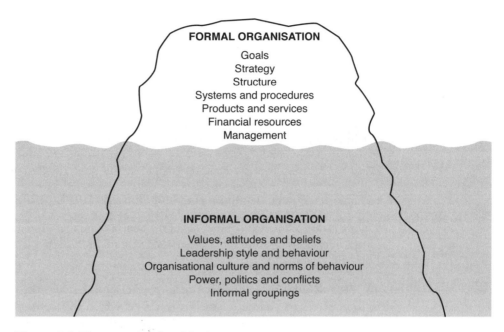

Figure 4.1 The organisational iceberg

iceberg. However, as with an iceberg, they may not become apparent until one collides with them unwittingly. Thus the difficulties in detecting the extent and characteristics of the hidden part of the iceberg are analogous to the difficulties encountered in examining and understanding the more informal, hidden aspects of organisational behaviour. Indeed, French and Bell (1990, p. 18) go so far as to say: 'Traditionally, this hidden domain either is not examined at all or is only partially examined.' The truth of this comment is debatable. However, whether it is wholly true or not, the acceptance that the informal organisation exists and can act powerfully to influence organisational activity is reason enough to examine how it impinges upon the extent to which organisations can deal with change.

The concepts of culture, politics and power have come to embrace much of what is included in the hidden part of the organisation. What is more, they play an important role in helping or hindering the process of change, as Morgan (1989) confirms in his statement: 'The culture and politics of many organisations constrain the degree of change and transformation in which they can successfully engage, even though such change may be highly desirable for meeting the challenges and demands of the wider environment.' Therefore, regardless of how well change might be planned in terms of the more formal organisational characteristics, it is the hidden informal aspects of organisational life which will act to help or hinder it. The discussion which follows, both in this chapter and the next, explores the nature and influence of culture and politics in terms of their significance for organisations in times of change.

● ● ● ● The meaning of culture

Many definitions of culture can be found in the literature and Kroeber and Kluckhohn (1952, p. 181) claim to have examined well over 100. It seems reasonable, therefore, to give their summary definition, which is:

> Culture consists in patterned ways of thinking, feeling and reacting, acquired and transmitted mainly by symbols, constituting the distinctive achievements of human groups, including their embodiment in artifacts; the essential core of culture consists of traditional (i.e. historically derived and selected) ideas and especially their attached values.

Another, often quoted definition is that of Hofstede (1981, p. 24) which is:

> Culture is the collective programming of the human mind that distinguishes the members of one human group from those of another. Culture in this sense is a system of collectively held values.

Both these definitions refer to culture on the 'grand scale'. In the first case, the definition refers to characteristics in terms of which different *societies* differ one from another. In the second case, Hofstede uses his definition to delineate one *national* culture from another. For instance, his reference to 'human groups' is taken to mean groupings based on nationality.

These definitions can be compared to those which are used more specifically to describe organisational cultures. The following three are chosen from a list given by Brown (1995) in his book entitled *Organisational Culture*. They span the years from 1952 to the present.

> The culture of the factory is its customary and traditional way of thinking and of doing things, which is shared to a greater or lesser degree by all its members, and which new members must learn, and at least partially accept, in order to be accepted into service in the firm. Culture in this sense covers a wide range of behaviour: the methods of production; job skills and technical knowledge; attitudes towards discipline and punishment; the customs and habits of managerial behaviour; the objectives of the concern; its way of doing business; the methods of payment; the values placed on different types of work; beliefs in democratic living and joint consultation; and the less conscious conventions and taboos. (Jaques, 1952, p. 251)

> A set of understandings or meanings shared by a group of people. The meanings are largely tacit among members, are clearly relevant to the particular group, and are distinctive to the group. Meanings are passed on to new group members. (Louis, 1980)

> Culture is 'how things are done around here'. It is what is typical of the organization, the habits, the prevailing attitudes, the grown-up pattern of accepted and expected behaviour. (Drennan, 1992, p. 3)

An examination of all these definitions illustrates a degree of overlap. Thus, in general, people are seen as being from different cultures if their ways of life as a group (whether societal or organisational) differ significantly, one from another.

Collectively, these definitions imply that culture is an objective entity which can be identified and which delineates one human grouping from another. It is clear that culture has cognitive (to do with thinking), affective (to do with feeling) and behavioural characteristics. However, this tends to give the impression that different cultures are easily identified and, on the whole, this is not so. Schein (1992, p. 6) sums this up by referring to organisational culture as:

> The deeper level of basic assumptions and beliefs that are shared by members of an organisation, that operate unconsciously and define in a basic 'taken for granted' fashion an organisation's view of its self and its environment.

The fact that these elements of culture operate 'tacitly' as Louis says, or 'unconsciously' as Schein says, reinforces the metaphor of the hidden part of the iceberg. What is also implicit in the use of this metaphor and these definitions is that culture is 'deep-seated' and is, therefore, likely to be resistant to change. However, as Bate (1996, p. 28) points out: 'Culture can be changed, in fact it is changing all the time.' The issue is the degree of change to which culture can be submitted over the short and long term and the process for doing this. Much depends on the perspective adopted and the type of change proposed. Three perspectives can be identified (*see* Ogbonna and Harris, 1998). These are: that culture *can* be managed; that culture *may* be manipulated; and that culture *cannot* be consciously changed. Most of the writing and research concerned with culture change subscribes to the first two of these perspectives. The last of these might be true if, for culture change to take place, some external (and perhaps unpredictable) forces are required to force it. However, even in these circumstances, the situation emerging from such events will need to be managed. This discussion, therefore, concentrates on issues associated with the first two of these perspectives on the assumption that much of what is said would apply if culture change occurs spontaneously rather than as a result of a more planned process.

Advice on how to *plan* culture change is not in short supply (for some examples see Bate, 1996; Carnall, 1995; Eccles, 1994; Ogbonna and Harris, 1998). There is general agreement that there is a need to (i) assess the current situation, (ii) have some idea on what the aimed for situation looks like and (iii) work out the 'what' and 'how' of moving the organisation, or section of it, away from its current culture to what is perceived to be a more desirable one. Of major importance is the need, before any attempt is made to alter the culture, to know more about the culture to be changed. Some ways of doing this are discussed in the next section.

Describing organisational culture

Methods for describing organisational cultures are varied. Some simply list what are seen to be the characteristics of culture. For instance, Brown (1995, p. 8) lists the following:

- artifacts
- language in the form of jokes, metaphors, stories, myths and legends
- behaviour patterns in the form of rites, rituals, ceremonies and celebrations
- norms of behaviour
- heroes
- symbols and symbolic action
- beliefs, values and attitudes
- ethical codes
- basic assumptions
- history.

It is then left to those attempting to describe a culture to frame their descriptions in terms of these characteristics. This is more or less easily done according to the precision with which the general characteristics are set out. In addition, not all writers are agreed on what should or should not be included in any list. For instance, a comparison of Brown's list with that of Robbins (2001) (*see* Illustration 4.1) illustrates well the two parts of the organisational iceberg in that Brown emphasises more strongly the more informal aspects of organisational life while Robbins includes some of the more formal elements.

Illustration 4.1

The characteristics of organisational culture

1 **Innovation and risk taking.** The degree to which employees are encouraged to be innovative and take risks.

2 **Attention to detail.** The degree to which employees are expected to exhibit precision, analysis and attention to detail.

3 **Outcome orientation.** The degree to which management focuses on results or outcomes rather than on the techniques and processes used to achieve those outcomes.

4 **People orientation.** The degree to which management decisions take into consideration the effect of outcomes on people within the organisation.

5 **Team orientation.** The degree to which work activities are organised around groups rather than individuals.

6 **Aggression.** The degree to which people are aggressive and competitive rather than easygoing.

7 **Stability.** The degree to which organisational activities emphasise maintaining the status quo in contrast to growth.

Source: Robbins, S. P. (2001), *Organizational Behavior,* 9th edn (Englewood Cliffs, NJ, Prentice Hall, pp. 510–11).

Identifying an organisation's culture using Brown's list could be done qualitatively or by constructing some kind of questionnaire type instrument. Activity 4.1 shows how a more quantitative method of identification can be used. The questionnaire there is based on Robbins's rather more precise culture characteristics.

Activity 4.1   Appraising your own organisation

The scales relate to the organisational culture characteristics listed in Illustration 4.1. Put a cross on each scale according to how you rate your own organisation (or one with which you are familiar). If possible, ask colleagues in different parts of the organisation to your own to carry out this rating process.

Organisational culture characteristics

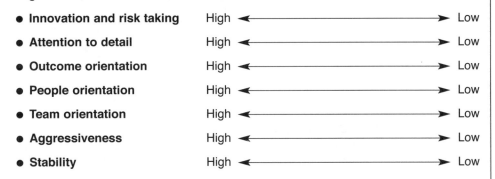

- **Innovation and risk taking**   High ⟵──────────────⟶ Low
- **Attention to detail**   High ⟵──────────────⟶ Low
- **Outcome orientation**   High ⟵──────────────⟶ Low
- **People orientation**   High ⟵──────────────⟶ Low
- **Team orientation**   High ⟵──────────────⟶ Low
- **Aggressiveness**   High ⟵──────────────⟶ Low
- **Stability**   High ⟵──────────────⟶ Low

Compare your own view of your organisation's culture with that of your colleagues. Where there are any differences, consider why their views might be different from your own.

Models of organisational culture such as those of Brown and Robbins do not make any attempt to link one culture characteristic with another. By contrast other writers suggest that different cultural characteristics *are* linked to one another through a hierarchy of 'levels' of culture. An example is shown in Figure 4.2. This illustrates the suggestions of Hofstede *et al.* (1990) that culture manifests itself at the deepest level through people's values and at the shallowest level in terms of the things which symbolise those values.

Other 'levels' models are those of Schein (1992) and Dyer (1985). Schein suggests three levels which are from the shallowest to the deepest: the *artifacts* level (the visible organisational structures and processes such as language, environment, rituals, ceremonies, myths and stories); the *espoused values* level (the organisation's strategies, goals, philosophies); and the *basic underlying assumptions* level (the unconscious, taken-for-granted beliefs, perceptions, thoughts and feelings which are the ultimate source of values and actions). Thus, the rituals, heroes and

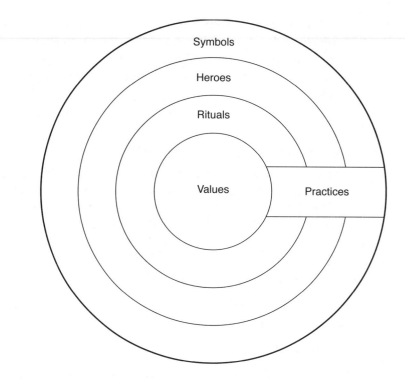

Figure 4.2 Different levels of culture

Source: Hofstede, G., Neuijen, B., Ohayv, D. D. and Sanders, G. (1990), 'Measuring organizational cultures: a qualitative and quantitative study across twenty cases', *Administrative Science Quarterly*, Vol. 35, p. 291.

symbols level of Hofstede *et al.* equates with Schein's artifacts level. However, Hofstede's values level is, apparently, split into two levels by Schein who distinguishes between the beliefs, values and attitudes associated with the espoused values level and the deeper level of basic assumptions. As far as Dyer's (1985) model goes, the only difference from that of Schein is that Dyer proposes four levels – *artifacts*, *perspectives*, *values* and *tacit assumptions*.

While the levels models have much in common with Brown's list of the elements of organisational culture, at first sight it seems that the seven characteristics of organisational culture identified by Robbins have little to do with them, yet Robbins's list appears much more amenable to being *used* to describe an organisation's culture in practical terms. However, it is possible to use the levels model to get some understanding of an organisation's culture. In this case, the process requires interpretation of signs and symbols, as well as language used, to assess the prevailing values and underlying assumptions about how the organisation should operate. Illustration 4.2 shows how a combination of Schein's and Dyer's models might be applied to the Beautiful Buildings Company whose structure is described in Chapter 3.

Illustration 4.2

Levels of culture in the BB Company

1 **Artifacts.** The annual report of the company includes policies concerned with employees as well as customers and shareholders. Building sites have well-kept, clean facilities for the workers. Gillian Lambeth is frequently referred to by her first name.

2 **Perspective.** It is acceptable for the trades union representatives to know what volume of work might be expected in the future, but the directors are not expected to talk about details of the proposed expansion until it becomes a well-established fact.

3 **Values.** Although there is a clear distinction between directors/managers and site workers, pay and conditions for workers should be fair and their views taken into account on matters pertaining to them. However, gaining contracts and satisfying customers is a priority.

4 **Basic/tacit assumptions.** All people should be treated with dignity whatever their level and function.

Objectivist and interpretive views of culture

Attempts to build models of organisational culture, such as those represented by Robbins's list and the levels models, throw up the issue of how to bring meaning to the concept of culture itself. In pursuit of this, Alvesson (1993), Bate (1996) and Brown (1995) all draw attention to the distinction between two classifications of culture. The first, of which Robbins's list and the levels models might be considered examples, treat culture as a critical variable which forms a partial explanation for differences in organisational operations. This can be termed the objectivist or functional view of culture (Alvesson, 1993). Alternatively, culture can be defined as a set of behavioural and/or cognitive characteristics (Brown, 1995). This view places culture alongside structure, technology and the environment (for instance) as one of the variables which influence organisational life and performance. In summary, this view of culture implies that organisations *have* cultures (*see* Brooks and Bate, 1994) and further implies that changing cultures is not that difficult given the correct way of going about it.

There is, however, a second view of culture, which interprets the meaning of culture as a metaphor for the concept of organisation itself. Thus, Pacanowsky and O'Donnell-Trujillo (1982, p. 126) say: 'Organizational culture is not just another piece of the puzzle. From our point of view, a culture is not something an organization *has*; a culture is something an organization *is*' [author's emphasis]. This view is echoed by Morgan (1986) who uses the metaphor 'organisations as cultures' as one of a range of metaphors which present different images of organisation. Morgan's definition of culture gives some sense of this. He says:

> Shared meaning, shared understanding and shared sense making are all different ways of describing culture. In talking about culture we are really talking about a process of reality construction that allows people to see and understand particular events, actions, objects, utterances, or situations in distinctive ways. These patterns of understanding also provide a basis for making one's own behaviour sensible and meaningful.
>
> (Morgan, 1986, p. 128)

Morgan maintains that, in doing this, members of organisations are, in fact, creating the organisation itself. In essence this means that organisations are *socially* constructed realities and that, rather than being defined by their structures, rules and regulations, they are constructed as much in the heads and minds of their members and are strongly related to members' self-concepts and identity. Taking this view of culture implies that, if understanding of an organisation's culture is to be reached, it is necessary to look at the routine aspects of everyday life as well as at the more obvious and more public signs, symbols and ceremonies, which are more frequently associated with organisational leaders. It also implies a requirement to examine how culture is created and sustained. This means recognising that culture is part of a much bigger historical pattern, and therefore, that 'more often it is a *recurrence* rather than just an occurrence' (*see* Bate, 1996, p. 29). A model of organisational culture which appears to bring together the idea of culture as congruent with everything that happens in an organisation is Johnson and Scholes's (1997) 'cultural web' as described in Illustration 4.3.

The cultural web

It can be seen from Illustration 4.3 that the cultural web is all-encompassing in the organisational elements which it includes. Johnson (1990) and Johnson and Scholes (1999) draw attention to the influence of prevailing organisational paradigms (i.e. the beliefs and assumptions of the people making up the organisation) in any attempt to bring about strategic change. The link between the beliefs and assumptions making up the paradigm and other aspects of organisational functioning is exemplified in the statement by Johnson and Scholes (1993, p. 61) that: 'It would be a mistake to conceive of the paradigm as merely a set of beliefs and assumptions removed from organisational action. They lie within a cultural web which bonds them to the day-to-day action of organisational life.'

Johnson and Scholes probably do not go as far as Morgan in equating culture fully with organisation, but neither do they completely objectify culture as separate from other aspects of organisational life. In addition, the subtitle of Johnson's (1990) article, 'The role of symbolic action', illustrates the emphasis put upon the rituals or routines, stories or myths, and symbols elements of the cultural web in any attempt to bring about change resulting in a shift in the organisational paradigm. For Johnson (1996), changing organisational structures, control systems and even power structures will not necessarily bring about a paradigm shift. He argues that, for this to happen, a much greater effort must be put into bringing about changes in the other elements of the cultural web.

Illustration 4.3

The cultural web

Johnson and Scholes explain the different elements of the cultural web as follows:

- The *routine* ways that members of the organisation behave towards each other and that link different parts of the organisation, comprise 'the way we do things around here', which at their best lubricate the working of the organisation and may provide a distinctive and beneficial organisational competency. However, they can also represent a taken-for-grantedness about how things should happen which is extremely difficult to change and highly protective of core assumptions in the paradigm.

- The *rituals* of organisational life, such as training programmes, promotion and assessment, point to what is important in the organisation, reinforce 'the way we do things around here' and signal what is important and valued.

- The *stories* told by members of the organisation to each other, to outsiders, to new recruits and so on, embed the present in its organisational history and flag up important events and personalities, as well as mavericks who 'deviate from the norm'.

- The more *symbolic* aspects of organisations, such as logos, offices, cars and titles or the type of language and terminology commonly used, become a shorthand representation of the nature of the organisation.

- The *control systems*, measurements and reward systems emphasise what it is important to monitor

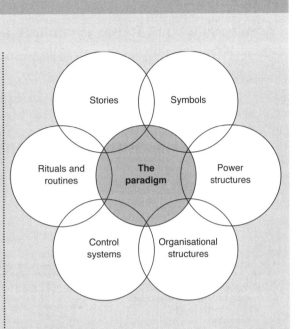

in the organisation and to focus attention and activity on.

- *Power structures* are also likely to be associated with the key constructs of the paradigm. The most powerful managerial groupings in the organisation are likely to be the ones most associated with core assumptions and beliefs about what is important.

- The *formal organisational structure* or the more informal ways in which the organisations work are likely to reflect power structures and, again, to delineate important relationships and emphasise what is important in the organisation.

Source: Based on Johnson, G. and Scholes, K. (1999), *Exploring Corporate Strategy, Texts and Cases*, 5th edn (Hemel Hempstead, Prentice Hall, pp. 74–8).

Activity 4.2   Creating a cultural web for your organisation

Illustration 4.4 shows the cultural web for an organisation involved in buying paper in bulk and then cutting and preparing it for sale to large-scale paper users.*

Using this as a guide, construct a cultural web for an organisation you know well (or if it is large, one particular division or department).

If you wished to institute change at the strategic level, how would you go about changing the rituals or routines, stories and symbols elements of your cultural web?

*Additional examples of the use of the cultural web can be found in Johnson and Scholes (1997, pp. 70 and 460–1) and Johnson and Scholes (1999, pp. 75).

Illustration 4.4

A cultural web of Paper Unlimited, a large UK-based paper distributor

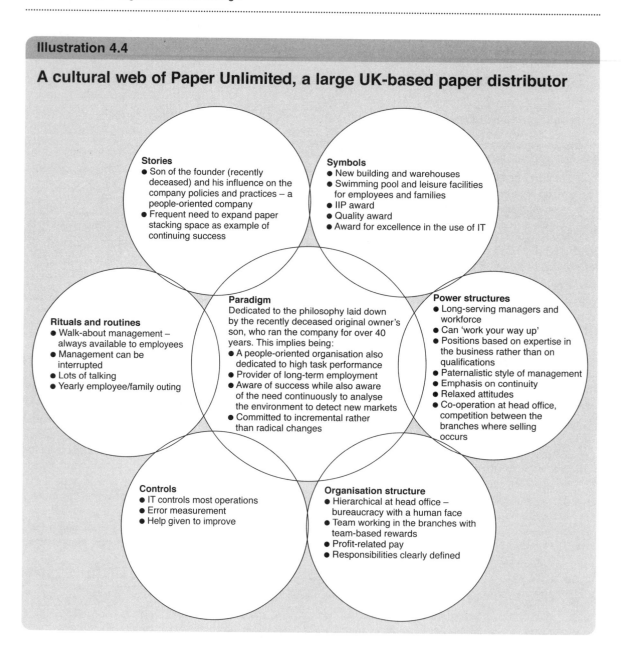

Stories
- Son of the founder (recently deceased) and his influence on the company policies and practices – a people-oriented company
- Frequent need to expand paper stacking space as example of continuing success

Symbols
- New building and warehouses
- Swimming pool and leisure facilities for employees and families
- IIP award
- Quality award
- Award for excellence in the use of IT

Rituals and routines
- Walk-about management – always available to employees
- Management can be interrupted
- Lots of talking
- Yearly employee/family outing

Paradigm
Dedicated to the philosophy laid down by the recently deceased original owner's son, who ran the company for over 40 years. This implies being:
- A people-oriented organisation also dedicated to high task performance
- Provider of long-term employment
- Aware of success while also aware of the need continuously to analyse the environment to detect new markets
- Committed to incremental rather than radical changes

Power structures
- Long-serving managers and workforce
- Can 'work your way up'
- Positions based on expertise in the business rather than on qualifications
- Paternalistic style of management
- Emphasis on continuity
- Relaxed attitudes
- Co-operation at head office, competition between the branches where selling occurs

Controls
- IT controls most operations
- Error measurement
- Help given to improve

Organisation structure
- Hierarchical at head office – bureaucracy with a human face
- Team working in the branches with team-based rewards
- Profit-related pay
- Responsibilities clearly defined

Johnson and Scholes's cultural web has been applied mainly to organisational cultures. In contrast, Morgan's proposal that organisations *are* cultures discusses (among other things) differences in national cultures, including the way these have formed through historical processes. The notion of culture as a metaphor for organisation also encompasses the concept of sub-cultures. This is reinforced by Alvesson (1993) who recommends combining perspectives at three levels. These are:

- the organisation as a culture (unitary and unique)
- the organisation as a meeting place for great cultures (which includes national ethnic and class cultures)
- local perspectives on organisational sub-cultures.

From this point of view, in order to analyse organisational culture, it is necessary to understand the mixture of cultural manifestations at all three levels. The methods for describing culture just discussed can be used to describe culture at the organisational and sub-organisational levels. However, the results of Hall's (1995) research offer a model which appears to accommodate descriptions of culture at all levels. Hall's compass model of culture and its associated culture typologies have been developed through an apparent interest in cultural differences in 'partnerships' by which she means intercompany relationships which may be in the form of alliances, mergers, acquisitions or some other form. From her research, she claims to have identified two components of behaviour or cultural styles of behaviour.

The first of these is *assertiveness*, which is the degree to which a company's behaviours are seen by others as being forceful or directive. She says:

> Companies which behave in high assertive ways are seen to be decisive, quick and firm. There is little hesitation in their action. If they introduce a new product or enter a new market they do so with full force. ... Low assertive companies behave in more slow and steady ways. They are careful to consider what they do before they take firm action. They introduce a new product or enter a new market step by step, keeping their options open. Unlike the one-track mind of the high assertive company, the low assertive company has a 'multi-track mind'.
>
> (Hall, 1995, p. 52)

The second behavioural component of culture is *responsiveness*, which is the degree to which a company's behaviours are seen by others as being emotionally expressed. Thus:

> Companies which behave in high responsive ways are seen to be employee friendly, relaxed or spontaneous. These companies give the impression that they compete on feelings more than on facts. In industry gatherings, high responsive companies tend to be very 'likable'. They seem more open than other companies. Low responsive companies behave in more reserved or closed ways. They are not so much liked as 'respected'. They tend to be more rigid, their employees serious. Low responsive companies compete more on facts than on feelings.
>
> (Hall, 1995, pp. 54–5)

Illustration 4.5 lists the behaviours which indicate high and low assertiveness and responsiveness. An example of a moderately assertive but more highly responsive organisation is given in Illustration 4.6.

Hall maintains that the four different combinations of the two behavioural components she has identified result in four different cultural styles. Figure 4.3 illustrates why this model is called the compass model in that each of the four styles is labelled as one of the four points of the compass.

Illustration 4.5

Assertive and responsive behaviours

Behaviours which indicate high and (low) assertiveness are:

- individualistic
- demanding rather than obliging
- taking control
- pushy
- authoritative
- charging ahead
- challenging
- hardworking
- quick moving
- (low) cautious (indecisive)

Behaviours which indicate high and (low) responsiveness are:

- sensitive
- loyal
- compromising
- trusting
- team players
- value harmony
- unpredictable
- (low) quantitative rather than qualitative
- (low) factual rather than emotional
- (low) precise rather than inexact
- (low) task rather than people oriented
- (low) consistent (methodological).

Source: Hall, W. (1995), *Managing Cultures. Making Strategic Relationships Work* (Chichester, Wiley, pp. 54–5).

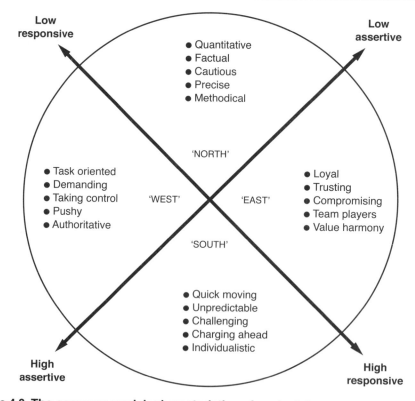

Figure 4.3 The compass model: characteristics of each style

Source: Reprinted by permission of John Wiley and Sons Ltd. Hall, W. (1995), *Managing Cultures. Making Strategic Relationships Work* (Chichester, Wiley, p. 58).

Illustration 4.6

RS Components – a moderately assertive but more highly responsive organisation

RS Components is a Corby-based company which supplies, from a mail order catalogue, a range of components varying from capacitors, bearings, bushes and seals to the cleaning agents, fastenings and power tools to trade organisations, other organisations and members of the public. However, as one of the product buyers says: 'The company sells just one thing and that is service to the customer.'

Visiting the company, one is struck by the quiet efficiency with which orders are taken by around 100 staff, working in specially designed open plan environments. Orders are taken at the rate of some 20,000 a day and a customer service standard of answering any telephone call within 5 seconds is maintained. In the order-taking areas, overhead displays give continuous information on the number of orders taken that day, the number of customers waiting and the number of staff available and waiting to take calls.

Within 15 minutes of an order being taken, it is received in the huge warehouse where product-collecting containers travel on rail-type tracks around the shelves holding the products to take the quickest route past 'pickers' who fill them to satisfy the order before continuing to the packing and despatch areas. The company guarantees delivery the day after the order is taken or the same day if required. The complete operation, from a customer requesting a product to its despatch, is computer controlled. At any time, computer displays give up-to-the-second information about any part of the process.

RS Components is not, however, just a distributor of products which are required in a hurry. It also offers technical advice and support on the range of products it sells, thus increasing the probability of achieving nearly 100 per cent satisfied customers.

Through its large, on-the-road sales staff and other market intelligence-gathering activities, it is successful in keeping up with projected market demands. Yet, it does not act hastily in offering a full service for the latest emerging products. If a new product appears to fit the company's selling policy, buyers will proceed cautiously in holding small stocks of the item until the demand can be more clearly discerned. As the demand becomes more established, the item will be stocked in quantities appropriate to meet customers' needs and the 'boast' to be able to supply the day after order.

Given the high level of computerisation which also allows almost every employee to be monitored, it might be thought that care for employees comes some distance after attention to the task. It is clear, however, to anyone spending time in the company, that care for employees is important. Every employee is identified by name, either by a name 'tag' attached to his or her computer (if one of the staff taking orders) or attached to their workstation (if in the 'pick and pack' warehouse). With a fairly large workforce, this enables everyone, whether known to each other or not, to address others by their name. The majority of staff work in teams which, although led by a team leader, are to a large extent self-managing.

Wages are slightly above the average for the type of work and pleasant restaurant facilities are available. The site which the company occupies includes garden areas where staff can sit or walk in the break times. A series of different start and finish times are available to suit the demands of the business, but which also provide flexible working hours to suit the different needs of different employees.

Hall claims, on the basis of her research, that the compass model with its four culture styles can be used to analyse culture, not only across a single organisation, but also with respect to individuals, departments and the industry and nation within which an organisation operates. Consequently, she claims that the model can be used to compare cultural relationships between organisations, nations and between one part of a multinational corporation and another. The choice of the 'compass' analogy seems to be derived from the identification of different national cultures and the positioning of these in terms of the points of a compass. As illustration of this, Figure 4.4 plots seven different countries on the assertiveness–responsiveness cultural style dimensions.

It should be noted that, in Figure 4.4, the further to the edge of the plot, the more extreme the cultural style. For instance, West Germany has a very high assertive, very low responsive cultural style, while Italy is more moderately placed on both of the cultural style dimensions. France is almost in the middle of the responsiveness dimension, but higher on the assertiveness scale. These results were based on a total of 211 responses from executives with experience of living and working in the seven countries represented. However, it should be noted that the executives were not, necessarily, of the nationalities on which they gave their

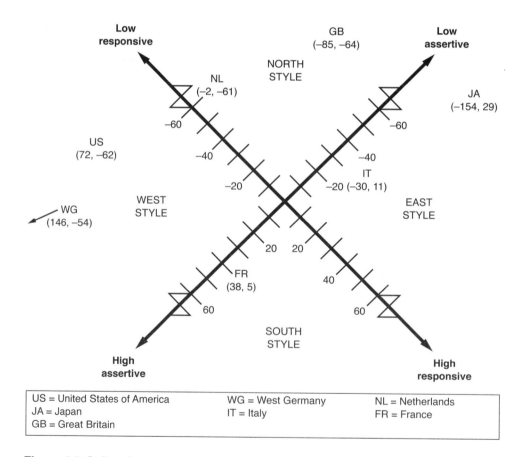

Figure 4.4 Cultural plots of nations

Source: Reprinted by permission of John Wiley and Sons Ltd. Hall, W. (1995), *Managing Cultures. Making Strategic Relationships Work* (Chichester, Wiley, p. 95).

views. These views were mainly those of executives who had, through their own work across national boundaries, experience of managers from the countries in the sample. It is not clear, therefore, how much the executives who were questioned were working from stereotypes of the managers on whom they were giving their views. In addition, the research used a sample of executives from two industries only – the automobile industry and the high-technology industry. Given these reservations, Hall's typology is detailed and comprehensive. It attempts to link Alvesson's (1993) three levels of culture and more. In addition, it points at one of the influences on organisational culture through its focus on differences between national cultures.

It is clear, however, that, in line with models of culture such as Robbins's discussed earlier, Hall's model is an example of an attempt to 'objectify', and so measure, culture. The result is to identify a number of different types of culture. Regardless of whether an objectivist or interpretive perspective on organisational culture is adopted, forming a 'typology' of cultures in this kind of way is useful as a device for describing organisational culture – even if it does not capture the richness of description which more qualitative, ethnographic studies of culture do. Consequently, it is useful to consider other organisational culture typologies which, as Hall's model does, allow a relatively easy comparison of one culture with another. These can, for the purpose of the discussion, be posed as 'dimensions' of organisational culture.

Dimensions of organisational culture

The structural view of culture

Structural views of culture inevitably draw on descriptions of different structural forms for their expression. One of the leading proponents of this view is Handy (1993) who draws on Harrison's (1972) studies in this respect. Handy refers to organisational culture as atmosphere, ways of doing things, levels of energy and levels of individual freedom – or collectively, the 'sets of values and norms and beliefs – reflected in different structures and systems' (p. 180). On the basis of Harrison's studies, he suggests four organisational culture types. Illustration 4.7 describes these.

Handy does not claim high levels of rigour for the descriptions given in Illustration 4.7, saying that a culture cannot be defined precisely. However, these descriptions could be used to determine a particular organisation's way of doing things. Pheysey (1993) builds on Handy's and Harrison's typologies to propose a categorisation of role, power, support and achievement cultures. The definitions of role and power cultures are those used by Handy, with support and achievement cultures having similar characteristics to Handy's task and person cultures. However Pheysey goes beyond Handy in linking her four types of

---

Illustration 4.7

A structural view of organisational culture

The power culture

Power cultures are those in which a single person or group tends to dominate. Handy refers to this culture as a *web* in the sense that the spider in the middle controls what happens throughout the organisation. Decision making is centralised. This type of culture is seen as, essentially, political in that decisions are taken on the basis of influence rather than through a logical rational process. Power is held by the centre by virtue of personal charisma or the control of resources. Family businesses, small entrepreneurial companies and occasionally trade unions are likely to have this type of culture. The strength of this type of culture depends on the strength of the centre and the willingness of other organisational members to defer to this power source. Handy likens this culture to the Greek god Zeus who ruled by whim and impulse, by thunderbolt and shower of gold from Mount Olympus.

The role culture

Handy likens role cultures to a *Greek temple*. The patron god here is Apollo, the god of reason, the argument being that role cultures work by logic and rationality. The pillars of the temple are strong in their own right and activity is controlled more by rules and regulations than by personal directive from the top. The pediment of the temple is seen as co-ordinating activity rather than overtly controlling it. Emphasis is on defined roles and occupants are expected to fulfil these but not overstep them. Role cultures flourish in stable situations and a sellers' market.

The task culture

The task culture is represented by a *net*. The dominant concept in a task culture is project work associated with matrix-type structures. Handy pushes the Greek god association somewhat here in suggesting Athena whose emphasis was on getting the job done. The task culture, therefore, is not particularly concerned with personal power or hierarchy, but with marshalling the required resources to complete work efficiently and effectively. Decision making is devolved to the project groups to enhance flexibility of working method and speed the outcomes. The task culture is said to flourish where creativity and innovation are desirable, particularly in organisations concerned with such activities as research and development, marketing, advertising and new ventures.

The person culture

According to Handy, this culture is an unusual one. It exists only to service the needs of the participating members. It does not have an overarching objective such as is found in more conventionally structured organisations. Examples of person cultures are barristers' chambers, doctors' centres, hippy communes and small consultancy firms. Person cultures have minimal structures and can be likened to a cluster or galaxy of individual stars. Handy proposes Dionysus as its patron deity who is the god of the self-oriented individual.

Source: Based on Handy, C. (1993), *Understanding Organizations* (London, Penguin, pp. 183–91).

---

culture not only to organisational structure (i.e. the design of organisations) but also to control systems, employee motivation, leadership styles and organisation development.

Activity 4.3   The strategy/structure–culture link

Look back at the discussion of Miles and Snow's typologies of strategic behaviour and Mintzberg's organisational forms in Chapter 3 and come to a conclusion as to how well or poorly they fit with the types of culture proposed by Handy and Pheysey.

Organisational culture and the external environment

It is hoped that the results of Activity 4.3 show how a view of culture, such as those of Handy and Pheysey, link closely to organisational structure and, by extension, to the strategies which organisations pursue. These culture typologies are mainly concerned with the internal environment of organisations (*see* discussion in Chapter 1). By contrast, Deal and Kennedy's (1982) four culture types of the tough-guy, macho culture, the work-hard/play-hard culture, the bet-your-company culture and the process culture, link more closely to the external environment (the marketplace) of the organisation. Illustration 4.8 gives a detailed description of these.

Illustration 4.8

The Deal and Kennedy typology

From their examination of hundreds of companies Deal and Kennedy (1982) claim to have identified four generic cultures.

The tough-guy, macho culture

These organisations are peopled with individuals who regularly take high risks and receive rapid feedback on the outcomes of their actions. Examples cited are police departments, surgeons, publishing, sports and the entertainment industry. In tough-guy, macho cultures the stakes are high and there is a focus on speed rather than endurance. Staff in these cultures tend to be young and financial rewards come early, but failure is punished severely through 'the sack'. Burnout is likely before middle age is reached. Internal competition and conflict are normal and this means tantrums are tolerated and everyone tries to score points off each other. However, while tough-guy cultures can be highly successful in high-risk, quick-return environments they are less suited to making long-term investments. Being unable to benefit from co-operative activity, these organisations tend to have a high turnover of staff and thus often fail to develop a strong and cohesive culture.

The work-hard/play-hard culture

This culture exists in organisations where there is low risk but quick feedback on actions – the world of sales organisations which incorporate hard work and fun. Examples are Avon, Mary Kay cosmetics

and encyclopaedia companies as well as companies like McDonald's. Persistence, keeping at it and working to recognised procedures are typical of work-hard/play-hard cultures. In these cultures, the risks are small because no individual sale will severely damage the salesperson. In addition production systems are built to withstand temporary hitches or deviations from normal. However, being selling oriented, all employees gain quick feedback on their performance. Heroes in these organisations are the super salespeople who turn in volume sales. Contests, conventions and other means of encouraging intense selling are used. Yet the culture emphasises the team because it is the team which makes the difference, not the achievements of single individuals. However, although work/play cultures can achieve sales volumes, this can be at the expense of quality – they frequently forget that success may be 'one shot' only.

Bet-your-company culture

These cultures are typical of organisations where the risks are high and the feedback on actions and decisions takes a long time. Bet-your-company organisations are those which invest millions or billions in projects which take years to come to fruition. Examples include large aircraft manufacturers such as Boeing, oil companies like Mobil and large-systems businesses. In contrast to tough-guy cultures, people working in bet-your-company cultures

▶

Illustration 4.8 *continued*

bet the company rather than themselves. Consequently, there is a sense of deliberateness which manifests itself in ritualised business meetings. All decisions are carefully weighed and based on careful research. Decision making tends to be top down, reflecting the hierarchical nature of the organisation. The survivors in these organisations respect authority and technical competence and have the stamina to endure long-term ambiguity with limited feedback. They will act co-operatively, and have proved themselves over a number of years – immaturity is not tolerated in this culture. Bet-your-company cultures lead to high-quality inventions and major scientific breakthroughs, but their slow response times make them vulnerable to short-term economic fluctuations in the economy. However, it is said that these companies may be those which the economy most needs.

The process culture

This culture is typical of organisations where there is low risk and slow feedback on actions and decisions. Examples are banks, insurance companies, public and government organisations and other heavily regulated industries. Working with little feedback, employees have no sense of their own effectiveness or otherwise.

Consequently, they tend to concentrate on the means by which things are done rather than what should be done. Values tend to focus on technical perfection, working out the risks and getting the process right. Protecting one's back is what most employees will do, so the people who prosper are those who are orderly and punctual and who attend to detail. The ability to weather political storms and changes becomes a desirable trait. In process cultures, there is considerable emphasis on job titles and status and the signs which symbolise them, such as style of office furniture. Position power is desired. Staying with the organisation is revered by the institution of long-service awards. Process cultures are effective when dealing with a stable and predictable environment, but find it difficult to react quickly to changing circumstances. On a positive note, they offer a counterpoint to the other three cultures just described.

Deal and Kennedy's typology was constructed in the early 1980s. While the cultural types may still be relevant and can be found in today's organisations, it is arguable whether the examples of each type that Deal and Kennedy give still hold today. For instance, banks (as examples of process cultures) have evolved more into sales-type organisations but do not, perhaps, yet fit the work-hard/play-hard culture suggested for sales-oriented companies.

Many government agencies in the UK have become 'privatised' in the way they operate and are moving away from the process-oriented culture of old. It is also clear that organisations do not always fit neatly into one typology or another. This, inevitably, gives rise to difficulties in describing a particular organisation's culture and in choosing which framework of typologies to use.

Organisational culture, structure, strategy and the external environment

The discussion so far has addressed perspectives on organisational culture which link it, separately, to the internal and external environments of the organisation in terms of organisational structure and the marketplace in which organisations operate. Someone who brings these two dimensions together along with a third one is Scholz (1987) who uses the terms evolution-induced, internal-induced and external-induced culture dimensions. The external-induced dimension of organisational culture draws directly on the work of Deal and Kennedy and Scholz uses Deal and Kennedy's four culture types to represent this dimension. The internal-induced dimension identifies three culture types (production, bureaucratic and professional) which are derived from organisational structure characteristics. The final cultural dimension, which is where Scholz goes beyond the earlier models, is the evolution-induced dimension. This dimension is related to the strategic orientation of the organisation. Five possible culture types are identified as follows:

1 *Stable*, with a time orientation towards the past and an aversion to risk.
2 *Reactive*, with a time orientation towards the present and an acceptance of 'minimum' risk.
3 *Anticipating*, also oriented towards the present but more accepting of 'familiar' risks.
4 *Exploring*, with a time orientation towards the present and the future and an acceptance of increasing risk.
5 *Creative*, looking forward to the future and accepting risk as normal.

Scholz's three dimensions of culture cover both internal and external aspects of an organisation's functioning in terms of structure, strategy and the operating environment and, consequently, offer a possibility of describing organisational culture in a more complex way than that offered by Handy's and Deal and Kennedy's culture types. However, there is no suggestion of how cultures of one type rather than another can be identified. This is in contrast with Robbins's and Hall's methods of describing culture, which can be done using questionnaire-based, quantitative techniques.

By the same token, some researchers, particularly those who subscribe to the interpretive view of culture, would say that organisational culture is much too complex a phenomenon to be measured through questionnaire and other similar quantitative-based methods. They suggest the need to use more qualitative techniques such as observation, interviews, focus groups and an ethnographic approach, as exemplified in Brooks and Bate's (1994, p. 178) study of a UK government agency through '(immersion) in the minutiae of everyday life' of the organisation.

What is more, qualitative techniques for identifying culture are more likely to reveal something of the sources from which current cultures spring.

Activity 4.4   *Compare and contrast Scholz's evolution-induced dimension with Miles and Snow's identification of the evolution of organisational forms in Table 3.1 in Chapter 3. How far can you 'map' each of Scholz's evolution-induced types of culture to each of Miles and Snow's corporate strategies and forms?*

● ● ● ● The sources of organisational culture

The influence of organisational history

The account, in Illustration 4.9, of Ford Motor Company's collection of long-standing sub-cultures which have evolved through the company's 95-year history and particularly their capacity, until recently, to resist change is echoed by the results of research studies of a major food retailing organisation (*see* Ogbonna and Harris, 1998) and a newly semi-privatised British civil service department (*see* Brooks and Bate, 1994).

An account of overcoming cultural barriers to change associated with the incorporation of a college, which provided pre- and post-registration nursing and midwifery education, into a much larger institution, within the university sector (*see* Hill and McNulty, 1998), tells a similar tale of the large influence that historical factors and the long-standing cultures of each institution had on the process of the change. All these accounts confirm the views of a well-known academic researcher in this field who commented, back in 1981, that: 'The subculture of an organization reflects national culture, professional subculture, and the organization's own history' (Hofstede, 1981, p. 27).

Regarding the last of these, Robbins (2001) emphasises how the philosophy of the organisation's founder and, as time passes, the top management define acceptable behaviour. The importance of leadership as a source of organisational culture is discussed by Brown (1995), who cites the example of Henry Ford who started the Ford Motor Company, as well as Ken Olsen at Digital Equipment Corporation and Gerard and Anton Philips at Philips. Sir John Harvey-Jones is well known for his influence at ICI and is an example of a leader continuing, through his writings, to influence the business scene with his views beyond his retirement. The cultural web of Paper Unlimited (*see* Illustration 4.4) is almost wholly derived from the way the company founder's son and long-time managing director established an organisational philosophy while setting up the organisation's structure, operating systems and procedures, criteria for recruitment and promotion and the style of management to be observed. Through his own behaviour, he was an example of how he wanted the company managed and run.

The influence of history is not, however, limited to the influence of particular people of importance to an organisation. A broader influence is referred to by Hofstede (1981, p. 27) who says: 'The rules of behaviour in industrial workshops in the nineteenth century were modelled after those in armies and monasteries. The structure and functioning of organizations are determined not merely by rationality, or, if they are, by rationality that varies according to the cultural environment.' Goodman's (1995) discussion of the different ages of wealth creation described in Chapter 1 is evidence of the way historical processes influence all aspects of organisational functioning including an organisation's culture. Even so, these processes and their timing are not the same for every society. They will be modified to some extent by the national culture in which they take place.

Illustration 4.9

Driving change: an interview with Ford Motor Company's Jacques Nasser

In an interview for the *Harvard Business Review* (1999) Jacques Nasser, Chief Executive Officer of Ford Motor Company, speaks of his attempt to bring about radical change in the company 'mind-set' of everyone working there. According to the interview account, Nasser is asking his employees (apparently all 340,000 in 200 countries) 'to think and act as if they own the company'. (In fact they do, to the extent of 20% of the outstanding stock.) 'To adopt, in other words, the capital markets' view of Ford – to look at the company in its entirety, as shareholders do.' Nasser says that this is 'a radically different mentality for Ford'. This mentality (or culture as it might be termed in the context of this discussion) is very different from the one which has, apparently, prevailed for much of the time since the company was formed 95 years ago – one which Nasser describes as: 'A collection of fiercely independent fiefdoms united under the flag of their functional or regional expertise.' Each division in this 'collection' appears to have its own organisational sub-culture for which, as Nasser comments, there were 'legitimate historical reasons'.

Elaborating on this he says: 'Think about Ford's history in three chunks: from its founding in 1905 to the early 1920s, the late 1920s through to the 1950s, and the 1960s through the 1980s.' The first period was one of 'colonization' and the opening of assembly plants (that were smaller versions of the original company in Detroit) in other countries, but with very little competition from other automotive companies. The second period was one of 'intense nationalism' with large automotive companies growing up in the UK, France, Germany, Australia, all making their own vehicles and exporting them to others – but in their own regions. The third period saw the rise of regionalism and the emergence of the European common market and the North American Free Trade Association (NAFTA). It was this period that saw the entrenchment of the regional and functional fiefdoms.

Nasser comments that, given the prevailing environment at that time, this arrangement worked very well: squeezing 'every last ounce of efficiency out of the regional model'. However, he goes on to say that this model does not work any more in the current environment of increasing globalisation of capital, communications, economic policy, trade policy, human resources, marketing, advertising, brands – and so on. Consequently, there is a perceived need to 'reinvent' Ford as a global organisation with a single focus on consumers and shareholder value.

Nasser talks of striving for some kind of DNA that drives how Ford does things everywhere. This includes a global mind-set, an intuitive knowledge of customers and a strong belief in leaders as teachers. However, this does not mean that the same products are produced and sold everywhere. What it does mean is that, although Ford cars have many common systems which bring scale efficiencies, they can also be tailored to individual local markets. What is more, although Ford would like to see common reward systems for staff wherever they work, Nasser recognises that different cultures have different attitudes to pay and rewards, for instance about the balance between fixed and variable rewards. What is also clear is that in some countries (with Australia as an example) the tax and other laws require different attitudes to employment, stock purchase and so on.

Having said all this, it is clear that Nasser is looking for a significant cultural shift from one suited to the conditions of the past to one which recognises the conditions of the present and the future. The article describes, in some detail, the approach being taken to help this to happen – an approach based on a multi-faceted teaching initiative, led by senior and middle managers and aimed, eventually, at all Ford employees wherever they are located. Nasser says: 'The Ford you see today has no resemblance to the Ford of five years ago. If you dissected us and inspected every blood vessel, we're different; our DNA has changed. I don't think we'll go back.'

Source: Based on Nasser, J. and Wetlaufer, S. (1999), 'Driving change: an interview with Ford Motor Company's Jacques Nasser', *Harvard Business Review*, March–April, pp. 76–88.

The influence of national culture

A survey of the literature on the cultural similarities and differences between nations identifies a long-standing debate known popularly as the convergence–divergence debate. In summary, those who support the convergence view argue that the forces of industrialisation (for instance, *see* Kerr, Dunlop, Harbison and Myers, 1960) and the use of similar technologies (*see* Castells, 1989; Woodward, 1965) as well as increasing size (*see* Chandler, 1962; Hickson and MacMillan, 1981; Pugh and Hickson, 1976) will push organisations, whatever their location, towards particular configurations with respect to strategy, structure and management. In addition, the growth of international organisations and those who trade abroad increases the need for 'international managers' who bring common management practices to all parts of their organisations wherever they are in the world. In support of this view, Ohmae (1991) puts forward the concept of the 'global organisation' which has no national allegiance, only an international common purpose. Furthermore, Ohmae argues for 'getting rid of the headquarters mentality', implying the possibility that an organisation's national cultural base will have no influence on the culture of the organisation itself. While not directly advocating what Ohmae says, the account of Jacques Nasser's change programme at Ford Motor Company (*see* Illustration 4.9) is an example of Nasser's vision to eliminate the regional 'fiefdoms' built up over a long period of time. He speaks of the markets valuing a global approach to business – 'an approach in which a company's units, divisions, teams, functions, and regions are all tightly integrated and synchronized across borders' (p. 78).

In contrast to this view is the notion that differences in countries' languages, religions, social organisation, laws, politics, education systems, and values and attitudes (Hofstede, 1980; Tayeb, 1989; Wilson, 1992) will, of necessity, mean that one nation's culture will diverge significantly from another's. For instance, Knightley (2000) in his book *Australia: Biography of a Nation* maintains that the geographic isolation of the country brought populations and cultures (Aboriginals, British and Irish convicts and their overseers, postwar refugees and Asian boat people) together into interaction which created a society with its own peculiar ways of doing things. It is interesting to note that Jacques Nasser (*see* Illustration 4.9) had to make separate arrangements for Australia regarding his Ford Motor Company-wide policy to roll out a worldwide employee stock-purchase programme because of the different tax regime there. It is still too early to know what influence E-commerce (both business to customer and business to business) and the increasing pressures on organisations to operate globally will have on the convergence or continuing divergence of national cultures. However, there is sufficient evidence of national cultural differences for the influence of national culture on organisational culture to be taken seriously.

The diversity of national cultures

There is an expanding body of research that claims to have identified *how* cultures vary. Illustration 4.10 summarises a frequently referenced framework – that of Kluckhohn and Strodtbeck (1961) who claim there are six basic dimensions which describe the cultural orientation of societies.

Both Adler (1997) and Robbins (1996) draw on Kluckhohn and Strodtbeck's framework in their discussions of societal and national cultures. In her book, Adler gives many examples of differences between societies and nations on these cultural dimensions. Regarding the good–evil dimension or trust–mistrust dimension, the way one group of people regard another will differ according to whether they set off with the assumption that people are trustworthy or that all people will cheat if given the opportunity. This translates, for instance, into whether things are kept locked up or not, whether information is freely available and how one group's actions are interpreted by another. Adler contrasts the North Americans

---

Illustration 4.10

Six different cultural orientations of societies

- *People's qualities as individuals in terms of whether people are seen as basically good or basically bad.* Societies that consider people good tend to trust people while those that consider people bad tend to start from a premise of mistrust and suspicion.

- *People's relationship to their world.* Some societies believe they can dominate their environment while others believe the environment and themselves to be inseparable and, therefore, they must live in harmony with it.

- *People's personal relationships in terms of individualism or collectivism.* Some societies encourage individualism and the notion of being self-supporting and achievement is based on individual worth, while others are more group oriented, where people define themselves as members of clans or communities (which might be the work organisation) and consider the group's welfare to be more important than the individual.

- *An orientation to either doing or being.* Societies which are doing and action oriented stress accomplishments which are measurable by standards believed to be external to the individual; societies oriented to being are more passive, believing that work should be enjoyed and live more for the moment.

- *People's orientation to time.* Some societies are past oriented, believing that current plans and actions should fit with the customs and traditions of the past while future-oriented societies justify innovation and change in terms of future pay-offs, believing radical change to be desirable as well as acceptable.

- *People's use of space.* Societies differ on such matters as offices in relation to status, the designation of public space compared to private space, the separation of managers from subordinates.

with the Chinese and Navaho in terms of the former's belief that they can dominate nature and the latter's belief that they must live in harmony with nature.

She describes Americans' strong individualistic tendencies as evidenced in their language, such as 'trounced the opposition', and their recruitment and promotion practices based on criteria relating to individual knowledge and skills. This contrasts with more group-oriented societies such as Japan, China, Indonesia and Malaysia which put more stress on assignments, responsibilities and reporting relationships in collective terms. People in these societies are more likely to gain employment through personal contacts who can vouch for their trustworthiness and ability to work with others. Finding jobs for family and friends is not seen as unusual or nepotism as it might be in more individualistic societies. Adler makes an interesting comparison between doers and 'be'ers in their typically different reactions to a salary rise. The doers react to higher pay rates by working more hours because they can earn more. The 'be'ers react to higher pay rates by working fewer hours, arguing that they can earn the same money in less time, so leaving more time for enjoying life. Offering overtime bonuses may work in 'doing' societies but will not work in 'being' societies.

Adler points out that different time orientations can impact significantly on people's attitudes to time keeping and punctuality. Different time orientations also bring differences in the length of time someone might be given to show his or her worth in a job. If employees are recruited with the expectation of staying many years with an organisation they will not have to show achievement in the short time expected in societies which recruit in the knowledge that the person may move on before very long. Finally, Adler uses the examples of North Americans and Japanese to contrast different societies' attitudes to the use of space. The former prefer closed offices and meetings behind closed doors while the latter prefer open-plan working areas which include managers as well as subordinates. Other interesting differences can be seen in how close one desk is to another and whether an office can be entered without ceremony or whether people must wait outside for permission to enter.

Figure 4.5 is based on Robbins's summary of the Kluckhohn–Strodtbeck framework with a profile for the United States plotted on it. It is obvious, from a reading of these descriptions, that variations will occur within societies as well as between societies. However, evidence from a series of well-known pieces of research (Hofstede, 1980, 1981, 1993, 1994; Hofstede, Neuijen, Ohayv and Sanders, 1990) appears to support the concept of geographically identifiable, culturally differentiated regions which are based on national boundaries. The major piece of research referred to was carried out in IBM and involved the analysis of questionnaires from some 116,000 employees in 50 different countries. This analysis resulted in the identification of four dimensions, which were found to differentiate national cultural groups. A fifth dimension based on the philosophy of Confucianism (which Hofstede categorised as virtue versus truth or, more simply, long-term versus short-term orientation) was identified by Bond working with a team of 24 Chinese researchers (*see* Chinese Culture Connection, 1987). Illustration 4.11 describes these.

Dimensions	Variations		
Nature of people	Good	Mixed	Bad
Relationship to the environment	Domination	Harmony	Subjugation
Focus of responsibility	Individualistic	Group	Hierarchical
Activity orientation	Being	Controlling	Doing
Time orientation	Past	Present	Future
Conception of space	Private	Mixed	Public

Figure 4.5 Variations in Kluckhohn and Strodtbeck's cultural dimensions

Source: Based on Robbins, S. P. (1996), *Organizational Behavior, Concepts, Controversies, Applications* (Englewood Cliffs, NJ, Prentice Hall, p. 56).

Illustration 4.11

Hofstede's dimensions of national culture

Power distance

Power distance refers to how a society deals with the fact that people are unequal, for instance, in physical and intellectual abilities. Some societies let these inequalities grow over time into inequalities in power and wealth. Other societies try to play down inequalities in power and wealth. In high power distance societies, inequalities of power and wealth are accepted not only by the leaders, but also by those at the bottom of the power hierarchy, with corresponding large differences in status and salaries. In low power distance societies, inequalities among people will tend to be minimised, with subordinates expecting to be consulted by superiors over decisions which affect them and treated more as equals of those with the power.

Individualism/collectivism

Individualism/collectivism refers to relationships between an individual and his or her fellow individuals. In an individualistic society, the ties between individuals are very loose. Everybody is expected to look after self-interest and perhaps that of their immediate family. Individuals in these societies have a large amount of freedom of action. In collectivist societies the ties between individuals are very tight.

The concept of the extended family is important and can reach work groups and organisations. Everybody is supposed to look after the interests of their in-group, which will protect them when they are in trouble.

Masculinity/femininity

Masculinity/femininity refers to the degree to which social gender roles are clearly distinct. In high-masculinity societies, the social division between the sexes is maximised, with traditional masculine social values permeating the society. These values include the importance of showing off, of making money and of 'big is beautiful'. In more feminine societies, the dominant values – for both men and women – are those more traditionally associated with the feminine role of nurturing and caring, putting relationships before money, minding the quality of life and 'small is beautiful'.

Uncertainty avoidance

Uncertainly avoidance refers to how a society deals with the fact that time runs only one way – from the past to the future – and that the future is unknown and, therefore, uncertain. Some societies accept this uncertainty and do not get upset about it; others seek to reduce the uncertainty as much as possible.

▶

Illustration 4.11 *continued*

People in weak uncertainty-avoidance societies tend to accept each day as it comes and are comfortable with a higher degree of risk taking. Societies demonstrating strong uncertainty-avoidance characteristics socialise their people into trying to beat the future. Precision and punctuality are important in a context of fear of ambiguous situations and unfamiliar risks.

Long-term/short-term orientation

This dimension is about virtue versus truth. Societies with a long-term orientation look to the past and present for their value systems. People living in these societies have a respect for traditions and fulfilling social obligations. It is important that they 'save face'. They do not believe in absolute truths. Societies with a short-term orientation look towards the future cultivating habits of thrift and perseverance. People living in these societies value analytical thinking and the search for truths. This dimension is not as developed as the other four, not having been subjected to the amount of follow up research since Hofstede's original study.

Based on information given in an article written by Hofstede in 1993, Table 4.1 gives the results of Hofstede's research for a selected number of countries.

Figure 4.6 illustrates four possible organisational models which, according to Hofstede (1994), refer to empirically derived relationships between a country's position on the power distance/uncertainty avoidance matrix and models of organisations implicit in the minds of people from the countries concerned.

From this it can be seen how Hofstede uses the metaphors of a village market, a well-oiled machine, a pyramid and a family to describe different approaches to organising. Thus, people from countries with a 'village market' culture do not appear to have the same need for hierarchy and certainty as those from a pyramid type culture. These contrast with people from cultures reminiscent of 'well-oiled machines' – such as Germany – where hierarchy is not particularly required because there are established procedures and rules to which everyone works. People who live in countries located in the 'family' quadrant – such as India, West

Table 4.1 Culture dimension scores for ten countries

	Power distance	Individualism*	Masculine**	Uncertainty avoidance	Long-term orientation***
China	High	Low	Moderate	Moderate	High
France	High	High	Moderate	High	Low
Germany	Low	High	High	Moderate	Moderate
Hong Kong	High	Low	High	Low	High
Indonesia	High	Low	Moderate	Low	Low
Japan	Moderate	Moderate	High	High	High
Netherlands	Low	High	Low	Moderate	Moderate
Russia	High	Moderate	Low	Low	Low
United States	Low	High	High	Low	Low
West Africa	High	Low	Moderate	Moderate	Low

* A low score implies collectivism. ** A low score implies feminine. *** A low score implies short-term orientation.
Source: Adapted from Hofstede, G. (1993), 'Cultural constraints in management theories', *Academy of Management Executive*, February, p. 91.

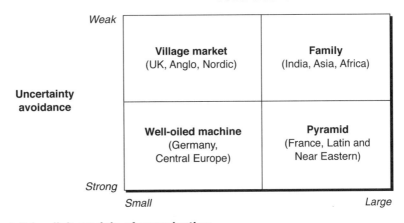

Figure 4.6 Implicit models of organisation

Source: Adapted from Hofstede, G. (1991), *Cultures and Organizations*, Maidenhead, McGraw Hill.

Africa and Malaysia – are said to have an implicit model of organisation which resembles a family in which the owner–manager is the omnipotent (grand)father.

It is clear that if, as Hofstede maintains, these differences between cultural groupings exist and any convergence across them will be very slow, then there is a good chance that they will influence organisational cultures in correspondingly different ways. It should not be forgotten, however, that Hofstede's research was carried out some time ago and mainly within a single multinational organisation. The clustering of countries into the four models depicted in Figure 4.6 is a simplification of the complexity of distinguishing one country's culture from another, let alone differences within countries.

There is, however, support for Hofstede's views on national cultural differences from research carried out by Laurent (1983). In contrast to Hofstede's research, which sampled the views of employees at all levels of a single organisation, Laurent's research focused on the views of upper and middle-level managers in a large number of different organisations, spread across nine European countries and the United States. Laurent's hypothesis was that the national origin of managers significantly affects their views of what proper management should be. The focus was, perhaps, slightly narrower than that of Hofstede, but had the advantage of sampling across several different organisations.

From his survey of 817 managers across the ten countries, Laurent identified four dimensions, which he labelled: organisations as political systems, organisations as authority systems, organisations as role-formalisation systems and organisations as hierarchical-relationship systems. Table 4.2 summarises the relative position of the ten countries on each of Laurent's dimensions. The results show France and Italy at the high end of the scores for all dimensions – meaning that they were politicised, hierarchical, had high degrees of role formalisation and believed in the authority of individuals. Denmark and the UK are positioned similarly to each other with low

Table 4.2 Summary of Laurent's findings

Dimension	Denmark	UK	The Netherlands	Germany	Sweden	USA	Switzerland	France	Italy	Belgium
Organisations as:										
Political systems	26	32	36	36	42	43	51	62	66	missing
Authority systems	46	48	49	34	46	30	32	65	61	61
Role-formalisation systems	80	80	67	85	57	66	85	81	84	81
Hierarchical-relationship systems	37	36	33	47	25	28	43	50	66	50

Source: Summarised from Laurent, A. (1983), 'The cultural diversity of Western conceptions of management', *International Studies of Management and Organisation*, Vol. XIII, Nos. 1–2, pp. 75–96.

levels of hierarchy and politicisation, moderate degrees of belief in individual authority and high levels of role formalisation. Sweden had the lowest score in terms of hierarchical relationships with moderate scores on the other three dimensions. Other similarities and differences can be seen from the table.

In contrast to the identification of national cultural characteristics typified by quantified data on defined dimensions, Illustration 4.12 is an example of a qualitative account of Danish managers and how to do business with them. However, as can be seen by Activity 4.5, it is possible to validate one set of results, obtained using one type of data collection technique, with another set of results using a different technique.

Illustration 4.12

On a wavelength with the Danes

FT

'Language is not a problem – but doing business with the "Italians of the north" requires tact', argues Sergey Frank

At first sight, doing business in Denmark may seem straightforward. The country is prosperous and an important trade partner in the European Union. Its people communicate in a friendly and direct way. Negotiators tend to be to the point, relaxed and informal. And the whole process is accompanied with a sense of humour. But do not fall into the trap of thinking you need only be yourself.

Throughout Scandinavia, communication is characterised by calmness and understatement. This applies to Danes, too, although they are known for being more temperamental than Swedes and Norwegians and are sometimes described as the 'Italians of the north'.

That does not make Copenhagen the same as Rome. Extrovert rhetoric and exaggeration are poorly

regarded in Denmark. The body language of Danes underlines this – especially on a first meeting. To touch someone's arm or to pat someone on the back while shaking hands is not appropriate when dealing with a Danish business partner. You should also keep enough distance from your counterpart for him or her to feel comfortable.

Danes tend to be open-minded when they deal with foreign business partners. A formal introduction from an international bank or sales representative, for example, is not absolutely necessary. Most Danish people speak and read English fluently. There is no need for an interpreter.

At the start of the negotiations, your Danish counterpart will tend to understate his or her own achievements, much as the English would. It is good

Illustration 4.12 *continued*

to be punctual and to structure the agenda. To display the sort of self-confidence that would strike extrovert cultures as quite normal would be inappropriate in Denmark.

One general principle of communication applies throughout Scandinavia: less is more. It is in your interest to provide a realistic initial offer with enough room for concessions. You should also avoid giving the impression that you think you are more successful than other people.

It is unwise to 'oversell' yourself and to reveal everything about yourself and your company. Instead, try to let your Danish business partner seek out the relevant information about a potential match with your company, your products and services. The same applies for presentations: a properly documented presentation aligned with a consistent argument goes down better than a hard sell.

Your Danish counterparts will be open, polite, flexible and ready to provide you with insights into their point of view. In brainstorming sessions they will be prepared to think up imaginative solutions and to evaluate them with you afterwards. In all this you should deploy humour, especially of the understated English variety.

However, you should be cautious in some respects. Danes do not start negotiations as quickly as, for example, Americans. They consider it rude for anyone to be interrupted in mid-sentence, especially if it is not to clarify something that has just been said. Be patient with the decision-making process: Danish executives do not like to be rushed.

The notion of 'fair play' counts for a lot in Denmark. It is reflected in social welfare and culture. Thus, your partner will usually try to find win–win solutions where both parties will receive a fair amount of profit – though Danes can drive a hard bargain.

The concern for fair play can be seen in Danish management culture: managers do not place much emphasis on hierarchy. Women have done well in Denmark, too. The country has the highest percentage of women in business in the European Union.

Most Danes are friendly, generous hosts. Entertaining is done at lunch or dinner, mostly in restaurants. An invitation to someone's home is a great honour. Wherever you are dining, you should arrive on time. Evening meals take place early but, unlike many east Asian business people, your Danish counterpart will expect you to stay and chat at the hotel bar.

Source: Frank, S. (2000), 'On a wavelength with the Danes', *Financial Times*, 23 October, p. 15.

Activity 4.5 *Compare and contrast the account in Illustration 4.12 with Laurent's findings with respect to the orientations of Danish managers in Table 4.2. Hofstede's results show Danish workers as having low power distance, low uncertainty avoidance, high feminine, and highish individualism characteristics and British managers as having low power distance, low uncertainty avoidance, high masculine and very high individualism characteristics. Does this accord with what is said about British managers in the account in Illustration 4.12?*

Compare the brief reference to American managers in this account with their positions on Hofstede's and Laurent's scales (as shown in Tables 4.1 and 4.2). How do you think American managers would fare doing business with Danish managers? In addition to using Hofstede's and Laurent's findings, use the profile for the USA on Figure 4.5 (Kluckhohn and Strodtbeck's cultural dimensions) to help you.

Hofstede's and Laurent's research are only two of many possible national culture models derived from the administration of questionnaires. However, they exemplify the way questionnaires can be used to demonstrate national cultural similarities and differences. Having said this, their methods can be criticised in terms of their attempts to 'objectivise' culture compared to more qualitative methods referred to in the previous discussion of organisational cultures. This criticism can, however, be balanced by other studies (e.g. d'Iribarne, 1989; Maurice, Sorge and Warner, 1980) which have found differences between national cultures, but which were based on in-depth, comprehensive examinations of similar organisations or organisational units in a limited number of countries.

A third method was used by Calori and De Woot (1994) when they used non-directive interviews with 51 human resource directors in 40 large international companies with headquarters or major operating units in Europe. On the basis of the results of these interviews, Calori and De Woot claim to have found country clusters which suggest a typology of management systems (*see* Figure 4.7). Illustration 4.13 summarises Calori and De Woot's conclusions on the characteristics typical of the first two levels of segmentation, that is the Anglo-Saxon, Latin and Northern Europe (using the German model as an example) groupings.

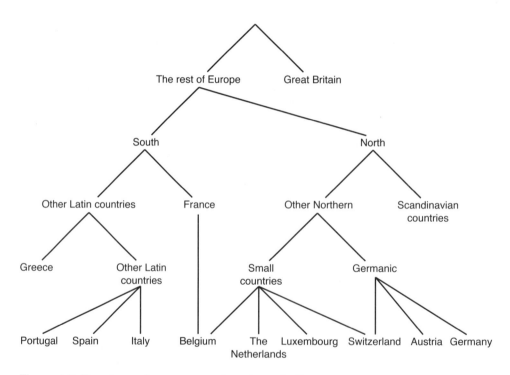

Figure 4.7 Typology of management systems in Europe

Source: Calori, R. and De Woot, P. (1994), *A European Management Model Beyond Diversity* (Hemel Hempstead, Prentice Hall, p. 20).

Activity 4.6	*Compare and contrast Calori and De Woot's country groupings and characteristics with the countries' positions on Laurent's cultural dimensions and the models presented in Figure 4.6. To what extent do any of these characterisations agree with your own experience, either through business dealings or as a tourist?*

Illustration 4.13

Differences between Great Britain, Southern Europe (including France) and Northern Europe (typified by Germany)

The United Kingdom, an exception in Europe

Management in the UK has more in common with the United States of America than the rest of Europe. It has:

- A short-term orientation (more than continental Europe).
- A shareholder orientation (whereas the rest of Europe has more of a stakeholder orientation).
- An orientation towards trading and finance (the importance of the stock market is more developed than in continental Europe).
- A higher turnover of managers.
- A greater liberalism towards foreigners (e.g. the Japanese).
- More freedom for top management *vis-à-vis* the workers and government.
- More direct and pragmatic relationships between people.
- More variable remuneration.

However, different from the United States of America, it has:

- Adversarial relationships with labour.
- The tradition of the manager as a 'gifted amateur' (as opposed to the professionalism of US managers).
- The influence of class differences in the firm.

The Latin way of doing business

Southern Europe (including France) differs from the rest of Europe in that it has:

- More state intervention.
- More protectionism.

- More hierarchy in the firm.
- More intuitive management.
- More family business (especially in Italy).
- More reliance on an élite (especially in France).

The German model

Characteristic of Germany, Austria and, to some extent, Switzerland as well as the Benelux countries, the German model is based on three cultural and structural characteristics:

- Strong links between banks and industry.
- A balance between a sense of national collectivity and the Länder (regional) system.
- A system of training and development of managers.

It has the following five components:

- The system of co-determination with workers' representatives present on the board.
- The loyalty of managers (and employees in general) who spend their career in a single firm, which then gives priority to in-house training.
- The collective orientation of the workforce, which includes dedication to the company, team spirit and a sense of discipline.
- The long-term orientation which appears in planning, in the seriousness and stability of supplier–client relationships and in the priority of industrial goals over short-term financial objectives.
- The reliability and stability of shareholders, influenced by a strong involvement of banks in industry.

Source: Based on Calori, R. and De Woot, P. (1994), *A European Management Model Beyond Diversity* (Hemel Hempstead, Prentice Hall, pp. 22–9).

National culture and organisational culture

The result of carrying out Activity 4.6 illustrates the complexity of attempting to build tight categories into which different national cultures can be put. It would be difficult to argue, however, that these differences do not occur. In addition, the evidence points to close relationships between national culture and organisational culture. For instance, a study by Furnham and Gunter (1993) provides examples of organisations in countries like Australia, Israel and Denmark which had low scores on Hofstede's power distance dimension also having common organisational structures. Their structures incorporated low centralisation of decision making and flatter pyramids of control, reminiscent of Handy's task organisational culture (Handy, 1993). These organisations' structures contrasted with those in countries such as the Philippines, Mexico and India, which scored highly on Hofstede's power distance dimension of culture. These latter organisations were typified by strict hierarchical structures and centralised decision making, reminiscent of Handy's role organisational culture.

Activity 4.7   *Look back at Figure 4.6 which positions four implicit models of organisation on Hofstede's power distance and uncertainty avoidance dimensions. Consider Deal and Kennedy's four culture types described in Illustration 4.8 and decide how far each can be related to one or more of Hofstede's organisational models.*

It is not difficult to link Deal and Kennedy's 'bet-your-company' culture with countries which score similarly to Germany on Laurent's dimensions of culture (*see* Table 4.1). In fact, because Laurent focused his questions on managers and their perceptions of organisational life, it is not surprising that there is a large overlap between his dimensions of national culture and others' dimensions of organisational culture. Both Hofstede (1994) and Adler (1991) draw attention to the way organisational theory (e.g. as it relates to motivation, decision making, leadership etc.) is culturally determined. Because most management and organisational theory derives from the work of scholars based in Western academic institutions, caution is advised about applying it indiscriminately to organisations in other parts of the world. For instance, organisational cultures which imply an adherence to participative styles of leadership and decision making and which are part of Western national cultures may not be welcomed in societies which see consultation on the part of leaders as a weakness and where workers would be embarrassed if consulted by their managers. Chambers (1996), in an article entitled 'Russia's different problems', points out a number of elements in Western guides to management which are of little practical use to Russian managers. For instance, the concepts of 'just-in-time' and 'lean production' make little sense in a situation of uncertainties of supply of both raw materials and components. In an environment of minimal structures for data collection and market intelligence and no framework of commercial law, Western sales and marketing strategies are of little use. Organisations in Russia are a product of a previous non-commercial culture and the infrastructure of business still reflects this.

It must not be forgotten, however, that, even though influenced to a smaller or larger extent by national culture, organisational cultures can change, although change is not easy. Conversely, some organisational cultures are more conducive than others to supporting organisational change.

● ● ● ● Organisational culture and change

Wilson and Rosenfeld (1990, p. 237) say: 'The pervasive nature of organisational culture cannot be stressed too much. It is likely to affect virtually all aspects of organisational life.' According to Schwartz and Davis (1981, p. 35): 'Culture is capable of blunting or significantly altering the intended impact of even well-thought-out changes in an organisation.' This is a popular view of culture and its implications for instigating any kind of change are clear. However, as the preceding discussion shows, organisational culture comes in many forms and, therefore, can be more or less supportive of change.

There are a number of different views on the relationship between culture and change. Figure 4.8 depicts various elements of organisational culture as they might influence organisational change.

Cultures in defence against, or supportive of, change

Figure 4.8 depicts the way some elements of organisational culture might support change while, at the same time, work against it – in other words how they might put up a defence against change. One element of organisational design which is particularly relevant to the ease with which change comes about is that of an organisation's structure. Some of the typologies of organisational culture

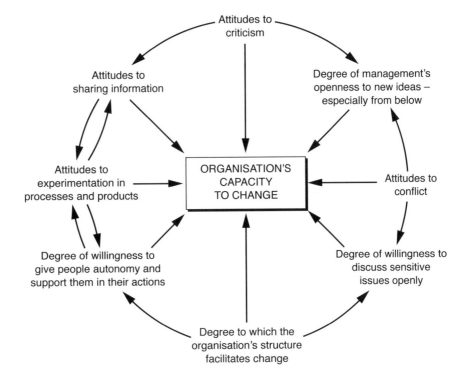

Figure 4.8 Organisational culture and change

(e.g. Handy, Harrison and Pheysey) discussed earlier in the chapter are related closely to types of organisation structure. Indeed, in these cases, culture and structure seem almost to be interchangeable. A similar case can be made for the mechanistic and organic organisational structures identified by Burns and Stalker (1961) and which were discussed in Chapter 3. Burns and Stalker's research is a good example of the merger of the concepts of structure and culture, as is seen in their argument that organic types of organisation are much more likely to be able to respond to the need for change than are mechanistic ones. However, it could be going too far to say that Burns and Stalker would have regarded mechanistic-type organisations to be *defensive* against change, because all organisations change, to some extent, incrementally, all the time. The use of the term 'defensive against change' is not, therefore, intended to imply, necessarily, that mechanistic and role-type organisational cultures will not support change. They are, however, unlikely to support, without serious trauma, the frame-breaking (*see* Tushman *et al.*, 1988), transformational (*see* Dunphy and Stace, 1993) or revolutionary types of change (*see* Johnson, 1987) discussed in Chapter 2. This is likely to be the case because of their structural characteristics, but might also be because of the attitudes, beliefs and values held by the people who work in them.

Kanter (1983) gives detailed descriptions of two extremes of organisational culture which not only are different in structural characteristics but also differ in the underlying attitudes and beliefs of the people working in them. The first she calls a 'segmentalist' culture and the other an 'integrative' culture. Illustration 4.14 summarises the characteristics of these two cultures.

In addition to the summary of a segmentalist culture given in Illustration 4.14, Kanter (1983, p. 101) offers the following ten 'rules for stifling innovation' as further elucidation of this concept:

1 Regard any new idea from below with suspicion – because it's new, and because it's from below.
2 Insist that people who need your approval to act first go through several other levels of management to get their signatures.
3 Ask departments or individuals to challenge and criticise each other's proposals. (That saves you the task of deciding; you just pick the survivor.)
4 Express your criticisms freely and withhold your praise. (That keeps people on their toes.) Let them know they can be fired at any time.
5 Treat identification of problems as signs of failure, to discourage people from letting you know when something in their area isn't working.
6 Control everything carefully. Make sure people count anything that can be counted, frequently.
7 Make decisions to reorganise or change policies in secret, and spring them on people unexpectedly. (That also keeps people on their toes.)
8 Make sure that requests for information are fully justified and make sure that it is not given out to managers freely. (You don't want data to fall into the wrong hands.)

Illustration 4.14

Segmentalist and integrative cultures

Segmentalist cultures
- Compartmentalise actions, events and problems.
- See problems as narrowly as possible.
- Have segmented structures with large numbers of departments walled off from one another.
- Assume problems can be solved by carving them up into pieces which are then assigned to specialists who work in isolation.
- Divide resources up among the many departments.
- Avoid experimentation.
- Avoid conflict and confrontation.
- Have weak co-ordinating mechanisms.
- Stress precedent and procedures.

Integrative cultures
- Are willing to move beyond received wisdom.
- Combine ideas from unconnected sources.
- See problems as wholes, related to larger wholes.
- Challenge established practices.
- Operate at the edge of competencies.
- Measure themselves by looking to visions of the future rather than by referring to the standards of the past.
- Create mechanisms for exchange of information and new ideas.
- Recognise and even encourage differences, but then be prepared to co-operate.
- Are outward looking.
- Look for novel solutions to problems.

Source: Based on the discussion in Kanter, R. M. (1983), *The Change Masters* (London, Routledge, Chapter 1).

---

9 Assign to lower-level managers, in the name of delegation and participation, responsibility for figuring out how to cut back, lay off, move people around or otherwise implement threatening decisions you have made. And get them to do it quickly.

10 And above all, never forget that you, the higher-ups, already know everything important about this business.

The Open University course 'Managing in organizations' (1985) discusses Argyris and Schon's (1978) identification of what appear to be the 'unwritten rules' governing some organisational relationships which mirror Kanter's rules for stifling change. These are:

1 Keep your views of sensitive issues private; enforce the taboo against their public discussion.

2 Do not surface and test differences in views of organisational problems.

3 Avoid seeing the whole picture; allow maps of the problem to remain scattered, vague and ambiguous.

4 Protect yourself unilaterally – by avoiding both direct interpersonal confrontation and public discussion of sensitive issues which might expose you to blame.

5 Protect others unilaterally – by avoiding the testing of assumptions where that testing might evoke negative feelings and by keeping others from exposure to blame.

6 Control the situation and the task – by making up your own mind about the problem and acting on your view, by keeping your view private and by avoiding the public inquiry which might refute your view.

The Open University material (pp. 47–9) contrasts this set of rules, which they say typifies what they call a 'defensive climate', with the following rules which they say are more typical of a 'supportive' climate:

1 Surface sensitive issues and encourage others to do so.
2 Ensure differences of view are publicly tested and that statements are made in ways that can be tested.
3 Bring together dispersed information and clarify vague and ambiguous data.
4 Do not avoid interpersonal confrontation even if it involves negative feelings.
5 Make protection of oneself and others a joint task oriented towards growth.
6 Control the task jointly.

It is clear from both Kanter and Argyris and Schon's writings that a segmentalist or defensive culture will mitigate against organisational change. Of additional interest is that many of the items in all the lists of rules frequently become the 'symbols' and 'symbolic acts' which Johnson (1990) says are so important to the maintenance or changing of organisational paradigms. They form the basis on which organisational learning and therefore organisational change may or may not take place.

Organisational learning and types of change

Argyris (1964) was one of the first people to point out the difference between two kinds of learning. The first, called *single-loop learning*, is indicative of a situation where an objective or goal is defined and an individual works out the most favoured way of reaching the goal. In single-loop learning, while many different possibilities for achieving personal or organisational goals might be considered, the goal itself is not questioned. Single-loop learning is also referred to as individual learning, that is, learning which an individual achieves but which seldom passes throughout the organisation in any coherent way.

This type of learning is contrasted by Argyris with *double-loop learning* where questions are asked not only about the *means* by which goals can be achieved, but about the *ends*, that is, the goals themselves. Johnson (1990) refers to this type of learning as *organisational relearning* which he says is a 'process in which that which is taken for granted and which is the basis of strategic direction – the paradigm – is re-formulated' (p. 189). Given that the organisational paradigm contains all the elements of Johnson and Scholes's (1993) cultural web, this implies change throughout the organisation in all aspects of its behaviour.

Individual or single-loop learning is most likely to be the dominant type of learning to take place within a segmentalist or defensive culture. The characteristics of this type of culture mitigate, significantly, against the sharing of information and openness which is required for organisational learning to take place. Therefore, while it could be said to be sufficient for the types of change which Dunphy and Stace (1993) define as 'fine-tuning' and 'incremental adjustment', it will be blind to the need for the kind of radical thinking required to bring about change in the organisation's direction, that is, strategic change. In addition, the inability of an organisation to operate double-loop learning contributes to the process of 'strategic drift' (Johnson 1987), which was discussed in Chapter 2, a process which can lead to change being forced upon an organisation.

Strong and weak cultures

'Organisational cultures differ markedly in terms of their relative strengths' (Brown, 1995, p. 74). Whether defensive or supportive, intuitively, the existence of a strong culture implies a commonly understood perspective on how organisational life should happen, with most organisational members subscribing to it. Conversely, a weak culture implies no dominant pervasive culture but an organisation made up of many different cultures, some of which will be in conflict with each other. Payne (1990) has suggested that the strength of an organisation's culture can be measured by, first, the degree to which it is shared by all members and, second, by the intensity with which organisational members believe in it. The greater the intensity of an organisation's culture, the greater the degree to which it pervades all levels at which culture manifests itself, that is, in influencing not only people's attitudes, but also their values, basic assumptions and beliefs.

The strength or weakness of organisational cultures is important in that it performs a number of functions for the organisation. A popular view is that it is the glue which holds the organisation together. Brown (1995) suggests the following functions at the organisational level.

Conflict resolution
As organisations can be characterised as grounds for disagreement and conflict, culture can be a force for integration and consensus. Knowing 'how things are done around here' can help avoid conflict.

Co-ordination and control
If a strong organisational culture helps avoid conflict, it will, conversely, facilitate the processes of co-ordination and control. Strongly held values and beliefs will ensure that all concerned will pull together in the same direction.

Reduction of uncertainty
For new recruits to an organisation, the more quickly they 'learn' the norms of behaviour, the more confident they will become in their assumptions about how others will behave and the way in which organisational processes are carried out. This has the advantage of reducing the complexity of the organisational world, neutralising uncertainties so that any actions taken are in tune with organisational rationalities as seen by the majority of organisational members.

Motivation
While extrinsic rewards such as pay, bonuses and promotions can motivate employees to perform well, a culture which can offer employees a means of

identification with their work, which can foster loyalty and assist their belief that they are valued, will add to their motivation and presumably the overall organisational performance.

Competitive advantage

A strong culture is said to improve organisational performance. Peters and Waterman (1982) and Kanter (1983) are just three well-known writers and consultants who claim to have found recipes for cultures which are presumed to link to performance. Their arguments are that the more closely an organisation sticks to their particular recipe, the greater the probability that it will be a high performer. It is debatable, however, whether a strong culture, even of the supportive kind, necessarily links to increased competitive advantage. For instance, Kotter and Heskett's (1992) research during the period 1977–88, identified ten large and well-known organisations (including Sears, Procter & Gamble and Goodyear), all of which had exceptionally strong cultures, but all of which had weak performances.

In some organisations, the existence of a weak dominant culture with multiple sub-cultures may be an advantage. Strong, all-pervasive cultures can be a disadvantage when they become so controlling that there is little potential for the nonconformity which brings innovation and the capacity to adapt to change.

● ● ● ● Changing organisational culture to bring about organisational change

The discussion in this chapter shows that it is difficult to deny the importance of culture as a dominant influence on the whole of organisational life. From this it could be deduced that, in order to bring about any kind of significant organisational change, the organisation's culture must be managed accordingly. This view is subscribed to by scholars such as Johnson and Scholes (1993) in their depiction of the cultural web. It is also evident in the arguments which recommend organisations to take on the characteristics of a supportive (integrative) culture (*see* Kanter, 1983) linked to an organic structure (Burns and Stalker, 1961) or those which will bring excellence in performance (*see* Peters and Waterman, 1982). From these points of view, permanent organisational change will only be brought about by first changing people's attitudes and values – in other words changing the culture at the deeper levels of its meaning as was illustrated in Figure 4.2.

However, changing an organisation's culture is not easy, as Schwartz and Davis (1981) point out from their observations of change at companies they researched. In relation to one of these – AT&T, which, in the late 1970s, undertook a large-scale corporate and organisational reorientation – Schwartz and Davis (1981, p. 31) say:

Despite the major changes in structure, in human resources, and in support systems, there is a general consensus both inside and outside AT&T that its greatest task in making its strategy succeed will be its ability to transform the AT&T culture. *It will probably be a decade before direct judgements should be made as to its success.* [author's emphasis]

Yet another example they quote is the case where the president of an engineering company resigned after six years of trying to change the company's culture from being production oriented to being market oriented. At this point he reckoned he had managed to dent but not change the culture.

Given this background, some means of measuring organisational culture and its relationship to organisational change appears desirable.

Assessing cultural risk

Activity 4.1 is one way of measuring organisational culture and this method can obviously be applied to any list of culture characteristics. For instance, Furnham and Gunter (1993) suggest this in relation to Schein's (1985) list of dimensions of corporate culture – a list not dissimilar to that of Robbins – and in addition give a list of various quantitative measures of culture. However, measuring organisational culture is, of itself, only a means to an end. The end is to determine how culture should be managed as part of the process of organisational change.

It was, therefore, in pursuit of this end that Schwartz and Davis devised a means of measuring culture in terms of descriptions of the way management tasks are typically handled in company-wide, boss–subordinate, peer and interdepartment relationships so as to assess the degree of cultural compatibility with any proposed strategic change. Figure 4.9 is an example of Schwartz and Davis's corporate culture matrix which they designed to carry out the first part of this process. It has been completed for the UK-based division of a company in the computer services industry.

Activity 4.8   *For any organisation you know well, use the basic matrix in Figure 4.9 to do the following:*

1 *Insert, in each cell of the main body of the matrix, words and/or phrases which encapsulate the different relationships (listed horizontally) according to the management of the tasks (listed vertically).*

2 *In the final column on the right, summarise the corporate culture for each task.*

3 *In the final row, summarise the corporate culture for each of the relationships.*

What do the summaries tell you about this organisation's overall culture?

Once you have carried out Activity 4.8, you can use the results of this analysis to assess the compatibility of the culture of this organisation to any proposed changes in the organisation's approach to its strategy, structure and operations. The framework for this comparative assessment is shown in Figure 4.10 as a

Tasks	Relationships				Summary of culture in relation to tasks
	Companywide	**Boss–subordinate**	**Peer**	**Inter-department**	
Innovating	Innovation if part of the mission	Bosses open to suggestions	Team work	Team work	Encourage creativity and innovation
Decision making	Has to fit in with strategy	Input from subordinates encouraged – boss has final word	Collective decisions	Work together to produce an integrated package	Collaborative decision making but boss has the final word; corporate strategy rules
Communicating	Easy, use of E-mail and phone	Friendly	Face to face and open	Easy, use of E-mail and phone	Easy, informal and friendly communications
Organising	Market focus	Democratic	Professional relationships	Collaborative	Organised on the basis of skills and professional relationships
Monitoring	Shareholder-led organisation	Meet short-term profit targets and	Project management deadlines	Project management	Need to meet short-term profit goals
Appraising and rewarding	Encourage performers	Hard work = good rewards	Results important	Results important	Meritocracy
Summary of culture in relation to relationships	Allow freedom to managers as long as they operate within the strategy and meet profit targets; output oriented	Friendly, rely on each other for success	Highly skilled professionals who help each other out	Work together to support sales	Overall performance and profit matter in a culture which welcomes dynamic and performance-related individuals

Figure 4.9 Corporate culture matrix

Source: Matrix adapted from Schwartz, H. and Davis, S. M. (1981), 'Matching corporate strategy and business strategy', *Organizational Dynamics*, Summer, p. 36; example from the author's own experience.

matrix which allows elements of the proposed strategy changes to be plotted against their importance to that strategy and the degree to which they are compatible with the culture. From this matrix, it can be seen that the nearer the elements of any proposed strategic change are to the top right-hand corner, the lower the chance that they will be accepted, given the prevailing culture. For instance, if a change to a matrix structure is of the utmost importance to a proposed strategic change, yet the culture is one which is reminiscent of Handy's (1993) 'role-oriented' culture or of Hall's (1995) 'north' culture, the need for a matrix structure would be positioned in the top right cell of the matrix in Figure 4.10. Other elements of the proposed change might still be low in level of culture compatibility but of low importance in the overall change strategy. They would, therefore, be positioned towards the lower right-hand part of the matrix.

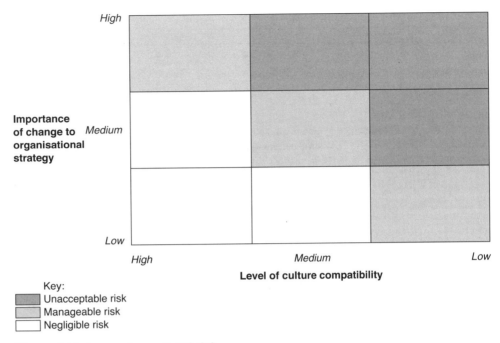

Figure 4.10 Assessing cultural risk

Source: Matrix adapted from Schwartz, H. and Davis, S. M. (1981), 'Matching corporate strategy and business strategy', *Organizational Dynamics*, Summer, p. 41.

The relevance of culture change to organisational change

Assessing cultural risk helps management pinpoint where they are likely to meet resistance to change because of incompatibility between strategy and culture. This further allows them to make choices regarding whether to: (a) ignore the culture; (b) manage around the culture; (c) try to change the culture to fit the strategy; or (d) change the strategy to fit the culture, perhaps by reducing performance expectations.

Ignoring the culture

Ignoring the culture is not recommended unless the organisation has sufficient resources to draw on to weather the subsequent storm and the possibility of an initial downturn in business.

Managing around the culture

The second option – managing around the culture – is a real possibility given that there are, in most cases, more ways than one of achieving desired goals. Figure 4.11 reproduces Schwartz and Davis's (1981) example of how to manage around an organisation's culture. This outlines four typical strategies that companies might pursue and what Schwartz and Davis call the 'right' organisational approaches to implement them. The final two columns set out the cultural barriers

	Strategy	'Right' approach	Cultural barriers	Alternative approaches
Company A	Diversify product and market	Divisionalise	Centralised power One-man rule Functional focus Hierarchical structure	Use business teams. Use explicit strategic planning Change business measures
Company B	Focus marketing on most profitable segments	Fine-tune reward system. Adjust management-information system	Diffused power Highly individualised operations	Dedicate full-time personnel to each key market
Company C	Extend technology to new markets	Set up matrix organisation	Multiple power centres Functional focus	Use programme co-ordinators. Set up planning committees. Get top management more involved
Company D	Withdraw gradually from declining market and maximise cash throw-offs	Focus organisation specifically. Fine-tune rewards Ensure top management visibility	New-business driven. Innovators rewarded. State-of-the-art operation	Sell out

Figure 4.11 How to manage around company culture

Source: Matrix adapted from Schwartz, H. and Davis, S. M. (1981), 'Matching corporate strategy and business strategy', *Organizational Dynamics*, Summer, p. 44.

to these 'right' approaches and the alternative approaches that could, therefore, be used.

Changing the culture

The third option, changing the culture to fit the desired strategic changes, is also a possibility but, as much of the literature cautions, this can be an extremely difficult and lengthy process, particularly if the culture is a strong one (Furnham and Gunter, 1993; Scholz, 1987). Furthermore, there are strong arguments (e.g. Hope and Hendry, 1995) against cultural change as a concept for present-day organisations given what Hope and Hendry (p. 62) describe as the move away from the large-scale hierarchies characteristic of the multinationals of the 1970s and 1980s, towards much leaner and more focused units.

According to Hope and Hendry, this move has been accompanied by an increase in the employment of what Drucker (1992) calls 'professional knowledge workers' but also by an erosion of security of employment and predictable career paths, with consequent difficulties of employee control. Two problems are said to arise from this. The first is that the 'knowledge workers' who are likely to flourish in these new types of organisation are least likely to be open to cultural manipulation. Second, any new managerial practice must allow for a degree of cynicism in the context of the downsizing which has removed several layers of middle management and therefore removed the opportunity for steady advancement once assumed as almost everyone's right. As a consequence of all this, 'employees in general may be less receptive to evangelical calls for shared cultural values' (Hope and Hendry, 1995, p. 62).

This view is supported by Beer, Eisenstat and Spector (1993) who argue that trying to change attitudes and values directly is futile; the way to bring about organisational change is first to change behaviour. The behavioural change will bring about the desired changes in attitudes and values. Thus, Beer *et al.* argue for changing the organisational context (people's roles, responsibilities and the relationships between them) first, which will then result in changed behaviour and associated attitudes. This view of change rests on the assumption that changing organisational structures, systems and role relationships, which comprise, in the main, the formal aspects of organisational life, will bring about desired cultural changes incorporating organisational members' attitudes and beliefs. Many models of planned change subscribe to this view and the 'Six steps to effective change' propounded by Beer *et al.* are an example of this (*see* Illustration 4.15).

Both Beer *et al.* and Hope and Hendry can be said to have their views supported by Hofstede (1981, p. 26) who quotes Bem (1970, p. 60) as saying: 'One of the most effective ways of changing mental programmes of individuals is changing behavior first'. He continues: 'That value change has to precede behavior change is a naive (idealistic) assumption that neglects the contribution of the *situation* to actual behaviour.'

The literature does not help in deciding whether cultural change is a real possibility or whether managers requiring organisational change should work

---

Illustration 4.15

Six steps to effective change propounded by Beer *et al.*

1 Mobilise commitment to change through joint diagnosis of business problems.

2 Develop a shared vision of how to organise and manage for competitiveness.

3 Foster consensus for the new vision, competence to enact it and cohesion to move it along.

4 Spread revitalisation to all departments without pushing it from the top.

5 Institutionalise revitalisation through formal policies, systems and structures.

6 Monitor and adjust strategies in response to problems in the revitalisation process.

Source: Beer, M., Eisenstat, R. A. and Spector, B. (1993), 'Why change programs don't produce change', in Mabey, C. and Mayon-White, B. (eds), *Managing Change* (London, PCP, pp. 99–107).

around the culture. Some methods of bringing about culture change depend upon education and persuasion or, in some cases, coercion, to help bring about changes in attitudes (Anthony, 1994). Others rely more on changing recruitment, selection, promotion, reward and redundancy policies to alter the composition of the workforce and so retain those who have the desired beliefs, values and attitudes associated with the desired culture (Dobson, 1988). It seems that a combination of approaches would be most effective unless the organisational changes proposed can, themselves, be changed to be more compatible with the existing culture.

Changing the strategy to match the culture

Schwartz and Davis (1981) give the merging of two organisations as an example of changing the strategy to be more compatible with the existing cultures. This choice for an organisation is similar to that of managing around the culture and further emphasises the possibilities inherent in the idea that organisations are able to choose the means by which they achieve their ends. In addition, those who view culture as a metaphor for organisations (Morgan, 1986) would find it difficult to preach wholesale cultural change. Some accommodation between changing the culture and adapting the strategy is more likely to be accepted.

Overall, compromise between these different approaches to managing organisational culture within a context of organisational change is counselled. Using a process which combines education and persuasion (to bring about attitude and value change) with changes in structures and systems (to bring about changes in behaviour) will help modify organisational culture as it is linked to organisational change on a broader scale. However, Pettigrew (1990) offers a timely reminder that cultural and strategic change is associated with organisational politics as well as with the core beliefs of the top decision makers. The next two chapters address these issues.

● ● ● ● Conclusions

The concept of culture is complex given its application to societies, organisations and groups, all of which interact one with another. The literature reviewed in this chapter has shown, to a considerable extent, the enduring differences between national or societal cultures, although there is evidence that some organisations can operate in very similar ways, regardless of where their different parts are located. The concept of national culture is, of course, not precise, when there are clearly differences in attitudes and norms of behaviour from one place to another within the same country. Even so, there are some generalisations which can be made and managers and others must clearly be aware that what they consider the norm might turn out to be something very different as national boundaries are crossed.

Regarding the concept of organisational culture, it is possible that when individuals join and work within particular organisations, they learn how to behave according to the expectations and norms of behaviour expected from them in that situation, even though outside the organisation whey may behave rather differently. Organisational culture might, therefore, be considered rather less enduring than national culture. Even so, the evidence shows that attempts to change organisational or sub-organisational cultures frequently run into difficulties. Given that the more organic and integrative organisational cultures are said to support change and, in particular, the increasing requirement for creativity and innovation in order for organisations to remain forward looking and competitive, it seems reasonable for many organisations to attempt to change their cultures in these directions.

It was seen in Chapter 3 that changing structures is not always easy, even though organisational structures are to a large extent visible and understood. By contrast, organisational culture, although allied to organisational structure, is much less visible and, with its many layers, dimensions and types, that much more difficult to change.

Consequently, as the later parts of this chapter show, there are occasions when attempting to change cultures is too risky and consideration must, therefore, be given to managing around the current culture or even changing the strategy to take account of the culture. What is more, as anyone involved in organisational change, some resistance to change is ever present not least because of perceived changes in position and therefore power base. Organisational politics and the politics of change are as embedded in organisations as are their structures and cultures. In recognition of this, the next chapter examines the issues of power, politics, conflict and change.

Discussion questions and assignments

1 Drawing on your experience or that of others, and with reference to the literature, explain why, in some cases, culture change seems to have been possible while in others this was not so.

2 To what extent does an organisation's structure influence its culture and its capacity to work with change? Justify your answer.

3 Review the evidence for and against the notion that, because of increasing globalisation of business and people's increasing knowledge of the attitudes and behaviours of people in different countries, national cultures are converging.

4 Prepare a presentation to demonstrate the degree of appropriateness of different types of organisational culture to different types of organisational change.

Case example

Culture clash may spark Schroders' exodus: bank's rivals have already started approaching top staff

FT

The telephones at Schroders' Cheapside headquarters were hot yesterday with the calls of headhunters and rival bankers trying to pick off some of the City's most prized corporate financiers. In what one Schroders banker described as 'ambulance-chasing of the worst kind', Schroders' rivals are hoping that its bankers will be demoralised by the news that they are to be bought by Citigroup, the world's largest financial services group.

Above all, they are stirring fears of a massive culture clash between Schroders and Salomon Smith Barney, Citigroup's investment bank into which they are to be integrated.

Salomon has the dubious distinction of having been the setting for two best-sellers: *Liar's Poker*, by Michael Lewis, a former bond salesman who wrote about his time at the firm, and Tom Wolfe's *The Bonfire of the Vanities*, about the 1980s tragicomic fall from grace of a $980,000-a-year Master of the Universe.

Both draw on Salomon Brothers' heritage of aggressive bond trading, especially on the firm's own account. Lewis tells how John Gutfreund, Salomon's chairman until 1991, liked to remind people that to succeed at the firm they had to wake up each morning 'ready to bite the ass off a bear'.

Other tales revolve around traders throwing phones at trainees' heads and filling each other's weekend bags with women's underwear.

This does not sit well with the patrician, traditionalist atmosphere inside the 182-year-old, family-controlled bank that lies a chunky cufflink's throw from St Paul's Cathedral.

But Sir Win Bischoff, Schroders' urbane chairman, was this week at pains to express his affection for Salomon Smith Barney.

'Of course, Salomon Smith Barney is different, but they have been building a business with the kind of people we employ,' he said.

It is certainly the case that the Salomon culture has softened since the 1980s, partly after it was merged with Smith Barney. The culture change has accelerated as proprietary trading has dwindled in importance for the firm.

The more substantial cultural difference between the two houses is in their approach to the business itself. Schroders turned client service and long-term relationships into a high principle.

Michael Carpenter, chairman and chief executive of Salomon Smith Barney, said his firm had also become client-driven. Most rival bankers are not so sure. 'They are still mainly product-driven,' one says. 'This is a marriage made in hell.'

At least one Schroders' banker wasted no time in planning his escape and had breakfast with a senior counterpart from Morgan Stanley Dean Witter about the possibility of moving jobs.

One banker said: 'Many of us liked working at Schroders. We felt part of the family and now feel the family's thrown us away.'

Citigroup is attempting to retain up to 200 key staff by earmarking about $250m (£152m) for loyalty bonuses. That alone will not be enough to retain the best bankers, but they are also expected to be offered equity. Many others at the firm were more optimistic, especially those bankers who had been pushing for some time for a link-up with a rival with financial muscle.

Pointing to Salomon's smaller European corporate finance business, one said: 'We're going to be very much in charge of the management structure and we have an opportunity to build something we wouldn't have been able to build on our own.'

The likelihood of some of Schroders' culture surviving under its new masters is good. Citigroup is itself in many respects a work in progress, after years of bolt-on acquisitions.

Source: Additional reporting by Gary Silverman in New York Copyright: The Financial Times Limited
Financial Times, 20 January 2000

Case exercise: Analysing the cultures of Schroders and Salomon Smith Barney

1   Using at least two of the ways of analysing an organisation's culture, discussed in the chapter, 'paint a picture' of the cultures of the two organisations in the case example.

2   Carry out some research (e.g. literature search, asking others, Web search) to come to a conclusion as to the possible pitfalls in forming alliances between organisations or merging organisations together. Start with two *Financial Times* articles which can be accessed through the FT global archive site entitled: 'Avoid merger most horrid' and 'When merging is hard to do'.

References

Adler, N. J. (1991), *International Dimensions of Organizational Behavior* (2nd edn), Belmont, CA, Wadsworth Publishing Company.

Adler, N. J. (1997), *International Dimensions of Organizational Behavior* (3rd edn), Cincinnati, OH, South Western College Publishing, ITP.

Alvesson, M. (1993), *Cultural Perspectives on Organizations*, Cambridge, Cambridge University Press.

Anthony, P. (1994), *Managing Culture*, Buckingham, Open University.

Argyris, C. (1964), *Integrating the Individual and the Organization*, New York, Wiley.

Argyris, C. and Schon, D. A. (1978), *Organizational Learning: A Theory of Action Perspective*, Reading, MA, Addison-Wesley.

Bate, S.P. (1996). 'Towards a strategic framework for changing corporate culture', *Strategic Change*, Vol. 5, pp. 27–42.

Beer, M., Eisenstat, R. A. and Spector, B. (1993), 'Why change programs don't produce change', in Mabey, C. and Mayon-White, B. (eds), *Managing Change* (2nd edn), London, PCP.

Bem, D. J. (1970), *Beliefs, Attitudes and Human Affairs*, Belmont, CA, Brooks/Cole.

Brooks, I. and Bate, S. P. (1994). 'The problems of effecting change within the British Civil Service: a cultural perspective', *British Journal of Management*, Vol. 5, pp. 177–90.

Brown, A. (1995), *Organisational Culture*, London, Pitman.

Burns, T. and Stalker, G. M. (1961), *The Management of Innovation*, London, Tavistock.

Calori, R. and De Woot, P. (1994), *A European Management Model Beyond Diversity*, Hemel Hempstead, Prentice Hall.

Carnell, C. (1995), *Managing Change in Organizations* (2nd edn), Hemel Hempstead, Prentice Hall.

Castells, M. (1989), 'High technology and the new international division of labour', *Labour and Society*, Vol. 14, Special Issue, pp. 7–20.

Chambers, D. (1996), 'Russia's different problems', *Financial Times*, 23 February, pp. 9–10.

Chandler, A. D., Jr (1962), *Strategy and Structure: Chapters in the History of the Industrial Enterprise*, Cambridge, MA, MIT Press.

Chinese Culture Connection (1987), 'Chinese values and the search for culture-free dimensions of culture', *Journal of Cross-Cultural Psychology*, Vol. 18, No. 2, pp. 143–64.

Deal, T. E. and Kennedy, A. A. (1982), *Corporate Cultures: the Rites and Rituals of Corporate Life*, Reading, MA, Addison-Wesley.

d'Iribarne, P. (1989), *La Logique de l'Honneur: Gestion des Entreprises et Traditions Nationales*, Paris, Seuil.

Dobson, P. (1988), 'Changing culture', *Employment Gazette*, December, pp. 647–50.

Drennan, D. (1992), *Transforming Company Culture*, London, McGraw-Hill.

Drucker, P. (1992), 'The new society of organisations', *Harvard Business Review*, September–October, pp. 95–104.

Dunphy, D. and Stace, D. (1993), 'The strategic management of corporate change', *Human Relations*, Vol. 46, No. 8, pp. 905–20.

Dyer, W. (1985), 'The cycle of cultural evolution in organizations', in Kilmann, R. H., Saxton, M. J. and

Serpa, R., *Gaining Control of the Corporate Culture*, San Francisco, Jossey-Bass.

Eccles, T. (1994), *Succeeding with Change Implementing Action-Driven Strategies*, Maidenhead, McGraw Hill.

Frank, S. (2000), 'On a wavelength with the Danes', *Financial Times*, October 23, p. 15.

French, W. L. and Bell, C. H., Jr (1990), *Organization Development. Behavioral Science Interventions for Organization Improvement* (4th edn), Englewood Cliffs, NJ, Prentice Hall.

Furnham, A. and Gunter, B. (1993), 'Corporate culture: diagnosis and change', in Cooper, C. L. (ed.), *International Review of Industrial and Organisational Psychology*, Chichester, Wiley.

Goodman, M. (1995), *Creative Management*, Hemel Hempstead, Prentice Hall.

Hall, E. T. (1981), *Beyond Culture*, London, Anchor Books, Doubleday.

Hall, W. (1995), *Managing Cultures. Making Strategic Relationships Work*, Chichester, Wiley.

Handy, C. (1993), *Understanding Organizations*, London, Penguin.

Harrison, R. (1972), 'How to describe your organization', *Harvard Business Review*, September–October.

Hickson, D. J. and MacMillan, C. J. (1981), *Organization and Nation: The Aston Programme IV*, Aldershot, Gower.

Hill, S. and McNulty, D. (1998). 'Overcoming cultural barriers to change', *Health Manpower Mangement*, Vol. 24, No. 1, pp. 6–12.

Hofstede, G. (1980), *Culture's Consequences: International Differences in Work-related Values*, London and Beverly Hills, Sage.

Hofstede, G. (1981), 'Culture and organisations', *International Studies of Management and Organizations*, Vol. X, No. 4, pp. 15–41.

Hofstede, G. (1983), 'The cultural relativity of organizational practices and theories', *Journal of International Business Studies*, Fall, pp. 75–89.

Hofstede, G. (1991), *Cultures and Organizations: Software of the Mind*, Maidenhead, McGraw Hill.

Hofstede, G. (1993), 'Cultural constraints in management theories', *Academy of Management Executive*, February, pp. 81–94.

Hofstede, G. (1994), 'Management scientists are human', *Management Science*, Vol. 40, No. 1, January.

Hofstede, G., Neuijen, B., Ohayv, D. and Sanders, G. (1990), 'Measuring organizational cultures: a qualitative and quantitative study across twenty cases', *Administrative Science Quarterly*, Vol. 35, pp. 286–316.

Hope, V. and Hendry, J. (1995), 'Corporate cultural change – is it relevant for the organisations of the 1990s?' *Human Resource Management Journal*, Vol. 5, No. 4, Summer, pp. 61–73.

Jackson, T. (ed.) (1995), *Cross-Cultural Management*, Oxford, Butterworth-Heinemann.

Jaques, E. (1952), *The Changing Culture of a Factory*, New York, Dryden.

Johnson, G. (1987), *Strategic Change and the Management Process*, Oxford, Blackwell.

Johnson, G. (1990), 'Managing strategic action: the role of symbolic action', *British Journal of Management*, Vol. 1, pp. 183–200.

Johnson, G. (1996), Lecture to Diploma in Management Studies students at Nene College of Higher Education, Northampton.

Johnson, G. and Scholes, K. (1993), *Exploring Corporate Strategy, Texts and Cases*, Hemel Hempstead, Prentice Hall.

Johnson, G. and Scholes, K. (1997), *Exploring Corporate Strategy, Texts and Cases* (3rd edn), Hemel Hempstead, Prentice Hall.

Johnson, G. and Scholes, K. (1999), *Exploring Corporate Strategy, Texts and Cases* (5th edn), Hemel Hempstead, Prentice Hall.

Kanter, R. M. (1983), *The Change Masters*, London, Routledge.

Kerr, C., Dunlop, J. T., Harbison, F. H. and Myers, C. A. (1960), *Industrialism and Industrial Man*, London, Heinemann.

Kluckhohn, F. and Strodtbeck, F. L. (1961), *Variations in Value Orientations*, Evanston, IL, Row, Peterson.

Knightley, P. (2000) *Australia: Biography of a Nation*, London, Cape.

Kotter, J. P. and Heskett, J. L. (1992), *Corporate Culture and Performance*, New York, Free Press.

Kroeber, A. L. and Kluckhohn, F. (1952), *Culture: A Critical Review of Concepts and Definitions*, New York, Vintage Books.

Laurent, A. (1983), 'The cultural diversity of Western conceptions of management', *International Studies of Management and Organisation*, Vol. XIII, Nos. 1–2, pp. 75–96.

Louis, M. R. (1980), 'Organizations as culture-bearing milieux', in Pondy, L. R. *et al.* (eds), *Organizational Symbolism*, Greenwich, CT, JAI.

McHugh, M. and Bennett, H. (1999), 'Introducing teamwork within a bureaucratic maze', *The Leadership & Organization Development Journal*, Vol. 20, No. 2, pp. 81–93.

Maurice, M., Sorge, A. and Warner, M. (1980), 'Societal differences in organising manufacturing units', *Organization Studies*, Vol. 1, pp. 63–91.

Mead, R. (1994), *International Management. Cross-Cultural Dimensions*, Oxford, Blackwell.

Miles, R. E. and Snow, C. C. (1984), 'Designing strategic human resource systems', *Organisational Dynamics*, Vol. 13, Part 8, pp. 36–52.

Mintzberg, H. (1983), *Structure in Fives: Designing Effective Organizations*, Englewood Cliffs, NJ, Prentice Hall.

Morden, T. (1999), 'Models of national culture – a management review', *Cross-Cultural Management*, Vol. 6, No. 1, pp. 19–44.

Morgan, G. (1986), *Images of Organization*, London, Sage.

Morgan, G. (1989), *Creative Organization Theory, A Resource Book*, London, Sage.

Nasser, J. and Wetlaufer, S. (1999), 'Driving change: an interview with Jacques Nasser', *Harvard Business Review*, March–April, pp. 76–88.

Ogbonna, E. and Harris, L. C. (1998), 'Managing organizational culture: compliance or genuine change', *British Journal of Management*, Vol. 9, pp. 273–88.

Ohmae, K. (1991), 'Getting rid of headquarters mentality', in *The Borderless World, Power and Strategy in the Interlinked Economy*, London, Fontana, pp. 101–24.

Open University (1985), Block III, 'Organizations', Course T244, *Managing in Organizations*, Milton Keynes, Open University.

Pacanowsky, M. E. and O'Donnell-Trujillo, N. (1982), 'Communication and organizational culture', *The Western Journal of Speech Communication*, Vol. 46, Spring, pp. 115–30.

Payne, R. L. (1990), 'The concepts of culture and climate', Working Paper 202, Manchester Business School.

Peters, T. J. and Waterman, R. H. (1982), *In Search of Excellence*, New York, Harper & Row.

Pettigrew, A. M. (1990), 'Is corporate culture manageable?' in Wilson, D. C. and Rosenfeld, R. H., *Managing Organizations, Text, Readings and Cases*, Maidenhead, McGraw-Hill.

Pheysey, D. C. (1993), *Organizational Cultures Types and Transformations*, London, Routledge.

Pugh, D. S. and Hickson, D. J. (1976), *Organizational Structure in its Context: The Aston Programme 1*, Aldershot, Gower.

Robbins, S. P. (1992), *Essentials of Organizational Behavior*, Englewood Cliffs, NJ, Prentice Hall.

Robbins, S. P. (1993), *Organizational Behavior, Concepts, Controversies Applications* (6th edn), Englewood Cliffs, NJ, Prentice Hall.

Robbins, S. P. (1996), *Organizational Behavior, Concepts, Controversies Applications* (7th edn), Englewood Cliffs, NJ, Prentice Hall.

Robbins, S. P. (2001), *Organizational Behavior: Concepts, Controversies Applications*, 9th edn, Englewood Cliffs, NJ, Prentice Hall.

Schein, E. H. (1985), *Organizational Culture and Leadership*, San Francisco, CA, Jossey-Bass.

Schein, E. H. (1992), *Organizational Culture and Leadership*, San Francisco, CA, Jossey-Bass.

Scholz, C. (1987), 'Corporate culture and strategy – the problem of strategic fit', *Long Range Planning*, Vol. 20, No. 4, pp. 78–87.

Schwartz, H. and Davis, S. M. (1981), 'Matching corporate strategy and business strategy', *Organizational Dynamics*, Summer, pp. 30–48.

Tayeb, M. (1989), *Organizations and National Culture: A Comparative Analysis*, London, Sage.

Tushman, M. L., Newman, W. H. and Romanelli, E. (1988), 'Convergence and upheaval: managing the unsteady pace of organizational evolution', in Tushman, M. L. and Moore, W. L. (eds), *Readings in the Management of Innovation*, New York, Ballinger Publishing Company.

Wilson, D. C. (1992), *A Strategy of Change, Concepts and Controversies in the Management of Change*, London, Routledge.

Wilson, D. C. and Rosenfeld, R. H. (1990), *Managing Organizations, Text, Readings and Cases*, Maidenhead, McGraw-Hill.

Woodward, J. (1965), *Industrial Organization: Theory and Practice*, London, Oxford University Press.

Chapter 5

The politics of change

Issues of power, co-operation and conflict are part of the politics of organisational life. Their importance is recognised in this chapter through a discussion of the sources of power and the way political action, as an expression of power, can be used in the management of change. This discussion is extended to include issues of powerlessness, with particular attention being paid to the position of women and members of minority groupings. A debate about the role of conflict concludes that not all conflict is dysfunctional to organisational performance and the ability of organisations to change.

Objectives

To:

- *explain the meaning of 'organisational politics'*
- *distinguish between different sources of power and ways of using power to influence people and events*
- *define and discuss the link between power, politics and conflict*
- *identify different types of conflict as a means of suggesting possible actions for conflict resolution*
- *discuss the relationship between power, conflict and change and ways of managing these.*

Organisational politics

Observation of small children left to their own devices shows a natural curiosity evidenced by a propensity to explore, experiment, form friendships with some children and not others and, quite frequently, thwart the intentions of their parents and other adults. These childlike characteristics do not disappear as children become adult and members of different organisations. In fact, learning how to thwart parents is probably good training for learning how to thwart the more formal aspects of organisational life such as rules and regulated procedures. Stacey (1996, p. 387) calls this type of activity 'self-organisation', that is, the self-forming patterns and processes which 'shadow' the formal organisation and which are endemic in all organisations. These patterns and processes are essentially political processes, which imply the exercise of power and the management of conflict. As such, they are of intrinsic interest in any discussion of organisational change.

The previous chapter discussed the culture of organisations as part of the informal or hidden part of organisational life; that is, part of the hidden section of the organisational iceberg. One conclusion about the nature of organisational culture is that it may be so all-pervasive that it is not so much hidden as not noticed until some kind of change occurs. The same might be said about the political processes, which appear to be an essential part of an organisation's functioning. Yet, the concepts of politics, power and conflict, particularly in the context of resistance to change, frequently appear in the role of the more undesirable aspects of organisational life. For instance, Robbins (2001, p. 351), drawing on the writings of Kanter (1979), says: 'Power has been described as the last dirty word. ... People who have it deny it, people who want it try not to appear to be seeking it, and those who are good at getting it are secretive about how they got it.'

A survey of attitudes towards change management and organisational politics involving 90 English managers during 1997 found that politics was a distracting side-issue compared to the issue of organisational performance (*see* Buchanan and Badham, 1999, p. 19). Fifty-three per cent of respondents agreed (against 24 per cent disagreement and 23 per cent neutral) that organisational politics is usually damaging, is a sign of incompetent management, and needs to be eradicated wherever possible. Contrariwise, 72 per cent agreed that, 'the more complex and wide-reaching the change, the more intense the politics become', with most agreeing that change agents (those facilitating or managing change) needed to be politically skilled. It seems that most managers would like to manage without the need to resort to political behaviour yet acknowledge the reality of it, particularly in the context of organisational change.

Defining power and politics

Defining 'power' and 'politics' is not straightforward. As Buchanan and Badham (1999, pp. 10–11) say: 'These are broad and vague concepts that have proved difficult to define or to measure, with precision and without ambiguity.' For their purposes, in discussing power, politics and organisational change, they offer the following:

> Power concerns the capacity of individuals to exert their will over others.

> Political behaviour is the practical domain of power in action, worked out through the use of techniques of influence and other (more or less extreme) tactics.

Consequently, power is an ability to make things happen and to overcome resistance in order to achieve desired objectives or results. Political behaviour, according to Buchanan and Badham, is 'the observable, but often covert, actions by which executives (and others) enhance their power to influence decisions'.

The concept of 'power in action' is echoed by Robbins (2001, p. 362) who maintains that this happens whenever people get together in groups and where an individual or group seeks to influence the thoughts, attitudes or behaviours of another individual or group. Acting politically is also a part of negotiation, as a means to overcoming resistance and of resolving conflict. It can, however, be the cause of conflict in that an individual or group seeks to affect, negatively, another individual or group. Thus, conflict may be the result of the use of power to affect others adversely. However, as Hardy (1994) points out, although power can be used to overcome conflict it can also be used to avert it. Therefore, as will be seen later in this discussion, political behaviour in organisations is not all bad.

Robbins divides the meaning of politics into 'legitimate' and illegitimate' political behaviour, the former being normal everyday politics such as bypassing the chain of command, forming coalitions, obstructing organisation policies and so on; the latter being deliberate sabotage, whistle blowing and groups of employees reporting sick. Robbins's (pp. 362–3) viewpoint can be summarised in his formal definition of political behaviour as follows:

> For our purposes, we shall define political behaviour in organizations as those activities that are not required as part of one's formal role in the organization, but that influence, or attempt to influence, the distribution of advantages and disadvantages within the organization.

This definition seems to accord with the views of Buchanan and Badham's sample of managers, discussed earlier, in their aversion to political behaviour in the normal course of organisational life. Having said this, Robbins clearly recognises the reality of politics when he refers to politics as a fact of life in organisations.

All these definitions appear to view political behaviour as one aspect of organisational life, which mirrors the 'objectivist' view of culture discussed in Chapter 4. Given Morgan's (1997) contrary views on organisational culture, it is not surprising that he poses organisations as political systems. As a consequence of this, he says that different types of organisations can be characterised as displaying different types of political rule. Illustration 5.1 describes the varieties of political rule, which Morgan claims can be found in organisations.

Illustration 5.1

Organisations and modes of political rule

- **Autocracy.** Absolute government where power is held by an individual or small group and supported by control of critical resources, property or ownership rights, tradition, charisma and other claims to personal privilege.

- **Bureaucracy.** Rule exercised through use of the written word, which provides the basis for a rational–legal type of authority or 'rule of law'.

- **Technocracy.** Rule exercised through use of knowledge, expert power and the ability to solve relevant problems.

- **Co-determination.** The form of rule where opposing parties combine in the joint management of mutual interests, as in coalition government or corporatism, each party drawing on a specific power base.

- **Representative democracy.** Rule exercised through the election of officers mandated to act on behalf of the electorate and who hold office for a specified time period or so long as they command the support of the electorate, as in parliamentary government and forms of worker control and shareholder control in industry.

- **Direct democracy.** The system where everyone has an equal right to rule and is involved in all decision making, as in many communal organisations such as co-operatives and kibbutzim. This political principle encourages self-organisation as a key mode of organising.

Source: Morgan, G. (1997), *Images of Organizations* (London, Sage, p. 157).

In his discussion of different types of political rule, Morgan draws attention to how the suffix *-cracy*, which appears in these terms, is derived from *kratia* which is a Greek term meaning power or rule. Thus the word autocracy implies the rule of one person, that is, the use of dictatorial power; the term bureaucracy is associated with people who sit at bureaux or desks making and administering rules; a technocracy is associated with the power of those with technical knowledge and skills; and democracy draws on the meaning of the prefix *demos* or populace, so that in democratic forms of organisation, power rests with the people as a whole or through their representatives.

Given these expressions of organisational politics, it is not difficult to conclude that politics are a part of everyday organisational life. That this is so becomes evident, most clearly, in the context of organisational change, particularly in the context of discontinuous, frame-breaking or transformational change discussed in Chapter 2. In order to understand, more thoroughly, the relationship between the political aspects of organisations and their ability to cope with change, some attention should be paid to power, conflict and resistance as component parts of organisational politics.

● ● ● ● Power in organisations

The characteristics of power

Buchanan and Badham's definition of power has been offered above. It is interesting to contrast this with a number of other definitions of power. For instance:

> Power influences who gets what, when and how.　　　　　(Morgan, 1997, p. 170)

> Power is the potential or actual ability to influence others in a desired direction. An individual, group, or other social unit has power if it controls information, knowledge, or resources desired by another individual, group, or social unit.
>
> (Gordon, 1993, p. 392)

> Power is defined as the potential ability to influence behaviour, to change the course of events, to overcome resistance, and to get people to do things that they would otherwise not do.　　　　　(Pfeffer, 1993, pp. 204–5)

> Power refers to a capacity that A has to influence the behaviour of B, so that B acts in accordance with A's wishes.　　　　　(Robbins, 2001, p. 352)

All these definitions have one thing in common – having power means being able to influence someone else's behaviour. Pfeffer's and Robbins's definitions bring in the added dimension of influencing that behaviour in a direction which the person or group would not, otherwise, have chosen. Robbins, in relation to his own definition, says it implies: a potential that need not be actualised to be effective; a dependency relationship; and the assumption that B has some discretion over his or her own behaviour. Power, therefore, is a function of relationships. It is not something a person 'has' regardless of what other people are thinking or doing; it only becomes valid when one person has something that the other values. For instance, a bank's ability to lend money to businesses gives it power over those businesses only if they are in need of finance and cannot obtain it anywhere else on the same terms.

Power also derives from differences between people and groups. Some people have more knowledge, expertise or resources than others do and, if these are scarce and desired, that person or group will have greater amounts of power than others. This can be referred to as the 'elasticity of power', a term taken from economics. In the field of higher education, staff with good research records are more highly valued than those without. Therefore, the power of staff to seek employment in many places is directly related to their publication records. The power of a head of department is inversely related to the strength of his or her staff's publication records.

Not all people in an organisational situation would agree on who has power, of whatever type, and who has not. Power exists, to a large extent, only in the eye of the beholder. It is not necessarily the resources or knowledge controlled that give someone power but the belief by others that he or she has that power of control. Many employees have not progressed in their organisations because they misjudged those who had the power to help them and those who did not. Others may potentially have power of one kind or another but perceive themselves to be powerless and thus miss the opportunity to exercise it on their own behalf. Handy (1993, p. 125) refers to the 'relativity of power' to describe the situation where one person or group perceives another to have power while a second person or group believes otherwise. As he says (*ibid.*): 'The group that overawes one person with its prestige and renown looks ludicrous to another. ... Bribes will sway some but repulse others.'

Handy also notes that power is rarely one-sided. Hitting back or saying no is an option open to those who are seemingly powerless. The dominance of one person over another depends on the power balance – how much one can put into the equation against the power of the other. One type of power can often be traded for another, for instance, money for image, as in the case of a company giving money to a university to fund a professorial chair which is intended to improve that company's image in the eyes of the community.

In summary, then, power is about the potential to influence as well as the actuality of influence and it is a function of relationships and differences between people, people's beliefs about it and how much one person has it in relation to another.

The relationship between power and influence

Many writers separate what power is from the means by which it is used. Handy (1993) distinguishes the concept of power from that of influence as evidence of this. Illustration 5.2 summarises Handy's descriptions.

Handy's classification of power and influence is useful, but life is not always as clear-cut as he suggests. For instance, a particular method of influence could be used in conjunction with several sources of power. In addition, the distinction between power and influence may, to some extent, be artificial, one shades into another. Morgan (1997), in his chapter entitled 'Organizations as political systems', does not differentiate between power and influence but discusses a list of 14 sources of power (*see* Illustration 5.3).

Paton (1994) discusses many of the sources of power found in Morgan's list but, usefully, divides them into what he calls 'visible' and 'invisible' sources of power. Many of these categorisations overlap with Hardy's (1994) identification of four 'dimensions' of power – decision-making power, non-decision-making power, symbolic power and the power of the system. Yet another example of a discussion of different types of power is that of Gordon (1993), but she also uses the concept of negotiation as a way of distinguishing the process through which desired outcomes are achieved. However, regardless of whose account is read, a number of common themes occur. The first of these is the recognition that power comes with position and the ability to control resources.

Illustration 5.2

Power and influence

Power as a source of influence

The possible sources of individual power which give one the ability to influence others are:

- *Physical power*: the power of superior force.
- *Resource power*: the possession of valued resources; the control of rewards.
- *Position power*: legitimate power; comes as a result of the role or position held in the organisation.
- *Expert power*: vested in someone because of their acknowledged expertise.
- *Personal power*: charisma, popularity; resides in the person and in their personality.
- *Negative power*: illegitimate power; the ability to disrupt or stop things happening.

Methods of influence

Different types of power are used in different kinds of ways. Particular methods of influence attach themselves (more or less) to particular types of power.

Some methods of influence draw on two or more sources of power:

- *Force*: derived from having physical power; physical bullying, hold-ups, loss of temper.
- *Rules and procedures*: derived from having position power, backed by resource power; devising rules and procedures to result in particular outcomes.
- *Exchange*: derived from having resource power; bargaining, negotiating, bribing.
- *Persuasion*: derived from having personal power; use of logic, the power of argument, evidence of facts.
- *Ecology*: derived from different power sources; manipulating the physical and psychological environment to achieve certain purposes.
- *Magnetism*: derives from personal and sometimes expert power; inspiring trust, respect; using charm, infectious enthusiasm.

Source: Based on Handy, C. (1993), *Understanding Organizations* (London, Pengiun, pp. 126–41).

Illustration 5.3

Morgan's sources of power in organisations

1 Formal authority.
2 Control of scarce resources.
3 Use of organisational structure, rules, and regulations.
4 Control of decision processes.
5 Control of knowledge and information.
6 Control of boundaries.
7 Ability to cope with uncertainty.
8 Control of technology.
9 Interpersonal alliances, networks, and control of 'informal organisation'.
10 Control of counterorganisations.
11 Symbolism and the management of meaning.
12 Gender and the management of gender relations.
13 Structural factors that define the stage of action.
14 The power one already has.

Source: Morgan, G. (1997), *Images of Organizations* (London, Sage, p. 171).

Position power and the control of resources

Almost all writers list position power or formal authority as an obvious source of power in organisations. Weber (1947), in his studies of organisations, drew attention to three types of authority. The first derives from tradition, that is, authority legitimised by custom and practice and a belief in the right of certain individuals to rule others. The second is charismatic authority which is legitimised through the leader's particular qualities being valued and an inspiration to others. The third type of authority is what Weber called 'rational–legal authority'. It is this type of authority that characterises the power held by people because of their position in some formal or understood hierarchy which has some independent standing with regard to the rules and procedures sustaining it. Position power bestows certain rights on those who have it, for instance, the right to order others to do things or to refuse other people's requests.

Handy (1993) links position power with resource power by arguing that if some control over resources does not come with the position, the source of this power will be invalid. This implies the backing of the organisation for the decisions of the individual concerned. In most modern organisations, some resource power accrues automatically to particular positions by virtue of the rational–legal basis on which the organisation is structured.

Resource power

Resource power comes with the power to distribute valued rewards or to withhold or withdraw something which someone else values. Illustration 5.4 describes two different, but related, strategies associated with the ability to withdraw or bestow valued rewards. These are 'push' and 'pull' strategies.

Illustration 5.4

Influencing others through push and pull strategies

'Push' strategies

Push strategies attempt to influence people by imposing or threatening to impose 'costs' on the people or group concerned if they do not do what is required. This may be done either by *withdrawing* something that the 'target' of your influence values, for example your co-operation and support or by threatening a sanction if your 'target' does not comply, for example disciplinary action, a poor appraisal, removal of a bonus or perk or often it may be public criticism or shaming. The ability to impose such costs will depend largely on a person's *position* and the *resources* that she or he controls.

'Pull' or 'reward' strategies

If push strategies are the stick, then 'pull' or 'reward' strategies are the carrot. They are 'the stuff' of theories of motivation that emphasise material, social and other extrinsic rewards. Rewards are often used to influence people by a process of *exchange*: 'I will give you so and so if you will do this for me.' Pull strategies may follow from any of the power bases: resources, for example extra pay or extra staff may be offered; expertise or information may be traded; increased status may be conferred or access to valuable contacts given. Less obvious, but perhaps more common, there are friendship and favour, approval, and inclusion in a group.

Source: Based on Handy, C. (1993), *Understanding Organizations* (London, Penguin, pp. 126–41).

Activity 5.1   *Describe some occasions when you have tried to use either a 'push' strategy or a 'pull' strategy to achieve an outcome you desired – perhaps to influence how other people acted.*

Were the strategies successful? If so, why do you think they worked?

If any of the strategies were not successful, why do you think this was so?

Invisible power

Control over resources such as determining other people's budgets or rate of promotion are examples of what Paton (1994) calls *visible assets* of the power holder. However, both Handy (1993) and Paton draw attention to what they term *invisible assets*. These are first, the power to control information, which is also referred to in Morgan's list of sources of power. Handy (1993, p. 129) says:

> A flow of information often belongs as of right to a 'position' in the organisation. If it does not already belong it can often be originated as a necessary input to that position. This can be horizontal information, i.e. information, often of a technical nature, from the same level of the organisation; vertical information, from above or from below but potentially trapped in the particular 'position' and to be dispersed with the agreement of the occupant. Information, above all else in life, seems to display the essential features of synergy. The whole is so often much more meaningful than the parts. An informational jig-saw, even though all the pieces are separately available, is nothing until put together. A 'position' can be, or can be made to be, simply by function of its position, a junction-box for information.

Morgan (1997, p. 179) echoes this by saying:

> These (people) are often known as 'gatekeepers' who open and close channels of communication and filtering, summarising, analysing, and thus shaping knowledge in accordance with a view of the world that favours their interests.

The ability to slow down or accelerate the flow of information gives power to many people who probably do not occupy 'high' positions, but who simply act as messengers or copiers of information from one part of the organisation to another. It is interesting that the advent of electronic mail and other means of electronic communication have become 'protected' by the use of personal passwords which control who gets what information and when. Illustration 5.5 is an example of invisible power which became visible only in one of its uses.

A second type of invisible asset (Handy, 1993) is that of right of access, which is similar to what Morgan refers to as having access to interpersonal alliances, networks and the 'informal organisation'. Certain positions in organisations give the right of entry to a variety of networks. While many of these are formal, there exist many informal networks and groupings to which entry comes more easily because of a person's position. Morgan (1997, p. 186) says:

Illustration 5.5

Listening in at the Beautiful Buildings Company

Just recently, the BB Company has secured contracts for three large-scale office buildings which are to be located in Manchester, Melbourne and New York. As a consequence of the need to maintain quick and reliable communications across the company, whose head office is currently in Milton Keynes, Gillian Lambeth, the Managing Director, and her co-directors have decided to install a technologically based information system to facilitate communications using systems such as electronic mail.

A few weeks after staff had been trained to use the E-mail system, Marcos Davidson, the Marketing Director, sent messages to his project manager in New York asking for information on another company's building which was similar to the one BB Company was erecting in Manchester.

Imagine his surprise when a message came back within an hour from Gillian Lambeth asking to be informed of the results of his enquiry. He thought that, with the use of his personal (secret) password, no one else but himself and whoever else he designated had access to his messages. What he did not know, until then, was that Gillian had asked the system installers to place her in a position where she could 'listen in' to any messages sent by anyone to anyone else on the system.

Marcos decided, there and then, to take care, in the future, about the type of message he sent and to use other communication channels for information he did not yet want Gillian to know about. Furthermore, he thought it might be a good idea if he had the same 'rights' over his staff that his managing director had over him!

> The skilled organisational politician systematically builds and cultivates such informal alliances and networks, incorporating whenever possible the help and influence of all those with an important stake in the domain in which he or she is operating.

An invisible asset mentioned by both Paton (1994) and Handy (1993) is the right to organise, which tends to be part of position power. Here again, this is not unlike Morgan's (1997) statement that a source of power is being able to use the organisation's structure, rules and regulations to suit one's own purposes. The right to organise is linked to methods of influence associated with ecology. An example is the power to say who occupies which organisational spaces or to waive certain rules according to convenience. Morgan and Paton both argue that organisational and work group structure can be used as a political instrument. Reorganisation always means a redistribution of power. Therefore, the power to restructure an organisation or part of it can be regarded as visible power. However, hidden agendas to use this process to accomplish other aims (e.g. reducing someone's access to certain information; changing someone else's committee memberships) are good examples of the use of invisible power.

Non-decision-making power

Position power almost always includes the right to make particular decisions. This is one of Hardy's (1994) dimensions of power – decision-making power. This power is frequently visible and unquestioned because of the power of the position. However, both Hardy (1994) and Paton (1994) show how issues which are

Illustration 5.6

Controlling the decision agenda

The marketing manager of an insurance company was on the brink of launching a large product development campaign. At the next management meeting, it had been decided to discuss poor profit performance in the previous two quarters. At issue was whether to deploy resources to expanding sales or to cutting costs by increasing automation (via electronic data processing). He knew that if this issue were to be raised at the meeting, he would be outvoted by a small minority of peers who leaned toward investing the funds in automation. However, he was convinced that automation didn't sell insurance! Therefore, he needed to find an issue that would rearrange the coalition structure currently against him. He realised that the key issue that he would prefer to have discussed was market share and not

profits, so he did three things. First, he sent a report to all the management committee members that showed how losses in market share could be regained by his proposal. Second, he sent to all members of the management committee a memo asking them to consider ways in which his proposed product development program could be carried out effectively and at a lower cost. Third, he persuaded the chief executive to place his project proposal first on the agenda. When the meeting started, the issue was not whether the product launch should take place or not, but what funds would be required to launch the product; the automation proposal was postponed, because some marginal members of the automation coalition had become committed to the market share issue.

Source: Paton, R. (1994), 'Power in organizations', in Arson, R. and Paton, R., *Organizations, Cases, Issues, Concepts* (London, PCP, p. 194).

not, strictly speaking, directly concerned with the decision itself, can, even so, be presented in such a way as to influence the outcome (*see* Illustration 5.6).

Wilson (1992, p. 54) refers to the type of power described in Illustration 5.6 as 'covert' power, saying: 'Here power is exercised through "non-decision making" rather than by means of attempts to influence readily identifiable (and commonly known) decision topics.' Invisible or covert power associated with decision making takes many forms. For instance, as shown in Illustration 5.6, it may take the form of the power to 'set' the agenda under which something will be discussed, limiting who may or may not take part in the discussion or defining the scope of the discussion. Hardy (1994) discusses the notion of 'safe' agendas where some issues do not even get discussed. Thus, some topics and people are deliberately excluded from the decision-making process. Exclusion from this process can also come about because participants do not have the knowledge or expertise to express a view or take part in any meaningful debate. The role of the 'expert' appears in many guises.

Expert or knowledge power

Paton (1994, p. 191) says: 'Organisations use specialist knowledge to cope with task and environmental uncertainty. This means that on certain issues they must rely on and accept the judgement of those who possess that knowledge.' Those who have specialist knowledge or expertise that is in scarce supply have resource power of a particular kind. Paton (1994, p. 191) gives an example of this:

> The middle-ranking research chemist who calmly says 'it just can't be done' can stop the marketing director of a chemical firm dead in his or her tracks. If the director is unwise enough to press the point he or she simply invites a lecture on, say, some finer points of polymer chemistry, whereupon – whether he or she pretends to understand and agree, or instead admits to not understanding and refuses to agree – the point is irretrievably lost.

However, as Handy (1993, p. 130) says, 'expert power is hedged about by one major qualification; it can only be given by those over whom it will be exercised'. Therefore, unless someone's claim to expertise is recognised, it will not become a power source for that person.

Morgan (1997, p. 184) says: 'From the beginning of history technology has served as an instrument of power, enhancing the ability of humans to manipulate, control, and impose themselves on their environment.' Knowledge of how to design and operate information technology systems is a special form of expert power. So many organisational functions and processes are dependent on information technology. Therefore, those who can solve the frequently recurring operating problems have power, often above their status. Many of these people are classed only as technicians, yet they have the power to reduce, instantly, the frustrations of others who are reduced to sitting impotently in front of a computer or prolong those frustrations through operating their own informal queuing system of those in need of help.

An interesting aspect of expert power (Handy, 1993) is that it is relative. To accumulate expert power, the expertise does not have to be very much greater than that of other people. A small amount of extra expertise can bring large amounts of power. However, as Handy points out, this power can easily be lost if someone comes along who has even a small degree of further expertise. As he says (p. 131): 'In the country of the blind the one-eyed man is king – until he with two eyes comes along.'

Symbolic power

In an article in *The Guardian* (26 July 1996) on the selling of copied computer software programmes alongside religious amulets, John Ryle says:

> An amulet is an ally, a reminder of an exemplary life, but its deepest meaning is decipherable only by priests and scholars. Likewise with software: the programs promise power and knowledge, but can be fully exploited only by cognoscenti (especially if the manufacturers, anticipating piracy, have protected them from encryption devices).

He goes on to say that the pleasure found in CD-ROMs does not necessarily relate to their use. This pleasure and feeling of power-knowledge relates more to the 'mystical potency (ascribed) to the software inscribed – invisibly – on its surface'. Implicit in this story is the concept of expert or knowledge power. However, the CD-ROM is also spoken of as an icon or symbol of pure information which, although invisible, is perceived as incorruptible. Such is the power of symbols, in this case a physical symbol representing something more profound.

Hardy (1994) draws attention to this aspect of symbols – that they stand for something other than themselves. The power which comes from the ability to manipulate symbols comes, therefore, from their capacity to signal to others the meaning, not of the symbol itself, but of what they stand for. This is implicit in Morgan's (1997) reference to symbolism as the management of meaning.

Symbolic power is, therefore, the power to manipulate and use symbols to create organisational environments and the beliefs and understandings of others to suit one's own purposes. Hardy includes the use of language, rituals and myths as examples of symbolic power. The use of phrases such as, 'all pulling in the same direction', 'we are a happy team', 'flatten the opposition' or 'argumentative (as opposed to conciliatory)' all give their own specific, covert messages about expected behaviour. The use of phrases such as, 'we are a happy team', negates the necessity to say, 'conflict and disagreement are not tolerated in this organisation'. Rituals involving who sits where at meetings and how people greet each other are indications of who holds power in relation to whom. Leaving the chair at the head of the table free for the most senior person or addressing someone as 'boss' symbolises one person's power in relation to another's. If a high-status person deliberately chooses to position her or himself next to a particular person, this could very well symbolise the chosen person's 'favourable' standing with regard to the other.

Morgan (1997) uses the term 'theatre' to describe the physical settings, appearances and styles of behaviour that can add to someone's power. He says (p. 189) of those who seek to add to their power in this way: 'Many deserve organisational Oscars for their performances.' Examples of the use of theatre are the size and furnishing of offices, the seating of visitors and the (unspoken) rules of dress. Morgan says (p. 190):

> Style also counts. It's amazing how you can symbolise power by being a couple of minutes late for that all-important meeting where everyone depends on your presence, or how visibility in certain situations can enhance your status.

He gives an example of how some people visiting the American president in the White House turn up early so as to be seen by as many people as possible while waiting for their appointment, thus dramatising their supposed importance.

As discussed in the previous chapter, Johnson and Scholes (1993) include symbols, rituals and routines and stories as elements of their cultural web. They present these as representative of the dominant culture of an organisation, thus providing clear evidence that symbols of power are inevitably intertwined with an organisation's culture and are, frequently, an outward expression of it. In summary, therefore, any analysis of power in organisations must take account of not only the types of power which are exercised over the content of decisions, but also the types of power that influence attitudes and behaviour, frequently in ways that those influenced are hardly aware of. Activity 5.2 presents some questions, the answers to which can be used to increase understanding of how symbolic power is used in a particular organisation.

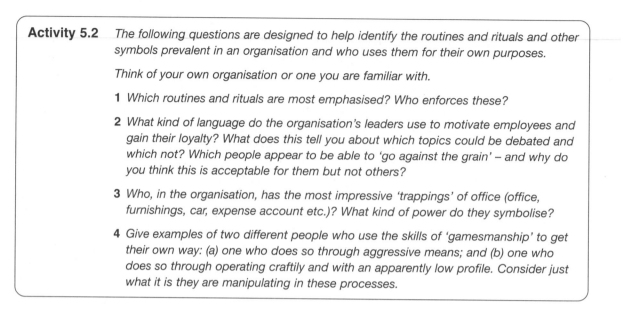

Activity 5.2 *The following questions are designed to help identify the routines and rituals and other symbols prevalent in an organisation and who uses them for their own purposes.*

Think of your own organisation or one you are familiar with.

1 *Which routines and rituals are most emphasised? Who enforces these?*

2 *What kind of language do the organisation's leaders use to motivate employees and gain their loyalty? What does this tell you about which topics could be debated and which not? Which people appear to be able to 'go against the grain' – and why do you think this is acceptable for them but not others?*

3 *Who, in the organisation, has the most impressive 'trappings' of office (office, furnishings, car, expense account etc.)? What kind of power do they symbolise?*

4 *Give examples of two different people who use the skills of 'gamesmanship' to get their own way: (a) one who does so through aggressive means; and (b) one who does so through operating craftily and with an apparently low profile. Consider just what it is they are manipulating in these processes.*

Individual power

The characteristics of power discussed earlier derive from sources associated with how an organisation is structured and the roles played by those working within it. Buchanan and Badham (1999, p. 48) refer to Pfeffer (1992) who adds another source of power – that which derives from the personal characteristics of those wielding power. These include:

- energy, endurance and physical stamina
- ability to focus energy and to avoid wasteful effort
- sensitivity and an ability to read and understand others
- flexibility and selecting varied means to achieve goals
- personal toughness; willingness to engage in conflict and confrontation
- able to 'play the subordinate' and 'team member' to enlist the support of others.

It is interesting, when considering this list, that power derived from these sources is potentially available to anyone given its non-dependence on position, status or control of knowledge or resources. However, it is unlikely to succeed unless used in conjunction with these. This leads to the issue of those who lack power – in other words the issue of powerlessness.

The politics of powerlessness

If there is one thing that symbols of power are intended to do, it is to make others who do not control these symbols feel their own lack of power. Conversely, many people are relatively powerless because of the way particular organisational factors affect them. In addition, some groups of people, for instance women and those from some ethnic minority groupings, appear powerless in relation to, on the one hand, men and, on the other, the majority groupings. Physically disabled people may be excluded from positions of status and decision making because of prejudice or simply a lack of physical access to the places where the exercise of power takes place.

Women's lack of power

A number of writers (Gordon, 1993; Handy, 1993; Kanter, 1979; Morgan, 1997) have discussed the position of women in relation to their perceived powerlessness compared to men. For instance, Morgan (1997) argues that formal organisations typically mirror what, in the West, has been (and, to a large extent, still is) a patriarchal society. Thus, those jobs which involve strategic decision making and the control of finances, as well as those which relate to machines and technology, are generally done by men. Jobs which involve caring, supporting others (e.g. secretaries), helping others (e.g. receptionists) tend to be done mainly by women.

Wilson (1995) has compiled a comprehensive summary of statistics showing that women earn less than men on average, that they occupy a much greater proportion of jobs at the lower levels of organisations relative to their overall numbers, and that they make up the vast majority of part-time workers (frequently doing more than one part-time job), thus having little employment protection, sickness benefits and, if they become unemployed, unemployment benefit. The Department for Education and Employment publication (2000) *Labour Market and Skills Trends 2000* reports that in 1999, 80 per cent of part-time employees in the UK were women. The same report shows that jobs held by women are disproportionately (compared to men) concentrated in a narrow range of industries and occupations, for instance, in clerical and secretarial occupations and in public administration, education and health.

Although women are reported as having a 54 per cent share of banking, finance and insurance jobs, they by no means occupy higher level jobs in City of London (Britain's financial centre) as Maitland (2000a) reports in an article which discusses the 'macho culture of long hours and big bucks' which discriminates against women becoming managers. Maitland reports Helena Dennison, Chair of the City Women's Network, as saying: 'The City is about ten years behind business. ... There's a lot of open discrimination, but there's also a lot of covert and very subtle discrimination, in running down women's confidence. *We're not talking about sexual issues but about power*' [author's emphasis].

Unfortunately, the situation regarding any increase in the proportion of women occupying higher-level jobs more generally is not encouraging. The report referred to earlier says (p. 15):

> In 1999, only a third of Managers and Administrators were women. This is a slight increase on 1992, but employment in managerial and administrative occupations continues to be dominated by men.

Illustration 5.7

Chipping away at the glass ceiling

The 26 July 1996 edition of *The Times Higher*, a newspaper mainly for people working in the higher education sector, reports data taken from *Beyond the Glass Ceiling*, a book by Sian Griffiths. The data illustrate the very low numbers of women academics promoted to the position of professor. Of 63 institutions of higher education surveyed, in only three were more than 15 per cent of professors female. Fifty of the institutions had fewer than 10 per cent female professors. Yet, as is pointed out, women occupy half the places on most university courses. Overall, the statistics reported include:

- Only 7.3 per cent of professors were women, although women made up 30 per cent of academics.
- New universities topped the league table for women professors.

- One university – UMIST – had no women professors.
- In engineering and technology the proportion of women professors dropped to 1 per cent.
- None of the professors in either agriculture or veterinary science was a woman.

The article also features two Oxford University women academics, who, in spite of international renown for their work, had only just been made professors. Each of them had worked at the university for some 20 years. One of the women, Gillian Morriss-Kay notes that, on the issue of promotion, 'the university had deliberately excluded "promotion" from its code of equal opportunities, on the grounds that it was an unnecessary complication'. Even with a much larger number of promotions in 1996 than usual, the proportion of women professors rose only to 8.1 per cent out of an eligible pool of 15 per cent.

Source: Based on *The Times Higher*, 26 July 1996, pp. 16–17.

The metaphor of the 'glass ceiling' has become well known in discussions of the lack of any significant number of women in middle to top management jobs. Wilson (1995, p. 153) features a cartoon by Amanda Martin which says: 'Girls, DO NOT shatter the glass ceiling – it hurts.' It goes on to give advice about the elaborate precautions that need to be taken in order to dismantle this kind of ceiling. Illustration 5.7 demonstrates the extent of discrimination against women academics in their attempts to become readers and professors. A week prior to the publication of the article referred to in Illustration 5.7, the same publication (*The Times Higher*, 19 July 1996) reported the advancement of Fay Gale, Vice-Chancellor of one of Australia's most prestigious universities, to head the Australian Vice-Chancellors Committee. At the time of writing she is only the third female to have held this position in almost 150 years of existence. Evidently, Professor Gale had long been a critic of the way the academic community is overwhelmingly male dominated. She is quoted as saying (p. 11): 'Australia does have positive discrimination in higher education – only it is men who enjoy the benefits.'

There are a number of explanations of why women occupy jobs characterised by low skills and low pay and, if they have achieved professional status, still do not rise in any significant numbers to the higher levels in their profession or the higher levels of management and thus, gain at least position power. One is that, because of the need to absent themselves for childbearing, women are not perceived to be committed to their work and employer. However, although it is clear that this belief about women prevails in the minds of many recruiters and senior managers, the evidence shows this to be a myth (Wilson, 1995). Women who commit themselves to a job and career do so in no way differently to men. A more complex reason which is put forward by a number of writers (e.g. Kanter, 1979; Morgan, 1997) is that the prevailing structures and power balances in organisations, which are predominantly based on a male model of what organisation and management is about, conspire indirectly to reduce the power sources of women. More recently, McKenna (1997) (as discussed in Buchanan and Badham, p.123) refers to the world of male politics in which: 'Sitting back and hoping for recognition is seen as passivity, a lack of fire, guts and ambition. Essential for success is self-promotion, and conformity to the "unwritten rules of success".' McKenna (1997, p. 51) says: '[Success is about] maintaining silence in the face of politics and backstabbing. ... It has little to do with performing good work or being productive and everything to do with pecking order and egos.'

All this is appears to be confirmed by articles in the press. For instance: 'Wanted: more uppity women: BOARDROOM APPOINTMENTS: Alison Maitland looks at the reasons why only 5 per cent of the directors of FTSE 100 companies are female' (Maitland, 2000b) and 'America's gender gap travels abroad: WOMEN IN BUSINESS: Almost half of US middle management is female but women get only 13 per cent of foreign postings' (Maitland, 2000c). However, there are some positive signs that the power balance might be shifting a little. In the former article, Maitland says: 'Headhunters argue that it is only a matter of time before women join the board in larger numbers. Some companies are explicitly asking for "balanced shortlists" of candidates.' She also reports on an Institute of Management survey which found that women account for 22 per cent of all British managers today, compared with just 8 per cent a decade ago. A Canadian newspaper, *Financial Post*, gives a more upbeat report on the increased number of women going into senior positions, to a large extent because of the 'flood tide of women over the course of the past 20 years who have worked their way up within organisations' (*Financial Post*, Canada, 2000). In other parts of the world such as the Middle East a 'bigger role for ... women in business (is) recommended' (Avancena and Saeed, 2000). PR Newswire (2000) also reports on a US Department of Commerce Women in Business Development Trade Mission to Cairo, Egypt; Nairobi, Kenya; and Johannesburg, South Africa.

If, as suggested here, the projections about increases in the numbers of women in management and senior management positions in traditionally male dominated occupations comes to pass, then this is predicted to alter the culture within which business is done. What is in general called the 'feminisation' of business (*see* for instance Gratton, 2000; McKenna, 1997) could very well alter the current view of organisational politics and power. What is not yet tested is whether the numbers of women opting out of 'large business' to start up their own companies (Gracie, 1998 reports this to be almost one-third of all new UK businesses in 1997) will be tempted to remain. Neither is it certain that feminisation of the workplace will make a difference to the endemic organisational issues of power imbalances and organisational politics, particularly when change implies redundancies and/or redesignation and redesign of jobs.

Activity 5.3 *Think of someone whom you consider does their job very well, but has been passed over for promotion. Assuming there is no reason why this person could not do the higher-level job (given time and training if necessary), why do you think they have not progressed?*

In your analysis, draw on the concepts of power discussed in the preceding sections and any explanations related to the possible lack of power of the person concerned.

Powerlessness because of cultural differences

The previous chapter discussed how national cultural differences can influence many aspects of organisational life. Care must be taken, therefore, not to assume that practices in one culture can be transferred, without question, to another. For instance, it would be unwise to assume that factors which motivate some groups of people will, similarly, motivate others; a leadership style which works well in organisations where a Westernised culture prevails may not be popular in countries where the power distance between levels in an organisation is much greater.

The implications of these cultural differences for a discussion of power and powerlessness hinge on the very issue of difference. For instance, as the previous chapter showed, there are definite differences in the behaviour of people from different cultures but, more importantly – because they are so difficult to change – in the values and attitudes which they bring to the workplace. Therefore, people from cultures scoring high on Hofstede's (1981) high power distance cultural dimension will expect managers to make all major decisions (and even some minor ones). However, in Western cultures, which characteristically score low on the power distance cultural dimension, these expectations can frequently be interpreted as a lack of ambition and unwillingness to take responsibility for actions. This, in turn, does not train these people to gain power sources such as 'control of decision processes' and 'formal authority', two of the sources of power given by Morgan (1997). Morgan also cites 'ability to cope with uncertainty' as another source of power. This relates directly to another of Hofstede's cultural dimensions – uncertainty avoidance. Consequently, if a minority group's cultural upbringing is one where ambiguity must be controlled, they will not be prepared to demonstrate attitudes and behaviour, which will gain them power in this direction.

A final example is the difference in orientation towards others that is found between different cultural groupings. The perspective of power in Western society is based mainly on the power of the individual, yet in many other societies (particularly in East Asian countries) people are expected to show loyalty to their group. It is the performance of the group that matters. Power is linked to the power of the group. Yuet-Ha (1996) points this out in her discussion of the differences between Western and East Asian work-related values and their relationship to work-related competencies. Her findings suggest that, for people from an East Asian culture, it is relatively easy to implement team working and shared responsibility and support. However, it is relatively difficult to implement such things as open communication, participation, decisiveness, empowerment, delegation of authority and responsibility, taking responsibility in leadership, and sharing information. Given that most of these competencies are ones favoured in Western societies, people from ethnic minority groups that favour other competencies are unlikely to progress when working in British, American and some European countries, unless they can change others' perceptions of their differences. As Morgan points out with one of his sources of power, their lack of power in the first place makes this difficult to achieve.

Positions of powerlessness

The discussion thus far demonstrates the relationship between powerful and powerless groups which mirrors the areas selected for legislation as attempts have been made to provide more equality of opportunity in an organisational world where power has, traditionally, gravitated to white men. Legislation has certainly helped to eliminate the more overt prejudices which have prevented women and people from ethnic minority groups from enjoying the benefits given to others, even if certain organisational and covert processes still contrive to reduce their access to power sources and forms of influence. However, there are other groups of people who do not have the benefit of legislation – because no particular prejudice is shown against them – yet still find themselves relatively powerless. These groups are not, as might be expected, those working at the lowest levels of the organisation. They are powerless because of the particular positions they occupy. It is nearly 20 years since Kanter (1979) singled out, among others, first-line supervisors and staff professionals as examples of people lacking power.

According to Kanter, power comes from access to resources, information and support to get a task done; as well as the co-operation of others in doing what is necessary. She maintains that both of these capacities derive not from leadership style and skill but from a person's location in the formal and informal systems of the organisation. This includes both the way the job is defined and the types of connections to other important people in the organisation. Three 'lines' of organisational power are defined: (1) lines of supply; (2) lines of information; (3) lines of support. These have been discussed already as being basically related to resource and position power. Of additional relevance here is the power which comes from *connections* with other parts of the organisational system. Kanter identifies this as deriving from two sources – job activities and political alliances. She says (pp. 65–6):

1 Power is most easily accumulated when one has a job that is designed and located to allow *discretion* (nonroutinised action permitting flexible, adaptive, and creative contributions), *recognition* (visibility and notice), and *relevance* (being central to pressing organisational problems).

2 Power also comes when one has relatively close contact with *sponsors* (high level people who confer approval, prestige, or backing), *peer networks* (circles of acquaintanceship that provide reputation and information, the grapevine often being faster than formal communication channels), and *subordinates* (who can be developed to relieve managers of some of the burdens and to represent the manager's point of view).

When people are in situations where they have strong lines of supply, information and support, their job allows them discretion and their work is recognised as being relevant to the organisation's purposes, they can more easily let go of control downwards and, thereby, develop their staff more effectively. In contrast to this situation, Kanter (1979, p. 67) says:

> The powerless live in a different world. Lacking the supplies, information, or support to make things happen easily, they may turn instead to the ultimate weapon of those who lack productive power – oppressive power: holding others back and punishing with whatever threats they can muster.

This situation is quite frequently that of the first-line supervisor. Illustration 5.8 shows how multiple causes combine to influence the attitudes and behaviour of first-line supervisors and people in similar positions and increase their feelings of powerlessness.

Kanter also discusses the position of staff professionals, that is, those people who act as 'advisers behind the scenes'. These are people who must 'sell' their knowledge and expertise and bargain for resources, but who, quite often, do not have power to bargain with – they have few favours to offer in exchange. Experience of many organisations shows that people working in human resource or personnel departments are frequently in this situation. They frequently have little line experience and, therefore, are not involved in the mainstream organisational power networks. Being specialists, their ability to cross functions or undertake general management positions is restricted. They are, therefore, likely to get 'stuck' in a limited career structure. Having little power themselves, they cannot pass it on to others. In addition, they are prey to having their work contracted to agencies or consultants outside the organisation. The effect of this relative powerlessness is that they tend to become 'turf-minded', protecting their patches, drawing strict boundaries between themselves and other functional managers. These various aspects of powerlessness, collectively, lead to conservative attitudes which are resistant to change. Activity 5.4 asks you to assess a job in terms of its capacity to generate power for its occupant.

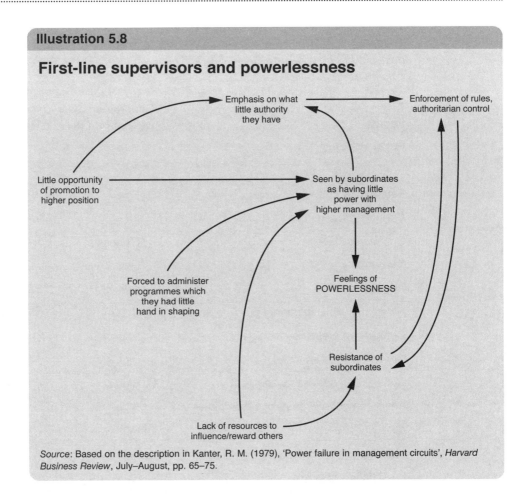

Illustration 5.8

First-line supervisors and powerlessness

Source: Based on the description in Kanter, R. M. (1979), 'Power failure in management circuits', *Harvard Business Review*, July–August, pp. 65–75.

● ● ● ● The link between politics, power and conflict

In the first section of this chapter, politics was described as the use of power. However, as Robbins (1996) points out, political behaviour, although defined as those activities undertaken to influence others, is particularly relevant to those activities which are not part of someone's formal organisational role. In an ideal organisational world there would probably be no need to behave other than in accordance with one's formal role. However, because the organisational world is made up of human beings, each of whom has his or her own set of values, interests and beliefs, there are bound to be differences of opinion as to the very many issues which pervade everyday organisational life, let alone those that prevail in conditions of change. Even in organisations which apparently have a strong dominant culture, the experience of that culture will vary for individuals and groups who carry with them their own subcultures. What is more, a dominant culture will not solve one of the perennial issues in all organisations – the existence of scarce resources, which are never sufficient for everyone to have all they want.

Activity 5.4   *The following is a list of factors which contribute to power or powerlessness. For your own job, or one you know well, take each factor in turn and tick the middle or last column as appropriate.*

Factor	Generates power when factor is:	Generates powerlessness when factor is:
Rules in the job	☐ Few	☐ Many
Predecessors in the job	☐ Few	☐ Many
Established routines	☐ Few	☐ Many
Centralised resources	☐ Few	☐ Many
Communications	☐ Extensive	☐ Limited
Task variety	☐ High	☐ Low
Physical location	☐ Central	☐ Distant
Relation of tasks to current problem areas	☐ Central	☐ Peripheral
Competitive pressures	☐ High	☐ Low
Net-forming opportunities	☐ High	☐ Low
Contact with senior management	☐ High	☐ Low
Advancement prospects of subordinates	☐ High	☐ Low
Authority/discretion in decision making	☐ High	☐ Low
Meaningful goals/tasks	☐ High	☐ Low
Participation in programmes, meetings, conferences	☐ High	☐ Low

Consider the overall picture obtained of the job. How powerful might the person occupying it be?

Source: Based on factors suggested by Kanter, R. M. (1979), 'Power failure in management circuits', *Harvard Business Review*, July–August, pp. 65–75; and Gordon, J. R. (1993), *A Diagnostic Approach to Organizational Behavior*, Allyn & Bacon, p. 425.

As the previous section discussed, the control of resources is an important source of power in organisations and, as resources (of whatever kind) are almost always scarcer than most people would like, additional resource power is frequently being sought. This, in its turn, results in individuals and groups seeking to gather more power to themselves. In other words, they will compete for power. The issue then becomes one of whether this type of competition is helpful to the achievement of organisational performance or whether it becomes dysfunctional. Handy (1993, p. 298) appears in no doubt about this when he says, 'competition for power nearly always turns to conflict', with the implication that, while competition is not necessarily undesirable, conflict is. However, whereas Handy's discussion of conflict implies some disapproval, Morgan (1997) takes a more pragmatic view indicating that conflict is a familiar feature of life in an organisational society. His argument rests on the assumption that, because organisations are designed as systems which, at the same time, promote competition as well as co-operation, one of their outputs will, inevitably, be conflict.

This view emphasises the plural nature of interests, conflicts and sources of power and has become known as the 'pluralist' frame of reference (Morgan, 1997, p. 199). This stands in contrast to the 'unitary' frame of reference which emphasises the philosophy that organisations have goals to which all organisational members subscribe, with all working towards their attainment. Whereas managers holding a pluralist view of the way organisations should operate stress the idea of a coalition of divergent interests which will sometimes result in conflict, managers subscribing to a unitary philosophy consider conflict as an aberration from the normal state of affairs which recognises only formal authority as the legitimate source of power. Thus, from a unitary frame of reference, managers are considered as the only people with the 'right to manage' while others are expected to subordinate their own personal interests to the good of the organisation. From this point of view, the only type of power recognised is formal position power. Expert power might be recognised but, in the main, only as a facet of position power.

Robbins (1990, p. 414) prefers the term 'traditional' to describe this view that assumes that all conflicts are bad. He says: 'The traditional approach treats conflict synonymously with such terms as violence, destruction, and irrationality. Consonant with this perspective, one of management's major responsibilities is to try to ensure that conflicts don't arise and, if they do, to act quickly to resolve them.' The ideas of Taylor (1911) and his principles of scientific management are examples of a unitary approach to managing. The idea, still current in many places, that all industrial action by workers is wrong stems from this view. The difficulty in accepting a unitary view of organisational life, as the human relations theorists showed (e.g. Barnard, 1938; McGregor, 1960; Mayo, 1933), is that it leaves no room for dealing with the multiplicity of interests which are now accepted as part of a democratic way of doing things; hence the formulation of the concept of 'pluralism'. Illustration 5.9 summarises these two different views.

A consideration of the unitary frame of reference, as portrayed in Illustration 5.9, shows that organisational politics, in the well-ordered world of the unitarist, should not exist. However, this view sits uncomfortably not only with the notion of a pluralist society, but also with the comments reported in Chapter 2 about the seemingly increasingly chaotic circumstances which are being predicted for organisations now and in the future. In such times political behaviour is to be expected, with its associated tendency to generate both competition and co-operation (of which conflict is a part). To ignore the role of conflict as a positive force as well as a negative force in the context of organisations and change is to ignore the realities of human living. Therefore, a more detailed understanding of the nature and sources of conflict and how to manage in situations of conflict is important for anyone involved in organisational change.

Illustration 5.9

The unitary and pluralist views of interests, conflict and power

	The unitary view	The pluralist view
Interests	Places emphasis upon the achievement of common objectives. The organisation is viewed as being united under the umbrella of common goals, and striving towards their achievement in the manner of a well-integrated team	Places emphasis upon the individual and group interests. The organisation is regarded as a loose coalition which has but a remote interest in the formal goals of the organisation
Conflict	Regards conflict as a rare and transient phenomenon which can be removed through appropriate managerial action. Where it does arise it is usually attributed to the activities of deviants and troublemakers	Regards conflict as an inherent and ineradicable characteristic of organisational affairs and stresses its potentially positive and functional aspects
Power	Largely ignores the role of power in organisational life. Concepts such as authority, leadership and control tend to be preferred means of describing the managerial prerogative of guiding the organisation towards the achievement of common interests	Regards power as a variable crucial to the understanding of the activities of an organisation. Power is the medium through which conflicts of interest are alleviated and resolved. The organisation is viewed as a plurality of power holders drawing their power from a plurality of sources

Source: Burrell, G. and Morgan, G. (1979), *Sociological Paradigms and Organisational Analysis* (London, Heinemann Educational Books Ltd, p. 204).

● ● ● ● Conflict in organisations

The previous section established a link between power, politics and conflict. However, the concept of conflict itself is by no means uncontentious. What one person calls conflict, another might call 'hard bargaining'. A number of definitions of conflict can be found in the organisational behaviour literature. Examples of these are:

> We can define conflict … as a process that begins when one party perceives that another party has negatively affected, or is about to negatively affect, something that the first party cares about.　　　　　　　　　　　　　　　　　　(Robbins, 1996, p. 505)

> For our purpose we can see conflict as: behaviour intended to obstruct the achievement of some other person's goals.　　　　　　　　　　　　　　(Mullins, 1996, p. 723)

> Conflict is the result of incongruent or incompatible potential influence relationships between and within individuals, groups or organisations.　　　(Gordon, 1993, p. 448)

> Conflict can be a disagreement, the presence of tension, or some other difficulty between two or more parties. … Conflict is often related to interference or opposition between the

parties involved. The parties in conflict usually see each other as frustrating or about to frustrate, their needs or goals.   (Tosi, Rizzo and Carroll, 1994, p. 436)

These definitions, collectively, include the following aspects of conflict. First, it must be perceived by the parties to it, otherwise it does not exist. Second, one party to the conflict must be perceived as about to do, or actually be doing, something which the other party (or parties) do not want – in other words there must be opposition. Third, some kind of interaction must take place. In addition, almost all accounts of conflict agree that it can take place at a number of levels: between individuals, between groups or between organisations. Gordon (1993) also points out that an individual may experience conflict within themselves; that is, they may experience internal conflict. This might be because of the incompatibility of goals set for them or a confusion over the roles they are asked to play. Conflict, however, is not a unidimensional concept. It comes in different guises according to its degree of seriousness and capacity to disrupt or, in some cases, improve a difficult situation.

The nature of conflict

Organisational conflict can be thought of as occurring in 'layers' (Open University, 1985) as shown in Illustration 5.10.

Illustration 5.10

The 'layers' in organisational conflict

Misunderstandings
These are 'getting the wrong end of the stick' – genuine misconceptions about what was said or done.

Differences of values
These are the other end of the scale, as it were, from misunderstandings. Conflicting values lead to the most serious disagreements. The values involved may be based on ethical considerations such as whether to take bribes (e.g. sales commissions) or not; the level at which safety should be set; whether to deal with regimes which condone particular ways of behaving (e.g. imprisoning those who disagree with them) which would not be acceptable in the home country. Differences of values may also involve disagreements about the purpose of the organisation, that is, the ends for which it exists. Thus differences of values are almost always about ends or goals or objectives.

Differences of viewpoint
Different parties may share the same values but have differences of view on how particular goals or purposes should be attained. Thus differences of viewpoint are disagreements on the means by which particular ends should be achieved. For example, two parties may agree on the goal to increase profitability but disagree on how to do this. One may argue for increasing price, the other may argue for keeping price stable and cutting costs.

Differences of interest
Status, resources, advancement and so on are all desirable 'goods' that most people want and, if they have them, they want to keep hold of them. The distribution of these goods is not a once and for all process; it is constantly being adjusted through budget setting, organisational restructuring, strategic planning

▶

Illustration 5.10 *continued*

and so on. Therefore, competition between individuals and, particularly, departments is ever present.

Interpersonal differences

These are what most people would refer to as 'personality clashes'. For whatever reason, some people find it difficult to get on with one another.

This might be because of differences of temperament, style or ways of behaving. Care should be taken, however, not to mistake other types of differences for personality clashes. Accounting for conflict under this heading is often used as an excuse for not facing up to differences which might be occurring for other reasons.

Source: Based on Open University (1985), Units 9–10 'Conflict' course T244, *Managing in Organizations* (Milton Keynes, Open University, p. 57).

The identification of 'layers' of conflict is useful in demonstrating that not all conflict is of the 'do or die' variety; it depends on what has caused the conflict. Handy (1993) argues that all conflicts start from two types of difference. These are, first, differing goals and ideologies, which relate most nearly to the level of differences in values. The second cause is differences about territory, which relate most closely to the level of differences of interest. Other writers (e.g. Mullins, 1996; Pfeffer, 1981; Robbins, 1990; Tosi *et al.*, 1994), between them, offer the following list of sources of organisational conflict.

Interdependence

Different organisational groupings depend upon each other to a smaller or larger extent. Sometimes the dependence relationship is mutual. For instance, the marketing department is dependent on the production department to produce the goods said to be desired by the customer. Production is dependent on sales and marketing for gaining customers who want the products and thus keep the production workers in jobs. At other times, the dependence is more one-way. The direction of dependence is related to power balances between groupings. Robbins (1990) draws attention to the fact that nearly all line-staff relations are based on one-way task dependence.

Organisational structures

Conflict is likely because of the power imbalances which prevail in hierarchical structures. This sort of conflict, of course, overlaps with the concept of dependence. However, horizontal differentiation brings its own problems. Both Robbins (1990) and Tosi *et al.* (1994) refer to research by Lawrence and Lorsch (1969) which demonstrated how research, sales and production departments all had different orientations towards formality of structure, interpersonal relationships and time scales. They both argue that increased differentiation between departments, with each becoming more specialised in its activities, will lead to increased potential for conflict between them. Tosi *et al.* describe the value differences between mechanistic and organic organisational forms.

Rules and regulations

Robbins (1990), in particular, mentions the role of rules and regulations in reducing conflict by minimising ambiguity. For Mullins (1996) this impacts on the clarity of definition of the roles people are expected to play. Robbins maintains that where there is high formalisation (i.e. standardised ways for people and units to interact with each other) there are fewer opportunities for disputes about who does what and when. Conversely, where there is low formalisation, the degree of ambiguity is such that the potential for jurisdictional disputes increases. Robbins maintains that conflict is more likely to be less subversive in highly formalised situations. In situations where the rules are vague, the opportunities to jockey for resources and other power bases increases. What is more, these activities can take place as easily through covert as through overt means. In contrast to this, Tosi *et al.* warn that rules and procedures do not necessarily guarantee an absence of conflict. In situations of over-regulation, people can become frustrated by their lack of autonomy and a perceived lack of trust of them by their superiors.

Limited resources

One of the sources of power in organisations is access to resources and the ability to bestow desired rewards on others. In good times, when resources are plentiful, the potential for conflict through competing for resources is reduced. In conditions of reducing profits or revenues or when redundancies are occurring, the potential for conflict over reduced resources rises. In addition, in economically hard times, gaining resources and extra rewards for subordinates is much more difficult, with the attendant potential for increased dissatisfaction among the workforce.

Cultural differences

The previous chapter identified a number of ways in which people from different nationalities and societies differ. Therefore, conflict can arise through misunderstandings or through inappropriate behaviour on the part of those with one set of cultural characteristics towards those with other characteristics. In addition, it would not be surprising to find cross-cultural differences in relation to resolution of conflicts. For instance, people who come from a collectivist culture, such as Japan, are more likely to avoid outright confrontation than people who come from more individualistic cultures such as the United States. People from cultures scoring high on Hofstede's (1981) power distance dimension are more likely to appeal to a higher authority and use bureaucratic rules and regulations to resolve conflict than people from cultures which score low on the power distance dimension.

Environmental change

Mullins (1996) lists this as one of his sources of conflict. He mentions shifts in demand, increased competition, government intervention, new technology and changing social values as possible causes of conflict. At the time of writing, the United Kingdom government is threatening to withdraw subsidy from the further and adult education sector for the training of sports coaches. This has resulted in articles and letters in newspapers as well as items on news programmes. If the subsidy is withdrawn, it is likely to affect the number of people enrolling on these courses and, therefore, the employment of the tutors concerned.

The identification of different sources of conflict is helpful in understanding more about organisational conflict but is not as straightforward as it looks. The relationship of sources of conflict to the layers of conflict identified earlier is complex. Many situations involve more than one layer of conflict. For instance, almost all types of conflict will include elements of misunderstanding and differences of values are often entwined with interpersonal differences. In addition, differences of viewpoint are closely linked to differences of interest. For example, the means which are thought appropriate to gain particular goals (for instance, the formulation of rules and procedures) are intimately related to issues about control, status, resources and so on. The Open University material referred to in Illustration 5.10 makes a useful comment on the relationship between interests and views, as follows:

> Interests are not only shaped by our views, they are also masked by them. The pursuit of personal or departmental advantage is a largely covert affair. Interests are modest to the point of prudishness; they do not walk naked through the corridors of organizations but go heavily clothed, preferably in a fashionable attire woven from the latest ideas about the best way to achieve organizational goals. (1985, p. 59)

This quotation shows how conflict is not necessarily expressed in loud arguments or fights. It also shows how political behaviour is frequently the outcome of differences resulting in conflict. However, conflict resolution does not necessarily imply political behaviour as defined by Robbins at the beginning of the chapter – that is, activities outside the formal organisational role requirements – as some of the strategies for resolving conflict show.

Approaches to conflict

Strategies for managing conflict will vary according to the frame of reference of an organisation's management. The orientation of managers subscribing to a unitary philosophy of organisation will be to suppress conflict whenever possible. Conflict is likely to be seen as the work of agitators and the dominant strategy will, therefore, be one of denigrating those thought to be the cause or dismissing them from the organisation. The paradox is, however, that, in a democratic society, this strategy will either cause further, more extreme conflict behaviour or drive the expression of conflict underground. The suppression of conflict within a unitary frame of reference will be successful so long as those without power fear the consequences of conflict (e.g. lockouts, dismissal, unemployment) sufficiently to avoid it. However, as soon as acceptable alternatives to the prevailing situation are available (e.g. alternative employment, successful industrial action), then conflict will again manifest itself, thus reinforcing the view that organisations cannot, in

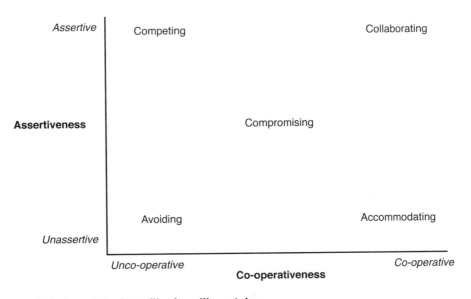

Figure 5.1 A model of conflict-handling styles

Source: Adapted from Thomas, K. W. (1976), 'Conflict and conflict management', in Dunnette, M. D. (ed.), *Handbook of Industrial and Organizational Psychology* (Chicago, Rand McNally, p. 900).

general, be managed as unitary wholes. Recognition of their pluralist characteristics is required if conflict is to be managed successfully.

Most writers on the subject of organisational conflict offer advice on how to manage conflict. Schelling (1960) suggests that parties to a conflict can act in three different ways. The first is to compete, in which case one party wins and the other loses. The second is to co-operate, in which case both parties win. The third is mixture of these two where the parties both compete and co-operate, with both winning something but not all they had hoped. A more comprehensive model of conflict resolution behaviours is Thomas's (1976) conflict-handling styles (*see* Figure 5.1).

Reference to Figure 5.1 shows that Thomas identifies five styles for handling conflict: competing; collaborating; avoiding; accommodating; compromising. Each style is positioned on two axes representing two different concerns. The vertical axis represents a concern to satisfy one's own needs. The horizontal axis represents a concern to satisfy the other party's needs. Illustration 5.11 identifies the situations when it would be most appropriate to use each conflict-handling style.

Each conflict-handling style has an outcome in terms of its capacity to tackle the content of the conflict and the relationship with the other party as follows:

1 *Competing*. This creates a win/lose situation, therefore, the conflict will be resolved to suit one of the parties only. The win/lose situation can lead to negative feelings on the part of the loser and damage the relationship.

2 *Collaborating*. This creates a win/win outcome, where both parties gain. It frequently brings a high quality solution through the results of the inputs of both

Illustration 5.11

Situations in which to use the five conflict-handling styles

Competing

1 When quick, decisive action is vital – e.g. emergencies.
2 On important issues where unpopular actions need implementing – e.g. cost cutting, enforcing unpopular rules, discipline.
3 On issues vital to company welfare when you know you're right.
4 Against people who take advantage of non-competitive behaviour.

Collaborating

1 To find an integrative solution when both sets of concerns are too important to be compromised.
2 When your objective is to learn.
3 To merge insights from people with different perspectives.
4 To gain commitment by incorporating concerns into a consensus.
5 To work through feelings which have interfered with a relationship.

Compromising

1 When goals are important, but not worth the effort or potential disruption of more assertive modes.
2 When opponents with equal power are committed to mutually exclusive goals.
3 To achieve temporary settlements to complex issues.
4 To arrive at expedient solutions to complex issues.

5 As a backup when collaboration or competition is unsuccessful.

Avoiding

1 When an issue is trivial, or more important issues are pressing.
2 When you perceive no chance of satisfying your concerns.
3 When potential disruption outweighs the benefits of resolution.
4 To let people cool down and regain perspective.
5 When gathering information supersedes immediate decision.
6 When others can resolve the conflict more effectively.
7 When issues seem tangential or symptomatic of other issues.

Accommodating

1 When you find you are wrong – to allow a better position to be heard, to learn and to show your reasonableness.
2 When issues are more important to others than to yourself – to satisfy others and maintain co-operation.
3 To build social credits for later issues.
4 To minimise loss when you are outmatched and losing.
5 When harmony and stability are especially important.
6 To allow subordinates to develop by learning from mistakes.

Source: Thomas, K. W. (1977), 'Toward multi-dimensional values in teaching: the example of conflict behaviours', *Academy of Management Review*, Vol. 12, p. 487.

parties. Win/win outcomes result in both sides being reasonably satisfied. They require openness and trust and a flexibility of approach.

3 *Compromising*. The needs of both parties are partially satisfied. It requires a trading of resources. Openness and trust may not be as great as for collaboration but compromise might set up a relationship which, in the future, could move to collaboration.

4 *Avoiding*. This does not tackle the problem. It creates a no-win situation. It does, however, allow a cooling-off period and allows the parties to (perhaps)

gather more information to begin negotiations afresh or decide there is no conflict after all. It can give rise to frustration on one side if they think the issue is
important while the other side do not.

5 *Accommodating.* This can create a lose/win situation, but retains a good relationship between the parties. It involves recognising when the other party might
have a better solution than oneself. It is used when relationships are more
important than the problem. It builds goodwill.

Activity 5.5   *Think of a conflict from your own organisational experience.*

*Analyse it to identify which one or more of the levels of conflict described in Illustration
5.11 apply to it.*

*If it has already been resolved, which of Thomas's approach(es) to conflict were used?
If it is still happening, which of Thomas's approaches do you think is most appropriate
to its resolution?*

Sometimes, however, as Morgan (1997) has pointed out, conflict is of a different
kind altogether. Rather than having a philosophy of pluralism, some organisations
are 'radicalised' to the extent that divisions between managers and other employees are almost irreconcilable. Thus, the radical frame of reference which
characterises these organisations derives from a view of society as comprising
antagonistic class interests which will only be reconciled when the differences
between the owners of production and the workers have disappeared. Based on a
Marxist perspective, this view does not usually in the West prevail to the extent
that behaviour in conflict situations goes so far as to cause the downfall of organisations and the social structures which support them. While occasionally, as a
result of industrial action on the part of workers and management, organisations
may close down, in the long run the power of the owners tends to prevail.

Activity 5.6   *Read the following story.*

Raheel and Veronica both worked at the same level in the sales department of Keen Machine, a
large motorcycle agency which held the sole rights to sell one of the leading brands of
motorcycle. They each managed a team of salespeople. Each team was responsible for a
different geographical area. Although the teams operated independently of each other, they
shared the services of two administrators who dealt with orders, invoicing etc. The administrators
also carried out typing and other administrative work for Raheel and Veronica. This work was
done by whoever was available at a particular time.

Every year, all the sales people had to undergo performance appraisals which were performed
by their manager (either Raheel or Veronica). However, it seemed that the administrators had
somehow been 'missed out' from this process. The sales director decided therefore that they also
should be appraised and, to be fair to both, by the same person (either Raheel or Veronica).

Raheel's sales team had faced some difficulties on their 'patch' recently and Raheel was
having to work hard to recoup their previous good performance. The sales director, not wanting to
distract Raheel from this task, asked Veronica to carry out the administrative staff appraisals.

Activity 5.6 *continued*

Up to this time, Raheel had always had a good relationship with both administrators and had no complaint about their work for him. However, recently, he began to notice that, if both he and Veronica gave work to the administrators at the same time, Veronica's work seemed to get done first – this was in spite of the fact that he had always thought he had a better relationship with them than Veronica. He complained to the administrators, who both declared they did not show any 'favouritism' to either himself or Veronica. He was still not satisfied but could think of no reason why their behaviour towards him should have changed.

Attempt to explain this situation using concepts and ideas related to issues of power and conflict.

Most people will have a preferred conflict-handling style, depending on their personality, culture, socialisation and organisational experiences. However, effective management of conflict requires the use of any of these styles, depending on the circumstances.

Power and conflict in times of change

The discussion so far shows that power, politics and conflict are indisputable aspects of social and organisational life. They are, therefore, of crucial importance to the issue of organisations and change. On the issue of power, French and Bell (1990, p. 280) take a positive view, saying: 'The phenomenon of power is ubiquitous. Without influence (power) there would be no cooperation and no society.' Others (e.g. Robbins, 1996) speak of the 'functional' role of conflict. Yet, as some of the preceding discussion shows, power and conflict, turned into politics, can be used to negative effect. The issue for managers of organisational change, therefore, is to use power and conflict in positive ways to enhance the change process and reduce unnecessary resistance. However, this is, as they say, easier said than done.

The two faces of power

The idea that power has two faces was put forward by McClelland (1970) to explain the positive and negative aspects of power. In their discussion of McClelland's theories, French and Bell (1990, p. 280) say: 'The negative face of power is characterised by a primitive, unsocialised need to have dominance over submissive others.' Positive power derives from a more socialised need to initiate, influence and lead. Therefore, positive power recognises other people's needs to achieve their own goals as well as those of management and the organisation. Negative power is about domination and control of others; positive power seeks to empower, not only the self, but also others.

The terms 'constructive and destructive' can also be used in relation to different types of conflict and are clearly linked to the concepts of positive and negative power. The use of negative power almost inevitably results in destructive conflict, with the attendant breakdown in communications and unwillingness to contemplate any view but one's own. Discontent such as this tends to multiply in conditions of uncertainty which are an inherent part of situations of change. It is in such situations that power balances are upset and disagreements which might, normally, have been settled by compromise, escalate into destructive win–lose situations. Organisations facing conditions of change are, in many respects, at their most vulnerable to the political actions of those who stand to gain from the change as well as those who stand to lose.

The problems of change

It could be argued that some types of change are less problematic than others and, clearly, radical, frame-breaking change is more likely to bring the greatest conditions of uncertainty and fear of what the future may bring. Even so, small-scale, incremental change can upset the balance of power through small, but significant, redistributions of resources or changes in structure which make some people's skills or experience more desirable than those of others. However, regardless of the content of any change, most writers would agree that it is the process through which the organisation must go to get from one state to another that brings the most problems. Nadler (1988) suggests three major problems associated with this transition process. The first of these is the problem of resistance to change; the second the problem of organisational control and the third is the problem of power. Figure 5.2 builds on these ideas to illustrate some interconnections between power, conflict, change and political action.

Figure 5.2 shows some possible implications for people's attitudes and behaviour during periods of organisational change. Thus, the transition process from the current organisational state to the desired one, rather than being merely a series of mechanistically designed steps, is fraught with possibilities of conflict and political action.

Figure 5.2 illustrates the role of power and conflict during periods of organisational change. 'Behind' each of the elements are many of the concepts discussed in relation to power, conflict and their expressions in political action. For instance, some types of change will challenge some people's values and beliefs and so induce an internal state of conflict which, in turn, means they are likely to resist the change. In addition, because values and beliefs are involved, this resistance will have a moral imperative attached to it. Confusion about the means of organisational control – that is, who and what is being monitored and how – is closely associated with disturbances in the power balance which will most frequently be linked to position and resource power. During times of confusion such as this, opportunities present themselves for taking political action using invisible sources of power. In this context, conflict, viewed as a problem, is likely to be resolved, if at all, by the use of win–lose strategies.

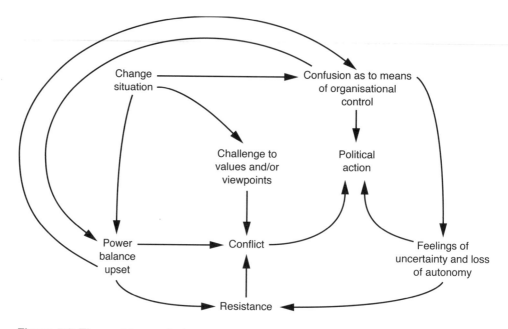

Figure 5.2 The problems of change

The role of symbolic action in the management of strategic change is discussed by Johnson (1990) and this will be considered further in the next chapter. Of interest here, however, is the fact that during periods of relative stability in organisations, symbols, such as stories and myths, rituals and routines and the more physical manifestations of status and power, play a major part in sustaining that stability. Consequently, in periods of organisational change, these same symbols (and their relationship with symbolic power) can be used in the process of resisting change. What is more, this argument holds whether the change is incremental or concerned with a shift in the organisational paradigm which was discussed in Chapter 4 as the cultural web. In addition, resistance, as a general term, to other than marginal changes incurs what was described in Chapter 2 as 'strategic drift' (Johnson, 1987, Johnson and Scholes, 1993). Thus the process of strategic drift, if allowed to continue without check, leads to confusion as to organisational goals and the means of achieving them. This in turn lays down the conditions for conflict and political action.

The problems of change sometimes appear overwhelming. However, as McClelland (1970) said, there is a positive face to power as well as a negative one. There is, equally, a positive face to conflict and political action in the context of organisational change.

The positive use of conflict and power

Robbins (1996) and the Open University (1985) use the terms functional or dysfunctional, and constructive or destructive conflict respectively. Indeed, with respect to functional conflict, Robbins refers to the interactionist approach to conflict which views it as not only a positive force, but also one that is absolutely necessary for a group to perform effectively. In support of this contention he argues that too low a level of conflict is just as dysfunctional as too high a level. Thus, there is a level of conflict – an optimal level of conflict – which engenders self-criticism and innovation to increase unit performance. Robbins says (1996, p. 533) about this:

> When conflict is at an optimal level, complacency and apathy should be minimised, motivation should be enhanced through the creation of a challenging and questioning environment with a vitality that makes work interesting.

The Open University draws attention to the fact that conflict acts to draw those on the same 'side' together in solidarity, but it can also create solidarity among those who are on different sides. This is because, as each side puts its point of view forward (even though in argument), information is revealed and shared and awareness of each other's goals and views is enhanced. Therefore, conflicts can result in *integrative* effects, but only if attempts to work through the conflict are non-coercive and use methods of openness and honesty.

Mills and Murgatroyd (1991, p. 159) talk about conflict and consent 'being in tension'. Most members of organisations will not revolt if they perceive that the methods of control used to achieve organisational purposes are based on some shared view of how these methods will be applied. For instance, Hofstede's (1981) concept of power distance as one of the dimensions of culture is useful in explaining why people from some cultures will accept a more authoritarian type of decision making and control than will people from other cultures. If an organisation's workforce is culturally inclined to risk taking and the tolerance of uncertainty, it will not be as comfortable with strict rules and regulations as one which, in Hofstede's terms, has high uncertainty avoidance.

Furze and Gale (1996) take an optimistic view of conflict in entitling their chapter on this 'Making conflict useful'. Illustration 5.12 lists a number of guidelines given by Furze and Gale for dealing with conflict. [The comments are not necessarily those of Furze and Gale.]

The guidelines for dealing with conflict (Illustration 5.12) are general ones and, if adhered to, may result in what Thomas (*see* Figure 5.2) called collaboration, where both parties stood to win. These same guidelines are also useful in the context of organisational change and are even more desirable in view of the increased potential for conflict at these times.

Care must be taken, however, to recognise the inevitability of shifting power balances, yet as Illustration 5.13 shows, the use of power in situations of change can be beneficial.

However, as the account of change in Illustration 5.13 shows, one result of the use of power by Brian Davies was to the detriment of the people who lost their jobs. Even so, because the basis on which people were chosen for the new style

Illustration 5.12

Guidelines for dealing with conflict

1 *Encourage openness*
This refers to the need to explore objectives, facts, views and the assumptions that surround the issues. Openness requires statements of who benefits and how. It assumes that conflicts cannot be resolved if issues associated with them remain hidden.

2 *Model appropriate responses*
The issue here is one of role modelling. If one party is prepared to make positive responses to contention, rather than being defensive or dismissive, this acts to encourage the other party to do likewise.

3 *Provide summaries and restatements of the position*
Doing this helps to keep communication going and is a helpful slowing down of the process when it becomes heated and points that are made are in danger of being ignored and lost.

4 *Bring in people who are not directly involved*
These outsiders can act as additional fact providers or take on the more process-oriented role of mediator or arbitrator. A mediator can facilitate a negotiated solution while an arbitrator can dictate one. Other possibilities are conciliators who act as communicators between the two parties (particularly if they won't communicate directly) and consultants. Instead of putting forward specific solutions, the consultant tries to help the parties learn to understand and work with each other.

5 *Encourage people to take time to think and reassess*
This means building in time for reflection and space apart. It may mean 'shelving' the problem for a short while but not as a means of avoiding it.

6 *Use the strengths of the group*
This refers to taking advantage of opportunities to use non-combative members of the group to which the combatants belong. Doing this brings others into the conflict, not to take sides, but to play a positive and creative role.

7 *Focus on shared goals*
Rather than concentrating from the start on differences, seek instead to identify where agreements exist – even if these are very small and, apparently, insignificant. These form a useful base on which to move outwards to assess just where differences exist. Parties to a conflict are often surprised at the amount of agreement which is there but of which they were unaware.

8 *Use directions and interests to develop areas of new gain*
Concentrating on other people's ideas can identify areas of potential gains. Then using guideline 2, summarise these in order to move forward.

9 *Try to build objectivity into the process*
Objectivity can be encouraged by asking those involved to express both the strengths and weaknesses of their position. What must be recognised, however, is that objectivity will always be tempered by people's value systems.

10 *Adopt an enquiring approach to managing*
This means probing through what appear to be the symptoms of conflict to understand the actual causes. Unless the fundamental cause is identified, the conflict will continue to flare up at regular intervals.

Source: Based on Furze, D. and Gale, C. (1996), *Interpreting Management. Exploring Change and Complexity* (London, Thompson International Press, pp. 312–17).

company was seen to be open and fair – not based on politics or tribal allegiances – the changes appear to have been accepted and new confidence instilled in the employees. As far as can be gained from this account, the use of power has been put to positive effect.

Illustration 5.13

Flight to revival

FT

Joel Kibazo reports on Kenya Airways' turbulent path to privatisation

When Brian Davies became managing director of soon-to-be privatised Kenya Airways, he realised he would have to draw on more than just experience to transform the African loss-making state carrier.

A former general manager at British Airways, Davies, together with Malcolm Naylor, the finance director, and Des Hetherington, who has since left the airline, had been part of Speedwing, the British Airways consultancy that carried out a 1992 study of the airline and recommended plans for its revival.

The consultancy team had found an airline on the verge of collapse. There was little cost control, which had contributed to the growing losses which hit $50m (£33m) in 1992. And senior management posts were awarded on the basis of political affiliation and tribal loyalty, with the result that the management hierarchy not only mirrored that of the Kenyan civil service but could have been a case study of the country's social structure.

The board of the company, chaired by the late Philip Ndegwa, a former governor of the central bank of Kenya, subsequently asked the Speedwing team to take over the running of the company and prepare it for privatisation.

Looking back over the last four years, Davies, who prides himself on having a direct but firm management style, says it has been a turbulent but interesting flight. As expatriates they have had to face the additional problem of a press campaign that labelled them 'white colonialists'.

One of the first things Davies had been warned about was the local custom of never doing anything on time. Arriving an hour late is not always considered rude.

'I have a personal fetish about time and I was warned that you can't do things on time in Africa.' Having decided on times of meetings, he would lock the doors to the meeting room and start without the late-comers. Initially this led to meetings with only about half the number of senior management staff but, as he says, 'the late-comers were soon embarrassed. It worked.'

Management's new promptness clearly percolated through to operations, where the airline's poor record of flight departures was a central issue. 'Today,' he says with pride, 'around 90 per cent of flights leave on schedule and around 85 per cent within 15 minutes of the set departure time. This made me determined to show that other things could also be tackled'.

Another target was staffing. The new team arrived after some 900 people had already been laid off, easing the burden of the staff reorganisation. Yet given the tribal traditions it still proved to be one of the most sensitive operations. The management asked employees to resign and reapply for their jobs.

The reorganisation was complicated by the company's six-tier management structure. Naylor remembers: 'I could not ask for a file without the message having to be passed down a chain of six people. It was crazy but that is how things had always been done here. You have to understand that in this culture position and seniority are very important.'

Following the review, the management was streamlined to three tiers, with each manager given specific tasks and budget responsibilities together with spending targets. Nine managers, said to have owed their positions to political or tribal affiliation, were sacked. But Davies says the review brought a new confidence to the staff. 'Everyone was able to see we had not based this on tribe or politics.'

Over the last four years the staff has fallen by a further 400 to 2,300 through a voluntary redundancy scheme, the first such scheme in a Kenyan state-owned company. Losses were reduced to $30m in 1993 and in 1994 the airline recorded its first profit, $7m, which rose to $17m last year. In 1994, the government assumed responsibility for all the airline's external debt arrears of about $82m and converted $33m owed to it into equity. Profits this year are expected to be ahead of the $22m expected by analysts.

Most of the changes in the first year were carried out against a background of a local press campaign against the new management. As the management

▶

Illustration 5.13 *continued*

came from the UK a commonly held view was that it was simply preparing the carrier for sale to British Airways. The more enterprising reporters published the management's hotel bills. Davies admits that at times he wondered what he had let himself in for. 'But in the end I knew we had a job to do and I wanted to see it through.' He says a Time Manager International (TMI) course early on in his career at British Airways, which emphasised putting people first, had been useful.

He moved to introduce some elements of TMI into courses he organised at Kenya Airways. 'If you show you value the employees then they too will treat the customer with the same care and attention.'

While arranging a course he discovered that 75 per cent of his staff had never been on an aircraft. 'This meant that they simply had no idea of what we were about.' A lunch aboard an old Boeing 707 aircraft was quickly arranged.

It would have been difficult to usher in so many changes without friction and Davies does admit to a number of misgivings. 'People misunderstood our open management style. We called each other by our first names and openly argued about a point. Here, they observe niceties and people were offended by our way of discussing things. It was an Anglo-Saxon way of doing things.' It took a word from the then

chairman to highlight the error of the new team's ways.

Davies also says he underestimated the effects of tribal allegiances. 'We would say we are only interested in the Kenya Airways tribe. But in fact we were ignoring reality. Tribe is a powerful aspect that cannot be ignored. For example, people find it difficult to discipline someone from their own tribe. Things are getting better but we have had to learn to live with that factor.'

Last year, the Kenyan government invited international carriers to take a stake in the airline. In January KLM, the Dutch national carrier, announced it had taken a 26 per cent stake. The management is now engaged in a series of briefings for international and local investors ahead of next week's flotation of 48 per cent of the company's shares, to be quoted on the Nairobi stock exchange. The government will retain a 23 per cent holding while 3 per cent of the shares will be used for an employee share ownership scheme.

Those expecting Davies to bow out of the company he has transformed have been wrong footed. He and Naylor have just accepted a two-year extension to their contracts. 'The last three years have been challenging. The next two years will be ones of fun as we enter the growth stage.'

Source: Kibazo, J. (1996), 'Flight to revival', *Financial Times*, 22 March, p. 12.

Action on power, conflict and change

The story of Brian Davies and his management of change at Kenya Airways (Illustration 5.13) appears to have followed (though not deliberately as far as is known) the four action steps which Nadler (1988) proposes for shaping the political dynamics of change. These actions are proposed in response to what Nadler perceives as one of the problems of change mentioned earlier in the chapter – the problem of power. The first of these is to ensure or develop the support of key power groups. This involves identifying those individuals and groups who have the power either to assist change or to block it. As Nadler says, not all power groups have to be intimately involved in the change. However, some groups will need to be included in the planning of any change to guard against their ultimately blocking it, not because it might affect them adversely, but because they had been ignored.

The second of Nadler's action steps is using leader behaviour to generate energy in support of the change. The guidelines for dealing with conflict, listed in Illustration 5.12, could very well be guiding principles here. In addition, sets of leaders working in co-ordination can significantly influence the informal aspects of organisational life. The third action step is using symbols and language to create energy. This has already been discussed in reference to the use of symbolic power and, in particular, Johnson's (1990) discussion of the role of symbolic action in managing strategic change. Finally, the fourth action step for shaping the political dynamics of change is the need to build in stability. This is the use of power to ensure some things remain the same. These might be physical locations, group members, even hours of work. It is helpful to provide sources of stability such as these to provide 'anchors' for people to hold on to during the turbulence of change. In addition, there is a need to let people know what will remain stable and what is likely to change.

Activity 5.7 *Apply Nadler's action steps for shaping the political dynamics of change to the account of Brian Davies's management of change at Kenya Airways.*

How far do you think Brian Davies's actions mirrored those suggested by Nadler?

The discussion in this chapter set out to show the importance of power and conflict as elements in the politics of change. Managers who, in times of change, can reasonably assess who has what power and the way in which it will be used – with possible consequences for potential and actual conflict – have a good chance of implementing the change they seek. The chapter concludes, therefore, with a description of one way of analysing the potential for action of individuals and groups according to: (a) their power to block change and (b) their motivation to do so.

The first step in analysing the potential for action, in favour of or against change, is to identify who holds sufficient power to assist change or, alternatively, to work against it – that is, to carry out a 'power audit'. This can be done by using a questionnaire such as is shown in Figure 5.3. This is based on the descriptions of the characteristics and sources of power discussed earlier in the chapter.

The questionnaire in Figure 5.3 should be used for each individual or group that is considered to be significant for the success or otherwise of any change process.

The second step is to compare the power of any individual or group to block change with their desire or motivation to do so. Assessing motivation to block change is not straightforward. It can be gauged, however, by considering whether the changes proposed will alter the degree of power held. As a general rule, if this is likely to be lowered, then resistance to change can be expected and vice versa. Figure 5.4 allows any individual or group to be categorised according to their power to block change and their motivation to do so.

Each cell of the matrix shown in Figure 5.4 represents a different situation and strategy to deal with it. Thus, if an individual or group has little power to block

Indicators of power to help or hinder change	*Individual Group A**	*Individual Group B**	*Individual Group C**
Position			
1. Status in hierarchy/formal authority			
2. Power to change organisational structure, rules, and regulations			
3. Control of strategic decision processes			
4. Control of operational decision processes			
Resources			
5. Control of scarce resources			
6. Control of budgets			
7. Control of technology			
8. Ability to reward or punish staff			
Personal characteristics			
9. Involvement in interpersonal alliances and networks, with links to the informal organisation			
10. Able to exert 'charismatic' leadership to get others to follow			
11. Able to cope with uncertainty			
Knowledge and expertise			
12. Information specific to the change situation			
13. Skills specific to the change situation			
14. Knowledge and expertise unique to situation concerned			
Symbols			
15. Quality of accommodation			
16. Use of expenses budget			
17. Membership of high-level decision-making committees			
18. Receipt of company 'perks'			
19. Unchallenged right to deal with those outside the organisation			
20. Access to the 'ear' of top management			

* Indicate, against each indicator, the degree of power for each individual or group, according to whether it is high (H), medium (M) or low (L).

Figure 5.3 Assessing power

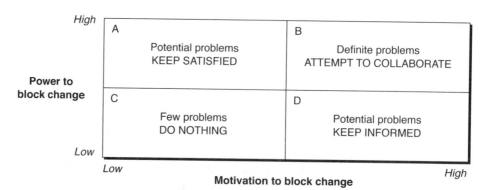

Figure 5.4 The power and motivation to block changes

change and, in addition, little motivation to do so (as represented by cell C), no immediate action needs to be taken. However, if there is both power to block change and the motivation to do so (cell B) this represents a serious situation in terms of the need to negotiate with those concerned and, if possible, to reach a collaborative agreement.

A potential danger to any change is represented by those who fall into cell A of the matrix – those with a high degree of power but little motivation to do anything about the change. This is because, if the situation itself changes, their interest could be increased and this might then move them into cell B. A strategy towards these people, therefore, should be one of 'keeping them satisfied'. This means maintaining their awareness of how the change might benefit them.

Cell D of the matrix represents a different kind of problem. It might be tempting to ignore these people but, because change situations are dynamic – particularly situations of incremental change – the people categorised into cell D might begin to gain power and thus move into the more contentious group represented by cell B. Consequently, these people should be kept informed of change developments, with some effort being made to persuade them that the change might bring them benefits. However, it must be recognised that these people may be the ones who, in any radical restructuring or change in systems, lose their jobs. Containment in the short term might, therefore, be the most appropriate strategy.

The axes of the matrix in Figure 5.4 are presented in negative terms in relation to organisational change. It is equally possible to label the axes 'power to facilitate change' and 'motivation to facilitate change'. The categorisation of individuals and groups according to this framework would not necessarily be the converse of that used in Figure 5.4. Therefore, it is worth completing two matrices for a fuller analysis of power, conflict and change.

The capacity for organisations to change, both incrementally and radically, depends on the multiplicity of different interests and values which are part of organisational life. Power and conflict can be used to further the aims of change, but can also be used to resist them. However, there is some evidence (e.g. Roberts, 1986) that most organisations, both publicly and privately owned, adopt a 'mixed' approach to organisational life generally. Thus, members of organisations will share some common interests and also have some conflicting ones. The traditional concept of the use of power and conflict as 'weapons' represents only a small part of organisational life. An alternative view is that power derives from collective and co-operative action (Roberts, 1986). Care should be taken, however, as the exercise of power and the management of conflict may differ cross-culturally, as is evident from the discussion in Chapter 4.

Finally, the style and function of leadership in the sharing or withholding of power and the management of conflict are crucial for organisational life generally but, particularly, in times of change, and in particular the function of leadership. The next chapter completes Part Two of the book by addressing the role of leadership in organisations and change.

● ● ● ● Conclusions

Power and politics in organisations are analogous to modes of political rule. In countries where a Western-type democracy prevails, the dominant form of organisation has been based on the notion of rational–legal authority in the form of bureaucracies. Much of what is written today, however, urges organisational managements to adopt more organic forms of organisation where rules are more fluid and co-ordination and co-operation are seen as the way forward. A work-force operating on co-operative lines is likely to be more innovative and productive than one where individuals and groups are in constant conflict with each other.

However, as the discussion in this chapter shows, some individuals and groups have larger and more varied sources of power than others and, in the nature of a competitive society and environment, will choose to use them to influence others in desired directions. In addition, some groups are relatively powerless, not because of their diminished abilities, but as a reflection of the position occupied in the wider society. The discussion also referred to perspectives on conflict which say that some level of conflict can be constructive by contrast to other levels and types of conflict being destructive. A characterisation of power proposed by Buchanan and Badham (1999, p. 56) is helpful, as a shorthand, in remembering what power encompasses. This is:

1 Power is a *property of individuals*, defined across a number of identifiable power sources or bases, some structural, some individual, and exercised in attempts to influence others.
2 Power is a *property of relationships* between members of an organisation, identified by the extent to which some individuals believe, or do not believe, that others possess particular power bases.
3 Power is an *embedded property* of the structures, regulations, relationships and norms of the organisation, perpetuating existing routines and power inequalities.

Issues of changing power balances and the accompanying increase in conflict levels almost inevitably come to the fore in situations of organisational change. Figure 5.3 brings together statements representing many elements which contribute to the degree of power held by individuals and groups. It might be thought somewhat tedious to have to answer questionnaires, such as the one in Figure 5.3, when the excitement or the fear of change approaches. However, without some form of analysis of power distribution and the propensity for political behaviour and conflict, change managers or change agents will find themselves facing the problems of change depicted in Figure 5.2. Changing structures and cultures, as discussed in Chapters 3 and 4, will almost certainly bring with them changing power balances and bring out the propensity for people to act politically to get the best 'deal' for themselves and their close associates. Consequently, managers and others working with change ignore the politics of change at their peril.

Discussion questions and assignments

1 Drawing on the types of power suggested by different writers and researchers, give examples of each based on your organisational experiences.

2 Discuss the idea that power and powerlessness are simply two sides of the same coin.

3 Discuss the proposition: 'In times of change, conflict between individuals and groups is inevitable.'

Case example

Testing the rhetoric of empowerment

FT

Everyone says they are in favour of delegating, but truly effective proponents of the art, being creative, are rare

For decades, management gurus have preached the benefits of pushing decisions down the line, allowing those doing the work to say how resources should be used. This has been given various names – delegation, empowerment, involvement, commitment. And the logic is irrefutable. More can be achieved, people will be motivated, managers are free to think about strategy, and so on. Yet every day I am struck by the number of minor decisions blocked by head-office diktat.

As a group, managers are not good at delegating. In surveys, 70 per cent of managers rate it one of their weakest skills. And they get worse at delegating once they reach their late forties, say their staff.

Of the 30 per cent who think they are effective delegators, only one in three are thought to be good by their subordinates. The rest are rated as 'dumpers' who believe delegation means clearing their desk by dumping accumulated trivia on to everyone else.

In the past week alone, I encountered three examples of poor delegation. The first was a large European business with annual sales of £56m and 5000 staff. One 45-year-old divisional head has worked for the company for 25 years. He is totally trustworthy and very experienced but he has no control over the salaries he pays his people.

A global financial services company I visited is little better. In the past financial year, one employee, a 36-year-old woman, generated a fee income of £2m for her employer. Yet she has to seek approval from her boss in New York before hiring an assistant.

And on Monday, I attended the morning meeting of partners in a firm of accountants. The senior partner monopolised the entire meeting, while his supposed 'colleagues' sat in total silence.

I have learnt five things about delegation. First, 'empowerment' is more about rhetoric than sharing power. Second, other centralising forces, such as information systems, minimise the impact of that movement. Third, work organisations remain the least democratic and centralised power structures in most Western societies. Fourth, those who criticise bosses for not delegating are usually guilty of the offence themselves. And fifth, the poor record of delegation often reflects a mutually convenient arrangement between bosses and their direct reports.

When you observe people's career progress, it soon becomes clear why delegation is such a difficult issue. Managers in their twenties know little about delegation. Childhood hardly encourages it: schools are familiar with the practice of a pupil delegating maths homework to a friend. It is called cheating.

However, young managers are eager to control the decisions that affect them. They are usually highly critical of their boss's unwillingness to delegate.

During these early years, managers do learn something: that delegation is much easier in theory than in practice. That is partly because the effect of decisions can be dramatically different from what they anticipated. To commit a serious cock-up is a relatively simple – and frighteningly public – achievement. Because

▶

Case example *continued*

delegation is a political process, understanding its politics is essential.

Armed with these insights, managers move into their thirties and middle-management. At that moment, they realise that it becomes clear to a majority that preserving the status quo is more attractive than foisting revolution. Delegation is all very well, but exposes them to uncomfortable scrutiny. Before long, these middle-managers tend to look for havens where they can sit on resources and watch for threats.

Do not misunderstand me: many are brilliant managers of the status quo. Routine services are their forte. They centralise control, minimise delegation and insist that others follow their systems. And it works – until the all-powerful central figure leaves or retires.

Among these middle-managers are some real delegators. These people get rid of what they are doing now and badger their bosses for more power and excitement. There are notable exceptions, but most are in their thirties or early forties and will not rest. They learnt in their twenties that their future depended on delegating. They are risk-takers who delegate courageously and expect others to deliver.

But even among this small number of high-flyers, time will eventually tell. Younger managers leave to create their own excitement. Older managers become less willing to take risks. The head office tightens its grip.

Can people who are poor delegators learn to do better? Surveys by London Business School's Interpersonal Skills Programmes suggest it is not easy. We can reiterate the logic that others develop when tasks are delegated, but most managers know this already.

They ignore the advice, because it suits them and their direct reports. The bosses can continue under the illusion that they are indispensable. Their subordinates are guaranteed an easier life – after all, everyone seeks some stability. It is a mutually beneficial arrangement that kills most attempts to improve delegation.

Delegation is an individual choice that requires effort. You have to want to change the way you manage. If you do want to improve, then begin by asking some basic questions: Why do you end up with all the work? What sort of impression are you giving others about your capability for bigger things?

Learn to say 'No'. Be especially wary of 'dumpers'. After any transaction ask: 'Who ended up with the work?' There is no prize for being everyone's workhorse; it is not an admired role in work organisations.

Source: Professor John W. Hunt, *Financial Times*, 13 October 2000

Case exercise: Can you delegate

How easy is it to delegate? John Hunt, the author of this piece above, asks these questions. Can you answer them and what do the answers tell you about adopting a participative style of leadership?

Questions

If your experience in delegation has been disappointing, examine how you went about it. Was the task clear? Did you agree to a schedule? Was the person capable or did they need training? Did you delegate or abdicate? Did you regularly monitor the work and coach the person so that they knew exactly what you wanted, by when and in what format? In short, were you, in your own way, one of the 'dumpers'?

References

Adler, N. J. (1991), *International Dimensions of Organizational Behavior* (2nd edn), Belmont, CA, Wadsworth.

Avancena, J. and Saeed, A. (2000), 'Bigger role for gulf women in business recommended', *Saudi Gazette*, Middle East Newsfile, 26 May.

Barnard, C. I. (1938), *The Functions of the Executive*, Cambridge, MA, Harvard University Press.

Buchanan, D. and Badham, R. (1999), *Power, Politics and Organizational Change*, London, Sage.

Burrell, G. and Morgan, G. (1979), *Sociological Paradigms and Organisational Analysis*, London, Heinemann Educational Books Ltd.

Department for Education and Employment (2000), *Labour Market and Skills Trends 2000*, Crown Copyright, London, Department for Education and Employment.

Department of Employment Group Skills and Enterprise Network (1996), *Labour Market and Skill Trends 1996/97*, Crown Copyright, London, Department of Employment.

Financial Post (2000), 'Cracking the glass ceiling: a new girl's network of top women takes its place in Canada's business firmament: power and influence: its no longer lonely at the top for women in business', *Financial Post*, Canada, 4 March.

French, W. L. and Bell, C. H. (1990), *Organization Development. Behavioral Science Interventions for Organization Improvement*, Englewood Cliffs, NJ, Prentice Hall.

Furze, D. and Gale, C. (1996), *Interpreting Management. Exploring Change and Complexity*, London, Thompson International Press.

Gordon, J. R. (1993), *A Diagnostic Approach to Organizational Behavior*, Needham Heights, MA, Allyn & Bacon.

Gracie, S. (1998), 'In the company of women', *Management Today*, June.

Gratton, L. (2000), *Living Strategy: Putting People at the Heart of Corporate Purpose*, Hemel Hempstead, Prentice Hall.

Handy, C. (1993), *Understanding Organizations*, London, Penguin.

Hardy, C. (1994), *Managing Strategic Action. Mobilizing Change, Concepts, Readings and Cases*, London, Sage.

Hofstede, G. (1981), 'Culture and organisations', *International Studies of Management and Organizations*, Vol. X, No. 4, pp. 15–41.

Johnson, G. (1987), *Strategic Change and the Management Process*, Oxford, Blackwell.

Johnson, G. (1990), 'Managing strategic change; the role of symbolic action', *British Journal of Management*, Vol. 1, pp. 183–200.

Johnson, G. and Scholes, K. (1993), *Exploring Corporate Strategy. Text and Cases* (3rd edn), Hemel Hempstead, Prentice Hall.

Kanter, R. M. (1979), 'Power failure in management circuits', *Harvard Business Review*, July–August, pp. 65–75.

Kibazo, J. (1996), 'Flight to revival', *Financial Times*, 22 March, p. 12.

Lawrence, P. R. and Lorsch, J. W. (1969), *Organization and Environment: Managing Differentiation and Integration*, Homewood, IL, R. D. Irwin.

McClelland, D. C. (1970), 'The two faces of power', *Journal of International Affairs*, Vol. 24, No. 1, pp. 29–47.

McGregor, D. (1960), *The Human Side of Enterprise*, New York, McGraw-Hill.

McKenna, E. P. (1997) *When Work Doesn't Work Anymore: Women, Work and Identity*, New York, Hodder & Stoughton.

Maitland, A. (2000a), 'Sexual incrimination: MANAGEMENT WOMEN IN THE CITY: The macho culture of long hours and big bucks has been highlighted by two bankers' discrimination cases, but there are signs of change', *Financial Times*, 20 January.

Maitland, A. (2000b), 'Wanted: more uppity women: BOARDROOM APPOINTMENTS: Alison Maitland looks at the reasons why only 5 per cent of the directors of FTSE 100 companies are female', *Financial Times*, 7 November.

Maitland, A. (2000c), 'America's gender gap travels abroad: WOMEN IN BUSINESS: Almost half of US middle management is female but women get only 13 per cent of foreign postings', *Financial Times*, 20 October.

Mayo, E. (1933), *The Human Problems of Industrial Civilization*, New York, Macmillan.

Mills, A. J. and Murgatroyd, S. J. (1991), *Organizational Rules. A Framework for Understanding Organizational Action*, Buckingham, Open University.

Morgan, G. (1997), *Images of Organizations*, London, Sage.

Mullins, L. J. (1996), *Management and Organisational Behaviour*, London, Pitman.

Nadler, D. A. (1988), 'Concepts for the management of

organizational change', in Tushman, M. L. and Moore, W. L. (eds), *Readings in the Management of Innovation* (7th edn), New York, Ballinger Publishing Company, pp. 718–32.

Open University (1985), Units 9–10, 'Conflict', Course T244, *Managing in Organizations*, Milton Keynes, Open University.

Open University (1991), Book 8, 'Power, leadership and empowerment', Course B789, *Managing Voluntary and Non-profit Making Enterprises*, Milton Keynes, Open University.

Paton, R. (1994), 'Power in organizations', in Arson, R. and Paton, R., *Organizations, Cases, Issues, Concepts*, London, PCP.

Pfeffer, J. (1981), *Power in Organizations*, Marchfield, MA, Pitman.

Pfeffer, J. (1992), *Managing with Power: Politics and Influence in Organization*, Boston, Harvard Business Press.

Pfeffer, J. (1993), 'Understanding power in organizations', in Mabey, C. and Mayon-White, B. (eds), *Managing Change* (2nd edn), London, PCP.

PR Newswire (2000), 'Department of Commerce Acting Assistant Secretary and Director General to lead women in business development trade mission to Egypt, Kenya, South Africa', 1 October.

Robbins, S. P. (1990), *Organization Theory, Structure Design and Applications*, Englewood Cliffs, NJ, Prentice Hall.

Robbins, S. P. (1993), *Organizational Behaviour* (6th edn), Englewood Cliffs, NJ, Prentice Hall.

Robbins, S. P. (1996), *Organizational Behavior. Concepts, Controversies Applications* (7th edn), Englewood Cliffs, NJ, Prentice Hall.

Robbins, S. P. (2001), *Organizational Behavior. Concepts, Controversies Applications* (9th edn), Englewood Cliffs, NJ, Prentice Hall.

Roberts, N. C. (1986), 'Organizational power styles: collective and competitive power under varying organizational conditions', *Journal of Applied Behavioral Science*, Vol. 22, No. 4, pp. 443–58.

Ryle, J. (1996), 'Soft silverware', *The Guardian*, 26 July, p. 3.

Schelling, T. C. (1960), *The Strategy of Conflict*, Cambridge, MA, Harvard University Press.

Stacey, R. (1996), *Strategic Management and Organisational Dynamics*, London, Pitman.

Taylor, F. W. (1911), *Principles of Scientific Management*, New York, Harper & Row.

The Times Higher (1996).

Thomas, K. W. (1976), 'Conflict and conflict management', in Dunnette, M. D. (ed.), *Handbook of Industrial and Organizational Psychology*, Chicago, Rand McNally, pp. 889–935.

Thomas, K. W. (1977), 'Toward multi-dimensional values in teaching: the example of conflict behaviors', *Academy of Management Review*, Vol. 12, pp. 484–90.

Tosi, H. L., Rizzo, J. R. and Carroll, S. J. (1994), *Managing Organizational Behavior*, Oxford, Blackwell.

Weber, M. (1947), *The Theory of Social and Economic Organization*, London, Oxford University Press.

Wilson, D. C. (1992), *A Strategy of Change*, London, Routledge.

Wilson, F. M. (1995), *Organizational Behaviour and Gender*, Maidenhead, McGraw-Hill.

Yuet-Ha, M. (1996), 'Orientating values with Eastern ways', *People Management*, 25 July, pp. 28–30.

Chapter 6

The leadership of change

One of the major debates concerning organisational change relates to the role of those who lead it. This chapter addresses the issue of leading change. It includes a discussion of whether there is one style of leadership best suited to managing change or whether different styles of leadership are required according to different change situations. Issues regarding resistance to change and the identification of strategies for managing it are also recognised.

Objectives

To:

- *identify those characteristics which distinguish leadership from management*

- *discuss whether there is 'one best way' of leading or whether leadership style and behaviour should vary according to the circumstances*

- *explain the possible relationship between organisational life-cycle theories and different leadership styles and behaviours*

- *assess the compatibility of different leadership approaches with different types of change situations*

- *discuss the issue of resistance to change in terms of its implications for leading the processes of planning and implementing change.*

● ● ● ● Management and leadership

The issue of leading change links strongly to everything already discussed – both in Part One and in the three preceding chapters, which make up the remainder of Part Two of the book. For instance, the management and leadership of organisations is played out through formal organisational structures with their accompanying rules and regulations – as discussed in Chapter 3 – yet the practice of both management and leadership influences, and is influenced by, an organisation's culture, the way power is distributed and the approach taken to conflicts. Thus, management and leadership are both parts of the formal and informal aspects of organisational life, as Illustration 6.1 shows.

A distinction can, however, be made which places management rather more firmly in the context of the formal organisation with leadership more naturally associated with the informal aspects of organisations. This chapter is mainly about the role of leadership as part of organisational life and, in particular, its relationship to organisational change. However, it is useful to be clear about the relationship between management and leadership before discussing leadership in more detail.

Management can be thought of as a function that is part of an organisation's formal structure. This is evident in Mullins's (1999, p. 166) statement that he regards management as:

- taking place within a structured organisational setting and with prescribed roles;
- directed towards the attainment of aims and objectives;
- achieved through the efforts of other people; and
- using systems and procedures.

He goes on to say:

It is through the process of management that the efforts of members of the organisation are co-ordinated, directed and guided towards the achievement of organisational goals. Man-

---

Illustration 6.1

Tough transition for hard-bitten banker

The drive and passion which James Wolfensohn has brought to his job as World Bank president, coupled with his skills as a lawyer and banker, make the former Australian air force pilot and Olympic fencer a formidable figure. Nine months into the job he needs all these qualities and more if he is to restore drive, purpose, and confidence to an institution which many believe has lost its way.

The Bank's record in Africa – its most formidable challenge – has been mixed at best. Accused of undue secrecy and poor performance by many of its projects, it is seen as cumbersome, bureaucratic and sometimes aloof from other development bodies.

Mr Wolfensohn, 62, a naturalised US citizen, has already made a mark on the Bank, forging closer links with non-governmental organisations as well as the private sector. But it has been a difficult transition for him – from tough-spoken hard-bitten international investment banker, used to getting his way, to a role which requires him to be a diplomat, personnel manager, and catalyst for change in an organisation as large as the Bank and still so set in its ways.

Source: Holman, M. and Waldmeir, P. (1996), 'World Bank chief's cry from the heart', *Financial Times*, 29 March, p. 4.

agement is therefore the cornerstone of organisational effectiveness, and is concerned with arrangements for the carrying out of organisational processes and the execution of work.

This definition draws on the idea that management is a particular function, which is embedded in the organisational structure and which involves a number of different kinds of activities which are, nevertheless, associated with each other. Thus, Fayol (1949) proposed five elements of management – planning, organising, commanding, co-ordinating, and controlling – which can be seen to relate to formal organisational systems.

Other writers and researchers have concentrated more on the *roles* that managers play, that is, what managers do. For instance, Illustration 6.2 describes the

---

Illustration 6.2

Mintzberg's managerial roles

Figurehead
In the figurehead role, the manager acts as the representative or symbol of the organisation. Examples of this role are attending meetings on behalf of the organisation, giving out long-service awards, or appearing on 'platforms' as a representative of local business.

Leader
The manager, as leader, is concerned with interpersonal relationships, what motivates his or her staff and what needs they might have.

Liaison
The liaison role emphasises the network of contacts with others in and outside the organisation. Liaising with others allows the manager to collect useful information. In the liaison role, a manager might belong to a professional institution.

Monitor
Monitoring the environment to keep informed of competitors' activities, new legislation, changes in the market and so on, are all examples of a manager's monitoring role.

Disseminator
The role of disseminator includes keeping staff and others within the organisation informed. This could be done in a variety of written and spoken forms and may be on a one-to-one basis or through group meetings.

Spokesperson
As spokesperson, the manager gives information to others outside the organisation. He or she speaks on behalf of the organisation, for instance on the organisation's policies and activities.

Entrepreneur
The role of entrepreneur is associated with innovation and change. It includes the design and implementation of different types of change from small-scale job redesign to large-scale organisational restructuring depending on the level of the manager concerned.

Disturbance handler
The manager in this role acts to solve problems that arise, often unexpectedly. Thus, managing to intervene in a conflict situation or find a solution to a machine breakdown are examples of this role.

Resource allocator
The majority of managers control some kind of resource (e.g. money, labour, time) which they can use, or allocate, at their discretion. Allocating money according to budgets is one aspect of this role. Other possibilities are the scheduling of subordinates' work and allocating equipment.

Negotiator
All managers have to play the role of negotiator when they debate who will do some things and who will do others. Coming to agreements on the scope of people's jobs and their pay are examples of negotiating.

Source: Based on Mintzberg, H. (1979), *The Nature of Managerial Work* (Englewood Cliffs, NJ, Prentice Hall).

ten roles, which Mintzberg (1979) suggested as a result of his study of chief executive officers in both small and large organisations.

Mintzberg (1979) grouped managerial roles into three sets: interpersonal roles (figurehead, leader, liaison); informational roles (monitor, disseminator, spokesman); decisional roles (entrepreneur, disturbance handler, resource allocator, negotiator). An examination of these categories and the roles within them highlights the ambiguity of the relationship between management and leadership. As this framework shows, leadership is just one aspect of a manager's job, a view that is echoed by Handy's (1993) contention that leading (which he takes to include the roles of figurehead, leader and liaison) is mostly concerned with the interpersonal aspects of a manager's activities. Consequently, although a manager must also be a leader, a leader does not always have to be a manager. Kotter (1990), as shown in Illustration 6.3, gives a useful summary of the differences between leading and managing.

Illustration 6.3

Comparing management and leadership

	Management	Leadership
Creating an agenda	Planning and Budgeting – establishing detailed steps and timetables for achieving needed results, and then allocating the resources necessary to make that happen	Establishing Direction – developing a vision of the future, often the distant future, and strategies for producing the changes needed to achieve that vision
Developing a human network for achieving the agenda	Organizing and Staffing – establishing some structure for accomplishing plan requirements, staffing that structure with individuals, delegating responsibility and authority for carrying out the plan, providing policies and procedures to help guide people, and creating methods or systems to monitor implementation	Aligning People – communicating the direction by words and deeds to all those whose cooperation may be needed so as to influence the creation of teams and coalitions that understand the vision and strategies, and accept their validity
Execution	Controlling and Problem Solving – monitoring results vs. plan in some detail, identifying deviations, and then planning and organizing to solve these problems	Motivating and Inspiring – energizing people to overcome major political, bureaucratic, and resource barriers to change by satisfying very basic, but often unfulfilled, human needs
Outcomes	Produces a degree of predictability and order, and has the potential of consistently producing key results expected by various stakeholders (e.g. for customers, always being on time; for stockholders, being on budget)	Produces change, often to a dramatic degree, and has the potential of producing extremely useful change (e.g. new products that customers want, new approaches to labor relations that help make a firm more competitive)

Source: Reprinted with the permission of The Free Press, a division of Simon & Schuster, from *A Force for Change: How Leadership Differs from Management* by John P. Kotter. Copyright © 1990 by John P. Kotter Inc.

Both Mintzberg's and Kotter's distinctions between leadership and management agree with Mullins's (1999) conclusion that management is concerned with activities within the formal structure and goals of the organisation, while leadership focuses more on interpersonal behaviour in a broader context. His statement (p. 254) that 'leadership does not necessarily take place within the hierarchical structure of the organisation' typifies this view. To support this contention, he refers to Watson's (1983) 7-S organisational framework of: strategy, structure, systems, style, staff, skills and superordinate (or shared) goals. Based on this, Watson maintains that management is more concerned with strategy, structure and systems, while leadership is more concerned with what he calls the 'soft' Ss of: style, staff, skills and shared goals. Leadership, then, is concerned with establishing shared visions and goals; with interpersonal relationships and communication; and with motivation and getting the best out of people. Basically, leadership is about influencing others in pursuit of the achievement of organisational goals.

However, as Smith (1991) points out, rather than being about absolute influence, leadership is about relative influence, in that 'a leader is someone who has more influence over others than they have over him or her' (p. 207). This introduces the idea of the leader and the *group*, thus implying the importance of *followers*. The discussion that follows shows that other factors also influence people's perception of what constitutes 'good leadership'. It will become evident also that there is no universally agreed view as to what this is. There are, however, a number of approaches which offer ways to understanding leadership and its relationship to organisational performance and organisational change.

● ● ● ● Approaches to leadership

There is a range of theories which purport to explain what makes a person a good and effective leader. These can be put into two broad categories. The first includes those theories which contend that there is 'one best way' of exercising leadership and, therefore, that there is a particular set of characteristics which 'good' leaders should possess. The second category says the opposite, that there is no one best way, but a range of leadership styles which should be applied differentially according to the situation in which leadership is required.

The 'one best way' to lead

Traits of leadership

The first of the approaches to leadership under this heading is not really a theory of *how* to lead. It is more a theory of what leaders should be like, in other words what traits (e.g. physical and personality characteristics, skills and abilities and social factors such as interpersonal skills, sociability and socio-economic position) are indicative of a successful leader. However, a survey of the research on this issue shows that there is a degree of confusion as to whether there are certain personality and other characteristics which, when present, 'fit' a person to be a leader. Early research (Mann, 1959; Stodgill, 1948) came to the conclusion that there were few relationships between the traits possessed by leaders and their performance. The notion of 'born to lead' did not hold up under scrutiny. However, more recent studies reveal stronger evidence of an identifiable set of personality and cognitive traits which are said to characterise successful leaders.

The first of these is a meta-analysis (one which surveys and brings together the results of other studies) carried out by Lord, De Vader and Alliger in 1986 which concluded that there could be six traits which distinguish successful leaders from others. These are:

- intelligence
- having an extrovert personality
- dominance
- masculinity
- conservatism
- being better adjusted than non-leaders.

A few years later, Kirkpatrick and Locke (1991) also surveyed existing leadership studies and suggested their own list of six leadership traits, which are:

- drive (achievement, ambition, energy, tenacity, initiative)
- leadership motivation (personalised or socialised)
- honesty and integrity
- self-confidence (including emotional stability)
- cognitive ability (the ability to marshal and interpret a wide variety of information)
- knowledge of the business.

In 1996, Dulewicz and Herbert (1996) reported on their original research on a sample of 72 managers who, on the basis of several indicators of success, could be identified as either 'high-flyers or low-flyers'. What these two researchers did was to administer two different personality tests to these managers to determine what characteristics differentiated the high-flyers. The results showed that the high-flyers scored higher than the low-flyers on the following:

- risk-taking
- assertiveness and decisiveness
- achievement
- motivation
- competitiveness.

They also showed exceptional managerial skills of:

- planning and organising
- managing staff
- motivating others.

Activity 6.1   *Read Illustration 6.1 again. Which of the leadership traits do you think James Wolfensohn possesses? Do you think the description 'hard-bitten' has positive or negative connotations in this context? Justify your conclusions.*

Look in newspapers and magazines such as Management Today *and* People Management *for articles on top managers, business leaders or managers and leaders in the business of sport. See if you can construct your own list of leadership traits which, according to what is said in the accounts, indicate a successful leader. How does your list compare with those of Lord and his colleagues, Kirkpatrick and Locke and Dulewicz and Herbert? How far are you convinced that your or others' lists are valid in this respect? How would you design a piece of research to test trait theories of leadership?*

It is interesting to compare and contrast these three lists. For instance, the trait of intelligence comes up in the first two studies mentioned and this is given further confirmation in Fiedler's (1989) Cognitive Resource Utilisation Theory (CRUT). This says that, under normal circumstances, a leader's intelligence will add crucially to his or her success as a leader. Consequently, a leader's intelligence is an important resource for any group. However, as Fiedler points out, there are some situations which can prevent leaders using the intelligence they possess – for instance, poor relations with their boss, poor interpersonal relationships and a non-directive style. Therefore, intelligence on its own is not sufficient to guarantee a successful leader. The characteristics of dominance (Lord, De Vader and Alliger, 1986), drive and self-confidence (Kirkpatrick and Locke, 1991) and almost all the characteristics listed by Dulewicz and Herbert (1996, p. 16) are required to support the use of a leader's cognitive capacities. What is particularly relevant about Dulewicz and Herbert's list, in comparison to the other two, is the addition of the characteristic of risk taking which is probably most relevant in times of organisational change. Two statements from their article make this point:

> Our most successful general managers are also willing to take risks rather than seek comfort in familiar situations; are determined to see things through to completion; set stretching targets for themselves and others; and are highly competitive and poor losers.
> … the competencies required of high-flyers will tend to concentrate on the ability to cope with change and uncertainty and the promotion of innovation.

The concept of 'innovation' associated as it is with 'creative thinking' (*see* Henry, 1991 and Henry and Walker, 1991), which appears in the latter statement, brings in a leadership trait which does not appear in the three lists mentioned earlier. Innovation is a process which finds expression in much of the literature relating to organisational behaviour in environments responding to strong triggers for change. It implies a set of leadership characteristics, which are related more to what is commonly known as 'right-brain' thinking as opposed to 'left-brain' thinking; that is, a preference for thinking and decision making which uses intuition in addition to, and just as much as, reason and logic. Lank and Lank (1995, p. 19) define intuition as:

a brain skill; operating largely from the right hemisphere; capable of entering awareness at physical, emotional and mental levels; whose sources are the subconscious, unconscious and/or superconscious; and which enters consciousness without rational thought or careful analysis and quantitative calculation.

Bennett III (1998, p. 590) links intuition to tacit knowledge which he conceptualises as:

idiosyncratic, subjective, highly individualised store of knowledge and practical know-how gathered through years of experience and direct interaction within a domain.

All three of these writers contrast intuition (or intuitive processing) and decision making with analytical, rational, logical thinking and decision making. They argue that, particularly in situations of uncertainty and turbulence (that is situations which in Chapter 2 were characterised as ill-structured, messy or soft), intuition is just as important for decision making as more explicit decision making processes based on the collection of 'facts' and logical reasoning. However, both Lank and Lank's and Bennett III's articles are theoretical rather than empirically based.

By contrast, Andersen (2000) offers a good argument based on an empirical study of 33 managers working in an organisation in the service sector in Sweden. Although a small study, one interesting aspect of Andersen's research is the method of identification of the managers' decision-making styles. For this, he used Keegan's Type Indicator (KTI) which measures preferences in terms of the way issues and problems are perceived and the way decisions about them are made. Based on the theories of Jung (1976), individuals use either *sensing* (respect for facts and information) or *intuition* (respect for possibilities and tacit knowledge and reasoning) for perceiving issues associated with problems and either *thinking* (respect for analysis, particularity, precision and logic) or *feeling* (based on their own values, but with respect for other people's feelings and emotions) for making judgements about what to do. Completion of the KTI identifies an individual as preferring *either* sensing *or* intuition *and* thinking *or* feeling to guide their behaviour in terms of decision making. What is more, within each pair of preferences (sensing and thinking; sensing and feeling; intuition and thinking; intuition and feeling) one will be 'dominant' and the other 'auxiliary'.

Using a fairly robust method of measuring leadership effectiveness – what the company termed 'gross profit margin' – Andersen found that the managers with dominant intuition combined with auxiliary thinking decision-making styles (what they term a 'creative-innovative' decision-making style) were the more effective ones. He concludes:

This study suggests that intuition as the dominant decision-making function is related to organisational effectiveness. The focus on future opportunities and threats as well as actions to preserve flexibility and handle uncertainty appears to be the reason why intuition in managers is effective.

This conclusion must remain a possibility only, given the limited nature of this research. However, other writers, not only academics (see Bunting's (2000) newspaper article 'Rewiring our brains' and the Website of the Institute of Personnel

Development's magazine *People Management* at www.peoplemanagement.co.uk/ women.htm), have coined the phrase 'the feminisation of business leadership' to extol the virtues of intuition as expressed more in the way female managers operate compared to what is seen as the more traditionalist 'command and control' styles of male managers. Pollock (2000, p. 19) describes how: 'Companies are turning to music, storytelling, visual art and even comedy in order to develop their people, engender creativity in the workplace and enhance their corporate image.' She quotes Nicholas Janni, teacher at the Royal Academy of Dramatic Art and visiting fellow at the Cranfield School of Management, in saying:

> The old style of management – control, protect and know everything – is no longer effective. That's a very masculine thing, which is not wrong, but it has big limitations. Arts-based learning is about using different parts of your brain. ...we're talking about using your imagination. This relates to what could be, as opposed to knowledge, which is limited to what is.

This discussion of the perceived need for managers to use intuition, as well as the more deliberately applied cognitive skills of reasoning and logic, can be compared to another trait which is being discussed as necessary for leaders to be successful. According to Goleman (1998, p. 93), who is reckoned to have developed the concept, '*Emotional intelligence* is the sine qua non of leadership' [author's italics]. On the basis of an examination of competency models in 188, mostly large, global companies, Goleman claims to have found which personal capabilities drove outstanding performance in these organisations. He grouped the capabilities into three categories: purely technical skills, cognitive abilities and competencies demonstrating emotional intelligence which he defines as having the five components of: self-awareness; self-regulation; motivation; empathy; social skills. While not decrying the need for leaders to have technical skills (such as accounting and business planning) and cognitive capabilities (such as analytical reasoning), he claims these are 'threshold capabilities'; that is, while being *necessary* to successful leadership they are not *sufficient* without the addition of emotional intelligence.

An examination of the components of emotional intelligence, however, might suggest that there is little new in these in terms of the psychological and social characteristics of individuals defined by psychologists throughout the ages. As evidence of this is a closely argued article by Woodruffe (2000) who draws on other people's work, as well as his own detailed arguments, to rebut the claim that emotional intelligence adds anything more to what is already known about the behaviours and competences of leaders and others. What Woodruffe does concede is that EI (as it is now known) has popularised the need for leaders to exhibit these capabilities in the service of bringing greater effectiveness to their management of people and the tasks they are involved in. This may be no bad thing if it encourages managers and leaders at all levels in organisations to pay attention to the need to use what Beer and Nohria (2000) call 'soft' *as well as* 'hard' approaches to leading organisational change. In addition, looking over the lists of leadership traits identified earlier in the chapter, only one of the components of emotional intelligence appears there.

Activity 6.2 *Think of two leaders you know, or have known, well. One should be a person whom you judged to be successful as a leader and the other quite the opposite – that is, unsuccessful. On the following scales, indicate the extent to which each person possesses that particular trait.*

If possible, ask some other colleagues to carry out the same activity.

	Very high	High	Average	Low	Very low
Need to achieve					
Need for power					
Leadership motivation					
Self-confidence					
Honesty and integrity					
Intelligence					
Knowledge of the business					
Assertiveness and decisiveness					
Competitiveness					
Emotional stability					
Extrovert personality					
Willingness to take risks					
Intuition and use of tacit knowledge					
Self-awareness					
Self-regulation					
Empathy					
Social skills					

From your results, what conclusions can you form as to whether successful leaders possess some traits which others do not? Compare your results with those discussed in the literature and with other people's views.

The results from doing Activity 6.2 are only an indication of the applicability of trait theories of leadership – after all, if you did this on your own, you have a sample of only two leaders! These theories do, however, appear to offer something in relation to the type of person best suited to lead others.

This idea certainly appears to find favour in the many descriptions of supposed leaders of change – what Reich (1991) calls 'the entrepreneurial hero'. This notion that there are some people who are, characteristically, leadership material is supported by implication when Kanter (1991, p. 54) says: 'I discovered the skills of change masters [by which she means those successfully bringing about change] by researching hundreds of managers across more than a half-dozen industries. I put change-master skills in two categories: first, the personal or individual skills and second, the interpersonal ones, how the person manages others.' She goes on to identify what she calls 'kaleidoscope thinking' as well as the ability to communicate visions, and be persistent. Coalition building and working through teams are aspects of her second category of skills. Other researchers have come to similar conclusions about the nature of leadership. For instance, Westley and Mintzberg (1989) claim to have identified a range of what they term 'salient capacities' of five well-known leaders (Edwin Land, Steven Jobs, Rene Levesque, Lee Iacocca, Jan Carlzon). The capacities of imagination, sagacity and foresight are prominent among them.

Yet Reich (1991) warns against the idea of the leader as hero with some set of hero-like characteristics. The concept of successful leadership is seen as more complex than this, as is evident in the title of Reich's article, 'The team as hero'. In support of Reich is the argument of Landrum, Howell and Paris (2000) that, while many writers claim that 'strong' (by which they generally mean charismatic) leadership is what is required for strategic and 'turnaround' change, there is also a 'dark side' to charismatic leaders. These writers comment that charismatic leaders can lead followers in directions unhelpful to the organisation. They also point out a possible propensity for narcissism and quote the words of Post (1986, p. 679) who stated that the charismatic leader: 'Requires a continuing flow of admiration from his audience in order to nourish his famished self. Central to his ability to elicit that admiration is his ability to convey a sense of grandeur, omnipotence, and strength.' Landrum *et al.* refer to *unethical* charismatic leaders who are controlling, manipulative and self-promoting – characteristics which can jeopardise and even sabotage the turnaround efforts of the organisation. To mitigate these possibilities and overcome the difficulties of leaders being all things to all people and situations, Landrum *et al.* argue for a team approach to designing and implementing strategic change, which incidentally is not unusual in more 'collective' societies (*see* Chapter 5), such as are found in the Far East.

Having said this, Western thinking is still more likely to veer towards the idea that there is still one best way to lead. However, instead of trying to find a set of characteristics to describe *what* a successful leader is, these ideas concentrate more on *how* a leader ought to *behave* in order to be successful.

Leadership behaviour

Bass (1990) lists no fewer than 29 different systems for classifying leadership behaviour. However, Wright (1996), in commenting on this, maintains that many of the concepts are so similar that four main leadership styles of behaviour can be identified. These are (p. 36):

1 *Concern for task.* The extent to which the leader emphasises high levels of productivity, organises and defines group activities in relation to the group's

task objectives and so on. (Also called concern for production, production-centred, task-oriented and task-centred leadership.)

2 *Concern for people.* The extent to which the leader is concerned about his or her subordinates as people – their needs, interests, problems, development etc. – rather than simply treating them as units of production. (Also called person-centred, person-oriented and employee-centred leadership.)

3 *Directive leadership.* The extent to which the leader makes all the decisions concerning group activities him- or herself and expects subordinates simply to follow instructions. (Also called authoritarian or autocratic leadership.)

4 *Participative leadership.* The extent to which the leader shares decision making concerning group activities with subordinates. (Also called democratic leadership.)

Given this classification of leadership style, it might be supposed that there are differences in the effects of using one style rather than another. However, Wright's review of a range of studies attempting to link leadership style with high performance and subordinate satisfaction found little evidence of a single style. Consequently, no one style seemed to emerge as the most appropriate in all situations and where, for instance, a participative leadership style was related to high performance and satisfaction of subordinates, it was not clear whether the leader's style was the causal variable or vice versa. Given this, it is interesting to note that two famous studies of leadership (Likert, 1961; Stodgill and Coons, 1957), known respectively as the University of Michigan studies and the Ohio State studies, separately identified two independent dimensions of leadership which were, in essence, a combination of the four types of behaviour described earlier. The Ohio researchers named these 'consideration' and 'initiating structure'.

Consideration is the degree to which a leader builds trust and mutual respect with subordinates, shows respect for their ideas and concern for their well-being. This dimension is linked to a participative, human relations approach to leadership. It therefore combines the 'concern for people' and 'participative leadership' styles identified by Wright.

Initiating structure is the degree to which a leader defines and structures his or her own role and the interactions within the group, towards the attainment of formal goals. It has elements of both the 'directive leadership' and 'concern for tasks' styles described earlier.

The University of Michigan researchers used the terms employee-centred and production-centred leadership for these dimensions but they were virtually the same in description to those of the Ohio researchers. The main point about these dimensions is that, because they are deemed to be independent of each other, a leader's behaviour can be categorised in four different ways. Thus, leaders can be:

- high on consideration and high on initiating structure
- high on consideration and low on initiating structure
- low on consideration and low on initiating structure
- low on consideration and high on initiating structure.

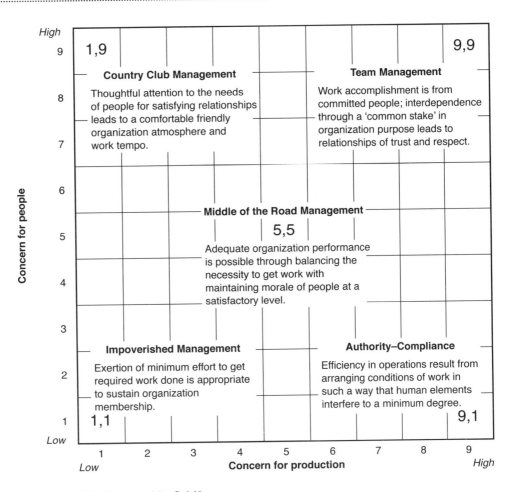

Figure 6.1 The leadership Grid®

Source: Blake, R. and McCanse, A. A. (1991), *Leadership Dilemmas: Grid Solutions* (Houston, TX, Gulf Publishing, p. 29). Copyright © 1991 by Robert R. Blake and the Estate of Jane S. Mouton, Austin, Texas. Used with permission. All rights reserved. The Grid® designation is the property of Scientific Methods Inc. and is used here with permission.

The relationship of these two-dimensional theories to the idea of a 'one best way' of leading manifests itself most clearly in the way Blake and Mouton (1964) built on these concepts to propose that the most effective leadership style is one which is high on both dimensions. Figure 6.1 gives the positions of five different leadership styles on a later version of Blake and Mouton's managerial grid – now called the 'Leadership Grid' (Blake and McCanse, 1991).

The different combinations of concern for people and concern for production set out in Figure 6.1 result in different combinations of leadership characteristics as follows.

The 9,1 Authority–Compliance leader has a high concern for the task and little concern for people, emphasising efficiency and the organisation's needs at the expense of the needs of people. There is a belief that production can only be achieved if people are closely supervised and controlled. According to Blake and McCanse (p. 55): 'A Grid style like 9,1 is unlikely to elicit the cooperation, involvement, or commitment of those who are expected to complete the task.'

The 1,9 Country Club leadership style is based on the assumption that productivity will follow if the needs of people are satisfied. These leaders believe that people cannot be pressured into doing things – they need to be well treated to get them to perform well. According to Blake and McCanse, however, this leadership style, although encouraging friendly and pleasant relationships, produces results where productivity suffers. Creativity and innovation are undermined because of the possible conflict which might surface as a result of challenges to existing ways of doing things.

The 1,1 Impoverished Management or laissez-faire leadership style is characterised by minimum concern for both production and the needs of people. The 1,1 leader's desire is to remain as uninvolved as possible with other people, compatible with fulfilling the requirements of the job and sustaining organisation membership. Conflict is deliberately avoided by remaining neutral on most contentious issues.

The 5,5 Middle of the Road leadership style is concerned with moderate rather than high performance. This results from a desire to balance the contradiction between production and people's needs through compromising in the face of conflict. It includes a willingness to yield on some points in order to gain on others. This is a team-oriented style, but because negativity is not tolerated, complacency can set in and the team can lose sight of reality.

The 9,9 style of Team Management incorporates high concern for production with a high concern for people. In contrast to the 5,5 leadership style which assumes an inherent contradiction between production and people, the 9,9 leadership style assumes that concern for both is necessary and that they do not inherently contradict each other. There is an emphasis on working as a team which recognises the interdependence of people with each other, together with the task to be done. Relationships between people are based on mutual trust and respect, and work is assumed to be accomplished only if employees are committed to the task, team and organisation.

Activity 6.3   *Read the following extract from an article about Mrs Isabella Beeton, famous for her book on household management which was written in 1859.*

Mrs Beeton: management guru

Mrs Beeton's approach can be summarised in three principles, which would certainly appear in most modern management texts: setting an example and giving clear guidance to staff; controlling the finances; applying the benefits of order and method in all management activities.

An example to staff
(In her own words)
'Early rising is one of the most essential qualities ... as it is not only the parent of health but of other innumerable advantages. Indeed when a mistress is an early riser, it is almost certain that

Activity 6.3 *continued*

her house will be orderly and well managed. On the contrary, if she remain in bed till a late hour, then the domestics, who … invariably partake somewhat of their mistress's character, will surely become sluggards.'

'Good Temper should be cultivated … Every head of a household should strive to be cheerful, and should never fail to show a deep interest in all that appertains to the well-being of those who claim the protection of her roof.'

'The Treatment of Servants is of the highest possible moment … If they perceive that the mistress's conduct is regulated by high and correct principles, they will not fail to respect her. If, also, a benevolent desire is shown to promote their comfort, at the same time that a steady performance of their duty is enacted, then their respect will not be unmingled with affection, and they will be still more solicitous to continue to deserve her favour.'

Source: Wensley, R. (1996), 'Mrs Beeton: management guru', *Financial Times*, 26 April, p. 15.

The article continues to quote from Mrs Beeton's book on the need to keep 'a housekeeping account-book … punctually and precisely'. On the issue of order and method she says: 'Cleanliness, punctuality, order and method are essentials in the character of a good housekeeper.'

Can you place Mrs Beeton on the Leadership Grid of Blake and McCanse? Justify your positioning.

The Leadership Grid assumes that there is one best style of leadership, that of the 9,9 'Team Management' style – regardless of the situation.

The Leadership Grid is a simplified way of categorising different aspects of leadership behaviour. There are, however, other categories of leadership behaviour which overlap with these, but which are more detailed in their descriptions; for instance, the 'powers of the person' discussed in an article by Useem (1996) who says that these kinds of behaviours transcend those of particular value to particular situations. These are:

- challenging the process
- searching for opportunities
- experimenting
- inspiring a shared vision
- envisioning a future
- enlisting others
- enabling others to act
- strengthening others
- fostering collaboration
- modelling the way
- setting an example
- celebrating accomplishments
- recognising contributions.

In addition to these, Useem, drawing on a study of 48 firms among the Fortune 500 largest US manufacturers, gives the following behaviours as characterising the most successful chief executive officers:

- being visionary
- showing strong confidence in self and others
- communicating high-performance expectations and standards
- personally exemplifying the firm's vision, values and standards
- demonstrating personal sacrifice, determination, persistence and courage.

This is yet another study which implies that there are certain desirable leadership qualities whatever the situation. What is important about this last list, however, is that these are behaviours which can be likened to those actions said to be characteristic of *transformational* leadership as compared to the less visionary styles of leadership associated with *transactional* leadership (*see* Illustration 6.4) and, therefore, more likely to be effective in times of change.

Illustration 6.4 compares and contrasts transactional and transformational leadership. The essential differences have been neatly summarised by Tichy and Ulrich (1984, p. 60) as follows:

> Where transactional managers make only minor adjustments in the organisation's mission, structure, and human resource management, transformational leaders not only make major changes in these three areas but they also evoke fundamental changes in the basic political and cultural systems of the organisation. The revamping of the political and cultural systems is what most distinguishes the transformational leader from the transactional one.

According to Bass (1990), transactional leaders are those who initiate structure and are considerate to employees – they might, therefore, be considered to be 9,9 leaders. However, transformational leadership goes beyond this as confirmed by Robbins

---

Illustration 6.4

Transactional and transformational leaders

Transactional leader
- *Contingent reward*: contracts exchange of rewards for effort, promises rewards for good performance, recognises accomplishments.
- *Management by exception (active)*: watches and searches for deviations from rules and standards, takes corrective action.
- *Management by exception (passive)*: intervenes only if standards are not met.
- *Laissez-faire*: abdicates responsibilities, avoids making decisions.

Transformational leader
- *Charisma*: provides vision and sense of mission, instills pride, gains respect and trust.
- *Inspiration*: communicates high expectations, uses symbols to focus efforts, expresses important purposes in simple ways.
- *Intellectual stimulation*: promotes intelligence, rationality and careful problem solving.
- *Individualised consideration*: gives personal attention, treats each employee individually, coaches, advises.

Source: Bass, B. M. (1990), 'From transactional to transformational leadership: learning to share the vision', *Organizational Dynamics*, Winter, p. 22.

(2001, p. 200) who says: 'Transformational leadership is built *on top of* transactional leadership – it produces levels of subordinate effort and performance that go beyond what would occur with a transactional approach alone.' The relationship between transformational leadership and team and organisational performance is discussed by Tichy and Ulrich through reference to some well-known leaders of American corporations, the conclusion being that transformational leaders are those most likely to 'revitalise organisations ... transform the organisations and head them down new tracks' (p. 60). Robbins quotes evidence from studies with American, Canadian and German military officers as well as managers at Federal Express to support the superiority of transformational leadership over transactional leadership in terms of being correlated with lower turnover rates, higher productivity and higher employee satisfaction. What is more, the effects of transformational leadership on subordinates is confirmed in Behling and McFillen's (1996) model of charismatic/transformational leadership where the leader's behaviour is said to give rise to inspiration, awe and empowerment in the followers, resulting in exceptionally high effort, exceptionally high commitment and willingness to take risks.

It would appear that transformational leadership behaviours add to the two dimensions of leadership identified in both the Ohio State and Michigan University studies. This view is supported by the results of work by researchers in Finland and Sweden (Ekvall and Arvonen, 1991; Lindell and Rosenqvist, 1992a, 1992b) which shows early evidence of a third dimension related to development-oriented leader behaviour – in other words, behaviour related specifically to leadership in an organisational change context. What is not clear is whether transformational leadership is the most recent leadership behaviour to be recommended whatever the circumstances or whether it is simply an additional leadership behaviour to be used in situations of radical change. Tichy and Ulrich (1984) and Bass (1990) seem to argue that transformational leadership is the best way to lead whatever the circumstances. Indeed, Bass (1990, p. 20) goes so far as to say that transactional leadership is, in many instances, 'a prescription for mediocrity', arguing that only transformational leadership can make a difference in an organisation's performance at all levels. By contrast, Ekvall and Arvonen and Lindell and Rosenqvist seem to suggest that behaviours approaching transformational leadership may be most appropriate in conditions of change.

The question remains, therefore, as to whether one particular way of leading can be appropriate regardless of the stage of development of an organisation, the environment in which it exists or the people who work in it; or whether different leadership styles and behaviours are required according to the different situations prevailing as organisations' environments change, along with associated changes in strategy and functioning.

Contingency approaches to leadership

From the discussion so far, it is clear that trait and simple behavioural theories of leadership have some support. However, as Figure 6.2 shows, there are many

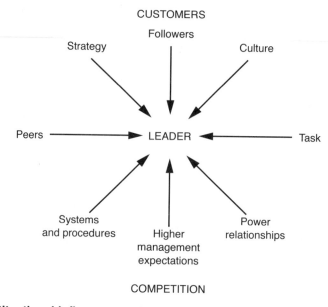

Figure 6.2 Situational influences on leadership effectiveness

things which can influence organisational outcomes in addition to those associated with a leader's qualities and behaviour.

Therefore, in contrast to theories of leadership which argue for a universal view of what traits and/or behaviours leaders should have, other theories maintain that a leader's behaviour should be contingent upon the organisational situation prevailing.

Behaviour along a continuum

One of the best-known theories of leadership, which takes into account situational factors, is that of Tannenbaum and Schmidt (1973) which arranges leadership behaviour along a continuum not dissimilar to the 'directive' and 'participative' leadership styles which contribute to the dimensions of the Ohio State and Michigan studies discussed previously.

At the 'boss-centred leadership' extreme, which assumes a high level of leader power, leaders *tell* subordinates what to do. At the other, 'subordinate-centred leadership' extreme, leaders and subordinates *jointly* make decisions. Moving along the continuum between these two positions, from the area of greatest freedom for leaders to the area of greatest freedom for subordinates, the leadership style becomes increasingly less authoritative and more participative. To this extent, the styles of leadership suggested are little different from those identified by the Ohio State and Michigan University studies, except in the degree of independence of the dimensions. What is different from the 'one best way' theories is that Tannenbaum and Schmidt do not support one preferred leadership style. On the contrary, they suggest that a leader should move along the continuum, selecting the style that is most appropriate to the situation prevailing, for which they use a threefold categorisation according to the 'forces' which they say should determine the style of leadership to use. These three forces are in the manager, in the subordinate and in the situation.

- *Forces in the manager.* Each manager will have his or her own combination of personality characteristics, skills and knowledge, values and attitudes which predisposes the adoption of one particular style of leadership or another.
- *Forces in the subordinate.* Subordinates vary in their characteristics such as the degree of support needed, experience in and knowledge of the work, commitment to organisational goals, expectations as to how leaders will behave, previous experience of different leadership styles. As Smith (1991, p. 212) says: 'Inexperienced, immature and uncommitted subordinates may force even the most participative manager to adopt an autocratic, telling, style.'
- *Forces in the situation.* These divide into two categories: first, the nature of the task or problem itself and, second, the general context in which the leadership activity takes place. This can include: the time available to make a decision, the organisational culture and power balances between the different participants in the situation and general opportunities and constraints arising from organisational structures and processes as well as environmental and societal influences. A simple example is that should a fire break out (a well-defined problem with an objective criterion of success), an appropriate leadership style would *not* be to call a meeting to discuss what should be done. A more relevant example is the case of new government regulations which must be adhered to and over which there is little opportunity for flexibility in implementation. In some cases, changes in the organisational environment are so sudden and severe that a more authoritative leadership style is the only one relevant to the situation. In other cases, the prevailing organisational structure and culture may force a more participative style of leadership. Illustration 6.5 is an example of the application of these concepts to leadership in a situation facing the Beautiful Buildings Company (BB Company) in one of its ventures to build luxury apartments in Japan.

Illustration 6.5

Little room to manoeuvre

Jayne was pleased that she had been put in charge of BB Company's latest building venture, the second of its kind to take place in Japan. She had limited experience of working in this country but had spent some time talking to staff working on the other Japanese site about how to approach the management of those employed on the building works. She knew, therefore, that there were a number of factors she would need to take into account when deciding on her own leadership approach.

The diagram illustrates the situation Jayne faced.

▶

Illustration 6.5 *continued*

	Directive style of leadership	Participative style of leadership

Jayne's preferences

Subordinates' preferences

Task structure

Context

The length of rules on the diagram indicate the degrees of freedom available to Jayne in the situation which faced her. The line indicating her own leadership style shows her preferences were for a more consultative/ participative style which she had been accustomed to using with staff in Britain. However, most of the Japanese employees were accustomed to a more formal management–subordinate relationship and were likely to work in this type of relationship, given the fact that Jayne was a woman. The task of building the apartments was complex but, in many ways, defined. Much of what was required had been worked out beforehand. However, as with all building works, unknown factors such as the weather and possible unexpected problems with the ground, let alone any industrial relations problems which could arise, contributed to there being certain unstructured elements to the situation. If any two of these factors combined, some extensive negotiations might need to be held between management and workers or their representatives. The BB Company prided itself on its care for its workers, so the organisational context was one which veered more towards a human-relations type of approach than an authoritarian one. Even so, profit was profit and the industry was a very competitive one. The organisation did not want anything to go wrong.

What the diagram shows is that Jayne has not much room for manoeuvre in deciding what approach to take as a leader in this situation. The overlap between all the forces is not large. If she cannot influence any of the factors associated with the subordinates, the task and the context, she must make sure to adopt a leadership style which tends towards the directive end of her preferences.

Fiedler's contingency model of leadership

The task-oriented/people-oriented continuum of leadership styles is also the centrepiece of Fiedler's (1967) contingency theory of leadership. In this case, however, the three situational variables said to determine the style of leadership to be adopted are:

- *Leader–member relations*: the extent to which a leader has the support of her or his group members. To determine this, questions might be asked about the willingness of group members to do what the leader tells them, the degree of trust existing between the leader and the followers and the extent to which followers will support the leader's decisions.
- *Task structure*: the extent to which the task or purpose of a group is well defined and the outcomes can be seen clearly to be a success or failure. To determine this, questions about the measurability of the outcomes might be asked. In other

words, is it possible to judge 'success' objectively or might there be different views on how the outcomes should be assessed?

- *Position power*: the amount of power (particularly reward power) which the leader can use to accomplish his or her, and the group's, purposes. The issue here is whether leaders have the support of higher management for the way they deal with subordinates.

A comparison of Fiedler's variables with those of Tannenbaum and Schmidt (1973) shows the 'task structure' variable to be similar in both cases. However, the other variables are different one from another. The underlying 'contingency' argument, though, remains the same. Consequently, according to Fiedler, the style of leadership adopted should take account of particular situational conditions in terms of the three variables identified and the subsequent degree of favourability, or otherwise, of the total situation. What is different about Fiedler's findings is that the relationship of leadership style to the favourableness/unfavourableness of the situation is a curvilinear one. In other words, when the situation is very favourable or very unfavourable, the most effective leadership style is said to be a task-oriented, more directive one, rather than a person-oriented one.

When the situation is of moderate favourability to the leader, the style recommended is a person-oriented one. Table 6.1 illustrates this in a simplified form. Of course, in reality, the relationship is not as simple as this. However, the argument that a more consultative and participative style is necessary in situations of confusion and maybe suspicion seems logical. When the situation is very favourable to the leader, he or she can probably take a more directive style, given the trust and support to be expected from group members. In very unfavourable situations, the leader must emphasise the need for task accomplishment in order to push the group towards its goals. This requirement, in turn, dictates a more directive, task-oriented approach.

Implicit in Fiedler's contingency theory is that leaders can adapt their leadership styles to the prevailing situation. However, Fiedler believes this to be difficult – as the allusions in Illustration 6.1 show – and, therefore, suggests either that leaders should be chosen so that their management style fits the situation or that elements of the

Table 6.1 Fiedler's contingency theory of leadership

	Leader–member relationships	Task structure	Position power	Leadership style
1	Good	Structured	High	Task-oriented
2	Good	Structured	Low	style recommended
3	Good	Unstructured	High	
4	Good	Unstructured	Low	Person-oriented
5	Poor	Structured	High	style recommended
6	Poor	Structured	Low	
7	Poor	Unstructured	High	Task-oriented
8	Poor	Unstructured	High	style recommended

situation need to be modified. However, neither strategy seems easy, thus confirming the existence of certain difficulties in 'matching' leaders and leadership situations.

Hersey and Blanchard's situational theory

Another difficulty with contingency theories is the question of how much importance should be attached to each contingency factor. Clearly, the task and the amount of power held by the leader are important, but it seems logical that the characteristics and expectations of group members or subordinates are more important in deciding what style of leadership to adopt – after all, it is these people who must carry out the task.

This would appear to be the case with Hersey and Blanchard's (1993) situational leadership theory which puts greatest stress on one major situational factor – the readiness of what they term the leader's 'followers'. According to this theory, a leader's behaviour should depend on the readiness of followers to accept responsibility and to be willing to make their own decisions. As with the other theories already discussed, the leadership behaviour is defined by Hersey and Blanchard in terms similar to those used for the initiating structure and consideration behaviours identified by the Ohio State researchers. The theory agrees with these researchers that these two behaviours are independent of one another. Therefore, a leader could be low on both task and relationship behaviour, high on both or high on one and low on another. As a result any leader's behaviour may fall into one of four quadrants – which go from 'telling' through 'selling' and 'participating' to 'delegating'. The readiness of followers also falls into four categories, each of which, in an ideal world, should trigger one of the four types of leadership behaviour. Gordon (1999, pp. 234–6) refers to this theory as a 'life-cycle' model of leadership, presumably because the followers move from being both unable and unwilling (or too insecure) to take on responsibility for their own actions, to being either unable but willing (or confident) or willing but unable, to the highest state of readiness where they are both able and willing to take responsibility for decisions and actions.

Figure 6.3 shows how a leader's behaviour should change according to the quadrant into which the followers' readiness falls.

An examination of Figure 6.3 shows the similarity of the four quadrants to the four corners of Blake and McCanse's (1991) leadership Grid. This is not surprising given the two leadership styles and the combinations available. However, while Blake and McCanse argue for a 'one best way' of leader (the 9,9 way) for all occasions, Hersey and Blanchard argue that a leader's style should be contingent upon the characteristics and attitudes of those who are led. In contrast to, for instance, Fiedler's views, both theories assume a leader's style is flexible enough to change according to the prevailing situation and, in Hersey and Blanchard's case, that it can presumably change in the presence of different groups and as the followers 'mature' through the cycle referred to by Gordon. Illustration 6.6 is a good example of how forces in the leader, the subordinates and the situation could be said to influence the leadership style to be adopted.

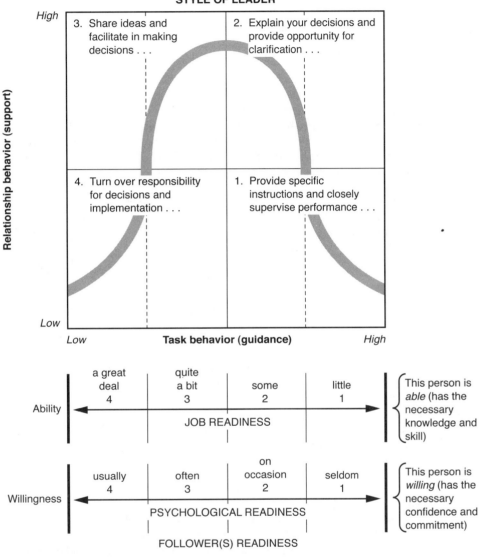

STYLE OF LEADER

High

3. Share ideas and facilitate in making decisions . . .

2. Explain your decisions and provide opportunity for clarification . . .

4. Turn over responsibility for decisions and implementation . . .

1. Provide specific instructions and closely supervise performance . . .

Low

Relationship behavior (support)

Low — Task behavior (guidance) — High

	a great deal 4	quite a bit 3	some 2	little 1	
Ability					This person is *able* (has the necessary knowledge and skill)

JOB READINESS

	usually 4	often 3	on occasion 2	seldom 1	
Willingness					This person is *willing* (has the necessary confidence and commitment)

PSYCHOLOGICAL READINESS

FOLLOWER(S) READINESS

Figure 6.3 Hersey and Blanchard's theory of situational leadership

Source: Hersey, P. and Blanchard, K. H. (1993), *Management of Organizational Behavior: Utilizing Human Resources*, 6th edn (Englewood Cliffs, NJ, Prentice Hall, p. 197).

Activity 6.4   *Using any of the theories already discussed, carry out an analysis of the situation facing James Wolfensohn in his new role at the World Bank.*

If you were James Wolfensohn, what leadership style would you adopt to help gain the objectives he mentions? Justify your views (see Illustration 6.6).

World Bank chief's cry from the heart

Michael Holman and Patti Waldmeir on Wolfensohn's passionate appeal to senior management

FT

Seldom if ever can a World Bank president have made a speech as impassioned and as critical as the one Mr James Wolfensohn made to senior management at a meeting in Washington on March 12.

It was a cry from the heart of a man who seeks to inspire as much as to lead, but who has seen that inspiration blocked by cynicism and distrust. For 90 minutes before 300 senior colleagues, Mr Wolfensohn fought that cynicism with the rhetorical weapons he uses so well: frankness, sincerity, passion and hyperbole.

He concluded on a high note, adopting the tone of enthusiasm he hopes will infect the work of his subordinates around the world: 'I am ... talking about a new atmosphere of change and a new atmosphere of hope and a new dream ... where we can say we are affecting the lives of people in the world (more) positively than anyone else, and we are doing it brilliantly.'

He spoke of a 'humanised' Bank, of a future when 'we can say that we care, that we can cry about poverty, that we can laugh when people have a good time, that we can embrace our clients, that we can feel part of them, where we can tell our kids we made a difference.' He had even invited two of his own children to earlier inspirational sessions, 'because I want them to be proud of me, I want them to think that what I am doing is different'.

But these comments came at the end of an extraordinarily critical session in which the new Bank chief, reviewing progress after nine months as head, alternately cajoled, chastised, implored and berated his listeners. Participants say the atmosphere was by turns subdued, and electric.

The issues were wide-ranging. But again and again, Mr Wolfensohn hammered home one central message with a vivid metaphor: there was a 'glass wall' which was standing in the way of his efforts to ensure that the Bank was more efficient as a development agency.

The Bank chief's frustration was palpable: he has staked his reputation on revolutionising the internal culture of the organisation, as an essential pre-

requisite to improving the Bank's ability to deliver development worldwide.

Among other things, Mr Wolfensohn wants success in the Bank to be judged by the performance of projects rather than the number of loans approved.

At times, his tone bordered on despair: 'I don't know what else we can do, in terms of standard or even non-standard approaches, to try to bring change in the institution. I just don't know what else to do.

'How can we get a new basis for working inside the bank? How can we change the atmosphere? How can we move from cynicism, distrust and distance, to risk-taking and involvement? ... there is so much baggage. There is a need, somehow, to break through this glass wall, this unseen glass wall, to get enthusiasm, change and commitment,' he said.

'I cannot have a situation where we as a group don't have that sense of excitement, commitment, and trust. I don't expect it overnight, but I have to tell you we have got to change this, and I don't know how to do it. I just don't know how to do it.'

Bank insiders say his comments were partly designed to shock his audience – the managers whose past performance has inspired widespread distrust among the staff. They say Mr Wolfensohn does not believe his experiment in more effective management is in peril.

But the evidence from internal Bank studies of personnel, cited by him in the meeting, is grim. Results of Bank 'focus' (study) groups 'undeniably show that there is a lack of trust in management, a huge sense of cynicism and there is some distance which I cannot get my hands on between expressed desire to move forward for change, and commitment in the organisation ... there is a palpable reservation in the air.'

The distrust is hampering efforts to restructure the organisation. Mr Wolfensohn is keen to improve the Bank's relationships with its clients by creating posts for 'country managers' who would be the main point of contact for governments. These country managers

Illustration 6.6 *continued*

would then draw on specialist skills within the Bank through an internal market.

Senior officials say that staff support the principle of this plan, but fear that it will be exploited by the chosen managers, who will exercise favouritism and patronage in the way they use resources elsewhere in the organisation.

This sometimes operates among people of the same nationality and sometimes under 'fiefdoms' which have developed over time, officials say.

The studies show that 40 per cent of Bank employees do not trust management. Bank insiders believe this is partly the result of past personnel policies: 'When good people don't always get promoted and those promoted are not always good, then the management responsible for that does not engender trust,' said one participant in the meeting.

Such a personnel issue was high on the agenda at the meeting: senior staff were unhappy about alleged favouritism on the part of Mr Wolfensohn and his top

aides in the choice of individuals for a new training initiative. But questioners soon moved on to other issues. One senior manager took the opportunity to complain: 'Up to now, I've had the impression that you thought you had all the answers, and that the message was "get on board, or get off the ship".'

Others spoke of a 'culture of approval, a culture where people don't express their opinions forthrightly' for fear of jeopardising career prospects. For his part, Mr Wolfensohn said he was astonished at 'the lack of interpersonal generosity (and) the lack of a team, a sense of team'.

He appealed to his colleagues to do their own independent thinking about change: 'I do not have a monopoly on the ideas ... I am enfranchising every one of you ... to come up with some ideas of how we can bring about the change,' he said, adding, 'there is just something here which the surveys show, and which I can feel, which is inhibiting us ... and I just beg you to think about it.'

Source: Holman, M. and Waldmeir, P. (1996), *Financial Times*, 29 March, p. 4.

Path–goal theory of leadership

The assumption of a flexible style of leadership in Hersey and Blanchard's (1993) theory is also true of what has come to be called the 'path–goal' theory of leadership, which also argues that leadership style (directive, supportive, participative or achievement oriented) is contingent upon various situational factors. Originally developed by House (1971), path–goal theory maintains that the leader should use the style of leadership which is most effective in influencing subordinates' perceptions of the goals they need to achieve and the way (or path) in which they should be achieved. The theory relates directly to expectancy theories of motivation in that a leader will be judged successful if she or he can help subordinates reach their goals. In other words effective leadership will help subordinates turn effort into appropriate and high-level performance.

Two dominant situational factors are relevant to this theory. These are, first, the characteristics of the team or group members, that is the subordinates; and, second, the nature of the task or job and the immediate context in which it takes place. The task of the leader is, therefore, to use a style which is congruent with the skills, motivation and expectations of subordinates and with the goals to be achieved, the design of the jobs and the resources and time available. Figure 6.4 is a generalised diagram of these factors which are presumed to intervene between the effort put into doing a job and the subsequent performance.

The subordinate characteristic of 'locus of control' in Figure 6.4 is of interest as it has not appeared in any of the other main leadership theories considered so far.

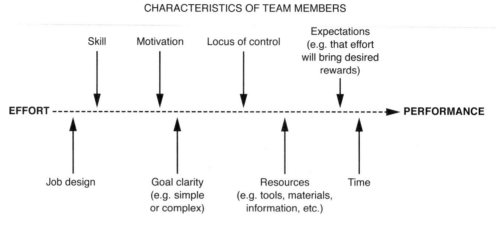

Figure 6.4 **Factors intervening between effort and performance**

In the same way as leaders may, characteristically, veer towards one style more than another, subordinates also have preferences for the way they are managed and this is influenced by their locus of control, that is, their beliefs about who controls their lives. Smith (1991, p. 220) describes the concept of locus of control as follows:

> The locus of control concerns a person's beliefs about who controls their life. People with an internal locus of control believe that they control their own lives. People with an external locus of control believe other people control their lives. According to path-goal theory of leadership non-directive styles of leadership should be used with 'internals' and a directive style should be used with externals. Internals like to be asked, externals like to be told.

Robbins (2001, p. 325) gives the following hypotheses connecting leadership style with path–goal theory situational factors:

Directive leadership leads to greater satisfaction when tasks are ambiguous or stressful than when they are highly structured and well laid out.

Supportive leadership results in high employee performance and satisfaction when subordinates are performing structured tasks.

Directive leadership is likely to be perceived as redundant among subordinates with high perceived ability and with considerable experience.

The more clear and bureaucratic the formal authority relationships, the more leaders should exhibit supportive behaviour and de-emphasise directive behaviour.

Directive leadership will lead to higher employee satisfaction when there is substantive conflict within a work group.

Subordinates with an internal locus of control (those who believe they control their own destiny) will be more satisfied with a participative style.

Subordinates with an external locus of control will be more satisfied with a directive style.

Achievement-oriented leadership will increase subordinates' expectancies that effort will lead to high performance when tasks are ambiguously structured.

Robbins refers to the work of Keller (1989) and Wofford and Liska (1993) as examples of support for path–goal theory, saying (p. 325): 'The research evidence generally supports the logic underlying the path–goal theory. That is, employee performance and satisfaction are likely to be positively influenced when the leader compensates for things lacking in either the employee or the work setting.' While this is likely to be true, effective leaders are also those who can match their leadership approach to the strategic focus and values of the organisation in which they operate.

Matching organisational models and leadership roles

The discussion thus far has identified a number of situational variables, which might be said to influence the style and behaviour of leaders. These are:

● leaders' predispositions to one style rather than another
● the strength of their power base to deliver rewards to their followers
● the expectations and skills of the followers and their preparedness for different degrees of autonomy in their own actions
● the nature of the task to be achieved
● the many factors (e.g. organisational structure, culture, time and resources available) which make up the organisational context in which leadership operates.

With respect to the latter, it could be argued that an organisation's strategic focus together with preferred forms of control will determine many of the other factors and, therefore, the particular leadership style adopted. Two different pieces of research pick up on these ideas to suggest links between different organisational models and different approaches to leadership.

The first of these is that of Quinn (1988) who proposes four organisational models distinguished on the basis of two bipolar dimensions (*see* Table 6.2). These are:

(a) the adaptability and flexibility of the way organisations operate as opposed to the desire for stability and control
(b) whether organisations are outward looking (towards the environment and the competition) or internally focused towards the maintenance of systems and procedures.

Table 6.2 summarises the different characteristics of the four organisational models which result from combining these four different organisational orientations. (Figure 6.5 shows these in diagrammatic form.) Quinn uses the terms 'the hierarchy', 'the firm', 'the adhocracy' and 'the team' as a shorthand way of describing the internal process, rational goal, open systems and human relations organisational models respectively.

Table 6.2 Summary of Quinn's (1988) four organisational models

Human relations model (adaptable and internally focused)	Open systems model (adaptable and externally focused)	Rational goal model (stable and externally focused)	Internal process model (stable and internally focused)
Towards: ● Flexibility ● Decentralisation ● Differentiation ● Maintenance of the socio-technical system	Towards: ● Flexibility ● Decentralisation ● Differentiation ● Expansion ● Competitive position of overall system	Towards: ● Centralisation ● Integration ● Maximising output ● Competitive position of overall system	Towards: ● Centralisation ● Integration ● Consolidation ● Continuity ● Maintenance of socio-technical systems
Values: ● Human resources ● Training ● Cohesion ● Morale	Values: ● Adaptability ● Readiness ● Growth/acquisition ● External support	Values: ● Productivity ● Efficiency ● Planning ● Goal setting	Values: ● Information ● Management ● Communication ● Stability ● Control
THE TEAM	THE ADHOCRACY	THE FIRM	THE HIERARCHY

Source: Based on Quinn, R. E. (1988), *Beyond Rational Management: Mastering the Paradoxes and Competing Demands of High Performance* (San Francisco, Jossey-Bass, p. 48).

What is interesting about the framework illustrated in Figure 6.5 is Quinn's linking of different dimensional positions with leadership style and the roles leaders should play. An examination of Figure 6.5 shows leadership styles positioned around the outer edge of the framework with the leadership roles inside them. From this, it can be seen that different leadership styles and behaviour 'fit' different organisational models.

A second piece of research, by Farkas and Wetlaufer (1996), came to similar conclusions to Quinn about the dependence of leadership style and behaviour on the needs of the organisation and the business situation at hand. On the basis of interviews with 160 chief executives around the world, these researchers found five distinctive approaches to leadership, each of which was associated with different emphases in terms of strategic planning, research and development (R&D), recruitment and selection practices, matters internal to the organisation or matters external to it and with whom, and how, they spent their time. According to Farkas and Wetlaufer (p. 111) the leadership approach to be adopted depends on answering questions such as: 'Is the industry growing explosively or is it mature? How many competitors exist and how strong are they? Does technology matter and, if so, where is it going? What are the organisation's capital and human assets? What constitutes sustainable competitive advantage and how close is the organisation to achieving it?' To these questions, one could also add: 'What kind of changes is the organisation facing and what do these mean for the role of leadership?'

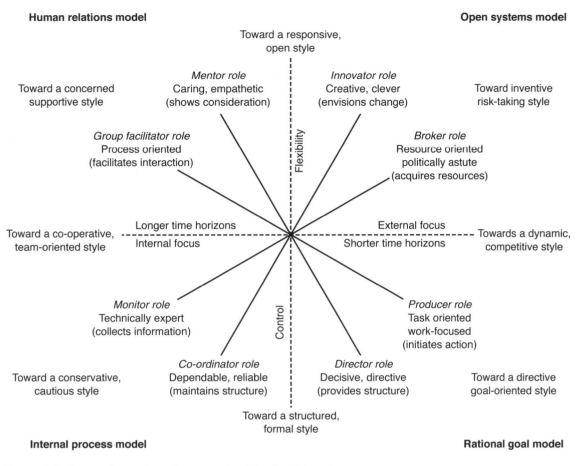

Human relations model

Toward a responsive,
open style

Toward a concerned
supportive style

Mentor role
Caring, empathetic
(shows consideration)

Innovator role
Creative, clever
(envisions change)

Open systems model

Toward inventive
risk-taking style

Group facilitator role
Process oriented
(facilitates interaction)

Flexibility

Broker role
Resource oriented
politically astute
(acquires resources)

Toward a co-operative,
team-oriented style

Longer time horizons
Internal focus

External focus
Shorter time horizons

Towards a dynamic,
competitive style

Control

Monitor role
Technically expert
(collects information)

Producer role
Task oriented
work-focused
(initiates action)

Toward a conservative,
cautious style

Co-ordinator role
Dependable, reliable
(maintains structure)

Director role
Decisive, directive
(provides structure)

Toward a directive
goal-oriented style

Toward a structured,
formal style

Internal process model

Rational goal model

Figure 6.5 Competing values framework of leadership roles
Source: Quinn, R. E. (1988), *Beyond Rational Management: Mastering the Paradoxes and Competing Demands of High Performance* (San Francisco, Jossey-Bass, p. 86).

● ● ● ● Leadership in times of change

The discussion so far suggests a number of conclusions, not all compatible, about leadership in times of organisational change. The first, which relates to the 'one best way' of leading, is that most of the characteristics presumed necessary for successful leadership by the trait theorists appear relevant to leaders of change. However, Kirkpatrick and Locke's (1991) identification of drive, leadership motivation, honesty and integrity, self-confidence, cognitive ability and knowledge of the business seem most relevant – along with the trait of general intelligence and the recognition that intuitive decision making is not out of place or 'second class' to other decision making processes based on rationality and logic. The second is that, given these characteristics, there might be a particular type of leadership behaviour which is most appropriate to leading change. This is the development-oriented behaviour which the researchers Ekvall and Arvonen (1991) and Lindell and Rosenqvist (1992a, 1992b) claim to have found. The third is that transformational leadership seems almost tailor-made for leading change. For instance, in their book entitled *The Transformational Leader*, Tichy and Devanna (1990) put forward a dramatic analogy of transformational leadership when they propose triggers for change emerging from what they call 'the prologue' of the new global playing field. Acts I (Recognising the need for revitalisation), II (Creating a new vision) and III (Institutionalising change) all follow on from this prologue. The 'epilogue' of 'History repeating itself' serves to emphasise the continuous nature of change and, therefore, the necessity for continuous transformation of organisations and the people in organisations having the continuing need for transformational leadership.

If these conclusions are accepted, the search for leaders of change could stop here. However, as the contingency theories of leadership show, leadership style and behaviour can vary according to the different characteristics of different organisational situations. In addition to those described, these situations also include an organisation's stage of development, the nature of the change process itself and the forces for or against any change, including individuals' and groups' resistance to change.

Leadership and the organisational life-cycle

The stages through which an organisation goes as it forms, develops and matures (and maybe disappears) were discussed in Chapter 2 with particular reference to the work of Greiner (1972). However, Greiner, as well as identifying these phases in an organisation's evolution, also sets out the different organisational practices required during each evolutionary phase. One of these practices is the style which top management should adopt according to an organisation's growth phase (*see* Table 6.3).

Clarke (1994, p. 12) elaborated on the phases and styles propounded by Greiner to suggest the following management styles:

- *Phase 1*: individualistic, creative, entrepreneurial, ownership
- *Phase 2*: strong directive
- *Phase 3*: full delegation and autonomy
- *Phase 4*: watchdog
- *Phase 5*: team oriented, interpersonal skills at a premium, innovative, educational bias.

Table 6.3 Matching top management style to organisational growth phases

Organisational growth phases	Phase 1 Growth through CREATIVITY	Phase 2 Growth through DIRECTION	Phase 3 Growth through DELEGATION	Phase 4 Growth through CO-ORDINATION	Phase 5 Growth through ELABORATION
Top management style	Individualistic and entrepreneurial	Directive	Delegative	Watchdog	Participative

Source: Derived from Greiner, L. (1972), 'Evolution and revolution as organizations grow', *Harvard Business Review*, July–August, p. 45.

Greiner's suggestions are helpful in drawing attention to the need for change in the management style of top management and other organisational leaders as organisations evolve and mature. This need is supported by suggestions by Clarke and Pratt (1985) who identify four different styles of managerial leadership required at different stages in the life of an organisation. These are:

- the *champion* to fight for and defend the new business
- the *tank commander* to take the business into its next stage of growth, someone to develop a robust team and direct the business into exploitable parts of the market
- the *housekeeper* to keep the business on an even keel as it enters the mature stage to provide efficiency as well as effectiveness
- the *lemon squeezer* to get the most out of the business as it is in danger of decline.

The idea that organisations at different stages of growth need different leadership approaches has also been taken up by Quinn (1988) whose work has already been discussed above (*see* Table 6.2 and Figure 6.5). For instance, Quinn argues that an organisation will start its life-cycle positioned predominantly in the open systems (the 'adhocracy') quadrant of the framework (*see* Figure 6.5). As it grows and develops, it will include the elements of the human relations model (the 'team') and a focus on productivity and accomplishment from the rational goal model (the 'firm'). As it reaches the stage of formalisation, it will become less oriented to the open systems and human relations models and will take on more of the characteristics of the internal process model (the 'hierarchy'). Finally, in its elaboration of structure stage, it will use elements of all the organisational models, but will refocus, in particular, back to the open systems model. The implications of this life-cycle for any organisation's management and its leadership approach are shown in Table 6.3. This implies that an inventive risk-taking style – typified by innovative, broker-type behaviour – is most appropriate in the early stages of an organisation's development. As the organisation develops towards an established collectivity, this should be tempered with a style more supportive of employees and more group oriented – in other words leaders should behave as mentors and group facilitators. As growth and development continue and the organisation enters a more formalised stage, a more conservative, cautious style is suggested and so the roles of monitor and co-ordinator become most important. Finally, in an organisation's most elaborated stage, leadership styles are required which are flexible enough to change orientation according to the complex, changing situations within the organisation itself, but with an emphasis on resource acquisition and innovation in anticipation of further change.

Activity 6.5   *Compare and contrast the leadership styles and behaviours described by Greiner, Clarke and Quinn in terms of their relationship to, and usefulness for, managerial leadership during the different phases or stages of an organisation's development.*

How do these leadership styles and behaviours accord with your own experience of effective and ineffective leadership at different organisational growth stages?

The results of completing Activity 6.5 may reveal some differences in the three classifications of leadership styles and behaviours surveyed. However, an issue which arises from all three descriptions is that of whether the same leaders can take the organisation through all these phases. Theories such as those of Hersey and Blanchard (1993) and path–goal theory (House, 1971) would say 'yes'. However, Fiedler (1967), in his exposition of a contingency theory of leadership, would advise caution in this respect. This is also the view of Clarke and Pratt (1985) and is further supported by evidence that, because different people have different thinking styles (Kirton, 1976) and preferred behavioural roles (Belbin, 1993), they will have different preferences for the way they interpret and cope with change. Care should be taken, therefore, not to assume that the same leader can be 'all things to all situations'. In addition, it may be that one style of leadership may be appropriate to a particular type of change while another may be appropriate to a different type of change.

Leadership and the nature of change

In Chapter 2, a range of different ways of defining change were reviewed. Table 6.4 is a reproduction of Table 2.2 in Chapter 2 which shows how different typologies of change might relate one to another and to the environmental conditions giving rise to them.

There is little in the literature to suggest which leadership styles and behaviours are most associated with each type of change. Two exceptions stand out. The first is the assumption that transformational leadership is associated with transformational or frame-breaking change. The second is the work of Dunphy and Stace (1993) who have, specifically, linked styles of leadership to types of change. Figure 6.6 shows the results of these linkings.

Table 6.4 Environmental conditions and types of change

Environmental forces for change			Types of change			
Ansoff and McDonnell (1990)	**Strebel (1996a)**	**Stacey (1996)**	**Tushman et al. (1988)**	**Dunphy and Stace (1993)**	**Grundy (1993)**	**Stacey (1996)**
Predictable	Weak	Close to certainty	Converging (fine-tuning)	Fine-tuning	Smooth incremental	Closed
Forecastable by extrapolation	Moderate	Close to certainty	Converging (incremental)	Incermental adjustment		Contained
Predictable threats and opportunities				Modular transformation	Bumpy incremental	
Partially predictable opportunities	Strong			Corporate transformation		
Unpredictable surprises		Far from certainty	Discontinuous or frame breaking		Discontinuous	Open ended

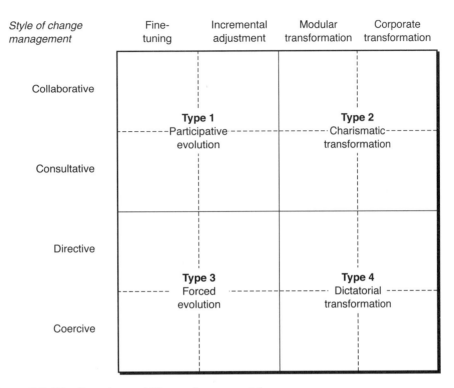

Style of change management	Fine-tuning	Incremental adjustment	Modular transformation	Corporate transformation

Figure 6.6 The Dunphy and Stace change matrix

Source: Dunphy, D. and Stace, D. (1993), 'The strategic management of corporate change', *Human Relations*, Vol. 46, No. 8, p. 908.

An examination of Figure 6.6 shows that any style of management can be used with any type of change. However, Dunphy and Stace's research with 13 service sector organisations which had gone through large-scale environmental change indicates that, for transformational change at the corporate level, a directive/ coercive style of leadership is likely to be most successful. What is interesting, however, is Dunphy and Stace's (p. 917) statement that: 'Once this basis for organ- isational renewal is in place, there is a choice to be made at the corporate level as to the mix of directive and consultative strategies needed to keep the momentum of change.' With regard to accompanying change at the business (operational) level, they suggest a more consultative style to win commitment of employees at that level.

Logic suggests that a more consultative style of management is more appropri- ate to converging, incremental types of change which are, in turn, likely to be associated with environmental forces for change which are predictable and of moderate strength, as shown in Table 6.4. However, Strebel (1996a) proposes a model which not only links leadership style and approach to environmental forces for change, but also links these to the degree to which an organisation is open to change initiatives. Consequently, any discussion of the leadership of change must take account of the capability and willingness of any organisation to remain either closed or open to the prospects of change. Leading change, therefore, will almost certainly be concerned with overcoming resistance to change.

Obstructing and facilitating processes for change

For the management of any organisation which is reacting to, or planning for, change there will be forces acting to facilitate the change and forces acting against it. Although these forces are important for any type of change, they become particularly important in the context of frame-breaking or transformational change. Newton (1993) discusses a number of processes which, she says, obstruct or facilitate change. Some of these factors and others are given in Illustration 6.7.

The forces *for* change listed in Illustration 6.7 are categorised into external and internal forces (in relation to the organisation). The forces *against* change are categorised into individual responses and organisational responses. Yet another distinction which could be made is between those forces which: (a) prevent a new perspective being formed, and (b) prevent implementation of change once the intentions for change are known (Ginsberg and Abrahamson, 1991).

External and internal forces associated with change

Forces for change originating in the external environment of an organisation were discussed in Chapter 1 as part of the PETS description of the organisational

---

Illustration 6.7

Forces for and against change

Driving forces for change
1 *External forces*:
- role of the state
- social pressures
- changing technology
- constraints from suppliers
- stakeholder demands
- competitor behaviour
- customer needs.
2 *Internal forces*:
- organisational growth
- pressures for increased performance
- managerial aspirations
- political coalitions
- redesign of jobs
- restructuring.

Driving forces against change
1 *Individual resistance*:
- fear of the unknown
- dislike of the uncertainty and ambiguity surrounding change
- potential loss of power base
- potential loss of rewards
- perceived lack of skills for new situation
- potential loss of current skills.
2 *Organisational resistance*:
- inertial forces deriving from the systemic nature of organisations
- interlocking aspects of structure, control systems, rituals and routines, signs and symbols
- inertial forces deriving from group norms
- potential loss of group power bases
- entrenched interests of stakeholders
- lack of organisational capability
- lack of resources
- threat to resource allocations.

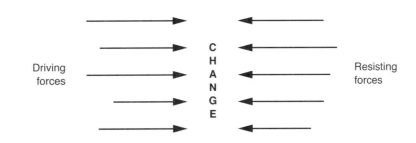

Figure 6.7 A force field diagram

environment. These, together with internal forces, such as the need for new product development or restructuring to accommodate new technological processes, are likely to facilitate change in that they are the triggers for change. However, these forces may be counteracted by other forces which resist change; for instance, those listed in Illustration 6.7 which, themselves, may be externally or internally generated. However, the role of leading change is more likely to be concerned with resistance from inside the organisation (which can be from individuals or be organisationally generated), this being the type of resistance most immediately manageable.

It is clear from an inspection of the factors listed in Illustration 6.7 that, for specific change situations, some forces will be stronger than others. One technique for depicting the range and strength of forces for and against change is that of *force field analysis*. Developed in the 1960s, force field analysis is based on the idea that, in any change situation, there are forces supporting change and forces opposing change. The theory, upon which the technique is based, implies that when the balance of the two sets of forces is equal, no change will occur. Thus, it is argued that, if change is desired, the forces supporting change need to be strengthened and those opposing change weakened. Figure 6.7 is a generic representation of a force field diagram, while Illustration 6.8 (drawing on the advice of Carnall (1995) and Huczynski and Buchanan (2001)) outlines the steps necessary for carrying it out.

Paton and McCalman (2000) suggest that force field analysis, as well as operating as a technique in its own right, can be incorporated into other change situation analyses such as the TROPICS test which is discussed in Chapter Two. The results of such analyses help in deciding the extent to which an organisation is open or closed to change. In this respect also, Strebel (1992, p. 67) offers the following advice.

1 Look for closed attitudes by examining what processes are in place for bringing new ideas into the industry, company, or business unit, especially at the highest levels; and by probing whether management is aware of the change forces.

2 Look for an entrenched culture by examining what processes are in place for reflecting on values and improving behaviour and skills; and by enquiring to what extent behaviour and skills are adapted to the forces of change.

Illustration 6.8

Force field analysis

Step 1: Define the problem in terms of the present situation, with its strengths and weaknesses, and the situation you would wish to achieve. Define the target situation as precisely and unambiguously as possible.

Step 2: List the forces working for and against the desired changes. These can be based on people, resources, time, external factors, corporate culture.

Step 3: Rate each of the forces for and against change in terms of strength: high, medium or low. Give the strength ratings numerical values: 5 for high, 3 for medium, and 1 for low; this allows totals for driving and resisting forces to be calculated.

Step 4: Using a diagram such as that in Figure 6.7, draw lines of different lengths to indicate the different strengths of the forces.

Step 5: Label each line to indicate whether that force is very important (VI), important (I) or not important (NI).

Step 6: For each very important (VI) and important (I) force supporting the change, indicate how you would attempt to strengthen the force. Then do the same for those forces opposing the change, but in this case indicate how you would weaken the force.

Step 7: Agree on those actions which appear most likely to help solve the problem of achieving change.

Step 8: Identify the resources that will be needed to take the agreed actions and how these resources may be obtained.

Step 9: Make a practical action plan designed to achieve the target situation which should include:

● timing of events
● specified milestones and deadlines
● specific responsibilities – who does what.

---

3 Look for rigid structures and systems, by examining when the organisation, business system, the stakeholder resource base, and the industry last changed significantly; and by enquiring to what extent the structures and systems are capable of accommodating the forces of change.

4 Look for counterproductive change dynamics by examining whether historical forces of change are driving the business; and by enquiring to what extent the historical forces of change have become the new force of resistance.

5 Assess the strength of the overall resistance to change by examining to what extent the various forces of resistance are correlated with one another; and by describing the resistance threshold in terms of power and resources needed to deal with the resistance.

Assuming assessments such as these can be done, Strebel's (1996a) juxtaposition of the level of intensity of forces for change (which he designates as weak, moderate or strong and which could be calculated from use of force field analysis) with the degree of resistance expected (that is, whether an organisation is closed to change, can be opened to change, or is open to change) is useful for determining the leadership behaviour and overall management approach to implementing change (*see* Figure 6.8).

The role of leadership in Strebel's model is most clearly spelt out in the case of weak environmental change forces in an organisational situation of being closed

Resistance	PROACTIVE	REACTIVE	RAPID	
Closed to change	Radical leadership	Organisational realignment	Downsizing and restructuring	Discontinuous paths
Can be opened to change	Top-down experimentation	Process reengineering	Autonomous restructuring	Mixed paths
Open to change	Bottom-up experimentation	Goal cascading	Rapid adaptation	Continuous paths
	Weak	Moderate	Strong	Change force

Figure 6.8 Contrasting change paths

Source: Strebel, P. (1996a), 'Choosing the right change path', *Mastering Management*, Part 14, *Financial Times*, p. 17.

to change. Of this situation, Strebel says that weak change forces imply proactive change; in an organisation unused to and closed to change, this implies radical leadership. By this, Strebel means an approach which will break the dominant culture of resistance by starting with top management and continuing through a process of shaking up others in the organisation. The proposed behaviour of change leaders (or, as Strebel refers to them, change agents) in this and the other situations shown in Figure 6.8 is summarised by Strebel as follows (1996a, p. 6):

> It is useful to distinguish between the different levels of 'change-force' intensity. Weak change forces are difficult to discern and require skill in communications and in identifying the value creating idea – but there is time for experimentation. Moderate change forces are those which have started to affect performance but do not threaten survival: getting people's attention is easier and multi-disciplinary teams should be employed.
>
> Those organisations with high resistance have very few 'change agents' and require a radical approach to break the dominant culture. The process should start with resistors at the top, can benefit from headstrong leadership (though can equally end in a disastrous ego trip), and requires some form of reorganisation. In organisations that can be opened to change, management has to help the change agents, and top-down experimentation is desirable. In organisations that are already open to change there is usually little risk in leaving the resistors until last. Bottom-up experimentation and goal cascading should be possible.

Strebel's model of paths to change is quite complex and, as this discussion is focused on leadership, the paths to change identified in the final column are only tangentially relevant – they are discussed further in Part Three of the book. What is important, here, is to note Strebel's comment (p. 5) that: 'Change leaders cannot afford the risk of blindly applying a standard recipe and hoping it will work. Successful change takes place on a path that is appropriate to the specific situation.'

Responding to resistance to change

Leadership can be conceptualised in terms of its three main functions within a group or organisation (Open University, 1996, p. 38). These are:

- the *strategic* function: developing a sense of direction in the group or organisation
- the *tactical* function: defining the tasks necessary to achieve the group's or the organisation's goals and making sure that these tasks are carried out effectively
- the *interpersonal* function: maintaining the morale, cohesion and commitment of the group or organisation.

It is important to note that these functions do not, necessarily, divide themselves among leaders at the top, middle and other parts of organisations. All the functions are carried out by all leaders whatever their status. However, it is reasonable to suggest that the strategic and tactical functions will feature more prominently in the planning and early stages of change, with the tactical and interpersonal functions featuring more prominently during the change process and when the change is in place.

Reducing or overcoming resistance to change depends on identifying the sources of resistance, as discussed earlier. It also depends on a leader's ability to be task oriented (both strategically and tactically) when the time requires it, but also relationship oriented to address the more individualised resistances to change. A first step is to recognise the conclusions of a number of writers (e.g. Clarke, 1994; Nortier, 1995; Rashford and Coghlan, 1989) that individuals faced with change often go through a traumatic process of shock and denial before they come to acknowledge and adapt to it. What must not be forgotten, however, is that change can be exciting and can bring new and positive opportunities for all. The notion of a vision and communicating that vision is important in this context, as exemplified by Clarke (1994, p. 124) when she says: 'It is a vision of a new future which provides the pull-through and momentum for change.' This view is reinforced by two articles (Beer, Eisenstat and Spector, 1990; Kotter, 1995) in the *Harvard Business Review*, both of which refer to the need for a vision to guide the change. This is, however, clearly not sufficient, as the other points of advice from these authors show (*see* Illustrations 6.9 and 6.10).

The advice on what to do given by Beer *et al.* (1990) and that on what *not* to do given by Kotter (1995) clearly overlap in content and intent and each element of advice is offered as relevant for all situations. By contrast, an earlier article by Kotter and Schlesinger (1979) is more circumspect in detailing a range of different approaches for dealing with resistance to change. These are:

- education and communication
- participation and involvement
- facilitation and support
- negotiation and agreement
- manipulation and co-optation
- explicit and implicit coercion.

Illustration 6.9

Six steps to effective change

1 Mobilise commitment to change through joint diagnosis of business problems.

2 Develop a shared vision of how to organise and manage for competitiveness.

3 Foster consensus for the new vision, competence to enact it and cohesion to move it along.

4 Spread revitalisation to all departments without pushing it from the top.

5 Institutionalise revitalisation through formal policies, systems and structures.

6 Monitor and adjust strategies in response to problems in the revitalisation process.

Source: Beer, M., Eisenstat, R. A. and Spector, B. (1990), 'Why change programmes do not produce change', *Harvard Business Review*, November–December.

Illustration 6.10

Why transformation efforts fail

According to Kotter (1995), transforming organisations fail through:

1 Not establishing a great enough sense of urgency.

2 Not creating a powerful enough coalition.

3 Lacking a vision.

4 Undercommunicating by a factor of ten.

5 Not removing obstacles to the new vision.

6 Not systematically planning for and creating short-term wins.

7 Declaring victory too soon.

8 Not anchoring changes in the corporation's culture.

In detailing the advantages and disadvantages of each method, Kotter and Schlesinger explain the particular set of circumstances where each approach might be used. For instance, if the change initiators possess considerable power, and change must come quickly, some form of coercion would be appropriate. By contrast, an approach associated with negotiation (or more collaboratively, participation) is more likely to succeed where the change initiators do not have complete information and where others have power to resist.

The value of Kotter and Schlesinger's analysis lies in the way it can help managers understand specific instances of opposition to change in order to work out an approach relevant to a particular situation. This, together with Illustrations 6.9 and 6.10, bring this chapter's discussion back to the beginning when the question was posed as to what leadership approach works best in situations of organisational change. Taken together, these illustrations show how leaders of change need to have certain attitudes and behaviours which are of benefit regardless of the prevailing situation, but they also need to understand that some behaviours are more effective in some situations and other behaviours more effective in other situations.

Conclusions

Leadership theories vary from those which maintain that there are a set of characteristics which leaders must have if they are to gain success in what they do to those which argue that no single leader can be successful regardless of their own preferences and the situation they find themselves in. Regardless of which set of theories gain attention at any time, agreement is becoming evident that leading change requires more than the command and control behaviours fashionable in times when organisations operated in stable predictable environments. The replacement of repetitive work with machines, the increasing emphasis on knowledge and the need to innovate to survive and prosper have brought a recognition that, for people to be creative, while working in situations of uncertainty, requires leaders who are able to harness the skills of others through working in collaborative rather than hierarchical ways.

This does not imply an emphasis on 'soft' approaches to leadership in neglect of hard decisions to be made in some circumstances. This view can be summarised in terms of Beer and Nohria's (2000) 'E' and 'O' change strategies. An E approach to change is based on economic value while an O approach is based on organisational capability. Thus, in an E approach to change (which the authors term a 'hard' approach), shareholder value is the only legitimate measure of corporate success. This implies heavy use of economic incentives, layoffs, downsizing and restructuring. Leaders who subscribe to an O approach (which can be termed a 'soft' approach) believe that they should aim to develop corporate culture and human capability through individual and organisational learning in a process of collaboration with others at all levels of the organisation.

Operating E and O approaches to change simultaneously is very difficult for most leaders of change. Combining the two could bring the worst of each and the benefits of neither. For instance, doubling or trebling shareholder returns through subscribing to an E approach could fail to build the commitment, co-operation and creativity which are necessary for sustained competitive advantage. Embracing an O approach could make it difficult to take tough decisions in times of economic downturn and the need to survive. Beer and Nohria advise that, unless organisations can find leaders who, exceptionally, have the will, skill and wisdom to work with both approaches, the way to proceed is to sequence them, with an E approach preceding an O approach. What is more, in the light of the doubts expressed earlier in the chapter, that one person can adopt different styles of leadership according to circumstances, there is a case for two leaders of change chosen for their contrasting traits and styles. Alternatively or additionally, the idea of team leadership is not unreasonable if the team is small with the members agreed on the vision and goals.

Leadership, together with the other aspects of organisational life discussed in this part of the book, comprise the context in which change takes place. With the description of this context now completed, we can proceed to the more practical considerations of how to design, plan and implement change, discussed in Part Three.

Discussion questions and assignments

1 Drawing on your own experience of organisational change, describe:

   (a) a situation where, in Reich's (1991) terms, someone acted as 'hero'
   (b) a situation where the notion of the leader as hero was less evident than Reich's concept of the 'team as hero'.

2 What were the advantages and disadvantages of these two different leadership situations? Justify your answer.

3 In the context of the discussion of different types of change posed in Chapter 2, and the idea that organisations must be alert to their ever-changing environments, debate the advisability of seeking managers at all levels who can act as transformational leaders.

4 Examine the concept of 'leaders of change' as it might apply across different societies and organisations.

Case example

From bureaucracy to teamwork

By means of a questionnaire survey of a sample of 346 employees of a large public sector social services-type organisation, McHugh and Bennett examined the feasibility of carrying out a large-scale transformational change in its structure, from one which was based on strict bureaucratic principles to one which favoured self-managed team working. The proposed change was in response to government initiatives to make such organisations more market oriented, responsive to clients, flexible in the way staff worked and generally to act more like a commercial company. They questioned the staff on: the degree to which they interacted with others in their day to day job; whether they considered themselves to work in teams; and what they thought was meant by team working. Having established that most (96 per cent) respondents could define team working (albeit using what might be a standard textbook definition); that the majority (89 per cent) indicated that their job required them to work as part of a team; but that only 66 per cent preferred to work together with others (31 per cent preferring to work independently), they examined a range of attitudes towards team working in the light of management's known views that this was to be the way forward.

The results showed a sizeable percentage (between 35 and 42 per cent) believing that management within the organisation did not understand the meaning of team work and that managers would find it difficult to give up their control, in order to encourage workforce democracy and empower others to make decisions. In spite of this, a large majority thought that

▶

Case example *continued*

the organisation should move towards team working, but only, it seemed, because top management had decreed it, even though the infrastructure required to make it work had not been given sufficient attention.

From the research, a number of factors emerged which would either facilitate or impede team working. Facilitating factors included: having managers and staff committed to communication; the freedom to make decisions; greater staff enthusiasm; training people to help them understand the concept of team working; and having team rewards. Impeding factors included: low staff motivation; lack of management and staff commitment; a reward system which sup-

ports competition rather than co-operation; no management and staff understanding of the concept; no acceptance of devolved responsibility; bureaucratic management styles; and adherence by management to the old ways of doingthings.

What was evident was that a number of 'trip wires', as defined by Hackman (1994), existed within the organisation which highlighted the strength of the impeding factors against the weakness of the facilitating factors in terms of the changes required for team working to become established as the preferred way of working.

The article goes on to elaborate on the trip wires.

Source: Based on McHugh, M. and Bennett, H. (1999), 'Introducing teamwork within a bureaucratic maze', *The Leadership and Organization Development Journal,* Vol. 20, No. 2, pp. 81–93.

Case exercise: What do you think?

Based on your knowledge, through either working in or being a customer of, organisations in the public sector, list the trip wires you can see in changing such organisations to permit: 'enhanced delegation, empowerment of staff and amongst those who occupy managerial roles, a commitment to the concept of team player as opposed to manager'.

Prepare a plan to help overcome the trip wires. In what order would you put each element of your plan? Make an estimate of the length of time required to implement each element of the plan.

References

Andersen, J. A. (2000), 'Intuition in managers: are intuitive managers more effective?' *Journal of Managerial Psychology,* Vol. 15, No. 1, pp. 46–67.

Ansoff, I. H. and McDonnell, E. J. (1990), *Implanting Strategic Management,* Englewood Cliffs, NJ, Prentice Hall.

Bass, B. M. (1990), 'From transactional to transformational leadership: learning to share the vision', *Organizational Dynamics,* Winter, pp. 19–31.

Beer, M. and Nohria, N. (2000), 'Cracking the code of change', *Harvard Business Review,* May–June, pp. 133–41.

Beer, M., Eisenstat, R. A. and Spector, B. (1990), 'Why change programmes do not produce change', *Harvard Business Review,* November–December.

Behling, O. and McFillen, J. (1996), 'A syncretical model of charismatic/transformational leadership', *Group &*

Organization Management, Vol. 21, No. 2, June, pp. 163–91.

Belbin, M. (1993), *Team Roles at Work,* Oxford, Butterworth-Heinemann.

Bennet III, R. H. (1998), 'The importance of tacit knowledge in strategic deliberations and decisions', *Management Decision,* Vol. 36, No. 9, pp. 589–97.

Blake, R. R. and McCanse, A. A. (1991), *Leadership Dilemmas: Grid Solutions,* Houston, TX, Gulf Publishing.

Blake, R. R. and Mouton, J. S. (1964), *The Managerial Grid,* Houston, TX, Gulf Publishing.

Bunting, M. (2000), 'Rewiring our brains', *The Guardian,* November 13.

Carnall, C. (1995), *Managing Change in Organizations* (2nd edn), London, Prentice Hall.

Clarke, C. and Pratt, S. (1985), 'Leadership's four-part progress', *Management Today*, March, pp. 84–6.

Clarke, L. (1994), *The Essence of Change*, Hemel Hempstead, Prentice Hall.

Dulewicz, V. and Herbert, P. (1996), 'Leaders of tomorrow: how to spot the high-flyers', *Financial Times*, 20 September, p. 16.

Dunphy, D. and Stace, D. (1993), 'The strategic management of corporate change', *Human Relations*, Vol. 46, No. 8, pp. 905–20.

Ekvall, G. and Arvonen, J. (1991), 'Change-centred leadership: an extension of the two-dimensional model', *Scandinavian Journal of Management*, Vol. 7, No. 1, pp. 17–26.

Farkas, C. M. and Wetlaufer, S. (1996), 'The ways chief executive officers lead', *Harvard Business Review*, May–June, pp. 110–22.

Fayol, H. (1949), *General and Industrial Management*, London, Pitman.

Fiedler, F. E. (1967), *A Theory of Leadership*, McGraw-Hill.

Fiedler, F. E. (1989), 'The effective utilisation of intellectual abilities and job relevant knowledge in group performance: cognitive resource theory and an agenda for the future', *Applied Psychology: An International Review*, Vol. 38, No. 3, pp. 289–304.

Ginsberg, A. and Abrahamson, E. (1991), 'Champions of change and strategic shifts: the role of internal and external change advocates', *Journal of Management Studies*, Vol. 28, No. 2, pp. 173–90.

Goleman, D. (1998), 'What makes a leader? IQ and technical skills are important, but emotional intelligence is the sine qua non of leadership', *Harvard Business Review*, November–December, pp. 93–104.

Gordon, J. R. (1999), *A Diagnostic Approach to Organizational Behaviour* (6th edn), Upper Sadldle River, Prentice Hall.

Greiner, L. (1972), 'Evolution and revolution as organizations grow', *Harvard Business Review*, July–August.

Hackman, R. (1994), 'Tripwires in designing and leading workgroups', *The Occupational Psychologist*, Vol. 23, pp. 3–8.

Handy, C. (1993), *Understanding Organizations*, London, Penguin.

Henry, J. (1991) *Creative Management*, London, Sage.

Henry, J. and Walker, D. (1991) *Managing Innovation*, London, Sage.

Hersey, P. and Blanchard, K. H. (1993), *Management of Organizational Behavior: Utilizing Human Resources* (6th edn), Englewood Cliffs, NJ, Prentice Hall.

Holman, M. and Waldmeir, P. (1996), 'World Bank chief's cry from the heart', *Financial Times*, 29 March, p. 4.

House, R. J. (1971), 'A path–goal theory of leader effectiveness', *Administrative Science Quarterly*, September, pp. 321–38.

Huczynski, A. and Buchanan, D. (2001), *Organizational Behaviour. Student Workbook* (4th edn), Hemel Hempstead, Financial Times/Prentice Hall.

Jung, C. G. (1976), TYPOLOGI. Till fragan om de psykologiska typerna, Typologie – Zur Frage der psychologischen Typen, Olten, Walter-Verlag AG, 1972 (translated from the German), Berghs Forlag, Stockholm.

Kanter, R. M. (1991), 'Change-motor skills: what it takes to the be creative', in Henry J. and Walker, D. (eds), *Managing Innovation*, London, Sage.

Keller, R. T. (1989), 'A test of the path–goal theory of leadership with need for clarity as a moderator in research and development organizations', *Journal of Applied Psychology*, April, pp. 208–12.

Kirkpatrick, S. A. and Locke, E. A. (1991), 'Leadership: do traits matter?' *Academy of Management Executive*, May, pp. 48–60.

Kirton, M. J. (1976), 'Adaptors and innovators: a description and a measure', *Journal of Applied Psychology*, Vol. 61, pp. 622–9.

Kotter, J. P. (1990), *A Force for Change: How Leadership Differs from Management*, New York, Free Press.

Kotter, J. P. (1995), 'Leading change: why transformation efforts fail', *Harvard Business Review*, March–April.

Kotter, J. P. and Schlesinger, L. A. (1979), 'Choosing strategies for change', *Harvard Business Review*, March–April.

Landrum, N. E., Howell, J. P. and Paris, L. (2000), 'Leadership for strategic change', *Leadership and Organization Development Journal*, Vol. 21, No. 3, pp. 150–6.

Lank, A. G. and Lank, E. A. (1995), 'Legitimizing the gut feel: the role of intuition in business', *Journal of Managerial Psychology*, Vol. 10, No. 5, pp. 18–23.

Likert, R. (1961), *New Patterns of Management*, McGraw-Hill.

Lindell, M. and Rosenqvist, G. (1992a), 'Is there a third management style?' *Finnish Journal of Business Economics*, Vol. 3, pp. 171–98.

Lindell, M. and Rosenqvist, G. (1992b), 'Management behavior dimensions and development orientation', *Leadership Quarterly*, Winter, pp. 355–77.

Lord, R. G., De Vader, C. L. and Alliger, G. M. (1986), 'A meta-analysis of the relation between personality traits and leadership perceptions: an application of validity generalization procedures', *Journal of Applied Psychology*, Vol. 71, pp. 402–10.

McHugh, M. and Bennett, H. (1999), 'Introducing team-work within a bureaucratic maze', *The Leadership and Organization Development Journal*, Vol. 20, No. 2, pp. 81–93.

Mann, R. D. (1959), 'A review of the relationship between personality and performance in small groups', *Psychological Bulletin*, Vol. 56, No. 4, pp. 241–70.

Mintzberg, H. (1979), *The Nature of Managerial Work*, Englewood Cliffs, NJ, Prentice Hall.

Mullins, L. J. (1999), *Management and Organisational Behaviour* (5th edn), London, Financial Times/Pitman Publishing.

Newton, J. (1993), 'Obstructing and facilitating processes in strategic change: a research approach', Proceedings of the British Academy of Management Conference, 20–22 September.

Nortier, F. (1995), 'A new angle on coping with change: managing transition', *Journal of Management Development*, Vol. 14, No. 4, pp. 32–46.

Open University (1996), Book 6. 'Managing people: a wider view', MBA Course, Milton Keynes, Open University.

Paton, R. A. and McCalman, J. (2000), *Change Management. A Guide To Effective Implementation*, London, Sage.

Pollock, L. (2000) 'That's infotainment', *People Management*, 28 December, pp. 18–23.

Post, J. M. (1986), 'Narcissism and the charismatic leader–follower relationship', *Political Psychology*, Vol. 7, No. 4, pp. 675–88.

Quinn, R. E. (1988), *Beyond Rational Management, Mastering the Paradoxes and Competing Demands of High Performance*, San Francisco, Jossey-Bass.

Rashford, N. S. and Coghlan, D. (1989), 'Phases and levels of organisational change', *Journal of Managerial Psychology*, Vol. 4, No. 3, pp. 17–22.

Reich, R. B. (1991), 'The team as hero', in Henry, J. and Walker, D., *Managing Innovation*, London, Sage.

Robbins, S. P. (2001), *Organizational Behavior, Concepts, Controversies, Applications* (9th edn), Englewood Cliffs, NJ, Prentice Hall.

Smith, M. (1991), 'Leadership and supervision', in Smith, M. (ed.), *Analysing Organizational Behaviour*, New York, Macmillan.

Stacey, R. (1996), *Strategic Management and Organisational Dynamics*, London, Pitman.

Stodgill, R. M. (1948), 'Personal factors associated with leadership: a survey of the literature', *Journal of Psychology*, Vol. 25, pp. 35–71.

Stodgill, R. M. and Coons, A. E. (1957), *Leader Behavior: Its Description and Measurement*, Columbus, Ohio State University Bureau of Business Research.

Strebel, P. (1992), *Breakpoints, How Managers Exploit Radical Business Change*, Cambridge, MA, Harvard Business Press.

Strebel, P. (1996a), 'Choosing the right path', Mastering Management, Part 14, *Financial Times*, pp. 5–7.

Strebel, P. (1996b), 'Breakpoint: how to stay in the game', Mastering Management, Part 17, *Financial Times*.

Tannenbaum, R. and Schmidt, W. H. (1973), 'How to choose a leadership pattern', *Harvard Business Review*, Vol. 51, May–June, pp. 162–80.

Tichy, N. M. and Devanna, M. A. (1990), *The Transformational Leader* (2nd edn), New York, Wiley.

Tichy, N. M. and Ulrich, D. O. (1984), 'The leadership challenge – a call for the transformational leader', *Sloan Management Review*, Fall, pp. 59–68.

Tushman, M. L., Newman, W. H. and Romanelli, E. (1988), 'Convergence and upheaval: managing the unsteady pace of organizational evolution', in Tushman, M. L. and Moore, W. L. (eds), *Readings in the Management of Innovation*, New York, Ballinger Publishing Company.

Useem, M. (1996), 'Do leaders make a difference?' Mastering Management, Part 18, *Financial Times*, pp. 5–6.

Vinnicombe, S. and Harris, H. (2000), 'A gender hidden', *People Management*, 6 January, pp. 28–32.

Watson, C. M. (1983), 'Leadership, management and the seven keys', *Business Horizons*, March–April, pp. 8–13.

Westley, F. and Mintzberg, H. (1989), 'Visionary leadership and strategic management', *Strategic Management Journal*, Vol. 10, pp. 17–32.

Wensley, R. (1996), 'Mrs Beeton, management guru,' *Financial Times*, 26 April, p. 15.

Woffard, J. C. and Liska, L. Z. (1993), 'Path–goal theories of leadership: a meta-analysis', *Journal of Management*, Winter, pp. 857–76.

Woodruffe, C. (2000), 'Emotional intelligence: time for a time-out', *Selection and Development Review*, Vol. 16, No. 4, pp. 3–9.

Wright, P. (1996), *Managerial Leadership*, London, Routledge.

PART TWO CASE STUDY

Selfridges, a study of change Part 2

Reactions to the changes

In 1997 the BBC (British Broadcasting Corporation) broadcast six half-hour television programmes of the 'fly on the wall' type but which included short interviews and comments by employees in the store. These programmes were filmed in the very early part of the change programme at the time that the large-scale changes were being introduced into the way Selfridges looked and operated and give some idea of the culture prevailing at that time. While many of the staff supported the changes, there were mixed reactions from some. It is instructive to consider what the programmes found then.

Throughout the six programmes, the word 'contemporary' kept coming up. For the two security staff featured, this meant seeking new ways of selling and new customers but, at the same time, not losing sight of existing customers, many of whom they said were local. For others, for instance the newly appointed furniture department buyer (who came from Habitat as Vittorio Radice had) this meant radical change from what he saw as bland, traditional furniture attracting 'bad-taste' customers. He wanted totally new customers who would perceive a *new* store. In pursuit of this vision, he wanted to get rid of most of the existing stock, which he perceived as 'low-brow'. This was clearly not the view of the departmental manager who maintained he would rather have 'traditional' furniture of which he could sell ten or so pieces, rather than one fancy expensive item which does not sell well. There was obviously a struggle between old and new.

One of the programmes showed that the introduction and setting up of a new Ralph Lauren concession of 'contemporary' menswear was not going well, with display units still to be erected and Ralph Lauren's own hangers to be located on the evening before the opening. Eventually the new concession was opened with the hangers having been found and some interim arrangements being made for the displays. What became clear from a meeting of the store General Manager with his departmental managers was the demanding environment in which managers worked in terms of targets to be met. When the furniture department manager mentioned that because of the difficulties encountered with the opening of the Ralph Lauren concession that this might affect sales, there was a veiled warning that if her department did not meet its targets, her job might not be safe. A sales assistant in another department had been severely criticised for not keeping the displays tidy and clean. His employment was terminated shortly after. As the General Manager and the 'visual' manager toured the store, they took photographs to record examples of poor displays, dusty counters and untidy spaces. These were used to confront the 'culprits' and to encourage improved performance in this respect.

There was clearly a competitive culture, between departments and managers, encouraged by senior managers which was evident in a management development sailing event where five teams of managers competed against each other. This was reflected in the intense competition between departments to recruit customers to register for Selfridges' gold credit card. There was even an attempt by the menswear department to take over one of the recruitment desks run by customer services. What was dubbed 'Gold card Sunday' ended in a prize being given to the department which had sold the most gold cards.

The changes associated with Christmas 1997 in terms of the move away from traditional Christmas images displayed in the windows and the reduction in size of Santa's Grotto brought doubtful reactions from customers. What is more, the Christmas period of that year did not deliver the hoped-for sales, bringing comments that the following year there would be a move back to more traditional Christmas displays and images.

Selfridges at the millennium

Turning around a department store is something like slowing down an oil tanker to turn it to face a new direction. The masterplan for Selfridges was to clear out the clutter and build brands which, although distinct one from another, continue to live in a unified environment.

'Department stores a hundred years ago used to be places you went to feel good. To shop, linger, lunch, experiment, and discover something new. I want to bring back that excitement,' explains Vittorio Radice.

At the time of writing, the new Manchester store had been open two and a half years with sales of £42.83 million for the year 2000/2001 – up from £34.8 million in 1999/2000. The target sales density of £300 per square foot, excluding VAT, was achieved six months ahead of schedule. Judith Waddell, the Human Resources Director, emphasised that it took only 18 months to get the Manchester store open. In recruiting staff to the new store, some managers were sent from London with others being recruited locally as people who knew the area, the socio-economic nature of the people and the buying culture in that part of the country. It is interesting to note that, in general, the London managers were less successful in the context of a greenfield site, which was totally different from London. Judith Waddell commented that some managers from London found it difficult to shake off the 'baggage' of the mother store.

Within a very tight time scale, a very large training programme was rolled out to all new staff. The staff of both stores is diverse in nature reflecting the diversity of the customers, particularly in London. The general managers of both stores are women, with 60 per cent of senior managers women. The six strong Board of Directors includes two women but, as yet, no people of colour.

Judith Waddell refers to the period of change at the London store combined with the opening of the Manchester store as 'a chaotic but dynamic' period. Profits fell in 1997 and 1998 and there was the push to get rid of old stock. Alison Straw, Head of Learning and Development, who joined the company in 1997, just after Judith Waddell, refers to herself and Judith 'doing a lot of learning'. Judith gave her the challenge of creating a learning company – a company that could learn from its mistakes. Alison says that at first she would go to meetings where people would say 'But we face these problems every year'. She maintains she does not hear that now.

Selfridges in 2001

According to Peter Williams, the Finance Director, there has had to be a change in the structure of the organisation and a questioning of the old ways of working. Previously, with the one store, many areas of responsibility and control got blurred, with buying and selling functions as one. The head office functions were subsumed in the retail functions making it difficult to see where responsibilities lay. It was difficult to make sure that people took on the roles and accountabilities they should do. The structure now is on a multi-site retail format. The five functional directors report to Vittorio Radice as Chief Executive. Each functional director has his or her own staff of senior managers as shown in Appendix A. Business managers (one each for menswear, womenswear, home and cosmetics) report to each of the general managers of the stores. Business managers, in turn, are responsible for sales managers, each of whom is responsible for one or more departments.

Peter Williams thinks the restructuring is good but says they do not want to lose (what Judith Waddell calls) the ambiguity of Selfridges. He says it is the creativity and the many things they do which are a little bit 'whacky' that is the attraction of the place to the customers, but also why some staff like to work there. He refers to Selfridges as a small city in itself. Part of the fun of it is, for instance, the Christmas Ball for staff held at London Zoo. He refers to the London store as a community, which has a buzz about it. They employ many young people for whom it is their first job. Socialising among staff members is encouraged.

There is a moderate turnover of staff, which is regarded as not necessarily bad. New people bring in new ideas gained from working in other parts of the industry. For instance, there is hardly anyone left in the finance team who was there at the beginning of the changes. Peter Williams says that the finance people now employed have a better capability. A large change in culture is that staff at the 'back of the house' now have a greater degree of empathy with what is going on at the 'front of the house'. He says: 'When the back of the house staff turn towards the front of house staff, they have to be the same as is expected of front of house staff towards customers.' Consequently, customer service is not just about customers who shop in the store, but about internal customers as well.

Appendix B reflects the attitudes encouraged towards the different stakeholders in the business. The concept of turning the values of stakeholders into value in terms of business success is one promoted by Judith Waddell, Human Resources Director and her staff. Judith comments: 'It is important that the values we express to the outside world are reflected internally. We must treat our employees in the same way we do our customers and our suppliers.' The core values Friendly, Aspirational and Bold (FAB) give Selfridges its point of difference in the retailing world and within the organisation these are the values which employees are encouraged to exhibit. A sound communications strategy and imaginative development programmes have been instrumental in changing the culture to one which is much more collaborative and receptive to change.

Training programmes aimed at increasing staff skills include a series of development workshops for those wanting a career in sales and those aspiring to a career in management. There are workshops with titles such as 'Presenting the products – lighting up your department', 'Dealing with difficult situations', 'Assertiveness', 'Succeeding at interviews' – and for aspiring managers 'Teamworking', 'Empowerment and delegation', 'Project capability', 'Strategic vision and direction setting' and 'Negotiating for a positive outcome'.

The training department has a relatively small budget but it has been protected when times have been less good. Head of Learning and Development, Alison Straw's key role in the past three years was all about change and adaptation. Her key role now is to work with managers, looking at their key competencies, helping them to set objectives and how to measure them. The aim of training and development is to make it fun as well as useful. There is now an emphasis on a coaching approach to help staff learn from their own experiences in contrast to traditional teaching and training. The Directors sponsor the management development programmes and managers, in turn, learn how to develop their staff.

Great emphasis is put on frequent communications with staff through magazines and videos. Vittorio Radice visits the Manchester store regularly with twice-yearly meetings with all managers there. There is a staff forum with representatives from unionised and non-unionised staff. Pay rates for sales associates is in the upper quartile. There is also the opportunity for everyone in the organisation to earn bonus based on personal, team or company performance.

Reflections

Judith Waddell, reflecting on the years of change, says they now have a better understanding of the effects of change and can explain it better. Considering how they might have done differently, she says they would not necessarily have done things very differently but would try to do them *better*. There was, perhaps, too much change of everything at once: systems, products, staff as well as the huge changes in the physical look of the store.

Commenting on the Board of Directors, she declares they are close-knit and cohesive, but with Vittorio Radice, the Chief Executive, quite definitely the leader. He is variously described in the press as 'a Modernist bent on shaking up a few traditions in the staid world of retailing', 'charismatic' and 'a retailer with style branded on his soul'. It is he who leads the vision and how he wants the stores to be. His focus is on continuous change, keeping 'just one step ahead' with the changing needs and wants of the market. He is able to cope with uncertainty and acts as much intuitively as with logical reasoning. The Directors, with their staffs, are charged with managing in line with the vision. While the Buying, Retail Operations and Marketing Directors concentrate on the products, the Human Resources and Development staff are clearly focused on the needs of employees, in terms of their personal development, but, more importantly, in terms of their performance as it contributes to the success of the store. The Finance Director keeps his eyes firmly fixed on spending with the needs of the shareholders clearly in view.

The London store has, in all likelihood, benefited from what a *Financial Times* newspaper article of November 1996 referred to as 'the return of the corporate spender (and) the reversal of the exodus of people and businesses seeking cheaper locations to live and work'. The article declares that: '[The exodus] peaked in the late 1980s but there are now more people returning to the city (i.e. London) than leaving it for the first time since the 1940s.' Vittorio Radice joined the store just as retailers were beginning to reap the benefits of a London revived by innovative art, music and theatre. Sales at the London store have risen consistently from that time with only blips due to the huge rail disruptions over Christmas 2000. At the Manchester store, sales have improved each year since its opening in 1998 and it is contributing significantly to the overall financial health of the company. (Appendix C contains an overview of the financial results for both stores.) Vittorio Radice says that the concept of brands is even stronger in Manchester than London. Selfridges is aiming to have at least six stores in its portfolio. It already has the one in Manchester at the out-of-town Trafford Park shopping centre and is planning the opening, in August 2002, of another one – this time in the centre of Manchester. A third (out-of-London) store, with another woman as General Manager, will open in Birmingham in 2003. Further stores are planned for other large cities in the UK. There are plans to develop the whole Oxford Street site to unlock the significant potential of the northern section where the hotel, car park and food hall are currently located.

When the question is asked as to whether the massive upheaval between 1996 and 1999 was worth the effort, attention is drawn to the continuing rise in sales and profits, with Selfridges' shares outperforming competitors such as Marks & Spencer, Harvey Nichols, Debenhams and the House of Fraser, ever since they launched themselves on to the stock market in 1998.

The future looks rosy, but will only turn out like that if constant watch is kept on what is, traditionally, a fickle market influenced by consumer confidence and the ability and willing-ness of people to spend on goods which are seen mainly to be at the luxury end of the market.

Appendix A: Selfridges plc organisation chart

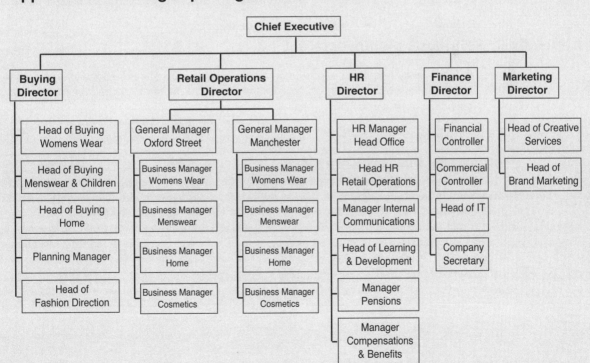

Appendix B: Values to value – the stakeholders

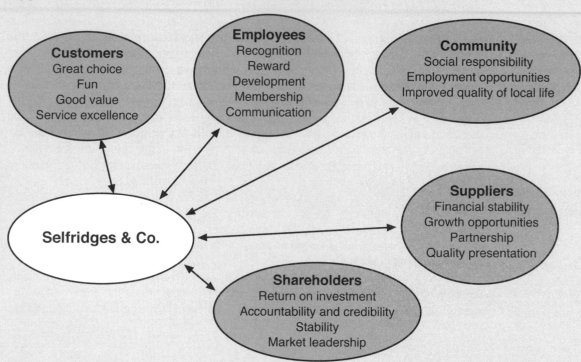

Appendix C: Selfridges plc financial review

In 2000 Selfridges continued to make major progress. Financial performance is again ahead, driven by strong sales growth and improved inventory management, in what continues to be a challenging market for many retailers.

(Selfridges plc annual report 2001)

Financial summary – two years to beginning 2001

Sales in the 53 weeks to 3 February 2001 were £392.1 million (1999/2000 52 weeks – £360.0 million), an increase of 8.9 per cent. The sales improvement reflects strong trading in both stores. Overall, trading profit increased by 30.1 per cent to £40.2 million.

Profit before tax increased by 39.9 per cent to £38.6 million (1999/2000 52 weeks – 15.9 per cent). Sales in week 53 amounted to £5.9 million and contributed £0.3 million to profit before tax. The underlying increase in like-for-like sales was 7.3 per cent, while profit before tax for 52 weeks increased to £38.3 million, an uplift of 38.8 per cent.

Oxford Street: sales and contribution to sales – two years ended 27 January 2001

	2000/2001 52 weeks £m	1999/2000 52 weeks £m	52-week change %
Sales	343.4	325.2	+5.6
Contribution	70.5	62.0	+13.7

Manchester: sales and contribution to sales – two years ended 27 January 2001

	2000/2001 52 weeks £m	1999/2000 52 weeks £m	52-week change %
Sales	42.8	34.8	+23.0
Contribution	3.5	1.3	+169.2

Dividend

A final dividend of 4.0 pence per share was paid on 1 June 2001, giving a total dividend for the year of 6.0 pence, an increase of 14.3 per cent over the dividend for 1999/2000.

Earnings per share

20.3 pence – up 28 per cent from 1999/2000.

Balance sheet

The Oxford Street freehold land and buildings were revalued at the balance sheet date, 3 February 2001, to £358 million on the basis of open market value and existing use. This value represented a £33.7 million increase on the previous revaluation on 1 February 1998.

Stock levels were reduced for the second year in succession, this year by 9.3 per cent to £21.4 million.

Current trading

Sales up 11 per cent in the first 6 weeks of 2001/2002.

Discussion questions and assignments

1 Assume you have been asked to advise Selfridges' Board of Directors on the organisational structure they could adopt when they have (say) five stores of different sizes in different parts of the UK. What would you advise? Justify your advice by reference to your reading of the chapters in Part Two of the book.

2 Carry out research on the Internet (in particular look for newspaper articles and copies of Selfridges' annual reports) to enrich the information given in the case on the prevailing culture at Selfridges. If you live within reach of London, you could visit the store to observe how things are done ('in the front of the house'). Construct, as far as possible, a cultural web for the organisation. How do you think this would differ from one constructed for the store around the late 1980s/early 1990s?

3 What sources of power do you think the Chief Executive, Vittorio Radice, has? What about the other Board Directors? Would these sources of power also be 'enjoyed' by each of the senior managers, team leaders and sales associates? Speculate on the reasons why the changes described in the case might be resisted and by whom? What might be the causes of conflict and between which individuals and groups?

4 What type of leader do you think Vittorio Radice is? How would he rate in terms of the list of traits in Activity 6.2 in Chapter 6? Look again at Illustration 6.2 in Chapter 6 and put forward an argument (adding some of your own assumptions about how a large store like Selfridges might operate) regarding which member(s) of the senior management (see Appendix A) might fill these different roles. Are any missing? Do you think all roles are necessary in all organisations? Which of Quinn's organisational models (see Table 6.2 and Figure 6.5 in Chapter 6) fits Selfridges? Will this model always be appropriate to the environment in which Selfridges operates? Position Selfridges' stage of development on Greiner's graph in Chapter 2. What might be Selfridges' next crisis point and next stage of development?

5 Obtain a copy of Beer and Nohria's article, referred to in Chapter 6, and analyse the change scenario at Selfridges in terms of the E and O approaches suggested there.

PART THREE

Strategies for managing change

Two major themes have emerged from the discussions in Parts One and Two of the book which have a bearing on the practical issues of preparing for, designing and implementing change in organisations. These can be grouped broadly into the categories of the content of change and the context in which it happens. Part One of the book concentrated on the content of organisational change and what causes it, while Part Two explored the formal and informal aspects of organisational life which influence the process of change and within which change happens.

This part of the book turns to the practicalities of *doing* change in the sense of designing, planning and implementing change – in other words concentrating on the processes through which change comes about. Two different approaches to change, each encompassing various methodologies, are discussed respectively in Chapters 7 and 8. These approaches relate directly back to the types of change discussed in Chapter 2, in particular, the concepts of hard and soft problems, that is, difficulties and messes. Consequently, Chapter 7 concentrates on change approaches which are based on rational–logical models of change which are most appropriate for situations of hard complexity where the 'people' issues are low. In contrast, Chapter 8 recognises that many change situations involve issues of organisational politics, culture and leadership (as discussed in Part Two of the book) which dictate an approach to change which can deal more easily with situations characterised by soft complexity.

Finally, Chapter 9 speculates about the future, both in terms of what future organisations might look like and the attitudes and behaviour of those working in them as they might impact on future organisational change.

Chapter 7

Hard systems models of change

There are a number of models for handling change in situations of hard complexity. This chapter describes one and, in order to demonstrate its use, applies it to a particular change situation. The limitations of this type of model are discussed.

Objectives

To:

- *recognise change situations (problems/opportunities) characterised mainly by hard complexity, where the use of hard systems methodologies are appropriate*

- *describe the main features of hard systems methodologies for defining, planning and implementing change*

- *explain the hard systems model of change (HSMC) as representative of hard systems methodologies of change*

- *discuss the limitations of hard systems methodologies of change and, therefore, the need for other change methodologies more suited to situations of soft complexity.*

● ● ● ● Situations of change

In Chapter 2, a number of different ways of categorising organisational change were discussed. These ranged from changes which happen incrementally, and which may affect only one part of an organisation, to the more radical, frame-breaking or discontinuous changes which pervade almost every aspect of an organisation's functioning. As Chapter 2 also showed, expectations with respect to the ease with which change happens vary according to its perceived complexity. Consequently, change in situations which are characterised by hard complexity is more likely to be enacted easily and speedily than change in situations which show soft complexity, that is, where issues are contentious and there is a high level of emotional involvement on the part of those likely to implement the change and those who will be affected by it.

There are many approaches to planning and implementing change. Some are more appropriate to situations of hard complexity – which Chapter 2 also described as 'difficulties' – while others are more appropriate to situations of soft complexity or, as Chapter 2 characterised them, 'messy' situations. Flood and Jackson (1991), using a systems perspective, classify various methodologies in a similar way but use the terms 'simple system' and 'complex system' instead of difficulties and messes. What is of more interest, though, is that Flood and Jackson also classify these methodologies according to their appropriateness of use in situations characterised by different ideological viewpoints. Three ideological viewpoints, representing three types of relationships between people, are defined. Two of these (the unitary and pluralist viewpoints) have been discussed already in Chapter 5 (*see* Illustration 5.9); all three are described in Illustration 7.1.

Using an extensive list of different methodologies for problem solving and change, Flood and Jackson suggest which ones are most appropriate in situations characterised as simple or complex systems but modified by whether relationships between people tend to be of a unitarist, pluralist or coercive nature. It is not the purpose here to consider all the possibilities. What is important, for this discussion, is to note that different logics dominate each possibility in terms of suggesting a particular approach to change. Consequently, in situations of hard complexity (e.g. where simple systems and a unitarist ideology of relationships prevails), a particular type of change approach will be appropriate, whereas in situations of soft complexity (e.g. where complex systems and a pluralist ideology of relationships prevails), a different type of change approach should be used. This chapter concentrates on the first of these situations, to describe an approach to change which is representative of those approaches which are best applied in the relatively bounded situations described variously as difficulties, simple/unitarist systems or, in more straightforward terms, 'hard' situations.

Illustration 7.1

Characteristics of unitary, pluralist and coercive relationships

Unitary
People relating to each other from a unitary perspective:

- share common interests
- have values and beliefs which are highly compatible
- largely agree upon ends and means
- all participate in decision making
- act in accordance with agreed objectives.

Pluralist
People relating to each other from a pluralist perspective:

- have a basic compatibility of interest
- have values and beliefs which diverge to some extent
- do not necessarily agree upon ends and means, but compromise is possible
- all participate in decision making
- act in accordance with agreed objectives.

Coercive
People relating to each other from a coercive perspective:

- do not share common interests
- have values and beliefs which are likely to conflict
- do not agree upon ends and means and 'genuine' compromise is not possible
- coerce others to accept decisions.

Source: Based on Flood, R. L. and Jackson, M. C. (1991), *Creative Problem Solving: Total Systems Intervention* (Chichester, Wiley, pp. 34–5).

●●●● Systematic approaches to change

Most people have the capacity to think logically and rationally. Indeed, some would say this is the only way to approach problem solving or responding to opportunities and, therefore, there can be one basic way of planning and implementing change. It is upon this premise that the more systematic approaches to managing change are based. Derived from earlier methods of problem solving and decision making such as systems engineering methods and operational research (Mayon-White, 1993), these 'hard' approaches rely on the assumption that clear change objectives can be identified in order to work out the best way of achieving them. What is more, a strict application of these approaches dictates that these objectives should be such that it is possible to quantify them, or at least be sufficiently concrete that one can know when they have been achieved. For instance, consider the situation described in Illustration 7.2.

Illustration 7.2 provides an example of what appears to be a difficulty about which most people could agree – it appears to have fairly defined boundaries. There are clearly some problems with the way IT faults are reported to the IT

Illustration 7.2

Dissatisfaction with the system for providing IT support services

Vernabelle, a member of staff of the Faculty of Art and Design at Singleton University, was making a telephone call to the office of the IT support service to report that the computer link from her office to the library was not working. As usual, there was no one there – she supposed the two staff employed in the office were somewhere in the Faculty of Art and Design seeing to someone else's computer. She decided, therefore, to send a memo but knew that, because of the time the internal post took, it would not get to the IT support office before the next day. Even then, from past experience, she suspected that when it was received, she would not receive a response without at least one reminder and perhaps two. Overall, she took a particularly dim view of the quality of IT support service provided and was sure that, if she were responsible for this service, she could improve its effectiveness without too much effort and resources.

---

support service and the way they are responded to when received. It is also clear that some quantitative indices could be devised on which to judge the system and which might give evidence of improvement if this were to take place. What follows is, first, a generalised description of a model of change which is most suited to situations such as that described in Illustration 7.2 – that is, in situations which are more of a difficulty than a mess and, second, a more fully worked out example of its use to plan and implement change in the Beautiful Buildings Company (BB Company).

● ● ● ● The hard systems model of change

Some of the clearest expositions of methods for planning and implementing change in 'hard' situations are those found in Open University course materials (1984, 1994) and the writings of Flood and Jackson (1991) and Paton and McCalman (2000). The methodology for change described here draws on all these sources. To avoid confusion with the Open University's latest model, the 'systems intervention strategy', and Paton and McCalman's 'intervention strategy model', the approach described here is referred to as simply the 'hard systems model of change' (HSMC).

Change in three phases

The HSMC is a method which has been developed for designing and managing change. Its roots lie in methods of analysis and change associated with systems engineering, operational research and project management, that is, where there is an emphasis on means and ends – in other words, on the means with which particular set goals are to be achieved. The HSMC is particularly useful when dealing with situations which lie towards the 'hard' end of the hard–soft continuum of change situations. It provides a rigorous and systematic way of determining objectives (or goals) for change; this is followed by the generation of a range of options for action; the last step is testing those options against a set of explicit criteria. The method is particularly useful where quantitative criteria can be used to test options for change. However, it is also possible to use qualitative criteria – a possibility which is discussed later in the chapter. The process can be thought of as falling into three overlapping phases.

- The *description* phase (describing and diagnosing the situation, understanding what is involved, setting the objectives for the change).
- The *options* phase (generating options for change, selecting the most appropriate option, thinking about what might be done).
- The *implementation* phase (putting feasible plans into practice and monitoring the results).

Within these three phases a number of stages can also be identified. These are shown in Illustration 7.3. What follows describes the stages in more detail.

Illustration 7.3

Stages within the hard systems methodology of change

Phases	Stages	Actions appropriate for each stage
Description	1 Situation summary	• Recognise need for change either to solve a problem or take advantage of an opportunity. • Test out others' views on the need for change • Using appropriate diagnostic techniques, confirm the presence of hard complexity and a difficulty rather than a mess
	2 Identify objectives and constraints	• Set up objectives for systems of interest • Identify constraints on the achievement of the objectives
	3 Identify performance measures	• Decide how the achievement of the objectives can be measured
Options	4 Generate options	• Develop ideas for change into clear options for achievement of the objectives • Consider a range of possibilities
	5 Edit options and detail selected options	• Describe the most promising options in some detail • Decide, for each option, what is involved, who is involved and how it will work
	6 Evaluate options against measures	• Evaluate the performance of the chosen options against the performance criteria identified in stage 3
Implementation	7 Develop implementation strategies	• Select preferred option(s) and plan how to implement
	8 Carry out the planned changes	• Involve all concerned • Allocate responsibilities • Monitor progress

The stages

Illustration 7.3 shows how the stages relate to the phases and provides an indication of likely actions at each stage. An important point to note, however, is that, although Illustration 7.3 presents the phases and stages as a series of sequential steps which follow logically on, one from another, this rarely happens so neatly in real life. There will, almost certainly, be times when there is a need for iteration or 'backtracking', from one stage to earlier stages, as insights generated at later stages reveal the requirement for modifications to previous ones.

Phase 1: Description

Stage 1: Situation summary

The basic idea in Stage 1 is to start by describing the system within which change is going to be made. This stage includes the following:

- Stating the commitment to the analysis and the reason for doing it. For example, statements like the following might be made:

   A commitment to ensuring the current product range is maintained after the takeover.

   A commitment to developing new markets while maintaining market share for existing services.

   A commitment to reducing the amount of floor space occupied by merchandise not achieving at least a 25 per cent profit margin.

- Describing, in words and with diagrams, the situation within which changes will be set.

At the end of this stage the scope of the study will be defined as will the range of problems and issues to be addressed.

Stage 2: Identification of objectives and constraints

In the context of stage 2, an objective can be defined as something which is desired; a constraint is something which inhibits or prevents achievement of an objective. In reality, objectives are likely to be things over which members of organisations may have some control. Constraints are frequently things in an organisation's environment (whether this is internal or external to the organisation) over which it has little control. This stage addresses both objectives and constraints. It involves being clear about where the decision makers want to go and which ways might be impassable or perhaps temporarily blocked. This stage involves the following:

- Listing objectives which are consistent with the themes which emerged from the diagnostic stage.
- Arranging the objectives into a hierarchy of objectives – an objectives tree. An example of a generalised objectives tree is shown in Figure 7.1. This shows how the high-level objective comes at the top, with lower-level objectives (sub-

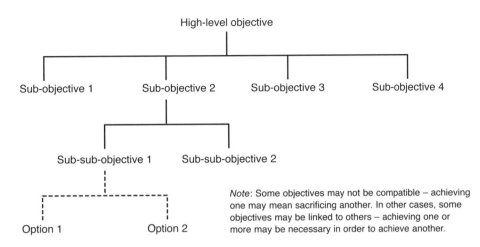

Figure 7.1 The structure of an objectives tree

objectives) arranged in descending order. Lower-level objectives 'lead to' or help the achievement of higher-level objectives.

● Listing constraints in terms of those which (a) are inviolable and (b) may be modified.

Stage 3: Identification of performance measures

The question to be answered in identifying performance measures is: 'How will I know whether or not I have achieved my objective?' If at all possible, use quantifiable measures, e.g. costs (in monetary terms), savings (in monetary terms), time (years, days, hours), amount of labour, volume etc. This stage includes:

● Formulating measures of performance which can be put against the objectives on the objectives tree.

It is possible that some objectives cannot be quantified. In this case, some form of rating or ranking can be used as a measure of performance. Figure 7.2 is an example of an objectives hierarchy for improving the effectiveness of an organisation's information technology support service. The measures of performance for each of the main objectives are in brackets.

Phase 2: Options

Stage 4: Generation of options (routes to objectives)

The setting up of objectives to be achieved is based on the concept of *what* needs to be done to bring about change. By contrast, the generation of options stage is the stage of finding out *how* to achieve the objectives. If the objectives tree is well developed, as Figure 7.1 shows, some of the lower-level objectives may actually be options. There will, however, almost certainly be more. In addition, therefore, to any options which 'creep into' the objectives tree, this stage involves the following:

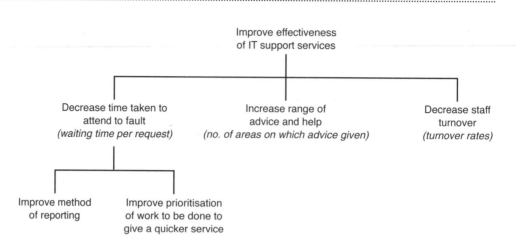

Figure 7.2 An objectives tree for improving the IT support services

- Drawing up a list of options. This can be done by making use of any number of creative thinking techniques such as:
  - brainstorming
  - ideas writing
  - questioning others
  - focus groups
  - interviews
  - research
  - meetings

At the end of this stage, a set of specific ideas should have been generated which will help the problem or opportunity – in the sense that they will further the achievement of the objective(s), rather than that they will break the constraints, and lead to beneficial changes to the situation described in stage 1. Figure 7.3 gives a list of options for the sub-sub-objective of 'Improve prioritisation of work to be done to give a quicker service' – which is one of the objectives in an objectives hierarchy for improving the effectiveness of the service given by an organisation's IT department in support of those who use computer-based programs to help with their work.

Stage 5: Editing and detailing selected options

At the stage of editing and detailing some options, it may be necessary to sort the options, in terms of those which are likely to be feasible given the particular situation described in stage 1 and the constraints identified in stage 2. The selected options should then be described in more detail – or 'modelled' – in terms of what is involved, who is involved and how it will work. It may be that some options cluster together and are better considered as a group. Other options will stand independently and must, therefore, be considered in their own right. There are many ways of testing how an option might work. The following are some

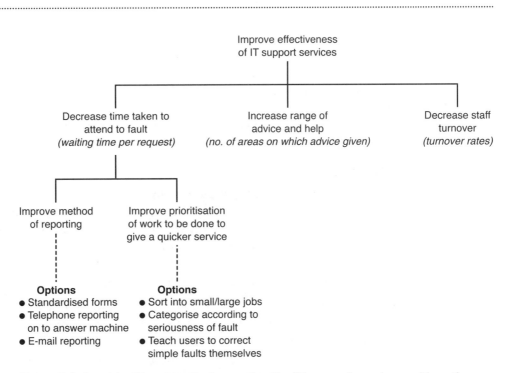

Figure 7.3 An objectives tree for improving the IT support services, with options generated for the two sub-sub-objectives

possibilities drawn from a comprehensive list produced by the Open University (1994, pp. 35–6).

(a) Physical models (architectural models, wind-tunnel test pieces, etc.).

(b) Mock-ups (make mock-ups of new products – sewing machines, aircraft, clothes dryers, etc.).

(c) Computer simulation models (for complex production systems, financial systems, etc.).

(d) Cashflow models (either manually produced or computer driven).

(e) Experimental production lines, or laboratory-scale plant.

(f) Scale plans and drawings (alternative office layouts, organisational structures, etc.).

(g) Cost/benefit analyses (as models of the likely trade-offs which would take place if a particular option were exercised; can be qualitative as well as quantitative).

(h) Corporate plans or strategies (any one plan or proposal represents a 'model' of how the corporation or organisation could develop its activities in the future).

(i) Organisation structure plans and proposals (for example, a chart of a new organisation structure would show how the formal communication links or reporting channels would work if the structure were adopted).

(j) Organisational culture analyses (methods of describing organisational cultures as the means of identifying effects of different options on the culture of the organisation).

Clearly, some of these processes can be time consuming and expensive. However, many options can be described or modelled through the use of diagrams (e.g. of different organisational structures, of input–output processes) or some form of cost-benefit analysis.

It is at this stage of the HSMC that each of the options generated for the objectives in Figure 7.3 would be explored in more detail, using the questions listed earlier about who would be involved, how it would work and what financial and other resources would be required for it to work. Some form of cost-benefit analysis could be used with costs and benefits being those of time as well as money.

Stage 6: Evaluating options against measures

The evaluation stage of the change process is a decision area. It allows choices of options to be made against the criteria identified in stage 3. Figure 7.4 shows a generalised evaluation matrix which compares one option against another on the basis of the measures set during stage 3.

Before making your recommendation, you should:

● Check that the model you have used is an accurate representation of the system.
● Consider whether the model seems to contain any bias or mistaken assumptions.
● Evaluate each option, or combination of options, according to how well it meets the performance measures. Rating the options overall on a scale (say of 1 for very good and 5 for very bad) is a useful guide.

Figure 7.5 is a rough estimate of the desirability of some of the options generated from the objectives in Figure 7.3.

A more detailed examination of each option in Figure 7.5 would show more precisely the impact, in terms of the performance criteria, on each objective listed. For the purposes of this example, however, an estimate has been made. On the basis of these, it is clear from the evaluation matrix in Figure 7.5 that some of these options could be combined. For instance, the best method of reporting should be combined with the best method for prioritising work to be done. On this basis, option 2 combined with option 3 seem to contribute most to the main objective. However, if an E-mail standard format of reporting were to be used, this

Objectives and related measures of performance	Option A	Option B	Option C	Option D
Objective 1, measure 1				
Objective 2, measure 2				
Objective 3, measure 3				

Figure 7.4 An evaluation matrix

Objectives and related measures of performance	Options			
	Telephone reporting on to answer machine	*E-mail reporting*	*Categorisation according to seriousness of fault*	*Use of written standardised reporting form*
Sub-objective Decrease time taken to attend to fault (*waiting time per request*)	Low cut in waiting time	Medium cut in waiting time	High cut in time for serious faults; low cut for simple faults	Low cut in time – delays through need to post
Sub-sub-objective Improve method of reporting (*fault reporting received more quickly and accurately*)	High increase in speed of reporting	High increase in speed and some increase in accuracy of reporting	No effect	High increase in accuracy of reporting
Sub-sub-objective Improve prioritisation of work to be done (*serious faults dealt with first*)	Difficult to estimate	Small improvement	Great improvement	Some improvement

Figure 7.5 An evaluation matrix for some options to improve the effectiveness of the IT support services

would also help speed and accuracy in reporting faults. It could also include space for indicating urgency in terms of lack of access to the particular program affected. The only problem with an E-mail solution is that this relies on this function not being the one which is at fault! If this is the case, written or telephone communication must be resorted to.

Phase 3: The implementation phase

Stage 7: Implementation

In problems of a definite 'hard' nature, implementation will rarely be a problem. With problems tending towards 'softness', implementation will be a test of how much people involved in the change have participated in its design.

There are three strategies for implementation:

(a) pilot studies leading to eventual change
(b) parallel running
(c) big bang.

Pilot studies help sort out any problems before more extensive change is instituted, but they can cause delay – a factor that is particularly important in a fast-moving dynamic situation.

Parallel running applies most frequently to the implementation of new computer systems, but can be applied to other kinds of change. The new system is run, for a time, alongside the old system, until confidence is gained that the new system is reliable and effective.

Big bang implementation maximises the speed of change, but can generate the greatest resistance to change. Big bang implementations carry a high risk of failure unless planned very carefully.

Implementation often involves a blend of all three strategies.

Stage 8: Consolidation – 'carry through'

It takes time for new systems to 'bed in'. It is at this stage that there tends to be a decline in concentration on the need to support the change, nurture it and the people involved. Yet this is one of the most crucial stages if the change is to be accepted and successful. Even after the implementation process, further changes can be forced on the situation at any time if the imbalance between the system and the environment becomes too great. There is no justification for 'sitting back'!

● ● ● ● Using the hard systems model of change

Illustration 7.4 describes concerns about the way large plant and machinery is acquired and maintained for use on the building sites of the Beautiful Buildings Company (BB Company). What follows is a description of the process Gerry Howcroft went through to identify a number of options for improving this situation to put before the senior managers' meeting. The description takes the form of notes made by Gerry, interspersed with comments on the method he used.

Illustration 7.4

Financial savings on the provision and maintenance of plant for use on building sites

'The next item on the agenda is the issue of the increasing costs of providing and maintaining major items of plant on the UK building sites. At our last meeting, we saw an earlier draft of this paper. We must now come to some decision as to which option to follow and how it will be implemented.'

So spoke Gillian Lambeth, the Managing Director of the Beautiful Buildings Company which was having one of its regular senior managers' meetings. The next item on the agenda was the increasing costs of purchasing and maintaining large items of plant (such as cranes, diggers and earth-moving equipment) used on the various UK building sites. The item had come to the fore because of the latest rises in the cost of purchasing and maintaining some of these large items of plant which were necessary components in any building project. What was more, in the case of plant breakdowns, getting the specialist maintenance services to effect speedy repairs was always problematical.

Gerry Howcroft, who was responsible for overseeing management of all the UK sites, had prepared a number of options for change which he believed would reduce these costs and improve the maintenance problems. These had already been discussed in rough form at a previous meeting. He had now gained more information on costs etc. of following the different options and had distributed the latest version of these to the managers before the meeting. The meeting now settled down to discuss what to do.

Change at the BB Company

> ### Gerry Howcroft's Note 1   19 May
>
> Need to think back to that course on managing change.
>
> Is this a difficulty or a mess?
>
> Application of criteria discussed in the book they gave us (Senior, 'Organisational Change' – Chapter 2 – Illustrations 2.7 and 2.8) ... situation is: bounded in terms of problem definition, people involved, timescale and resources available.
>
> Plus – situation is like Stacey's conditions of 'close to certainty' rather than conditions of 'far from certainty' (also mentioned in Senior's book – Chapter 2).
>
> Think, therefore, that this is more of a difficulty than a mess.
>
> So – think will have a go at using the HSMC.

Stage 1: Summarising the BB Company's concerns

As overall sites manager, Gerry was responsible for the acquisition and maintenance of plant and equipment deemed necessary for carrying out the complex activities which take place on any building site. In this role, he had to make sure that large plant such as cranes and diggers were fit to carry out the work required of them. This entailed his finding the best suppliers in terms of cost and service backup and ensuring proper maintenance of the plant. Recently, however, the costs of maintaining two large cranes and a digger, which were currently being used on two different sites, had begun to escalate and it seemed as if costs generally for using plant such as this were going up. Gerry wondered whether the equipment had been ill-used or not maintained well or whether it was simply beginning to wear out. As part of the first stage of applying the HSMC, he decided to visit the sites in question and talk to the site manager and any others who had views about the provision, use and maintenance of this type of plant. On his return he summarised his findings in another note (*see* Note 2).

> ### Gerry Howcroft's Note 2   21 May
>
> Visited Karen (site manager) at the Three Towers site who said cranes such as these should last 'forever' if looked after. Think this far-fetched given the way the guys use them. Didn't seem to be anyone personally responsible for servicing and maintaining them – one of the men got some overtime each week to hose them down – if they broke down and the operator couldn't fix it, the service agent was sent for. On the other hand, Jed (who operated the crane all the time at the Riverside site) said his crane was just so old that, in spite of good maintenance it had 'had its day' – this in spite of Jed's obvious feelings of 'ownership' towards the crane!
>
> Think there are many contributions to rising costs – a couple of diagrams might help – see Note 3.

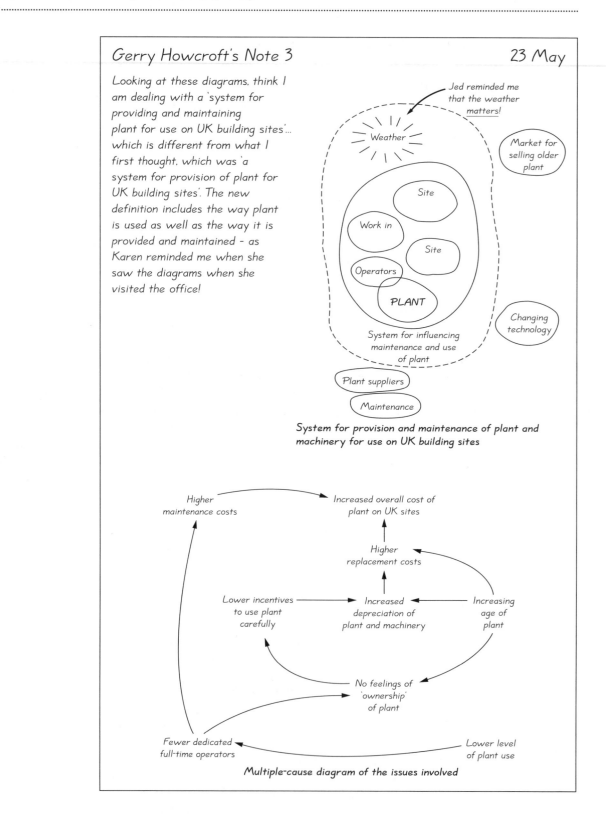

Gerry Howcroft's Note 3   23 May

Looking at these diagrams, think I am dealing with a 'system for providing and maintaining plant for use on UK building sites'... which is different from what I first thought, which was 'a system for provision of plant for UK building sites'. The new definition includes the way plant is used as well as the way it is provided and maintained - as Karen reminded me when she saw the diagrams when she visited the office!

Jed reminded me that the weather matters!

Weather

Market for selling older plant

Site

Work in

Site

Operators

PLANT

System for influencing maintenance and use of plant

Changing technology

Plant suppliers

Maintenance

System for provision and maintenance of plant and machinery for use on UK building sites

Higher maintenance costs → Increased overall cost of plant on UK sites

Higher replacement costs

Lower incentives to use plant carefully → Increased depreciation of plant and machinery ← Increasing age of plant

No feelings of 'ownership' of plant

Fewer dedicated full-time operators ← Lower level of plant use

Multiple-cause diagram of the issues involved

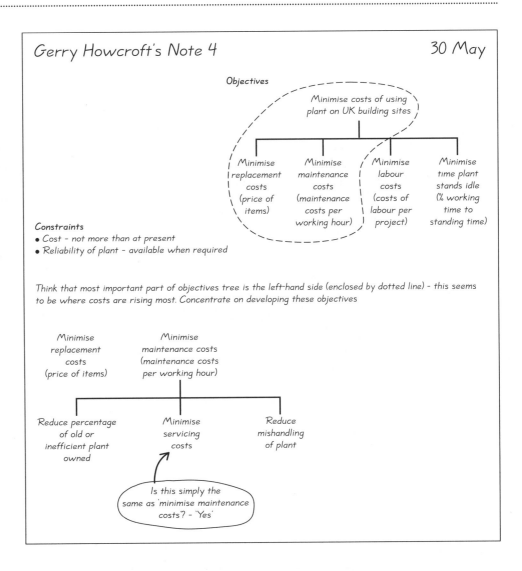

Gerry Howcroft's Note 4   30 May

Stage 2: Setting up objectives to be achieved and recognising constraints

Having summarised the situation regarding the issue of plant costs, Gerry's next step was to build a hierarchy of quantifiable objectives. His Note 4 shows the results of this activity. Gerry did not find this activity particularly easy, given the requirement of the HSMC methodology that lower-level objectives should logically contribute to higher-level objectives and contribute overall to the top objective, in this case of 'minimising the costs associated with the use of plant on UK building sites'. However, he recognised that some confusion of objectives was inevitable before a clear system of objectives began to emerge. Even so, he reminded himself that the characteristics of a good objective are that:

1 It should address the problem to be solved.
2 It must be relevant to the issues identified.

3 It should provide a guide on what needs to be done to make the change from the current situation to the desired situation.

4 It must be something which can feasibly be acted upon.

It can be seen from Gerry's Note 4 that he did not develop all the higher-level objectives into more detailed sets of sub-objectives. Given his knowledge of his management colleagues and their way of thinking, he made a decision to concentrate on the objective 'Minimise maintenance costs' to develop sub-objectives for further consideration, but also to consider the objective 'Minimise replacement costs'. With regard to the objectives 'Minimise labour costs' and 'Minimise time plant stands idle', he kept these 'in reserve' in case of need for further exploration of the issue.

Having developed his objectives hierarchy as far as he could in a direction thought feasible and achievable, the next step for Gerry was to develop further the measures of performance for the objectives identified (in brackets) in Note 4.

Stage 3: Identify performance measures

Note 5 shows the table Gerry compiled to ensure he had some idea of how he would tell if and when an objective had been achieved. From Gerry's Note 5, it can be seen that some objectives are more difficult to quantify, in *practice*, even if, theoretically, measures can be put upon them. In addition, the simple measure of 'price of items' for the objective 'minimise replacement costs' was not sufficient. The cost needed to be expressed for a certain period of time which could be related either to (say) a number of years or the period of a particular project. The measure for reducing mishandling of plant could, perhaps, have been formulated in monetary terms but, for the present, Gerry decided to use a scale to judge the likely effects of any option on this objective.

Gerry Howcroft's Note 5	*2 June*
Objective	*Measure*
1. Minimise replacement costs	Cost of replacing item of plant over a specified period of time averaged out per year (assume cost of new plant for now).
2. Minimise maintenance costs	Cost of maintenance (includes servicing and repair) averaged out on a working hourly basis – i.e. does not include time standing idle. Will need to get accounts to get these figures.
3. Reduce percentage of old/ inefficient plant	Say no plant to be more than eight years old.
4. Reduce mishandling of plant	Difficult to measure. May have to look at training given – assuming training improves standard of plant handling. Another measure might be cost of maintenance per operator – easier to do when operator full-time on plant. For now using a scale of 1 (low) to 5 (high) according to effect on plant might be okay.

Stage 4: Generate options for change

Having set up some objectives to be achieved – hopefully, to improve the situation – Gerry's next step was to generate a range of options which would enable the objectives to be achieved. He did this by asking Kerry, one of the site managers, and the accounts manager to help in 'brainstorming' ideas for change. The results of this brainstorm are shown in Note 6.

Gerry Howcroft's Note 6   *6 June*

Options for change

Objective:	*Minimise replacement costs*
Options:	*Find cheapest supplier*
	Stop buying plant
	Increase replacement time
	Get someone else to replace the plant
	Hire not buy
	Lengthen life of plant
	Buy secondhand
Objective:	*Reduce percentage of old/inefficient plant owned*
Options:	*Sell everything over a certain number of years old*
	Sell everything not used on a regular basis and hire occasionally as required
	Replace old plant with new plant more frequently
	Don't own any plant
	Borrow plant from others
Objective:	*Minimise servicing costs*
Options:	*Reduce number of services per period of time (say operating hours)*
	Obtain cheaper provision of services
	Don't service at all
	Operators do all servicing rather than just basics
	Use other people's plant and which they service
	Contract out servicing to lowest bidder
Objective:	*Reduce mishandling of plant*
Options:	*Train operators in plant handling*
	Institute operator gradings (linked to pay) based on handling performance
	Contract out operating to operators employed by specialist agencies

---

Stage 5: Edit options and detail selected options

Gerry considered all these options in the light of the constraint of maintaining a high level of reliability of plant. It seemed that the options might reduce to a few main themes. At this point, Gerry decided to try out the options list on a couple of colleagues (one of whom was the company accountant) to see which they thought might be feasible. He also used his own judgement. He eventually arrived at a list which included some options as they stood, amalgamated others, and eliminated others (*see* Note 7).

Gerry Howcroft's Note 7   *9 June*

Themes emerging from options list

- *Finding a cheaper source for buying plant (either new or secondhand)*
- *Don't buy plant – hire or borrow*
- *Use only plant which is less than eight years old (or whatever period seems appropriate considering rise in repair and maintenance as age increases)*
- *Increase the period of time before replacement*
- *Service plant less frequently than at present*
- *Train operators to do all servicing and maintenance*
- *Contract out operating to specialist firms*
- *Offer incentives for better operating practices*

Comments

Some of these options contradict each other, so if one is taken up another might be automatically cancelled – e.g. 'Increase time before replacement' conflicts with 'Use plant eight years old or younger'.

Given the importance the MD attaches to safety on sites, I am going to go for options which are in line with her concerns and which meet the constraint of 'reliability of plant'.

For the time being, therefore, I am going to turn an objective into a constraint and work to have plant which is no older than eight years.

Within these constraints, the following seem worthy of further consideration:

1 *Continue buying own plant (search for cheapest deals) with maintenance outsourced.*

2 *Continue buying own plant with maintenance done by own staff.*

3 *Continue buying plant which is used continuously and hire other for occasional use; maintenance of own plant done by own staff.*

4 *Continue buying plant which is used continuously and hire otherwise but outsource maintenance of own plant.*

5 *Hire all plant with maintenance as part of the deal.*

6 *Offer incentives for good performance in plant handling.*

I guess there are more permutations but, depending on how the costings come out on these, we can look at those later.

As Note 7 indicates the options available seemed to range from, at the one extreme, the BB Company's owning and maintaining all plant to, at the other extreme, hiring (or leasing) plant which was maintained entirely by the suppliers. A number of possibilities were clearly possible between these two. The options listed as 1 to 5 are a mix of these. What is evident from the range of possible options is that some quite detailed information is required before one option can be evaluated against another. In addition, option 6 might only be relevant if one of options 1 to 4 were chosen. If option 5 were chosen, incentives to operate the plant well might not be thought relevant if all maintenance costs were included in the hire contract.

Stage 6: Evaluate options against measures

The method of evaluating options against the measures of performance associated with each of the objectives to be reached varies according to the type of options generated. For example, if the options are different production systems, not only would these have to be evaluated on cost measures, but they might also involve evaluation through building some simulations of the different systems. These could, of course, be physical models but they could also be computer models. For Gerry's purposes, it was possible to construct an evaluation matrix which allowed comparison of options one against another in terms of the measures of performance for the defined objectives. Note 8 is a record of Gerry's first attempt, on very limited information, at an evaluation matrix.

Gerry Howcroft's Note 8						*16 June*
			Options			
Objectives and related measures of performance.	*1 Continue buying own plant with maintenance outsourced*	*2 Continue buying own plant with maintenance by own staff*	*3 Continue buying continuously used plant and hire plant which is used only occasionally: maintenance of own plant done by own staff*	*4 Continue buying continuously used plant and hire otherwise: outsource maintenance of own plant*	*5 Hire all plant with maintenance as part of the deal*	*6 Offer incentives for good plant-handling performance*
Minimise replacement costs (£ per year)	*High cost*	*Medium cost*	*Medium cost*	*Medium cost*	*Medium cost*	*Low cost*
Minimise maintenance costs (£ per working hour)	*High cost*	*Medium cost*	*Medium cost*	*Medium-high cost*	*Medium cost*	*Low cost*
Reduce mishandling of plant (scale of 1 to 5 - 1 being least effective, 5 being most effective)	*1*	*3*	*2*	*1*	*1*	*4*

Need to give some information on this to the senior managers' meeting on 23 June - only a week away! Have only got limited information on options - still, can make some guesses at this point and will take the views of colleagues as to which options to pursue - then must get better information on hiring etc.

Gerry took copies of the first draft of the evaluation matrix to the senior managers' meeting. The outcome of the discussion of what he had prepared was that he should get more information on options 3, 4 and 5 which involved different levels of hiring plant instead of purchasing it. What Gerry had, in effect, to do was to go back to stage 5 to get more detail about these options before preparing a final evaluation matrix. This took some time, what with getting information from the finance department (only to discover that it was not kept in a 'user-friendly' form!) and from companies which hired out plant and equipment. Eventually, however, having gathered as much information as he could, he prepared a final evaluation matrix for discussion at the meeting referred to in Illustration 7.4.

The outcome of that discussion is recorded in Gerry's Note 9.

Gerry Howcroft's Note 9   *5 August*

What a long discussion which went round and round in circles – difficult to decide between one option and another – the evaluation matrix was very helpful but then decisions are not always perfectly logical!

Eventually, decided on the hiring option with maintenance all-in – however we could not change overnight to this from where we are at present – just purchased a new digger on the Blackton site.

Will need to do a thorough survey of the state of plant on all the sites to determine when to make the changeover to hiring.

Interesting that the meeting decided to retain our own operators for now (even though could get an agency to supply these) – so will start talks with Personnel as to how we might give extra training and/or offer incentives to improve operator performance – after all, the maintenance costs part of the hiring contract is dependent on the amount of maintenance needed – large repairs will incur extra cost.

Seems an implementation strategy is required!

Stage 7: Develop implementation strategy

Gerry realised that the 'big bang' strategy for implementing change was not viable for his situation. Some of the plant had only recently been purchased, while other items were some years old. Overall, plant on the various sites was in different states of repair. Therefore, Gerry decided to go for the 'parallel running' implementation strategy where older and/or poorly maintained plant was replaced first. This would also offer the opportunity of monitoring the costs of hiring against owning *in reality* as against the theoretical case which the options had presented. If, after all, the savings proved negligible or negative, another evaluation of options could be done.

One good thing about retaining the company's own operators was that there were likely to be few problems from the workforce on the changeover. What might happen, however, was the occasional hiring of plant plus operator when it was required for a limited short period. This would give a chance to see how such hirings were received generally.

Stage 8: Carrying out the planned changes

For Gerry and the other senior managers, the changes, when implemented, will need monitoring. Changing from purchasing plant to hiring it may not mean much change in the way plant is operated on the building sites. However, the changes in the way maintenance and repairs are done will require operators and site managers to learn a new system of reporting and getting these done.

One of the benefits of going through the processes involved in applying the HSMC methodology was that Gerry realised how little monitoring of the costs of plant usage had been done up to the change. When trying to obtain the costs of the different ways of providing and maintaining plant, he became very much aware of the diffuse nature of much of the information he wanted. From now on, he was going to make sure that the finance department arranged its systems so that monitoring of large expenditures such as this could be monitored. This would, of course, mean yet more change but in a different part of the organisation. Gerry wondered whether this was another case of applying the HSMC!

Issues in using the hard systems model of change

The HSMC has been posed as a methodology for change which is most appropriately used in situations of hard complexity, or what have been termed difficulties. The case study involving Gerry Howcroft and the BB Company illustrates this use. In Gerry Howcroft's case, there is reason to believe that resistance to the planned changes will not be high. However, this is not always the case, as the discussion in Chapter 6 showed. Whenever and wherever possible, therefore, those people who are likely to be affected by the change should be consulted as early as possible. In addition, support from senior management is essential for any but the most localised, operational types of change.

It was clear that, in Gerry's case, the information he needed to construct an informative evaluation matrix was not easily obtainable – particularly with regard to that which he required from his own organisation. This stage of the methodology can, therefore, be quite long if a realistic evaluation of options is to be done. By the same token, it is possible to go through the stages of the methodology quite quickly to address key factors associated with the change situation. A small group of people could quickly drive a way through this methodology to suggest at least a tentative solution in a situation requiring change. In addition, as Paton and McCalman (2000, pp. 94–5) point out:

> A Q & D (quick and dirty) analysis can be a useful starting point for the change agents tackling a more complex problem. It will indicate key factors and potential barriers to change, it will highlight the principal players and give an indication of resource requirements. Such an analysis will at an early stage set the scene for things to come and provide the change agents with a valuable insight into the complexities of the transition process.

An example of using the HSMC as a starting point to an analysis of a more messy situation is given in Illustration 7.5. This demonstrates the early stages in considering how to expand the provision and delivery of open and resource-based learning in the further education colleges run by the local education authority of 'Shire County'.

Illustration 7.5

Change in the further education colleges of Shire County

Existing state of affairs

- Falling numbers of 16–19 year olds coming into further education (FE)

- Only small percentage of adults participating in FE

- Current FE provision not always accessible to needs of adults in terms of content, qualifications and mode of delivery

GAP

Desired state of affairs

- Increase proportion of 16–19 year olds in FE

- Signficant increase in number of adults in FE

- Improve accessibility for all learners, but for adults in particular, i.e. greater choice of content, qualifications and mode of delivery relevant to educational and training needs

This state of affairs brought forth the following commitment statement:

In an environment of decreasing numbers of 16–19 year olds and limited numbers of adults participating in further education, the aim for the future is to make it possible for more people to participate in education and training through the expansion of open and resource-based learning (O&RBL) both as an integral part of mainstream provision as well as an alternative but equally credible way of facilitating and accrediting learning.

A causal-loop diagram (see Figure 7.6) was constructed to provide further information about the forces operating for and against the desire to expand O&RBL. From this a range of objectives were formulated, together with a list of possible measures of performance.
An initial attempt at an objectives hierarchy is shown in Figure 7.7.
Possible measures of performance (not particularly attached to specific objectives):

- Establish O&RBL centres by ? (date).
- Extend availability of provision to 48 weeks per year by ? (date).
- Achieve x % of open and resource-based learners by ? (date).
- ? (number) of companies using O&RBL by ? (date).
- ? (number) of staff trained in the delivery of O&RBL by ? (date).
- ? (number) of students gaining qualifications through O&RBL by ? (date).
- Complete changeover to providing mathematics instruction in modules by ? (date).
- ? % increase in use of O&RBL in all mainstream provision by ? (date).

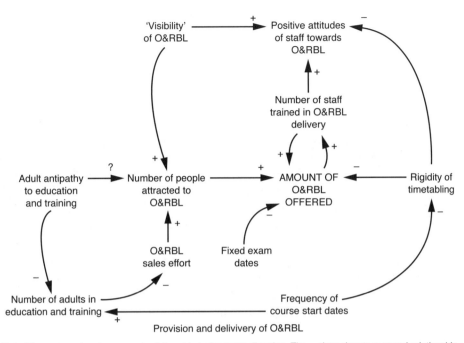

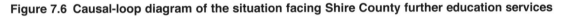

Note: The + signs denote a causal relationship in the same direction. The − signs denote a causal relationship in opposite directions

Figure 7.6 Causal-loop diagram of the situation facing Shire County further education services

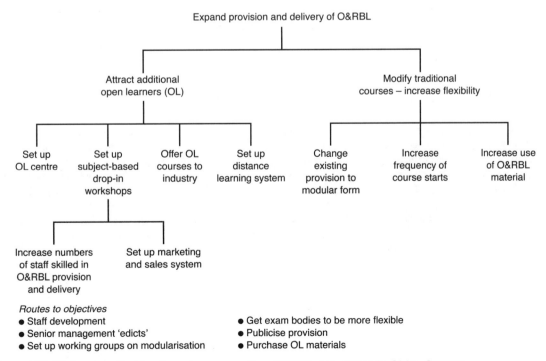

Figure 7.7 Hierarchy of objectives for expanding O&RBL provision in Shire County

Using the HSMC, in the case of Shire County, was useful for setting out the commitment to change, carrying out (with the help of diagrams) a situational analysis of the forces for and against the change and formulating some objectives and measures of performance in preparation for planning and implementing the change. What this methodology was less good at doing was identifying the political issues surrounding the implementation of radical change of this kind. In addition, current organisational, professional and institutional cultures were clearly going to work to make changes of this kind difficult to achieve.

This was a case where the changes desired were going to take some time to come to fruition and these would involve changes, not only to the buildings and teaching areas (i.e. physical changes) but also in people's attitudes and behaviours – changes which would include both staff and students (present and potential students). The changes being proposed here were more in line with what has been described as 'organisational development', that is, change which is ongoing, which involves most parts of the organisation and most of its members and which will not succeed without the involvement of all concerned at all stages in the change process. The next chapter describes in more detail a change process more relevant to situations of soft complexity – in other terms, situations known as messes.

Discussion questions and assignments

1 From your or other people's experiences, identify three change situations where application of the HSMC could prove useful. Then identify three situations where it would 'run into difficulties'. Justify your categorisation.

2 As far as is feasible, apply the HSMC to a change situation with which you are familiar.

References

Flood, R. L. and Jackson, M. C. (1991), *Creative Problem Solving: Total Systems Intervention*, Chichester, Wiley.

Mayon-White, B. (1993), 'Problem-solving in small groups: team members as agents of change', in Mabey, C. and Mayon-White, B. (eds), *Managing Change* (2nd edn), London, PCP.

Open University (1984), Block III, 'The hard systems approach', Course T301, *Complexity, Management and Change: Applying a Systems Approach*, Milton Keynes, Open University.

Open University (1994), 'Managing the change process', Course B751, *Managing Development and Change*, Milton Keynes, Open University.

Paton, R. A. and McCalman, J. (2000), *Change Management. A Guide to Effective Implementation* (2nd edn) London, Sage.

Stacey, R. (2000), *Strategic Management and Organisational Dynamics: The Challenge of Complexity*, London, Financial Times/Prentice Hall.

Chapter 8

Soft systems models for change

Through a revision of the concept of soft complexity, this chapter begins by challenging the notion of rationality as applied to organisational change. This is followed by a short description of Lewin's three-phase model of change as a prelude to a more detailed description and discussion of organisational development as an approach to change. Some limitations of organisational development as a change philosophy and as a change approach are discussed.

Objectives

To:

- *recognise that some change situations (problems/opportunities), by nature of their complexity and particular characteristics, require soft rather than hard systems approaches to change*

- *consider the philosophy, value orientation and theoretical underpinnings of organisation development (OD) as a generalised example of soft systems models for change*

- *outline and describe the processes and practices which comprise most OD approaches to designing and implementing organisational change*

- *discuss the limitations of OD approaches to managing change.*

● ● ● ● Managing change in situations of soft complexity

The previous chapter ended with an example of the need for change for which the HSMC had limited applicability. This was because the situation which gave rise to the requirement to expand open and resource-based learning in further education colleges in Shire County was characterised by elements of both hard and soft complexity. As Chapter 7 showed, it was possible, using the HSMC, to build an objectives hierarchy with measurable performance criteria and to generate some options for bringing about the necessary changes. However, while this was fine in theory, other factors – the organisational culture, entrenched power bases and established leadership styles, as well as the simultaneous reorganisation of the county education service which was driving the change – combined to make the process of change much more complex, diffuse and confused than it appeared at first sight. In summary, what faced those charged with bringing about the changes was much more of a mess than a difficulty, implying that a different approach to planning and implementing change was required.

In an article aptly named 'The art and science of mess management', Ackoff (1993) identifies three different 'kinds of things' that can be done about problems. He says (p. 47): 'They can be *resolved, solved or dissolved.*'

According to Ackoff, 'to resolve a problem is to select a course of action that yields an outcome that is good enough, that *satisfices* (satisfies and suffices)'. This is an approach which relies on common sense, based on previous experience as to what might work or not and, to some extent, on trial and error. People who use this approach (and Ackoff says most managers are problem resolvers) do not pretend to be objective in their decision making. They use little specially collected data, either of a quantitative or qualitative nature, justifying their conclusions by citing lack of time or lack of information or too complex a situation for anything other than minimising risk and maximising the likelihood of survival. Ackoff calls this the 'clinical' approach to dealing with messes, a metaphor which emphasises different people preoccupied with different aspects of the problem situation, but coming together to reach some consensus on how to proceed with resolving the problem. However, while this approach is likely to keep most people satisfied and 'on board' with the change, a major criticism is that, because of its commitment solely to qualitative-type thinking based on past experience and hunch, it lacks analytical rigour in its formulation of objectives and the means of evaluating their attainment. Therefore, it is never quite clear how far the objectives of the change have been met.

This criticism can certainly not be levelled at the 'solvers' of problems. By contrast with resolvers of problems, rather than using simple common sense and what might have been successful in the past, solvers of problems use approaches to problems which are much more heavily reliant on research-based scientific methods, techniques and tools. This means they eschew qualitative models in favour of quantitative models in their aspirations to be completely objective. Ackoff calls this the 'research' approach to mess management. It is much more likely to be used by management scientists and technologically oriented managers. This approach is akin to hard systems models of change in its emphasis on quantitative methods of analysis, objective setting and generation of options for change as demonstrated in the description of the HSMC in the previous chapter. However, while addressing the lack of 'hard' data in the clinical approach to mess management, the research approach is limited in that its techniques are more applicable to mechanistic systems (which lend themselves to performance definition and measurement) than to purposeful human behaviour (which includes many unmeasurable elements). In addition, given that a mess is not just one problem but a complex of problems interacting one with another, decomposing the mess to deal with one problem at a time (as this approach would suggest) loses the essential properties of the larger more complex whole. This is summarised well by Ackoff when he says (p. 51):

> Therefore, when a research-orientated planner decomposes a mess by analysis, he loses its essential properties. ... As a consequence, what he perceives as the hard facts of the mess are really soft fictions of his imagination, abstractions only loosely related to reality.

From this, it seems that both resolvers, with their clinical approaches to bringing about change, and solvers of problems, with their research approaches to change, are limited in their capacity to plan and implement change in unbounded soft situations characterised as messes. Consequently, Ackoff suggests a third approach, based on the concept of *dissolving* problems. Of this approach to problem solving, he says (p. 48):

> To *dissolve* a problem is to change the nature, and/or the environment, of the entity in which it is embedded so as to remove the problem. Problem dissolvers *idealise* rather than satisfice or optimise because their objective is to change the system involved or its environment in such a way as to bring it closer to an ultimately desired state, one in which the problem cannot or does not arise.

He calls this approach the 'design' approach in that problem dissolvers, in addition to using the methods and techniques of problem resolvers and problem solvers, seek to redesign the characteristics of the larger system containing the problem (for instance, changing the organisational culture, structure, systems and/or processes). Thus, they look for dissolution of the problem in the wider containing system rather than looking for solutions in the contained parts. Ackoff (p. 48) maintains that only a minority of managers use this approach and they are those, 'whose principal organisational objective is *development* rather than growth or survival, and who know the difference'. Of the concept of development he says (pp. 48–9):

> To develop is to increase and desire to improve one's quality of life and that of others. Development and growth are not the same and are not even necessarily related.

As an example of this, he refers to the fact that a heap of rubbish can grow without developing and a person can develop without growing.

As the situation for change unfolded in the further education system in Shire County, it became evident that this was not a problem to be resolved or solved, but a complex of problems which was likely to require the wider system containing it to be redesigned, if progress was to be made towards achieving the stated objectives. These objectives themselves were, incidentally, somewhat unclear and by no means shared by all.

It is not usual to find reference to 'dissolving' problems in the literature on change. Yet most of the change models associated with 'soft' situations and systems (i.e. those characterised by soft complexity) imply a need for redesigning systems at many levels of the organisation. These include issues associated with individuals and the groupings they form, as well as with organisational strategy, structure and processes. This means not only an emphasis on the *content* and *control* of change (as the hard systems models of change dictate), but also an emphasis on the *process* by which change comes about, or as Buchanan and Boddy (1992, p. 27) maintain, a need for 'backstaging' as well as 'public performance'. In other words, there is a need to be concerned with what Buchanan and Boddy (p. 27) call 'the exercise of "power skills", with "intervening in political and cultural systems", with influencing negotiating and selling, and with "managing meaning".'

The consequences of this are that designing change in messy situations must also include attention to issues such as problem ownership, the role of communication and the participation and commitment of the people involved in the change process itself. It also means, as evidenced in the following section, challenging the notion that planning and implementing change can be wholly rational, a notion that the majority of hard systems models of change assume.

The challenge to rationality

For some time, the literature on corporate strategy and strategic change (*see*, for instance, Carnall, 1995; Johnson, 1990; Kirkbride, Durcan and Obeng, 1994; Stacey, 2000) has put forward arguments challenging the idea that people make decisions and choices according to some rational model of decision making. For instance, Johnson (1993) argues strongly that rational models of change, with their associated scientific management techniques, overlook the significance of the cultural, political and cognitive dimensions of organisational life. The discussion, in Chapter 4, of Johnson and Scholes's (1997) cultural web is a strong indictment of the contention that managers and implementers of change always (or even frequently) act according to some abstract formulation of what is rational in any particular situation.

This is not to say, however, that people do not act rationally. It is to say, as Carnall (1995) would maintain, that they act according to their own view of what is rational for them. This will include their particular perspective of the causes, consequences and need for change, moulded by their values, culture, attitudes and political position within the organisation. Any case for change will not, therefore, be accepted according to some (supposedly) objective rational analysis. Change, in this scenario, will only be possible and effective if it is accompanied by processes which address, in particular, the feelings, needs and aspirations of individuals, the group processes which bind them together and the structures and systems which are forces for stability rather than change. Added to these are the cultural, political and symbolic processes which act to maintain the current organisational paradigm or 'the way things are done around here'.

Given all this, it appears that hard systems models of change, although necessary in some defined and agreed situations, are not sufficient to explain organisational messes and are extremely limited in providing a model for planning and implementing change in these situations. For instance, hard systems approaches to change require the setting of quantifiable objectives against which criteria for their attainment can be set. This assumes that there is little argument about *what* the change objectives are. These approaches are useful in situations where change is sought to the *means* whereby things are done and where a problem can be *solved* in the terms discussed by Ackoff in the previous section. By contrast, as the discussion in Chapter 2 showed, one of the distinguishing features of organisational messes is that there is no agreement on what constitutes the problem let alone what changes are required. Consequently, it is more likely that those involved in these types of situations are looking to challenge not just the *means* of doing things, but also to challenge *purposes* and *why* things are done like they are *at all*. In other words, they are searching for ways to *dissolve* rather than just *solve* problems in the terms discussed by Ackoff. In summary, therefore, what this latest discussion leads to is an argument for an approach to change which can cope more effectively with situations of soft complexity – in other words, some type of soft systems model for change.

There is neither the space nor the necessity to illustrate here all the different variants of models for bringing about change in soft, messy situations. What follows, therefore, is a generalised description of 'organisation development' (more commonly known as the OD approach) – an umbrella term for a set of values and assumptions about organisations and the people within them which, together with a range of concepts and techniques, are thought useful for bringing about long-term, organisation-wide change; that is, change which is more likely to dissolve problems than to resolve or solve them.

Organisation development – philosophy and underlying assumptions

According to French and Bell (1990, p. 17), in their book entitled *Organization Development, Behavioral Science Interventions for Organizational Improvement*, organisation development (OD) is:

A top-management-supported, long-range effort to improve an organization's problem-solving and renewal processes, particularly through a more effective and collaborative diagnosis and management of organization culture – with special emphasis on formal work team, temporary team, and inter-group culture – with the assistance of a consultant–facilitator and the use of the theory and technology of applied behavioral science, including action research.

Cummings and Worley (1997, p. 1) in their book entitled, *Organization Development and Change*, say organisation development is:

A process by which behavioural knowledge and practices are used to help organizations achieve greater effectiveness, including improved quality of life, increased productivity, and improved product and service quality. ... The focus is on improving the organization's ability to assess and to solve its own problems. Moreover, OD is oriented to improving the total system – the organization and its parts in the context of the larger environment that impacts upon them.

An examination of these definitions confirms some distinguishing characteristics of the OD approach to change. These are:

1 It emphasises goals and processes but with a particular emphasis on processes – the notion of organisational learning (Argyris and Schon, 1996; Pedler, Boydell and Burgoyne, 1991; Senge, 1990) as a means of improving an organisation's capacity to change is implicit in OD approaches.
2 It deals with change over the medium to long term, that is, change which needs to be sustained over a significant period of time.
3 It involves the organisation as a whole as well as its parts.
4 It is participative, drawing on the theory and practices of the behavioural sciences.
5 It has top management support and involvement.
6 It involves a facilitator who takes on the role of a change agent (Buchanan and Boddy, 1992).
7 It concentrates on planned change but as a process that can adapt to a changing situation rather than as a rigid blueprint of how change should be done.

The significance of people in organisations

The OD approach to change is, above all, an approach which cares about people and which believes that people at all levels throughout an organisation are, individually and collectively, both the drivers and the engines of change. Consequently, one underlying assumption is that people are most productive when they have a high quality of working life. In addition, there is an assumption that, in many cases (and perhaps the majority), workers are under-utilised and are capable, if given the opportunity, of taking on more responsibility for the work they do and of contributing further to the achievement of organisational goals.

Paton and McCalman (2000, p. 121) offer three 'fundamental' concepts with respect to the management of people and gaining their commitment to their work and organisation. These are:

1 Organisations are about people.
2 Management assumptions about people often lead to ineffective design of organisations and this hinders performance.
3 People are the most important asset and their commitment goes a long way in determining effective organisation design and development.

These assumptions are not new. Even so, many managers continue to believe in Taylorism and scientific management – which in Matsushita's (1988) words means: 'executives on one side and workers on the other, on one side men [sic] who think and on the other men [sic] who can only work'. Yet, Matsushita, drawing on his experience as head of the Sony organisation, went on to say:

> We are beyond the Taylor model; business, we know, is so complex and difficult, the survival of firms so hazardous in an environment increasingly so unpredictable, competitive and fraught with danger, that their continued existence depends on the day-to-day mobilisation of every ounce of intelligence.

The OD approach to change is entirely in line with these sentiments. What is more, these sentiments extend to a number of assumptions regarding people in groups. The first of these is that people are in general *social* beings. They will, therefore, form groups – whether these are legitimised by the organisation in terms of formal work teams or whether they are the more 'informal' groupings which form part of every organisation's functioning. French and Bell (1990, p. 45) reinforce this assumption by saying that: 'One of the most psychologically relevant reference groups for most people is the work group, including peers and superiors.' Consequently, the work group becomes increasingly important in any attempt at change. Yet, in many cases, work groups do not utilise effectively resources for collaboration. For instance, the formal leader of any group cannot perform all the leadership functions at all times and in all situations. Thus, for a group to become effective, all group members must share in problem solving and in working to satisfy *both* task and group members' needs. If work groups are managed in such a way as to engender a climate of mistrust and competition between participants, then any change will be seen as a threat rather than an opportunity and all the negative aspects of group functioning will come to the fore to work against the change. OD approaches to change assume, therefore, that work groups and teams are an essential element in the process of designing and implementing change. However, as individuals interact to form groups and other collective working relationships, so do groups interact and overlap to form larger organisational systems which, in their turn, influence an organisation's capacity to learn and change.

The significance of organisations as systems

One of the characteristics of OD approaches to change mentioned earlier in the chapter is that it involves the organisation as a whole as well as its parts – a characteristic which is exemplified by Pugh (1993, p. 109), when he refers to organisations as 'coalitions of interest groups in tension'. Chapter 1 introduced the idea that organisations are systems of interconnected and interrelated sub-systems and components which include more formal organisational structures and processes, as well as the more informal aspects of organisational life such as culture, politics and styles of leadership which are closely bound up with the values and attitudes people bring to their workplaces.

This idea is one of the most important assumptions of OD as a process of facilitating change. This is because, first, it reinforces the systemic nature of organisational life and the fact that changes in one part of the organisation will inevitably impact on operations in another part. For instance, the multiple-cause diagrams used in previous chapters to depict a number of different change situations are good illustrations of the *interconnectedness* of causes and consequences of complex messy situations.

Second, and related to this, it challenges the assumption that a single important cause of change with clear effects can be found, as well as the assumption that any cause and its effects are necessarily closely related in space and time. This is most clearly stated by Carnall (1995, p. 55) when he says:

> [The] causes of a problem may be complex, may actually lie in some remote part of the system, or may lie in the distant past. What appears to be cause and effect may actually be 'coincidental' symptoms.

Third, any organisation is a balance of forces built up and refined over a period of time. Consequently, proposed change of any significance will inevitably change this balance and will, therefore, almost certainly encounter resistance, particularly of the type which was categorised as 'organisational' resistance to change (*see* Illustration 6.7) mentioned in Chapter 6. Consequently, OD approaches assume that no single person or group can act in isolation from any other. For instance, if win–lose strategies are common to the behaviour of management, this way of dealing with conflict will permeate other workers' attitudes to settling disputes and disagreements. By way of contrast, if managers openly discuss problems and take views on how these might be addressed, then this culture of trust and co-operation will reach into other parts of the organisation's functioning – hence the belief that OD activities need to be led by top management if they are to succeed in bringing about successful change.

Fourth, because organisation development as a concept is assumed to operate throughout an organisation, the OD process is most definitely not a 'quick fix' to the latest management problem. This is articulated by French and Bell (1990, p. 48), who say that change 'takes time and patience, and the key movers in an OD effort need to have a relatively long-term perspective'.

Finally, OD approaches to change are essentially processes of facilitating *planned* change. Consequently, an effective manager of change:

> *anticipates* the need for change as opposed to reacting after the event to the emergency; *diagnoses* the nature of the change that is required and carefully considers a number of alternatives that might improve organisational functioning, as opposed to taking the fastest way to escape the problem; and *manages* the change process over a period of time so that it is effective and accepted as opposed to lurching from crisis to crisis.
>
> (Pugh, 1993, p. 109)

The significance of organisations as learning organisations

The ideas in the previous two sections (the significance of people in organisations and the significance of organisations as systems) come together in the assumptions that, for organisations operating in increasingly complex and turbulent environments, the only way to survive and prosper is to be a *learning organisation*.

The concept of a learning organisation and the associated concept of *organisational learning* were discussed briefly in Chapter 4 in the context of the broader discussion of organisational cultures. The concept of a learning organisation is built upon the proposition that there is more than one type of learning. In support of this proposition are writers such as Argyris (1964, 1992) and Argyris and Schon (1996) who distinguish between *single-loop* and *double-loop* learning or, as Senge (1990) terms them, *adaptive* and *generative* learning. The concepts of single- and double-loop learning can be explained in terms of systems for change that are either goal oriented or process oriented (Open University, 1985). In brief, a goal-oriented approach to change is directed towards changing the means by which goals are achieved. By contrast, those who subscribe to a process-oriented approach to change, while still concerned with goals, focus more on fostering a change process which enables the goals to be challenged. In other words, goal-oriented approaches are concerned with doing things better, while process-oriented approaches are concerned with doing the right things.

With a goal-oriented approach, the problem or issue is likely to be seen as an interesting, though possibly substantial *difficulty*; that is it is perceived, primarily as a technical and financial matter with a specific time horizon and hence fairly well bounded. The main focus is on increased efficiency of goal achievement. Management of this type of change is frequently done through a project team led by more senior managers concerned primarily with cost-benefit aspects (goals and constraints). A goal-oriented approach is analogous to thermostatically controlling the temperature of a heating system. The temperature is predetermined and the thermostat merely alters the means through which the temperature is maintained. In essence, what is not questioned is the initial setting of the goal. It is not difficult to see that goal-oriented approaches to problems, issues and change are basically congruent with hard systems models of change. Once the objective is identified, then the issue which remains is to establish the most efficient means of achieving it – hence the function of objective trees as described in the previous chapter.

By contrast, within a process-oriented approach, the problem is likely to be seen as distinctly *messy*. The changes might have long-term and, as yet unforeseen ramifications, which make the formulation of goals and constraints problematic. The problem is much more concerned with changing the behaviour of people and the structures and cultures within which they work. A process-oriented approach starts by identifying who must be involved in the process, what sort of issues should be addressed and how all this can be facilitated. The phases of the project are by no means as clearly defined as in a goal-oriented approach. It may take some time before the problem itself is agreed which will most likely challenge the goal itself. In these situations, single-loop learning is necessary as a means of monitoring the performance of organisational systems and subsystems in relation to the objectives set for them. However, single-loop or adaptive learning, which depends mainly on individualistic learning is not sufficient in situations, which require creative thinking to develop new visions and ways of doing things. Elkjaar (1999, pp. 86–7), writing in a book edited by Easterby-Smith, Burgoyne and Araujo (1999) entitled *Organizational Learning and the Learning Organization*, speaks of 'social learning' and that it is necessary to participate and be *engaged* in organizational projects. In a good exposition and critique of the learning organisation, Paton and McCalman (2000, p. 218) summarise the views of double-loop or generative learning as expressed by the main writers on learning organisations/ organisational learning as follows:

> They emphasize a collaborative, participative approach centred on team processes. They demonstrate a commitment to the creation of a shared vision of the future direction of the company and the necessary steps, structural and behavioural, to achieve that vision. They stress a proactive approach to learning, creating new experiences, continuous experimentation and risk-taking. Finally, they each emphasise the role of leaders to facilitate the change process and to foster a commitment to learning.

This quotation indicates that process-oriented/double-loop/generative learning involves issues associated with organisational structures, cultures and styles of leadership in terms of the capacity of these aspects of organisational life to support and facilitate this type of learning. It certainly draws attention to many of the issues discussed in Part Two of the book, the importance of people and the concepts associated with organisations as collections of subsystems interacting and reflecting the organisational system as a whole – concepts which are wholly in line with the organisational development approach to change.

The mind-map in Figure 8.1 summarises the philosophy and underlying assumptions of OD as a process for facilitating organisational change. The remainder of this chapter attempts to spell out in more detail the nature of the OD process itself.

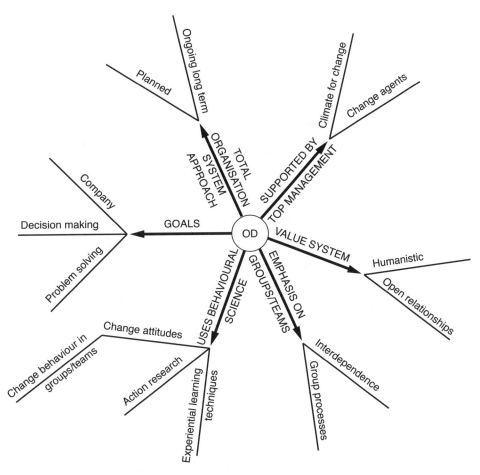

Figure 8.1 Basic assumptions of OD as a model for change

● ● ● ● The OD process

OD is at heart a process of facilitation of organisational change and renewal. It operates at all levels of the organisation – individual, group and organisational. It is a relatively long-term process for initiating and implementing planned change. It takes into account the messy nature of many organisational problems which involve unclear goals and differing perspectives on what constitutes the problems, let alone how to solve them. It recognises organisations as social entities where political as well as intellectual responses to change can be expected. It agrees with Benjamin and Mabey's (1993, p. 181) statement that: 'While the primary stimulus for change in organisations remains those forces in the external environment, the primary motivator for *how* change is accomplished resides with the people in the organisation.'

On the basis of these assumptions, organisation development as a process for instigating and implementing change has two important characteristics. The first is that it is a process of change which has a framework of recognisable phases which take the organisation from its current state to a new more desired future state. Second, within and across these steps, the OD process can be perceived to be a collection of activities and techniques that, selectively or accumulatively, help the organisation and/or its parts to move through these phases. The idea of phases can be most clearly demonstrated through a consideration of Lewin's (1951) three-phase model of change. This is followed by a more detailed description of OD as it has developed in more recent times.

Lewin's three-phase model of change

As already mentioned, most OD models of change consist of a series of phases (or steps/stages, depending on nomenclature). One such model, although based on work done many decades ago, is still referred to extensively in the literature on change. This is Lewin's (1951) model of the change process as one consisting of the three phases of: *unfreezing*, *moving* and *refreezing*.

Unfreezing

The first of these phases – unfreezing – concerns the 'shaking up' of people's habitual modes of thinking and behaviour to heighten their awareness of the need for change. This would probably include the introduction of information showing discrepancies between desirable goals and modes of operating and what is currently happening. According to Goodstein and Burke (1993), it might even include selectively promoting or terminating employees. For instance, in the case of the largest college, Pitford College, in Shire County (*see* Illustration 7.5), a member of staff was promoted to be Director of Open and Resource-based Learning (O&RBL). Other staff had their responsibilities changed to include 'tutoring' (rather than teaching) students working mainly in a self-service type of learning environment. All staff received news that a new O&RBL centre was to be built and that the timetables of all full-time students would be altered so that at least 20 per cent of their time would be spent learning in the new centre, using multimedia materials on a 'pick and mix' basis according to their needs. Part of this unfreezing process was the extensive consultation with heads of departments and other decision makers to discuss the new developments – which were seen as challenging the prevailing wisdom of how education and training in the further education sector should happen.

Moving

The second phase of Lewin's change process – moving – is essentially the process of making the actual changes that will move the organisation to the new state. As well as involving new types of behaviour by individuals, this includes the establishment of new strategies and structures, with associated systems to help secure the new ways of doing things. In Shire County, this involved a number of different activities. First, a series of staff seminars on the concept and operation of O&RBL were carried out. As a result, staff were concerned with redesigning their courses to include at least 20 per cent delivery of learning on O&RBL principles. In fact, some staff planned to deliver certain learning programmes as *predominantly* O&RBL programmes.

In addition, in Pitford College and one of the other two colleges in Shire County, large new O&RBL centres were built with multimedia teaching and learning facilities. Dignitaries representing education, industry and commerce were invited to the opening ceremonies which were used as a symbol for change as well as advertising the facilities to those who might support them. The inclusion of local employers' representatives emphasised the importance of providing for the needs of adult learners as well as those of the youngsters who had, traditionally, been the main 'customers' of these colleges. What is more, in the redefinition of teaching as 'facilitating learning' it was recognised that the managers of these new O&RBL centres did not necessarily have to be academics. This was further reinforced by associating the new centres very closely with existing library and computer services whose staff were not classed as academics.

Refreezing

Lewin's final phase in the change process – refreezing – involves stabilising or institutionalising the changes. This requires securing the changes against 'backsliding' and may include recruitment of new staff who are 'untainted' by the old habits. The continuing involvement and support of top management is crucial to this step. All of the elements of Johnson and Scholes's (1997) cultural web (*see* Chapter 4) are important in establishing new ways of doing things. Once strategy, structure and systems have been changed, it is equally important to reinforce the changes through symbolic actions and signs such as a change of logo, forms of dress, buildings design and ways of grouping people to get work done. The use of continuous data collection and feedback is essential to keep track of how the change is progressing and to monitor for further change in the light of environmental changes.

As an example of Lewin's three-phase change process, Goodstein and Burke (1993) make reference to the change British Airways (BA) made, from being a government-owned enterprise to being a privately owned one – a change which involved moving from what was basically a bureaucratic and militaristic culture to a service-oriented and market-driven one. Regarding the refreezing step, they mention how the continued involvement and commitment of top management helped ensure that the changes were 'fixed' in the way BA did business. Promotion was given to those employees who displayed commitment to the new values with a 'Top Flight Academy' being established to train senior management according to the new way of doing things. In addition, Goodstein and Burke (pp. 169–70) say: 'Attention was paid to BA's symbols as well – new, upscale uniforms; refurbished aircraft; and a new corporate coat of arms with the motto "We fly to serve".'

In the case of the colleges in Shire County, although the move to a culture of open and resource-based learning continued to some degree, it was constrained by a slackening off of commitment from top management as the environment in which the colleges operated changed yet again and brought new imperatives. Included in this were changes in the economic environment which brought changes in the political environment. These were increasing unemployment rates among young people and, as a result, a commitment on the part of government to increase training opportunities through funding further education provision for the 16–19 age group. In addition, there was an increase in training opportunities for adults. These opportunities operated outside the further education system, thereby, perhaps, lessening the requirement for more flexible provision within the further education colleges themselves. Consequently, the phase of 'moving' the current situation to the desired future one was never fully completed and the follow-through of refreezing – absorbing the change into the culture of the organisation – was thus put in jeopardy.

Lewin's three-phase model of organisational change can be criticised mainly for its concept of refreezing, that is, the idea of cementing the changes into place to create a new organisational reality. While this aim to prevent the backsliding mentioned earlier is laudable, it tends to ignore the increasingly turbulent environment within which many modern organisations operate and the need for *continuous* change. However, this should not detract from the debt which current OD approaches owe to the work of Lewin and his colleagues. This debt is summarised by French and Bell (1990, p. 25) when they say: 'Lewin's field theory and his conceptualizing about group dynamics, change processes, and action research were of profound influence on the people who were associated with the various stems of OD.' This remains the case to the present time.

Lewin's concept of organisational change as a *process* dominates much of OD theory. In addition there is widespread recognition that organisations must carry out an assessment of where they are now, where they want to be in the future and how to manage the transition from the one state to the other. Where current theories of OD are leading, however, is to a realisation that change is a process which is not linear and which is itself complex and messy, including many loops back and forth from one stage in the process to another. The following description tries to capture the essence of this. However, because of the limitations of the written word to describe something that is so dynamic in action, the process may appear more mechanistic than it is in reality. It should be remembered that what is being proposed is only a framework within which many variations may occur.

OD: an action–research-based model of change

According to Paton and McCalman (2000, p. 169), 'change is a continuous process of confrontation, identification, evaluation and action'. They go on to say that the key to this is what OD proponents refer to as an action–research model.

French and Bell (1990) give a detailed description of action research. Briefly, it is a collaborative effort of data gathering, data discussion, action planning and action between the leaders and facilitators of any change and those who have to enact it. Therefore, action research is, as its name suggests, a combination of research and action. This means collecting data relevant to the situation of interest, feeding back the results to those who must take action, collaboratively discussing the data to formulate an action plan and, finally, taking the necessary action.

A number of elements distinguish this approach from the hard systems model of change discussed in Chapter 7. First, it is not a 'one-off' event, which ends when a change has been completed. In their article describing the application of OD in an American electricity utility, Alpander and Lee (1995) illustrate this by saying: 'Organisations which are successful in maintaining their competitiveness have learned to view change not as a one-time event, but an ongoing process necessary to remain on the cutting edge in meeting customer needs.' This includes the ideas within the concept of a learning organisation discussed earlier. Second, it is an iterative or cyclical process which is continuous and which, if OD is taken as part of an organisation's philosophy of action, continues as part of everyday organisational life. Third, each of the components of the model (diagnosis, data gathering, feedback to the client group, data discussion and work by the client group, action planning and action) may be used to form each of the phases which make up a typical OD process. Furthermore, these components may, collectively, form cycles of activity *within* each stage of the OD process. Finally, the OD approach to change is firmly embedded in the assumption that all who are or who might be involved in any change should be part of the decision-making process to decide what that change might be and to bring it about. It is not, as some hard systems models of change suggest, a project planned and implemented by senior managers or some designated project manager, with the assumption that other workers in the organisation will automatically go along with it.

Building on the concept of action research, Figure 8.2 shows the stages of the OD model. These are now described in more detail. However, it is important to note that change on the scale involved in most OD efforts does not succeed without some established facilitation function. Hence, the emphasis on the role of the change agent, as evidenced by positioning this person or group in the centre of the diagram. The role of the facilitator or change agent, is discussed later in the chapter. What follows first is a more detailed description of the stages which make up the OD model itself.

Stages 1a and 1b: The present and the future

An examination of Figure 8.2 shows two stages strongly linked together in a symbiotic relationship. Hence the labelling of them as 1a and 1b – that is, two processes which are, in effect, intertwined and which could be regarded as one. The reason for this is that it is never clear whether a change process should start with the development of a vision for change (that is, where the organisation wants

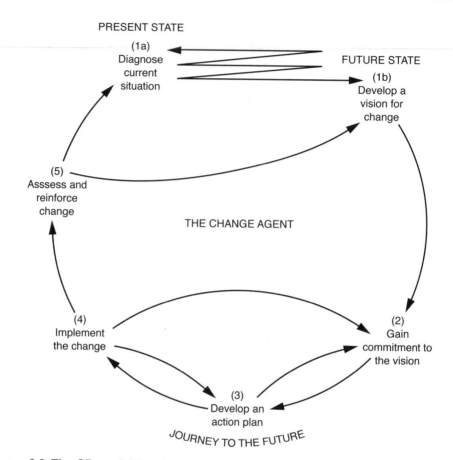

Figure 8.2 The OD model for change

to be), followed by a diagnosis of where the organisation is at present; or whether a start should be made with diagnosing 'what is', followed by statements about 'what could be'. For instance, Buchanan and McCalman (1989), in their four-step model of perpetual transition management, pose the 'trigger layer' (which examines environmental opportunities and threats) before the 'vision layer' (which defines the future). By contrast, Mabey and Pugh (1995) put as the first stage the process of agreeing the organisation's purpose/mission. This is followed by an assessment of the organisation's external and internal environments.

In reality, as the zigzag arrow in Figure 8.2 shows, these two processes act in parallel, with each process feeding the other as it proceeds until some idea of a future direction is achieved. However, for ease of description, stages 1a and 1b are discussed separately.

Stage 1a: Diagnose current situation

This stage is where the concept of PETS (political, economic, technological and socio-cultural factors) and the metaphor 'winds of change' (*see* Chapter 1) are useful as tools for diagnosing triggers for change that emanate from the external environment of the organisation. In addition the temporal and internal environments must be assessed. In an ideal world, this would be done on an ongoing basis (a) to detect strategic drift (*see* Chapter 2) and (b) to gather data on the organisation's capacity to respond to a change in direction or ways of operating. However, sometimes it takes a crisis to trigger this type of diagnosis. For instance, individuals in a newly created UK university (previously a polytechnic) had been pressing for several years for an increase in research activity supported by appropriate resources. It was only when the university lost valued government grant money that senior managers declared that 'something must be done' and a major investigation was instigated to ascertain what this might be and how it could happen.

Diagnostic processes such as these clearly call upon the data-gathering component of the action–research aspects of the OD model and the feedback of the results for discussion and verification by those concerned with, and involved in, the subsequent change. As mentioned earlier, in addition to data gathering about the organisation's external environment, there is also a need for a more detailed examination of such things as:

- individuals' motivation and commitment to their work and organisation
- recruitment practices, career paths and opportunities
- prevailing leadership styles
- employee training and development provision
- intra- and inter-group relationships
- organisational structure and culture.

Data gathering, therefore, is done at the individual, group and organisational levels and should include those things which form barriers to organisational performance as well as those which contribute to organisational success.

Activity 8.1   *Consider your own organisation or one with which you are familiar.*

If you were appointed as a change consultant to this organisation, what data would you want to collect and how would you go about doing this – without alienating the people concerned from the process?

Methods of collecting data include questionnaires, individual and 'focus-group' interviews, observation and examination of organisational documents. Price (1987) suggests collecting data on what people *think*, *feel* and *do* in terms of the *tasks* they perform, their *ways of working* and the *relationships* they have with each other. Many of the illustrations and activities in the chapters in Part Two are useful diagnostic tools for use at this stage in the change process.

Activity 8.2   *Go back to Part Two of the book and list those illustrations and activities which you think might be useful for the process of carrying out a diagnosis of the current state of your organisation or one with which you are familiar.*

It is clear that data collection and analysis is crucial to this stage in the OD process. It is important to note, however, the necessity for giving feedback on the findings to those from whom the data came, for further discussion and verification – a process particularly important in the case of data gained from the administration of questionnaires and through observation, where there is little interaction between questioner and questioned. This feedback process also serves the purpose of developing a vision for change – that is, where the organisation wants to be in the future.

Stage 1b: Develop a vision for change

An organisation's sense of what needs to change comes out of the process of organisational diagnosis and creative thinking. However, as we have already seen, this does not happen only when the diagnosis is complete. As the diagnosis proceeds and problem and success areas emerge, theories of what should be changed begin to form. These, in turn, bring demands for new information which will eventually move the process towards some definition of what the future should look like.

One way of looking at this stage of activity is to perceive it as a *creative* phase, in the sense that 'something new' is being looked for. This might imply a different strategy in terms of products, services or markets. It might also imply a change in structure and culture – including the way people are managed and led. Flood and Jackson (1991) suggest the use of metaphors as organising structures to help people think about their organisations. The examples given are: organisations as machines, organisms, brains, cultures, teams, coalitions and prisons. Thus, stage 1a would be concerned with identifying what metaphor most matched the current organisation and stage 1b would identify a metaphor to which its members might aspire.

Pat Snelson (1996), of RS Components (*see* Illustration 4.6 in Chapter 4), says that a vision must:

- drive the business forward
- inspire
- yield sustainable advantage.

Burnside (1991, p. 193) says:

> A vision can be described as a living picture of a future, desirable state. It is living because it exists in the thoughts and actions of people, not just in a written document. It is a picture because it is composed not of abstractions but of images.

On the concept of 'images', he quotes Lievegoed (1983, p. 75) as saying: 'Images are more meaningful than abstract definitions. Images always have a thought content, an emotional value, and a moral symbolic value' and goes on to say: 'A vision is thus integrative because it brings these dimensions together.' According to Burnside, there are two main aspects to visions – the strategic picture, which he calls the 'head' side, and the relational picture, which he calls the 'heart' side.

The charter and mission statements of the Body Shop reflect closely the views and ideals of its owners. In addition, considerable effort is put into spreading the messages they contain to everyone throughout the 1210 shops located in some 45 countries (as at February 1995). Indeed, the development of an extended Body Shop Charter was achieved through groups of employees from all levels of the organisation meeting off-site at intervals for many months (*see* Activity 8.3).

Activity 8.3   *How far do you think the following statements made by the Body Shop go towards meeting the definitions of a vision given above?*

THE BODY SHOP'S TRADING CHARTER

We aim to achieve commercial success by meeting out customers' needs through the provision of high quality, good value products with exceptional service and relevant information which enables customers to make informed and responsible choices.

Our trading relationships of every kind – with customers, franchisees and suppliers – will be commercially viable, mutually beneficial and based on trust and respect.

THE BODY SHOP'S MISSION STATEMENT – OUR REASON FOR BEING

- To dedicate our business to the pursuit of social and environmental change.
- To CREATIVELY balance the financial and human NEEDS of our stakeholders: employees, customers, franchisees, suppliers and shareholders.
- To COURAGEOUSLY ensure that OUR business is ecologically sustainable, meeting the needs of the present without compromising the future.
- To MEANINGFULLY contribute to local, national and international communities in which we trade, by adopting a code of conduct which ensures care, honesty, fairness and respect.
- To PASSIONATELY campaign for the protection of the environment and human and civil rights, and against animal testing within the cosmetics and toiletries industry.
- To TIRELESSLY work to narrow the gap between principle and practice, while making fun, passion and care part of our daily lives.

Source: *The Body Shop Case Study* (1995), Kellogg School of Management, Northwestern University, Evanston, IL, USA and The Body Shop International Plc, West Sussex, UK.

This example of employee involvement in the development of an organisation's vision underlines the close linking of stages 1a and 1b and their combined outputs in identifying an organisation's present and desired states in terms of two aspects of its functioning. These outputs are: first, the gap which represents the difference between an organisation's current strategy and goals and those to which it must aspire in order to respond to the forces and circumstances of the external environment; second, the gap between what Benjamin and Mabey (1993, p. 182) call: 'the core values as related internally to the ethos of the organisation'.

Stage 2: Gain commitment to the vision and the need for change

It is at the second stage of the process that feedback from the results of stages 1a and 1b are most important. Unless those concerned and involved with the change have been consulted and have participated in the process to this point, there will be little incentive for them to 'buy into' the new vision and the change process which will follow it.

This stage is akin to the 'conversion layer' of Buchanan and McCalman's (1989) model of perpetual transition management – the one which follows the trigger and vision layers which were mentioned earlier. However, gaining recruits for the change is not easy, as Pugh's (1993) four principles for understanding the process of organisational change show (*see* Illustration 8.1 and Activity 8.4). These principles in turn draw attention to the need for managers to use many different and interacting ways to gain the commitment and involvement of all concerned in the change programme.

Pugh's four principles draw attention to the need for, not just two-way, but many-way communication as part of the process of gaining commitment to the vision and the need for change. This is one of the reasons why most descriptions of OD-type models of change emphasise the importance of managing resistance through discussion, negotiation and active participation of those likely to have to make the changes. Established work groups and teams become particularly important at this stage, as is evidenced by French and Bell's (1990, pp. 126–7) statement that:

Illustration 8.1

Pugh's principles and rules for understanding and managing organisational change

Principle 1: Organisations are organisms
This means the organisation is not a machine and change must be approached carefully with the implications for various groupings thought out. Participants need to be persuaded of the need for change and be given time to 'digest' the changes after implementation.

Principle 2: Organisations are occupational and political systems as well as rational resource-allocation ones
This means that thought must be given to how changes affect people's jobs, career prospects, motivation and so on. It also means paying attention to how change will affect people's status, power and the prestige of different groups.

Principle 3: All members of an organisation operate simultaneously in the rational, occupational and political systems
This means that all types of arguments for change must be taken seriously. It is not sufficient merely to explain away different points of view. Rational arguments for change are as important as those which involve changes in occupational and political systems.

Principle 4: Change is most likely to be acceptable with people who are successful and have confidence in their ability and the motivation to change
This means ensuring an appropriate place (or set of people) from which to start the change and to ensure the methods used are relevant to those who are 'first in line' in accepting the change.

Source: Based on Pugh, D. S. (1993), 'Understanding and managing change', in Mabey, C. and Mayon-White, B. (eds), *Managing Change*, 2nd edn (London, PCP).

Collaborative management of the work team culture is a fundamental emphasis of organisation development programmes. This reflects the assumption that in today's organisations much of the work is accomplished directly or indirectly through teams. This also reflects the assumption that the work team culture exerts a significant influence on the individual's behaviour. ... Teams and work groups are thus considered to be fundamental units of organisations and also key leverage points for improving the functioning of the organisation.

Consequently, the process of gaining commitment to change must include working at the group level of the organisation and recognising the strength of influence of both formal and informal group leaders. In addition, it is more efficient of time and effort to communicate with individuals as groups than with them solely as individuals – even though this should not be the only means of communicating with them. It is not, however, sufficient merely to inform people of the vision and the necessity for change. This is because visions for change are rarely so clearly structured that information from all levels of the organisation can be ignored. As Smith (1995, p. 19), writing on the realities of involvement in managing change, says: 'No top manager can know at the outset [of any change] exactly what needs doing, what information is needed, or where it is located.'

Activity 8.4   *Identify a major change in an organisation with which you are familiar – preferably one in which you have been involved.*

Consider each of Pugh's principles and make notes regarding the following in terms of gaining people's commitment to the need for a new vision and associated change.

Principle 1
- *Were the implications for different groupings thought out?*
- *What (if any) methods were used to persuade people of the need for change?*

Principle 2
Was thought given to how the changes might impact on people's:

- *positions and prospects?*
- *status?*
- *power?*

Principle 3
Were the comments (supportive or otherwise) of different people and groups taken seriously and acted upon?

Principle 4
- *How much effort was made to increase people's confidence in the new vision?*
- *How much effort was made to identify those people and groups who were most likely to 'spearhead' the change?*

Jones (1994, p. 49), a colleague in the same consultancy practice as Smith, talks of 'listening to the organisation'. Reporting research with top management on the reasons why large-scale programmes of change often fail, Smith says that nearly all the managers interviewed reported on how much they had underestimated the importance of communication. However, as Jones says, this is not simply a question of senior management shouting louder from the top. This will not identify and bring to the surface the doubts that people have and their fears of what change might mean for them. Neither will it bring to the surface any problems with implementing the vision which top management may not be able to see for themselves.

Far from shouting from the top, the action–research cycle of collecting and analysing data and feeding back the results should be maintained here, as in the previous stages, so as to avoid widespread alienation of the workforce from the need to change and the vision to which it relates. Lloyd and Feigen (1997, p. 37) neatly summarise the dangers of not doing this when they say: 'Vision statements only work when the needs of those at the bottom of the organisation are integrated upwards with the needs of the market.' Accomplishing this means being sensitive, not only to people's worries about the way tasks and structures may be affected by the change, but also to what Mabey and Pugh (1995, p. 36) term the 'emotional readiness for change, the quality of existing relationships and the latent commitment to new ways of working'. Otherwise, any plan for action has little chance of being successfully implemented.

Stage 3: Develop an action plan

The development of an action plan can be thought of as beginning the phase of managing the transition from an organisation's current state to its desired future state, as shown by the 'JOURNEY TO THE FUTURE' label in Figure 8.2. However, it also continues the process of gaining commitment to the vision but with a somewhat changed emphasis on *how* that vision can come about.

A number of issues are important in this stage of the OD process. One is the issue of *who* is to guide the planning and, later, the implementation of the change. Another is the issue of precisely *what* needs to change to achieve the vision, while a third is *where* any intervention should take place. The following explores these issues in more detail.

The role of a change agent

The success of using an OD approach to facilitate change rests on the qualities and capabilities of those who act as the facilitators of change. Moving organisations from current to future changed states is not easy and requires knowledge and skills which some managers do not possess. In addition, many managers are so close to the day-to-day issues and problems of managing that they are unable to stand back from the current situation to take a long look at how things might be different. For these and other reasons, such as a need for managers themselves to learn how to manage change, the use of a change agent is usually deemed desirable in most OD approaches to change. However, the change agent as facilitator of change does not necessarily have to be from outside the organisation – he or she might very well come from another part of the organisation, not the one which is the focus of the change. Indeed, some large organisations have departments or divisions which are specifically set up to act as OD consultants to the rest of the organisation.

Buchanan and Boddy (1992) devote a complete book to the subject of the change agent. In it they give a helpful list of the competencies of effective change agents, based on research on how managers deal with change (*see* Illustration 8.2). For instance, when Selfridges began the process of the transformational change described in the case studies at the end of Parts One and Two, they employed, on a seconded basis, a consultant to act as Director of Strategic Change.

The list in Illustration 8.2 is a useful one and is reminiscent of the characteristics of 'transformational' leaders discussed in Chapter 6. However, this list must be considered in the context of how it came about. The evidence for constructing the list came mainly from questioning project managers – that is *internal* change

---

Illustration 8.2

Competencies of an effective change agent

Goals

1 Sensitivity to changes in key personnel, top management perceptions and market conditions and to the way in which these impact the goals of the project in hand.

2 Clarity in specifying goals, in defining the achievable.

3 Flexibility in responding to changes outwith the control of the project manager, perhaps requiring major shifts in project goals and management style and risk taking.

Roles

4 Team-building activities, to bring together key stakeholders and establish effective working groups and clearly to define and delegate respective responsibilities.

5 Networking skills in establishing and maintaining appropriate contacts within and outside the organisation.

6 Tolerance of ambiguity, to be able to function comfortably, patiently and effectively in an uncertain environment.

Communication

7 Communication skills to transmit effectively to colleagues and subordinates the need for changes in

project goals and in individual tasks and responsibilities.

8 Interpersonal skills, across the range, including selection, listening, collecting appropriate information, identifying the concerns of others and managing meetings.

9 Personal enthusiasm, in expressing plans and ideas.

10 Stimulating motivation and commitment in others involved.

Negotiation

11 Selling plans and ideas to others, by creating a desirable and challenging vision of the future.

12 Negotiating with key players for resources or for changes in procedures and to resolve conflict.

Managing up

13 Political awareness, in identifying potential coalitions and in balancing conflicting goals and perceptions.

14 Influencing skills, to gain commitment to project plans and ideas from potential sceptics and resisters.

15 Helicopter perspective, to stand back from the immediate project and take a broader view of priorities.

Source: Buchanan, D. and Boddy, D. (1992), *The Expertise of the Change Agent* (Hemel Hempstead, Prentice Hall, pp. 92–3).

agents who were concerned with changes in their own project areas. Perhaps, because of this, it emphasises more the *content* of the change and how to get ideas accepted, rather than the *process* skills of consultation and participation which form an essential part of the facilitation role. In this respect it can be compared with Paton and McCalman's list of the roles taken on by effective change agents. These are:

1 To help the organisation define the problem by asking for a definition of what it is.
2 To help the organisation examine what causes the problem and diagnose how this can be overcome.
3 To assist in getting the organisation to offer alternative solutions.
4 To provide direction in the implementation of alternative solutions.
5 To transmit the learning process that allows the client to deal with change on an ongoing basis by itself in the future.   (Paton and McCalman 2000, p. 182)

In contrast to the concept of a change agent, Kotter (1996) uses the concept of a 'guiding coalition' and suggests four key characteristics as being essential for it to be effective. These are (Kotter, 1996, p. 57):

1 Position power: Are enough key players on board, especially the main line managers, so that those left out cannot easily block progress?
2 Expertise: Are the various points of view – in terms of discipline, work experience, nationality, etc. – relevant to the task at hand adequately represented so that informed, intelligent decisions will be made?
3 Credibility: Does the group have enough people with good reputations in the firm so that its pronouncements will be taken seriously by other employees?
4 Leadership: Does the group include enough proven leaders to be able to drive the change process?

It is clear, however, that the guiding coalition cannot, by itself, cause widespread change to happen. What it can do is to set targets for change which, collectively, will move the organisation and its members much closer to realising the vision which was developed in stage 1b and further refined in stage 2. Having done this, the issue becomes: '*Who is do what, with what kind of involvement by others?*'

Responsibility charting

Beckhard and Harris (1987, pp. 104–8) have developed a technique called 'responsibility charting' which assesses the alternative behaviours for each person or persons involved in a series of actions designed to bring about change. They describe the making of a responsibility chart as follows:

Responsibility charting clarifies behaviour that is required to implement important change tasks, actions, or decisions. It helps reduce ambiguity, wasted energy, and adverse emotional reactions between individuals or groups whose interrelationship is affected by change. The basic process is as follows:

Two or more people whose roles interrelate or who manage interdependent groups formulate a list of actions, decisions, or activities that affect their relationship (such as developing budgets, allocating resources, and deciding on the use of capital) and record the list on the vertical axis of a responsibility chart [*see* Figure 8.3]. They then identify

Actors →											
Actions ↓											

Key:
R = Responsibility (not necessarily authority)
A = Approval (right to veto)
S = Support (put resources towards)
I = Inform (to be consulted before action but with no right of veto)

Figure 8.3 Example of a responsibility chart

the people involved in each action or decision and list these 'actors' on the horizontal axis of the form.

The actors identified can include:

R = the person who has the *responsibility* to initiate the action and who is charged with ensuring it is carried out

A = those whose *approval* is required or who have the power to *veto* the decision. This could be the responsible person's superiors

S = those who can provide *support* and resources to help the action to take place

I = those who merely need to be *informed* or consulted but who cannot veto the action

Certain ground rules are set out when making a responsibility chart. French and Bell (1990, p. 137) summarise these as follows:

First, assign responsibility to only one person. That person initiates and then is responsible and accountable for the action. Second, avoid having too many people with an approval–veto function on an item. That will slow down task accomplishment or will negate it altogether. Third, if one person has approval–veto involvement on most decisions, that person could become a bottleneck for getting things done. Fourth, the support function is critical. A person with a support role has to expand resources or produce something that is then used by the person responsible for the action. This support role and its specific demands must be clarified and clearly assigned. And, finally, the assignment of functions (letters) to persons at times becomes difficult. For example, a person may want A–V (approval–veto) on an item, but not really need it; a person may not want S (support) responsibility on an item, but should have it; or two persons each want R (responsibility) on a particular item, but only one can have it.

Activity 8.5   *Identify a change initiative in which you have been involved (or one with which you are familiar). You may find it helpful to use the example identified in completing Activity 8.4.*

To give you practice in using a responsibility chart, list some of the actions associated with that change and assign the people involved according to their responsibility role(s).

Consider whether Beckhard and Harris's ground rules for assigning roles were adhered to. If not, did this cause confusion of responsibilities and/or impede action?

This discussion of responsibility charting illustrates the 'chicken and egg' nature of planning organisational change. While it is right to consider *who* will lead and participate in implementing change, this has to be done in conjunction with *what* it is that needs to change.

The what and where of change

Pugh (1986) has devised a matrix of possible change initiatives based on the different issues which can hamper change and the level at which they occur. Figure 8.4 is a reproduction of what has become known as the 'Pugh OD matrix'.

The matrix reproduced in Figure 8.4 can be used to help with action planning (as represented by the initiatives listed in italics) about: (a) the type of intervention required to facilitate change in line with the organisation's vision (represented by the columns), and (b) the level at which it should take place (represented by the rows). For instance, at the level of the individual, problems may be occurring because there are few opportunities for promotion from the job of factory floor supervisor to higher levels of management, sales people see no reason to change given their current bonus plan and many middle managers have made their jobs to suit their own needs rather than those of the organisation. Problems at the inter-group level might include marketing and production arguing about the feasibility of setting up a new production line to satisfy what the marketing staff consider to be a market opportunity. Intervention is frequently required at the organisational level when an organisation's structure prevents the emergence of, let alone action upon, initiatives which could be beneficial to the organisation as a whole.

Beckhard and Harris (1987, p. 73) suggest the following organisational subsystems – any of which can be considered as a starting point for change:

- *Top management*: the top of the system.
- *Management-ready systems*: those groups or organisations known to be ready for change.
- *'Hurting' systems*: a special class of ready systems in which current conditions have created acute discomfort.

	Behaviour (What is happening now?)	**Structure** (What is the required system?)	**Context** (What is the setting?)
Organisational level	General climate of poor morale, pressure, anxiety, suspicion, lack of awareness of, or response to, environmental changes *Survey feedback, organisational mirroring*	Systems goals – poorly defined or inappropriate and misunderstood; organisation structure inappropriate – centralisation, divisionalisation or standardisation; inadequacy of environmental monitoring – mechanisms *Change the structure*	Geographical setting, market pressures, labour market, physical condition, basic technology. *Change strategy, location, physical condition, basic technology*
Inter-group level	Lack of effective co-operation between sub-units, conflict, excessive competition, limited war, failure to confront differences in priorities, unresolved feelings *Inter-group confrontation (with third-party consultant), role negotiation*	Lack of integrated task perspective; sub-unit optimisation, required interaction difficult to achieve *Redefine responsibilities, change reporting relationships, improve co-ordination and liaison mechanism*	Different sub-units' values, lifestyle; physical distance *Reduce psychological and physical distance; exchange roles, attachments, cross-functional groups*
Group level	Inappropriate working relationships, atmosphere, participation, poor understanding and acceptance of goals, avoidance, inappropriate leadership style, leader not trusted, respected; leader in conflict with peers and superiors *Process consultation, team building*	Task requirements poorly defined; role relationships unclear or inappropriate; leader's role overloaded, inappropriate reporting procedures *Redesign work relationships (socio-technical systems), self-directed working groups*	Insufficient resources, poor group composition for cohesion, inadequate physical set-up, personality clashes *Change technology, layout, group composition*
Individual level	Failure to fulfil individual's needs; frustration responses; unwillingness to consider change, little chance for learning and development *Counselling, role analysis, career planning*	Poor job definition, task too easy or too difficult *Job restructuring/modification, redesign, enrichment, agree on key competencies*	Poor match of individual with job, poor selection or promotion, inadequate preparation and training, recognition and remuneration at variance with objectives *Personnel changes, improved selection and promotion procedures, improved training and education, bring recognition and remuneration in line with objectives*

Figure 8.4 The Pugh OD matrix

- *New teams or systems*: units without a history and whose tasks require a departure from old ways of operating.
- *Staffs*: subsystems that will be required to assist in the implementation of later interventions.
- *Temporary project systems*: ad hoc systems whose existence and tenure are specifically defined by the change plan.

Activity 8.6 *What similarities and differences can be found between Pugh's levels of analytical focus and Beckhard and Harris's list of subsystems for intervention?*

In addition to the issue of where change interventions might take place, the planning of OD interventions must also take account of the degree of change needed, that is, the scope of the change activities. In terms of the Pugh OD matrix, this means considering whether: (a) people's *behaviour* needs to change, and/or (b) the *organisation's structure and systems* need to change and/or (c) the *context or the setting* needs to change. According to Mabey and Pugh (1995, pp. 40–1):

> The first (left-hand) column is concerned with current behaviour symptoms which can be tackled directly. Since it suggests methods and changes which address the symptoms without intervening into the required system or setting, this column comprises the least radical of the development strategies. Indeed in some cases the results may not be recognised as change at all – merely as overcoming some difficulties in the proper workings of the current system. Thus in one application, as the result of a team-building exercise with a Ward Sister and her staff, the functioning of the ward, the morale of staff, and the standard of patient care all improved. The Hospital Management Committee regarded this process not as a change, but one of getting the organisation to work properly.
>
> But it may be that this degree of intervention is not sufficient to achieve the required aims. It could be that, however improved the group atmosphere and leadership style, the group will not function well because it is not clear what the organisation requires of it, adequate information to carry out the group task is not available at the appropriate time, and the tasks are inappropriately divided and poorly allocated to the members of the group. In these circumstances, the second column, concerned with organising the required system, is the appropriate degree of intervention. This is a greater degree of intervention because it may require change in the structure, systems, information flows, job design, etc., which inevitably affects a much wider range of the 'organisational environment' of the particular group.
>
> Even this degree of intervention may be insufficient. The problems may lie in the contextual setting (changing market pressures, physical distance, poor group composition, poor promotion procedures, etc.). Then the degree of intervention in the third (right-hand) column is appropriate. This is a still greater degree of intervention requiring strategy changes, considerable expenditure of resources (both financial and human), and carrying with it greater likelihood of disruption with its attendant costs. It is not, therefore, to be undertaken lightly.

Mabey and Pugh go on to say that, as action moves from the left through to the right-hand column, a greater degree of intervention and commitment is required. Consequently, they suggest starting at the left column of the matrix and moving towards the right only as it becomes necessary because of the dictates of the problem. Activity 8.7 offers an opportunity to become more familiar with the content of the matrix and how it might be used in planning change.

As stated earlier, the process of developing an action plan for change should be done through consultation and collaboration with those who will implement the change, thus reinforcing commitment to change. Beckhard and Harris's (p. 72) concept of the action plan being a 'road map' for the change effort is a useful one. In addition, they say that an effective action plan should have the following characteristics:

- *Relevance*: activities are clearly linked to the change goals and priorities.
- *Specificity*: activities are clearly identified rather than broadly generalised.
- *Integration*: the parts are closely connected.
- *Chronology*: there is a logical sequence of events.
- *Adaptability*: there are contingency plans for adjusting to unexpected forces.

The last of these characteristics is particularly important. As anyone knows, it is all well and good, setting out on a journey with the route well defined beforehand. However, because of the many things which exist to thwart the best laid plans (for instance in the case of the road map and journey: traffic, passenger sickness, road works, accidents and so on), the plan must be flexible enough to adapt to the changing circumstances of not only *what* needs to change, but also possible changes in the transition process itself. Consequently, as Figure 8.2 shows, the development of an action plan must always be linked closely to its subsequent implementation.

Activity 8.7   *The best way to understand the Pugh OD matrix is to apply its different 'cells' to a real organisational example.*

Choose a situation from your own experience where a need for change has been established.

Go through the matrix and note which cells are appropriate for starting interventions which will help in the change process.

If you find this too difficult to start with, look at the following list of organisational problems and activities and note in which of the Pugh matrix cell(s) you would place them.

1 *The accounts department who 'lived' on the top floor always seemed to be at loggerheads with the research and development team who were 'housed' in an outside annex.*

2 *Since the redundancies, which were mentioned wherever you went in the organisation, people were moaning about the amount of work they had to do and the lack of recognition of this by senior management.*

3 *The staff in the post room appeared bored with their jobs. Admittedly, the work was rather repetitive.*

4 *It took so long to get an answer to queries, because the boss had always to be informed.*

5 *The members of the project group felt abandoned and without leadership.*

Stage 4: Implement the change

Any text dealing specifically with organisation development as a change methodology contains details of different techniques and methods for initiating and implementing change (*see*, for instance, Cummings and Worley, 1997; French and Bell, 1990). For the present purposes, the activities in italics in the Pugh OD matrix in Figure 8.4 can be used to illustrate ways of initiating organisational change. As the matrix illustrates, these relate to the different levels of analytical focus and the scope of the change activities. The following gives additional details of those activities which require further explanation. It should be noted however that, because these activities are mainly concerned with the behaviour column of the matrix, it *does not mean* that they are, necessarily, any more important than the activities concerned with structure and context. They are selected for further explanation simply because they may not be as familiar as some of the others.

Survey feedback

Surveys can be used to assess the attitudes and morale of people across the organisation and are used at different stages in the OD process. At the implementation stage, they are important for the effective management of the change. Feedback from these surveys to those involved in the change activities helps stimulate discussion of what is working and what is not and should result in modifications to the action plan or the way it is being implemented or, sometimes, to a reorientation of the vision.

For example, in 1994, Lloyds of London, one of the City's prestigious financial institutions, carried out an employee opinion survey on the progress of a large-scale change programme, the results of which were fed back to the staff involved for further discussion and appropriate action. Clarke, Hooper and Nicholson (1997, p. 29), writing about this, say:

> The process was designed to demonstrate to people that the corporation was not just saying: 'Your views are important', but that it actually meant it. Not only was the management team prepared to listen; it would also distribute the results openly and honestly. More importantly it would act on the views expressed. Sophisticated timetabling, communications, objective-setting and measurement ensured that this happened.

The survey was repeated 18 months later to identify progress on actions resulting from the first survey.

Organisational mirroring

'The organisation mirror is a set of activities in which a particular organisational group, the host group, gets feedback from representatives from several other organisational groups about how it is perceived and regarded' (French and Bell, 1990, p. 147). Organisational mirroring is different from interventions at the inter-group level, being concerned with relationships between three or more groups. It is a technique which benefits from the services of a change consultant who is not connected with any of the groups involved in the process. A 'fishbowl' technique is frequently used as part of organisational mirroring. This is where the group asking for feedback (the host group) first sits and listens to what the other group representatives have to say (without interruption). The representatives of the host group and the other group then exchange places to allow the host group to have their say (ask for clarification, information etc.) without interruption. Finally, the representatives of both groups are divided into small sets to work together on problems which emerge before all coming together to devise action plans, assign people to tasks and set target dates for improvements to be completed.

The techniques of survey feedback are most frequently associated with gaining information on people's attitudes and behaviour. It should not be forgotten, however, that other types of information gathering will be just as important – for instance with regard to progress against financial and other quantifiable measures of organisational performance.

Inter-group confrontation (with third-party assistance)

Although a technique of 'confrontation' sounds alarming, it enables two groups, which have their unique specialities, to confront organisational issues which go beyond their particular expertise. Mabey and Pugh suggest that an exercise such as this might require two days of work away from distractions and helped by a 'neutral' facilitator. The objective is to help the members of the two groups increase their awareness of the importance of each other's activities to the overall organisational performance and thus reduce a sense of 'them and us'.

French and Bell and Mabey and Pugh suggest a process where each group is asked to produce two lists. The first is the complaints 'we' have against 'them'. The second is the complaints that 'we' think 'they' would have about 'us'. Lists are then shared between the two groups. According to Mabey and Pugh, two characteristics usually emerge. First, some of the complaints can be dissolved fairly quickly, being the result of simple misunderstandings or lack of communication. Second, the lists of both groups show a surprising degree of congruency; in other words 'we' know what they think about 'us' and 'they' know what we think about 'them'. The lists form the basis for further discussion and exploration of how conflict can be resolved and more positive working relationships established.

Role negotiation

Role negotiation is a technique developed by Harrison (1972). Basically, it involves individuals or groups negotiating to 'contract' to change their behaviour on a quid pro quo basis. In general, it requires the help of a facilitator and (typically) during a day's workshop session, each set of participants is asked to say what they want the others to *do more of*, *do less of* or *maintain unchanged*. A follow-up meeting a month or so later assesses progress and, if necessary, renews or sets up new contracts. It is important to note that this *does not* involve probing people's likes and dislikes about each other. It concentrates solely on the roles they play and their behaviour as part of these.

Process consultation

This is rather more than a technique in that Schein (1987) has written a book entitled *Process Consultation*. From Schein's point of view, process consultation is a central part of organisational development. According to French and Bell (1990, p. 152): 'The crux of this approach is that a skilled third party (consultant) works with individuals and groups to help them learn about human and social processes and learn to solve problems that stem from process events.' The kinds of interventions which are part of process consultation are: agenda-setting interventions; feedback of observational data; coaching and counselling of individuals and suggestions about group membership; communication and interaction patterns; allocation of work, responsibilities and lines of authority. French and Bell say (p. 153):

> The process consultation model is similar to team-building interventions and intergroup team-building interventions except that in PC greater emphasis is placed on diagnosing and understanding process events. Furthermore there is more emphasis on the consultant being more nondirective and questioning as he or she gets the groups to solve their own problems.

Team building

Team building is an essential part of the OD process. Team-building techniques can be used for established long-term groups as well as for special, shorter-term, project groups. Processes included in team building are: (a) diagnosis of the task together with individuals' and group needs; (b) diagnosis and negotiation of roles; (c) responsibility charting; (d) understanding and managing group processes and culture. Usually, a change agent or independent consultant/facilitator is used to help in team building.

Life and career planning

There are a number of exercises which can help in career planning, which is part of life planning. One is to draw a life line representing the past, present and future. Past events are positioned according to important things which have happened in life, including things done well and things done not so well – 'ups' as well as 'downs'. Future desired events are also recorded on the line, and some indication is given of time of achievement. Another exercise is to write one's obituary as if death were to occur now and then as if death was some years in the future. The last exercise is intended to give some idea of what is hoped for in the near and far future.

Activity 8.8   *Think back to the change which you identified for Activity 8.5. Which of the techniques (at any level or scope) in Pugh's OD matrix were used as the change was implemented? Were they appropriate?*

The role of short-term wins

Implementing change which will ultimately transform an organisation is a *long-term process* and it is understandable if commitment to the vision becomes somewhat weakened on the way. Consequently, the achievement of 'short-term wins' (Kotter, 1996) is important, both as a motivating factor and as a mechanism for tracking the progress towards the longer-term goals. However, Kotter goes further than this in identifying six ways in which short-term wins can help organisational transformations. These are:

- *Provide evidence that sacrifices are worth it*: Wins greatly help justify the short-term costs involved.
- *Reward change agents with a pat on the back*: After a lot of hard work, positive feedback builds morale and motivation.
- *Help fine-tune vision and strategies*: Short-term wins give the guiding coalition concrete data on the viability of their ideas.
- *Undermine cynics and self-serving resisters*: Clear improvements in performance make it difficult for people to block needed change.
- *Keep bosses on board*: Provides those higher in the hierarchy with evidence that the transformation is on track.
- *Build momentum*: Turns neutrals into supporters, reluctant supporters into active helpers, etc.   (Kotter, 1996, p. 123)

Short-term wins do not, however, happen automatically as part of the change process. They have to be planned *deliberately* so that they become much more probabilities than possibilities. According to Kotter (pp. 121–2), a short-term win has three characteristics:

1 It's visible; large numbers of people can see for themselves whether the result is real or just hype.
2 It's unambiguous; there can be little argument over the call.
3 It's clearly related to the change effort.

An example of a short-term win is when a company reduces delivery time on one of its ten main products by a predetermined percentage in a predetermined time; or when the number of customer complaints reduces by (say) 50 per cent during the first half of the year; or when the jobs of a group of employees become easier to do because they are getting more relevant information in a more timely way. Short-term wins are not those of the type: 'We expect to increase our sales in the next couple of months'; neither is the fact that two previously sworn enemies are now talking pleasantly to each other a short-term win, unless the outcome is some further improvement in morale and organisational performance.

The setting and assessment of short-term wins links the implementation stage of the OD process to the more all-embracing assessment of the organisation's progress towards its vision and the continuing reinforcement of the change process itself.

Stage 5: Assess and reinforce the change

Assessing change

In organisational situations of hard complexity, it is relatively easy to assess the extent to which change has been achieved. The setting of 'hard' objectives and quantifiable performance measures makes this a more straightforward process. However, in the softer, more 'messy' situations where change methodologies of the OD type tend to be used, change is an evolving process concerned not only with changes in quantifiable performance objectives, but more frequently with changes in attitudes, behaviours and cultural norms where measurement is bound to be less precise. Even so, measurement of these things is possible. It is also desirable in terms of its role in providing positive feedback that the change process is 'working' and in testing how far the organisation has moved towards achievement of its vision.

A number of ways are available for measuring the softer issues associated with change. These are:

1 *A survey or cultural audit*, which can potentially cover all staff. Its results can be quantified and quickly disseminated. The audit can be done at regular intervals to provide repeated snapshot measures of an organisation's progress towards its change objectives. The Nationwide Building Society is an example of an organisation which uses such a system as part of its commitment to continuous improvement.

2 *Interviews with individuals or focus groups*, which allow the collection of more qualitative, in-depth information. An example of testing what a company's vision and values statement meant to staff was the exercise carried out by the Body Shop just after a public challenge to its integrity regarding its stance of being socially responsible in its policies and practices. The Body Shop called it 'gazing into the mirror'. It consisted of 44 meetings each with 20 different staff and managers from all parts of the organisation. All the meetings were attended by a board member and a moderator who later summarised the discussions to produce a report of the main themes arising and subsequent recommendations for action.

3 *An examination of turnover and absenteeism rates* as an indication of general morale and well-being.

4 *An analysis (through observation or questionnaire) of group performance* in terms of task achievement, but also in terms of the quality of meetings (including number of meetings and length) and leader performance.

5 *'Picturing the organisation'*, that is, asking staff to present their perception of the organisation in graphical or image terms rather than in words. This might include the use of metaphors in line with those suggested by Morgan (1986) in Chapter 4 or Flood and Jackson (1991) (*see* stage 1b earlier in this chapter). Alternatively, it might be in the form of a 'Rich Picture' (Checkland, 1981), that is, a collage of images represented by drawings and symbols connected by other symbols depicting the relationships between them. Illustration 8.3 is an example

Illustration 8.3

Rich picture of changes in the organisation of services for people with learning disabilities

of a rich picture depicting a situation of change from a centrally run service for people with learning disabilities. This meant a change from mainly hospital-based provision to provision which was in line with a 'care in the community' concept – that is, devolving care to a myriad much smaller units, the management of which had to 'sell' their services (in competition with others) to the national health authority which was charged with 'buying' them on behalf of the users.

When the rich pictures about an organisation start to resemble images closely related to the vision, management can have some confidence that the change has been successful in respect of how employees feel about it.

Reinforcing and consolidating change

Farquhar, Evans and Tawadey (1989, p. 49) say: 'A real danger in the process of organisational change is the failure to carry it through sufficiently far. Companies may be tempted to relax when the immediate crisis recedes while they still have not addressed the deeper organizational problems which generated the crisis.' The lesson from this is that the new order resulting from any change needs to be institutionalised. This is well put by Mabey and Pugh (1995, p. 50) when they say:

> Individuals need to be held personally accountable for prescribed initiatives; new working relationships and boundaries between different working groups need to be negotiated; ways of recognising and rewarding desirable behaviours and attitudes need to be devised to demonstrate that the organisation is serious about the change strategies that have been set.

It is pointless expecting people's behaviour to change if this is not reinforced by concomitant changes in personnel policies and practices, including appraisal, career development and reward systems. In addition, staff training and development needs to reorient itself to the needs of the new vision and the changes which help guide its attainment. According to Farquhar *et al.*, this is particularly important with regard to middle managers. While change can happen fast at the top (often through bringing in new people) and be accepted at the lower levels of an organisation (particularly if the rewards for change are clear), middle managers, who perform the bridging function between the two, may be slower to accept new cultures, policies and practices. Yet it is middle management which must make change work. They must, therefore, be given the new skills they will need – particularly when structures and cultures are expected to change.

More generally, the action–research model of data collection, data analysis and feedback for action is just as important at this stage of OD as at any other. Any change programme is stressful, but if employees continue to *own* change this stress will become not negative stress but, rather, positive pressure to accept that change can be the norm, with the adoption of innovative, change-oriented behaviour.

● ● ● ● An assessment of the OD model for change

The model of OD presented here departs to some extent from early OD models which emphasised mainly the attitudinal and behavioural aspects of organisational life and gave insufficient attention to aspects such as strategy, structure, technology and, in particular, the needs of customers or clients, let alone shareholders, and the financial environment within which most organisations operate. Not only has it drawn from these earlier models, but it has used elements of other more directive change models such as Kotter's (1996) eight-stage change process and Buchanan and McCalman's (1989) model of perpetual transition management.

Even so, organisation development as a philosophy and a process can be critiqued according to a number of criteria. The following are examples.

OD does not always face up to harsh realities of change

Almost all models of change include, in one form or another, the underlying concept of unfreezing. From an OD point of view this would be achieved through a typical action–research process of data collection, analysis and feedback as part of a participatory process of education for change. Yet, authors such as Clarke (1994) and Johnson (1990) describe this process of unfreezing in much harsher terms.

Thus, Clarke (pp. 147–8) talks of 'speeding up the unfreezing process' through *destabilising* people to detach them from the old order. She quotes the example of Centraal Beheer, an insurance company in the Netherlands, 'creating an anxiety greater than the risk of doing something different'. She goes on to say (p. 149): 'Pent-up anger and discontent are the motivators for change; no significant change is possible without them.' Clarke talks the language of crisis and even of engineering a crisis in order to speed up the unfreezing process.

Johnson (p. 190) goes further than Clarke with his talk of 'symbolic acts of questioning or destruction' to start the unfreezing process. He gives examples of John de Lorean trying to change his division of General Motors by promulgating stories to ridicule the dominant culture and of Lee Iacocca firing 33 out of 35 vice-presidents within three years of taking over at Chrysler. Johnson continues this line of thinking by saying (p. 190): 'As conflict and debate grows, managers may actually foster it by symbolic acts of conflict, destruction and degradation.'

However, care must be taken that crisis is not seen merely as a threat and, as Ferlie and Bennett (1993) point out, paradoxically reduces energy, creativity and flexibility. From an OD point of view crisis would be seen as an opportunity which, in Ferlie and Bennett's (p. 270) words, 'forces awkward issues up the agendas [when] we are likely to see continuing pressure from pioneers, the formation of special groups who evangelise the rest of the organisation, high energy and commitment levels, and a period of organisational plasticity in which anything seems plausible'.

Alternatively, as Farquhar *et al.* (1989, p. 37) point out: 'Not all companies see crisis as a prerequisite for major organisational change. The World Bank, for example, believes that a trigger of another kind may be sufficient. This could range from the aspirations of top management, through anxiety about an uncertain future, to a downturn in results.' Monitoring the internal and external organisational environments on a regular basis can detect potential crises in their early and most treatable phases. What needs to be recognised is that change without crisis is most frequently incremental and time is needed to build the momentum for larger-scale, more radical change.

OD is limited when change situations are 'constrained'

OD has been promoted as a change model for coping with situations of soft complexity where goals and also the means of achieving them are unclear. However, there are situations which have many of the characteristics of soft complexity yet are constrained in the sense that the goals are predetermined and the means of achieving them are to some extent set. In other words, change is dictated by top management or the precise requirements of some part of the organisation's external environment. For instance, health care is proscribed by the need to safeguard the public against malpractice and legislation regarding the use of treatments and drugs. Setting up a new doctor's practice must adhere to many different forms of regulatory requirement. Franchisees must often run their businesses according to the dictates of the franchiser.

It may be, of course, that, when change is desirable, a hard systems model of change is most appropriate. However, 'dictated' change is likely to bring resistance from those who must implement it. Therefore, although the earlier stages of the OD model may not be applicable, there is still the requirement to develop an action plan, implement, assess and reinforce change. In addition, gaining commitment to, and participation in, this part of the change process by those who must make the change is of the utmost importance. Consequently, even in highly constrained situations of change, implementation must be as carefully executed as in any other OD process.

OD in the public sector

Chapter 3 discussed the work of Burns and Stalker (1961) and illustrated the differences between mechanistic and organic organisational structures. A consideration of these shows how an organic structure, rather than a mechanistic structure, is more suited to organisations embracing an OD model of change. Consequently, the application of OD in the mechanistically structured, bureaucratic organisations which are typical of governmental and publicly accountable organisations is a difficult undertaking. Writing on organisational development in the public sector, McConkie (1993, pp. 634–42), writing from a North American perspective but one which applies generally, discusses a number of reasons why the application of OD in public sector organisations is likely to give rise to problems. These, together with others, are:

1 The basic philosophical differences between the assumptions and values of OD and those of the bureaucratic model (which is typical of most public sector organisations) are significant because public sector organisations typically reflect strong adherence to bureaucratic norms and behaviour patterns – forms and patterns foreign to those of OD – therefore making OD application difficult and sensitive, though not impossible.

2 Public sector organisations have multiple authoritative decision makers and multilevel accountability and reporting relationships. They are also 'supervised' by many interests, such as the general public, other government agencies, interest groups, the media and so on. All these make it difficult, first, to get support and gain approvals for an OD initiative and, second, to guide OD designs to fruition because so many people and interests 'get in the way'.

3 Financial support is difficult to obtain for OD work in public sector organisations. This is because, first, funding for consultancy (i.e. external change agents) is limited compared with that available in the private sector and, second, so many different people have to agree to the spending of funds.

4 In public sector organisations, the large variety of different and frequently conflicting interests, different political allegiances, reward structures and values make OD, as a system-wide effort, difficult to apply. OD interventions are, therefore, more likely to be of a small-scale nature in single departments or work groups.

5 McConkie (p. 640), on the writings of Golembiewski (1969), says: 'Five aspects of the public "habit background" … make it an inhospitable host for OD: public patterns of delegation, the legal habit, the need for security, the procedural regularity and caution, and the slowly developing image of the "professional manager".'

6 Decision making in public sector organisations tends to be pushed upwards towards the top. This contrasts with OD objectives which seek to increase self-control and self-direction of organisation members, something which is difficult if decisions must always be passed to upper levels of management. What is more, deciding where the 'top' is can be confusing. It might be the highest level of the administration, but it may be necessary also to take account of elected and appointed political interests – which may be at both local and national level. The generally accepted assumption that OD-type interventions should have the support of top management and, frequently, should be led by them, sits uneasily with the realisation that, in some instances, for political reasons the top may not want to be seen to be involved.

These points paint a depressing picture for the likelihood that any OD model for change could succeed in public sector organisations. However, as the public sector (in the UK for example, the health service, local authorities, some government departments) has become more privatised in its outlook and with regard to outcomes, the OD model for change becomes more realistic and easier to apply. Indeed, because of the extreme complexity of these organisations and the massive changes which they are having to face, change models which do not take account of the soft, messy situations they face have little likelihood of succeeding. What OD practitioners must realise is that they need to be very flexible in the way they apply their models for change in these particular types of change scenario.

OD in different cultures

The discussion in Chapter 4 identified issues associated with differences between people from different societal cultures. It also touched upon diversity of gender and race within national groupings. It is not difficult to find many organisations, large and small, which operate across the world.

This chapter and the previous one have described at least three ways of designing and implementing organisational change. In addition, ways of dealing with resistance and conflict have been addressed. What must be recognised, however, is the predominantly Western bias of much that is written about organisations and change. Consequently, writers such as Jaegar (1986) and more recently Adler (1997) do well to warn that not all change methods and techniques are transportable across national boundaries to other parts of the world or even to different ethnic groupings within single countries. This is particularly the case with the range of techniques associated with OD as a philosophy and a methodology for bringing about change.

In an extensive discussion of organisational development and national culture, Jaegar links typical OD values with each of Hofstede's (1980) dimensions of culture and concludes that they have a low correspondence with high power distance, high uncertainty avoidance, high masculinity and moderate individualism. Consequently, some OD-type interventions are unlikely to gain easy acceptance in societies which score high on these dimensions. This is confirmed by Cummings and Worley (1997) who give an example of people from Scandinavian countries as being sympathetic to OD change methods, which is in line with their scores on Hofstede's dimensions. They contrast this with people from Latin American countries (who score high on power distance, uncertainty avoidance and masculinity) who are unlikely to be comfortable with some of the OD ways of effecting change.

The OD philosophy of people-centred leadership and employee participation in the change process is unlikely to find favour in countries such as France and Italy where managers subscribe to ideals of hierarchy and formalised organisational systems (*see* Laurent, 1983). The title of Jack's (1997) article in the *Financial Times* – 'Caste in stone' and his comment, 'Challenge French corporate hierarchies at your peril' – say much of French managers' attitudes to the participative styles of leadership which are typical of OD approaches to change.

One consequence of these reservations about the degree to which OD approaches can be used wherever change occurs, is that there is a need for OD-type techniques to vary according to whether an organisation operates in what

Keegan (1989) terms an *ethnocentric* or *geocentric* way. Organisations with an ethnocentric orientation are those which tend to offer a standard product across the world and which operate with centralised decision making from the home country base. Managers, wherever they are located, are usually chosen from the home country nationals on the basis that operations and ways of managing 'abroad' should mirror those in the home base.

By contrast, organisations with a geocentric orientation accept that things might be done differently in different countries. Consequently, although there is still a degree of overall centralised co-ordination of activities, products, operations and methods of management are tailored to the different conditions in each country. In this type of organisation, instead of managers being 'sent out' (e.g. as expatriates) from the home country, the organisation trains and develops host country managers to operate in a decentralised, mainly autonomous way.

The consequences of this distinction are that similar approaches to change are more likely to be used in ethnocentrically operated organisations than those which organise on geocentric principles where approaches to change are more likely to be tailored to the cultures in which they are being used.

Having said that, there remain many OD techniques which can be used in spite of there existing less than propitious attitudes and beliefs on the part of those involved. Citing Harrison (1970), French and Bell (1990) use the concept of 'depth of intervention' to distinguish those techniques which interact mainly with the more formalised organisational systems (such as job enrichment, management by objectives, role analysis and attitude surveys) and those which go deeper into exploring the informal and more personal organisational systems – for instance, team building, encounter groups and interpersonal relationship explorations. Depth of intervention is a useful concept for deciding how 'deep' to go in the use of OD-type interventions as part of the process of change which involves people from different cultures. It is particularly relevant for those organisations that operate outside their home country environment.

● ● ● ● Conclusions

Soft systems models for change, of which OD is a well-known example, contrast with hard systems in being able to address the issues of soft complexity inherent in the type of 'messy' situations described in Chapter 2. Soft systems approaches to change emphasise not just the content and control of change but also the *process* by which change comes about. They require consideration of the cultural and political aspects of organisations as much as the structure and systems. 'Change agents' facilitating change using these approaches require influencing skills and the skills of negotiation. Because different individuals respond to their different *perceptions* of events, which will differ one from another, change agents need to understand the aspirations and feelings of those working in change situations as well as the group processes which bind them together.

Soft systems models of change are, essentially, *planned* approaches to change. This does not mean, however, that they cannot account for unexpected and surprising events. Indeed the requirement to iterate frequently around and across the different phases and stages of the model takes account of the probability that there will be 'changes within changes' occurring. Taken together, hard and soft systems models of change offer those working with change ways of addressing issues in their simplicity and complexity to enhance the work or organisations and the lives of those working in them.

Discussion questions and assignments

1 Debate the pros and cons of using external change agents compared to internal ones.

2 Compare and contrast the HSMC and the OD approach to change.

3 Draw a rich picture of life as experienced by you in your organisation.

References

Ackoff, R. L. (1993), 'The art and science of mess management', in Mabey, C. and Mayon-White, B. (eds), *Managing Change*, London, PCP.

Adler, N. J. (1997), *International Dimensions of Organizational Behavior* (3rd edn), Cincinatti, OH, South-Western College Publishing, ITP.

Alpander, G. G. and Lee, C. R. (1995), 'Culture, strategy and teamwork, the keys to organizational change', *Journal of Management Development*, Vol. 14, No. 8, pp. 4–18.

Argyris, C. (1964) *Integrating the Individual and the Organization*, New York, Wiley.

Argyris, C. (1992) *On Organizational Learning*, Oxford, Blackwell.

Argyris, C. and Schon, D. A. (1996), *Organizational Learning II*, Reading, MA, Addison-Wesley.

Beckhard, R. and Harris, R. T. (1987), *Organizational Transitions, Managing Complex Change* (2nd edn), Reading, MA, Addison-Wesley.

Benjamin, G. and Mabey, C. (1993), 'Facilitating radical change: a case of organization transformation', in Mabey, C. and Mayon-White, B. (eds), *Managing Change* (2nd edn), London, PCP.

The Body Shop Case Study (1995), Kellogg School of Management, Northwestern University, Evanston, IL,

USA and The Body Shop International Plc, West Sussex, UK.

Buchanan, D. and Boddy, D. (1992), *The Expertise of the Change Agent: Public Performance and Backstage Activity*, Hemel Hempstead, Prentice Hall.

Buchanan, D. and McCalman, J. (1989), *High Performance Work Systems: The Digital Experience*, London, Routledge.

Burns, T. and Stalker, G. M. (1961), *The Management of Innovation*, London, Tavistock.

Burnside, R. M. (1991), 'Visioning: building pictures of the future', in Henry, J. and Walker, D. (eds), *Managing Innovation*, London, Sage.

Carnall, C. (1995), *Managing Change in Organizations*, Hemel Hempstead, Prentice Hall.

Checkland, P. (1981), *Systems Thinking, Systems Practice*, Chichester, Wiley.

Clarke, J., Hooper, C. and Nicholson, J. (1997), 'Reversal of fortune', *People Management*, 20 March, pp. 22–6, 29.

Clarke, L. (1994), *The Essence of Change*, Hemel Hempstead, Prentice Hall.

Cummings, T. G. and Worley, C. G. (1997), *Organization Development and Change* (6th edn), Cincinnati, Ohio, South-Western College Publishing.

Easterby-Smith, M., Burgoyne, J. and Araujo, L. (eds) (1999), *Organizational Learning and the Learning Organization: Development in Theory and Practice*, London, Sage.

Elkjaar, B. (1999) 'In search of a social learning theory', in Easterby-Smith, M., Burgoyne, J. and Araujo, L. (eds), *Organizational Learning and the Learning Organization: Development in Theory and Practice*, London, Sage, pp. 75–91.

Farquhar, A., Evans, P. and Tawadey, K. (1989), 'Lessons from practice in managing organizational change', in Evans, P., Doz, E. and Laurent, A. (eds), *Human Resource Management in International Firms: Change, Globalization, Innovation*, London, Macmillan.

Ferlie, E. and Bennett, C. (1993), 'Patterns of strategic change in health care: district health authorities respond to AIDS', in Hendry, J., Johnson, G. and Newton, J. (eds), *Strategic Thinking, Leadership and the Management of Change*, Chichester, Wiley.

Flood, R. L. and Jackson, M. C. (1991), *Creative Problem Solving: Total Systems Intervention*, Chichester, Wiley.

French, W. L. and Bell, C. H., Jr (1990), *Organization Development, Behavioral Science Interventions for Organization Improvement*, Englewood Cliffs, NJ, Prentice Hall.

Goodstein, L. D. and Burke, W. W. (1993), 'Creating successful organization change', in Mabey, C. and Mayon-White, B. (eds), *Managing Change*, London, PCP.

Harrison, R. (1972), 'When power conflicts trigger team spirit', *European Business*, Spring, pp. 27–65.

Hofstede, G. (1980), *Culture's Consequences: International Differences in Work-related Values*, London and Beverley Hills, Sage.

Jack, A. (1997), 'Caste in stone: Challenge to French corporate hierarchies at your peril', *Financial Times* April 10.

Jaegar, A. M. (1986), 'Organization development and national culture: Where's the fit?' *Academy of Management Review*, Vol. 11, No. 1, pp. 178–90.

Johnson, G. (1990), 'Managing strategic change; the role of symbolic action', *British Journal of Management*, Vol. 1. pp. 183–200.

Johnson, G. (1993), 'Processes of managing strategic change', in Mabey, C. and Mayon-White, B. (eds), *Managing Change* (2nd edn), London, PCP.

Johnson, G. and Scholes, K. (1997), *Exploring Corporate Strategy. Texts and Cases* (4th edn), Hemel Hempstead, Prentice Hall.

Jones, P. (1994), 'Which lever do I pull now? – the role of "emergent planning" in managing change', *Organisations & People*, Vol. 1, No. 1, January, pp. 46–9.

Keegan, W. J. (1989), 'International-multinational-global marketing: a typology', Chapter 1 in Keegan, W. J. (ed.), *Global Marketing Management* (4th edn), Englewood Cliffs, NJ, Prentice Hall.

Kirkbride, P. S., Durcan, J. and Obeng, E. D. A. (1994), 'Change in a chaotic post-modern world', *Journal of Strategic Change*, Vol. 3, pp. 151–63.

Kotter, J. P. (1996), *Leading Change*, Boston, MA, Harvard Business School Press.

Laurent, A. (1983), 'The cultural diversity of Western conceptions of management', *International Studies of Management and Organisations*, Vol. XIII, Nos. 1–2, pp. 78–96.

Lewin, K. (1951), *Field Theory in Social Science*, New York, Harper & Row.

Lievegoed, B. (1983), *Man on the Threshold*, Driebergen, p. 75.

Lloyd, B. and Feigen, M. (1997), 'Real change leaders: the key challenge to management today', *Leadership & Organization Development Journal*, Vol. 18, No. 1, pp. 37–40.

Mabey, C. and Pugh, D. (1995), Unit 10, 'Strategies for managing complex change', Course B751, *Managing Development and Change*, Milton Keynes, Open University.

McConkie, M. L. (1993), 'Organization development in the public sector', in Cummings, T. G. and Worley, C. G., *Organization Development and Change* (5th edn), St. Paul, MN, West Publishing Company.

Matsushita, K. (1988), 'The secret is shared', *Manufacturing Engineering*, March, pp. 78–84.

Morgan, G. (1986), *Images of Organization*, London, Sage.

Open University (1985) Unit 8, 'Process', Course T244, *Managing in Organizations*, Milton Keynes, Open University.

Paton, R. A. and McCalman, J. (2000), *Change Management. A Guide to Effective Implementation*, London, Sage.

Pedler, M., Boydell, T. and Burgoyne, J. (1991), *The Learning Company*, London, McGraw-Hill.

Price, C. (1987), 'Culture change – the tricky bit', *Training and Development*, October, pp. 20–2.

Pugh, D. (1986), Block 4, 'Planning and managing change', *Organizational Development*, Milton Keynes, Open University.

Pugh, D. (1993), 'Understanding and managing change', in Mabey, C. and Mayon-White, B. (eds), *Managing Change* (2nd edn), London, PCP.

Schein, E. (1987), *Process Consultation Volume II: Lessons for Managers and Consultants*, Reading, MA, Addison-Wesley.

Senge, P. (1990), *The Fifth Discipline: the Art and Practice of the Learning Organization*, New York, Doubleday Currency.

Smith, B. (1995), 'Not in front of the children: the realities of "involvement" in managing change', *Organisations & People*, Vol. 2, No. 2, pp. 17–20.

Snelson, P. (1996), 'How to "deep six" strategic planning', Nene College of Higher Education/University of Leicester, MBA Speakers' Day.

Stacey, R. (2000*), Strategic Management and Organisational Dynamics: The Challenge to Complexity* (3rd edn), London, Pitman.

Chapter 9

A changing future

The material in this chapter builds on what has been discussed in the book, but takes a more 'futuristic' focus. It is, therefore, to some extent speculative. However, it is hoped that the material discussed will provide an impetus for considering two aspects of organisational change. The first is what organisations of the future might look like. The second is to speculate on the impact that more wide-ranging changes in society will have on people and their attitudes to work. The possible conflicts between the two are addressed with suggestions on some factors which might help to make organisational change a success.

Introduction

The two chapters in Part One examined the way organisations and the context in which they operate have changed throughout time as well as discussing the way political, economic, social and technological changes impact on the way organisations operate today. The concept of organisational change was shown to be heterogeneous in that there are many types of change occurring both sequentially and simultaneously, sometimes predicted and sometimes coming as a 'surprise'.

This picture was elaborated in Part Two by addressing aspects of organisational life which intervene to influence change outcomes in one direction or another. During this discussion, a variety of contrasting ideas on the nature of change and how it should be responded to and managed were advanced. Finally, in Part Three, two major methodologies of change were described. Given all this, it would be ideal if the overall outcome were an all-embracing, widely accepted theory of change with agreed guidelines on 'how to do it'. Unfortunately, this is not the case. This is particularly the case when organisational managers and others working with organisational change attempt to look into the future in the hope of predicting when and how their organisations, in whole or part, should prepare for what comes to pass. The purpose of this final chapter is, therefore, to examine some of the ideas which have been put forward – particularly as the millennium came and went – regarding what the future holds. It addresses issues associated with the way changing demographics, households and families, occupations and employment, education, lifestyles, communities, government and state are likely to influence and change the nature of organisational life, directly or indirectly, in the next decade and beyond. In doing this, and within the conventions of the systems approach described in Chapter 1, it provides a feedback loop and reiteration of what was said there but, in the case of the discussion here, takes a somewhat wider and more speculative perspective.

What is said here may be controversial, it may provoke agreement or disagreement, even though it is grounded in a variety of people's theories, research and opinions. It may lead to frustration in that the issues cannot be dealt with one by one, but interact in a systemic way one with another. In this it mirrors the soft complexity of much of organisational life. It is hoped, however, that it will lead to an improved process of debating the future of organisations and the way they operate, within an ever-changing, only partially predictable and, of itself, 'messy' organisational environment.

Some general trends

In August 1999, the Department of Trade and Industry in the UK published a report entitled *Britain towards 2010: The Changing Business Environment* (*see* Scase, 1999). It is recommended for anyone interested in and working with organisational change and can be ordered free from the DTI. A scenario called 'Foresight 2015' can also be accessed through the Forsight Website.

The report starts with a list of some major trends which are likely to affect industry, lifestyles and social structures and which, in turn, will affect organisations – their strategies, structures, how they are led, employment practices and the need to work with change. Eleven trends are mentioned. These are:

- *Individuality*: a decline in traditional family forms.
- *Choice*: an increase in choice of home, work, leisure.
- *Mobility*: an increase in the mobility of individuals regarding residence, working, and personal relationships.
- *Identity*: increased 'fluidity' in personal identities because of increased mobility and more transient working arrangements, personal relations and leisure.
- *Independence*: increased freedom from traditional obligations leads to more self-centredness, self-indulgence and hedonistic psychologies.
- *Anxiety and risk*: a more rootless society giving rise to feelings of insecurity; society perceived as perhaps high risk and threatening or exciting and challenging.
- *Creativity*: increased focus on self-interest and individuality will encourage personal creativity generating a more innovative society.
- *Globalisation*: increase in the international division of labour with greater global segregation between the developed and underdeveloped economies: Islamic and Christian societies, Russia, Central Europe and Euroland; the challenge to Britain is to become a leading-edge information economy.

- *Information and communication technologies (ICTS)*: increasing capabilities of ICTs leading to the decline in traditional forms of organisation including large public sector as well as commercial and voluntary organisations.
- *Bio-technologies*: genetic engineering; increased ability to control patterns of reproduction, not just sex of babies; technologies to improve health, both physical and psychological.
- *Socio-economic inequalities*: increased polarisation in cultural, educational and material living standards.

This list gives some idea of the tenor of this report. It is not intended to discuss all these in detail here but to discuss, in the context of other predictions, those issues of particular relevance to, and which have implications for, organisational change.

● ● ● ● Demographic changes

It is well known that Britain has an ageing population. According to Scase (1999) in the current decade (first decade of the twenty-first century), the population in Britain, like that of many European countries, will be static and possibly in decline. Kandola (2001) maintains that there will soon be 40 per cent of people who are over 50 years of age with only 5 per cent who are in the 15–19 age group. This implies an ageing population. Over the next 20 years, these trends will bring a fall in the proportion of people under 25 and a large increase in the middle-aged and over-65s.

Consequently, perceptions of what constitutes 'old age' will need to change. To quote Scase (1999):

> Today's over 50s – clad in their jeans, trainers and baseball caps – no longer view themselves as old. ... Middle age is no longer the beginning of the end but the beginning of a thirty-year period of personal enjoyment and self-indulgence.

If this is the case, the focus of much advertising and the design of wanted – rather than needed – goods and services will have to change. Leisure and entertainment industries will have to change orientation from concentrating on the under-35s to those who are older, particularly those who are 'time rich, cash rich'.

Set against this, the costs of caring for the very old, given longer life expectancy, will increase as will the demand for medical services. The increase in the numbers of very old people could drive the further development of ICTs in health care and welfare functions. Through the use of interactive, audio-visual monitoring the elderly could be enabled to live independent lives for longer periods than at present when many elderly people, with no one close by to help them, have to enter residential care.

Associated with these changes is the less known trend in the increasing number of single person households, the increase coming particularly from younger middle-aged people not yet engaged in 'live in' partnerships and especially women in the 15–44 age group as well as older widows given the propensity for men to die at a younger age than women. The institution of marriage in Britain has been losing popularity since 1981 – the Government Actuary Department (1999) predicts that this trend will continue and that by 2011, 31 per cent of women and 39 per cent of men will never have been married. By 2021, the prediction rises to 41 per cent women and 50 per cent men. This does not mean that all these people live alone – cohabiting will gain in popularity. However, statistics produced by the Department of Environment in 1995 predict that, by 2010, single person households will become the predominant household type in Britain, accounting for almost 49 per cent of all households. Alongside these changes, and coupled with the increasing emphasis on occupational and private pensions, there is likely to be a continued rise in the trend towards early retirement, even though in the future, UK women retiring will not draw their state pensions until they are 65 – as men do now.

Changing lifestyles

Many of these trends, including increasing migration in Europe, longer life expectancy and greater frequency of divorce and 'split-ups' among those living together, combine to suggest the need for between 4.4 and 5.5 million additional homes by 2015 (Scase, 1999). If elderly people are enabled to live longer in their own homes, this trend will add to the projected increase in the number of homes needed by single people and other groups just mentioned. Given the limitations on building in country areas, new or refurbished homes are likely to be built on 'brown sites' or in cities and towns leading to urban regeneration with the possibilities of reversing the current decline in inner city life and business. The provision of apartments, both up-market and for low-income single people, may be a significant part of this development. Whatever and wherever this building takes place, it is good news for the construction industry.

The sharp differences in lifestyles between single men and single women, for instance that women are likely to enjoy more intensive and broader social networks and to be more actively involved in leisure, recreation, education and cultural activities than men (*see* ESRC *British Household Panel Study*, 1998), suggest the need to practice gender-based market segmentation with market intelligence taking more account of these categories of consumers for marketing and retailing purposes. Businesses, perhaps small to medium in size, associated with the personal, more individualised requirements of people living on their own (for instance, a decrease in the demand for mass-produced clothes and other goods and corresponding increase in branded 'limited edition' fashion and 'state-of-the-art' household objects) will increase. Fear of crime and the demands for personal security systems will lead to greater demand for interactive communication technologies and household security products such as video surveillance systems.

The past two decades have begun to see changes in the roles of men and women, particularly with regard to domestic and child responsibilities. However,

Scase warns that although gender roles, particularly regarding household tasks, are likely to change with more sharing of domestic duties, any shift in this direction should not be exaggerated. The British Social Attitudes Survey covering 1984 to 1998 suggests that changes of this kind in the past have not been pronounced and, on this basis, are unlikely to be dramatic in the future. In addition, the burden of household responsibilities will continue to be heaviest on working-class women, sometimes as a result of 'serial' personal relationships. Men will continue to be able to avoid their domestic obligations. Where families can look after their longer-living elderly relatives, it is women on whom the majority of this care will fall. Middle-class women are more likely to be able to afford the emerging ICT systems of surveillance and use the Internet to order food deliveries for their elderly relatives than those from low-income families. Single low-income people will not be able to afford to buy and maintain their own home, having to rely on house sharing or low-cost rented accommodation.

Many of these trends – positive and negative – contrast, of course, with those in some other, particularly non-European countries where marriage with children is still the expected and perhaps preferred form of household and where elderly people are looked after by their families. In some countries, the expected life span for many people does not run into 70 years and over. Parker (1998) reports World Bank statistics showing that the number of men and women aged between 15 and 64 years of age in the global workforce increased by 100 per cent over the years from 1965 to 1995. The total number was 2.5 billion in 1995, of whom only 380 million lived in high-income countries. Daniels and Radebaugh (2001, p. 764) say: 'Demographers are nearly unanimous in projecting that populations will grow much faster in emerging economies (China being the exception) than in industrial countries, at least up to the year 2030.'

● ● ● ● Occupational changes

The figure in Illustration 1.4 in Chapter 1 shows the Institute for Employment Research's (2000) predictions regarding the percentage change in occupations of UK workers over the period 1998 to 2009. This suggests an increase in managerial and professional occupations related to a decline in those associated with skilled and semi-skilled manual and clerical tasks.

Two decades ago, the largest proportion of all UK jobs (30 per cent) was to be found in the manufacturing sector. As the millennium approached, this reduced to 17 per cent. The agricultural sector has decreased its share of the labour market over this period from 5 to 2 per cent. Sectors which have increased their hold on the labour market are distribution, hotels and restaurants (18 to 23 per cent); banking, finance and insurance (11 to 19 per cent); and, to a lesser extent, public administration, education, health and other services (24 to 28 per cent) (*see Labour Market and Skills Trends*, February 2000, available free from the UK Department for Education and Employment). According to this report, these trends are likely to continue for the next few years, with the shift in the balance towards the service sector becoming more pronounced.

These statistics relate to organisations in the UK. By contrast, Parker (1998, p. 313) shows by reference to World Bank statistics, that agriculture is still overwhelmingly the dominant occupation for workers in low-income countries. In fact, most of the world's workers are employed in the agricultural sector, fewer in services and fewer still in industry. However, as Western-based organisations become more global in their employment practices as well as in their marketing activities, the number of people in many of these countries involved in manufacturing and service industries is likely to increase with a corresponding decrease of people working on the land.

Changing employment policies and practices

Workforce diversity and the 'war for talent'

Robbins (1996, pp. 61–2) says:

> During the next decade, new worker growth in the United States will be occurring most rapidly among women and Hispanics. This is going to result in reshaping the overall labour force. By the year 2005, women will likely hold 50 percent of all jobs in the United States. ... Minorities will hold more than one out of four jobs. Whilst these small percentage changes may not seem important, they are! They indicate that the white-male working population is aging and the younger faces in organisations will belong to women, African-Americans, Latinos, and Asian-Americans.

Robbins goes on to say that this is happening not just in the United States but across the world:

> Take Western Europe as an example. Eight million legal immigrants and an estimated 2 million illegal immigrants now live in 15 nations of the European Union. A particularly large influx of Muslims and Africans in recent years has been changing the religious and racial composition of these countries. And in Asia, the big challenge in organisations is adjusting to the rapid increase in the number of women employees, especially in the managerial ranks. Although a distinct minority, women are making significant inroads into managerial positions throughout Asia ... even in Japan, long hostile to corporate women, females are increasing their presence in management.

With respect to Britain, Scase (1999) reports projected economic activity rates for women by 2006. The rates for women aged 25 to 54 and 60 to 64 years are projected to follow a rising trend, which has been observed since 1984. Economic activity rates for age groups 16–19 and 55–59 are projected as relatively stable. In summary, by 2006, approaching 80 per cent of women in Britain in the 25 to 54 age group will be economically active. Of particular interest is the rise in economic activity among women in the 60 to 64 age group – from 20 per cent in 1984 to 30 per cent in 1996 with a projected rise to 35 per cent in 2006.

Since 1970 an increasing proportion of women have obtained academic, professional and managerial qualifications and more and more are entering the medical, legal and management professions. However, Maitland (2000a) points out that only 5 per cent of directors of FTSE 100 companies are women. A *Financial Times* article of 20 January 2000 says: 'Women are still alien beings in certain parts of the City of London.' Even in the USA, where almost half of middle management is female only 13 per cent of women are offered foreign postings (see Maitland, 2000b). By contrast, the National Management Salary Survey (1998) reports a rising trend in the percentage of managers who are women – although the slope of the graphs is less steep as the level of management responsibility rises. The issue is the length of time that will need to pass before men and women are represented equally in high-level management and professional jobs and whether women will decide 'enough is enough' and set up organisations of their own. This is a similar situation for people from ethnic minority groups. Statistics quoted by Kandola (2001) indicate that although the percentage of graduates from ethnic minority groups is double the percentage of these groups in the general population, their chances, currently, of reaching the higher levels of organisations are low.

All this is in spite of issues such as the overall lack of population growth in Britain, coupled with fewer people active in the labour market, which are perceived by some as leading to what Kandola terms the 'war for talent'. In response to this concern, employment practices, which favour white men in middle and upper management roles, as well as in many of the higher paid sectors of industry, will need to change. Kandola maintains that there is 'lots of talent out there' and the war for talent will only continue to exist if employers continue to 'fish in fished out waters'. By this he means fishing in talent pools which exclude women and people from ethnic minority groups who are as well, if not more, qualified (54 per cent women and 13 per cent ethnic minorities which is double the number of people of ethnic minority origins in the general population) as white men. As many other European countries are also likely to face the perceived war for talent, the pressure will be on to encourage emigration from developing countries – although only those 'chosen' for their particular skills and abilities are likely to be welcomed. By contrast, jobs can be exported to developing countries where there is an ample supply of labour, a policy which has the advantage of being able to hire workers (frequently well qualified) at lower wages. Alternatively, or additionally, the push to adopting robotics and other labour saving devices will strengthen.

If employers and managers are to meet the increasing demands for knowledge workers and strive towards operating learning organisations, as discussed in earlier chapters, they will need to change their employment policies and practices not only to attract but also to retain, women and employees from minority groups. Difference among employees is something to be welcomed rather than something which is a matter for suspicion. People feel comfortable with other people who are like themselves in looks and attitude. However, homogeneity among employees is not a recipe for high organisational performance now or in the future, given that creativity and innovation are keys to organisational success.

Organisations will need to change to ensure they employ people of varied talents and skills and living/behaviour patterns if they are to meet the changing needs of the new sets of customers which demographic and lifestyle changes will bring. This in turn is likely to require modified ways of managing personnel and perhaps offering more flexible ways of working to suit the needs of those groups who cannot or do not want to take up full-time, five days a week working out of the home. In other words, offering a variety of patterns of employment.

Changing patterns of employment

A report entitled *1971–2006 – Review of the Economy and Employment* (1997/98) by the Institute of Employment Research at the University of Warwick suggests that the percentage of all employment taken up by part-time work and self-employment will increase respectively from 25 per cent to 30 per cent and from 12 per cent to 15 per cent in the next ten years. For instance, the results of a survey done by Bacon and Woodrow (1999) (*see* Bakhshi, 1999) show that the number of people in manual occupations becoming self-employed increased by more than 450 per cent between 1997 and 1998 and over the same period, self-employment among managerial and professional workers grew by almost 300 per cent. Small firms make up 93 per cent of all enterprises in the European Union – almost one-third of the workforce. In conjunction with these changes in employment patterns, many people are seeking more flexible ways of working, including part-time, sessional, contract and home working.

Flexible working

It is not easy to define 'flexible working'. For this discussion it is probably sufficient to define it fairly loosely as patterns of employment which do not conform to the standard full-time working week of 40 hours or so carried out over typically five-day periods away from the home.

There are advantages and disadvantages for both employers and employees in working more flexibly. From the employer's viewpoint, it offers flexibility in managing workforce requirements as the demand for products and services varies over the year and day to day. From the employees' viewpoint, non-standard working offers flexibility of working to fit in with family and other commitments. Given the continuing reliance on women to carry out domestic duties, including the care of children and elderly dependants, women, in particular, welcome the opportunities offered by flexible working to fit work into other aspects of their lives.

Men also seem to want more flexible working arrangements, in this case, working from home. An article in the *Financial Times* entitled 'Men outnumber women in working from home' (Bennett, 2000) reports on a UK government survey from the Skills and Enterprise Executive (2001) into work–life balance which shows that of the 7500 employees questioned, 24 per cent of those allowed to work from home were men and 16 per cent women. When the respondents were asked if they would like to work more at home, 38 per cent of men and 33 per cent of women said they would. By contrast, employers did not, overwhelmingly, appear to favour home working in that, of the 2500 companies surveyed, only 22 per cent allow staff to work from home. These figures mask findings that most people who get a chance to work from home are managers and professionals and that employers perceive working from home mainly as exceptional or an occasional arrangement.

One of the downsides of flexible working is that it does not always attract good pay rates and opportunities for career advancement are variable even if pay is good. Commitment to an organisation by its employees is still frequently evidenced by long working hours and 'visibility' at the workplace, even though the employees themselves do not see flexible working arrangements for others as particularly unfair (Bennett, 2000). Non-standard working can offer personal liberation. However, the pessimistic view is that some of these arrangements will simply lead to a greater proportion of low-paid jobs undertaken mainly by women, school leavers, students and older, pre-retired men. For instance, the decline in the number of small shops in favour of large supermarkets, the increase in call centres and the growing need for care assistants to care for an ageing population have all combined to introduce replacement but still part-time, low-paid jobs.

An accepted academic expert in this field, Cary Cooper (2001), in an article entitled 'Careers, work and life: ways of finding a better balance', argues that the defining characteristics of the 1990s were a short-term contract culture, with outsourcing, downsizing and *long working hours*. More flexible working, then, does not necessarily mean shorter working time as evidenced by the government survey discussed by Bennett, which indicated that the most commonly cited reason for wanting to work from home was 'to get more work done' rather than to fit work more easily around other responsibilities. Cooper argues forcibly that long working hours adversely affect the health and well-being of workers and their families. What is more, some types of flexible working (e.g. short-term contracts, seasonal working, working on an outsourced basis) engender high levels of job insecurity. In spite of this, Cooper (2001) sets out a variety of ways in which flexible working, rather than exploitation, can help employees to address their work–life balance issues at the same time as helping organisations to recruit and retain people of talent, whichever gender, social or ethnic grouping they come from.

A quotation from Scase (1999, p. 55) is an example of how some local government authorities have responded to their communities and provided work opportunities to meet the need of their employees. He says:

> New demands from communities will have implications for local government. The use of ICTs will encourage the adoption of new employment and work practices. Some local authorities are already ahead of many private sector organisations in adopting new management philosophies. They have embarked on strategic outsourcing and sub-contract many of their activities. Many have adopted 'family friendly' employment policies encouraging part-time and flexi-work, as well as job sharing. Some already operate as 'network' organisations, with a small core of purchasers negotiating quality control with

external providers. They are also encouraging homeworking, allowing employees to operate in virtual teams.

An entrepreneurial economy

In the light of the discussion thus far on the changes brought through changing demographics and lifestyles as well as the desire for different kinds of working arrangement, if industries and the organisations within them fail to respond to (a) the expectations of an increasingly educated workforce, many of whom are single persons who may wish to make work their central life interest and (b) couples who are interested in balancing work and home, then many people will be encouraged to set up their own business. As evidence that this may already be happening, an article in *Management Today* (*see* Gracie, 1998) reports that women founded almost one-third of all new businesses in 1997. A reasonable projection from the Bacon and Woodrow (1999) survey (*see* 'Changing patterns of employment' earlier in this chapter) is that this trend will continue but with significant differences across economic sectors. According to Scase (1999, p. 26): 'The numbers of self-employed will be greatest in the media and entertainment industries, hotel, catering and leisure, and in the financial services sector.' In line with the desire for more flexible forms of employment, many of these self-employed people will be on fixed-term, performance-related contracts – probably spending much of their time *as if* employed but responsible for their own employment costs. People such as this will be responsible for their own financial planning and pension costs thus relieving the organisations they work for of 'overhead' costs and their administration. The development of ICTs has assisted people to set up their own business and will continue to be a significant aspect of this. Current disadvantages of being a particular sex or age, coming from an ethnic minority origin or being physically challenged can, for some jobs, be overcome with the assistance of ICTs, allowing home working and communications regardless of distance. To summarise:

> These trends will lead to a more varied and flexible labour market in Britain. Long-term careers and employment in a small number of large corporations are likely to decline as employees are forced to be more adaptive, shifting between companies with greater frequency as well as embarking upon periods of self-employment. Entrepreneurship will be more pronounced as companies continue to outsource many of their corporate functions. At the same time, a more self-reliant and 'independent' culture among those who are technically and intellectually expert will reinforce this trend. (Scase, 1999, p. 26)

● ● ● ● Operating virtually

The discussion in the previous section indicates a trend towards an entrepreneurial economy in Britain. The discussion in Chapter 3 of a move in some sectors to organising 'virtually' reflects the increasing emphasis on the need for workers whose value lies in their knowledge and ability to innovate in an increasingly global economy. A thoughtful article by Ridderstrale (2000) entitled 'Business moves beyond bureaucracy' argues that organisations need new structures as the requirement for greater creative thinking and knowledge spreads. Ridderstrale refers to a study by McKinsey, which found that some 20 per cent of world output is open to global competition. The forecast is that in 30 years the percentage will be 80 per cent. He goes on to say: 'It is in Bangalore, India, where 140,000 IT engineers are challenging the hegemony of the West' (p. 14). The recent rise of ICT companies shows how conventional attitudes to employment and promotion of non-white males have been bypassed. In Silicon Valley, the home of so many telecommunications companies, employment of women, immigrants and people below 35 years of age is greater than employment of these groups in traditional US companies.

In the future, hierarchical management structures will be less evident. The management of intellectual capital will require skills that nurture creativity and innovation in workforces rather than compliance as in the past. The regimes of control and command will no longer suffice. In a world of outsourcing and contract working, managers will need skills to plan and co-ordinate 'associates' working in different parts of the world.

Ridderstrale (2000, pp. 14–15) suggests four ways that organisations can depart from the bureaucratic model. The first is to *flatten* the organisation, not by removing the middle management layers but by flattening from middle management up and down. The second way is to introduce *flexibility* in structures. This means moving away from vertically structured organisations to ones structured in such a way that people can move across functional and geographical borders. Third, managers and others need to know who can do what, where and how. This is reminiscent of organisations being learning organisations. It means 'the development of an inventory of core competences and "core competents", the people who make the competences happen'. Finally, Ridderstrale talks about the need for organisations to be more *tribal*. This means that information is held among all members of the organisation. The organisation as a tribe shares values, vision, attitudes, culture and norms but lets individuals and groups find best ways of achieving the vision. Ridderstrale maintains that this starts by hiring people with the 'right' attitudes. Interestingly, the by-line for another article by Kehoe (2000, p. 20) asserts: 'In the new economy (i.e. the "internet economy"), changing your attitude is more important than changing your software.'

Scase (1999, p. 27) says: 'Organisations of the future will be heavily dependent on information management. Supply chains will be characterised by co-operative relations between companies through joint ventures, strategic alliances and partnerships.' Employees of, and contractors to, virtual organisations will not work 'at the organisation', so smaller premises will be required. Organisations will make considerable cost savings in this way, but will have to provide the means for workers to come together at regular periods to socialise and to reinforce organisational cultures and values. All this, however, implies a change in the contract of commitment between organisations and those they employ – whether directly or indirectly in a plethora of different ways.

The changing psychological contract

Scase (1999, p. 29) says:

> In the workplace of the future, employees will have very different psychological expectations. Most employees will consider their organisational commitment to be temporary. They will have few expectations of long-term careers and will tend to regard employment contracts as short-term negotiated arrangements.

Sparrow (2000, p. 202) says, in the abstract to an article about the future of work:

> It is argued that we shall witness fundamental transitions in forms of work organisation. Initially, this will not compensate for the deterioration in the psychological contract that has been experienced by those who have lived through an era of downsizing. However, it will raise the need to develop new competencies to cope with the changes in work design.

Not everyone would agree with statements such as these about the changing workplace. However, discussions throughout the book and evidence from a number of 'future thinkers' appear to be sufficient to warrant a closer look at what this means in more detail, both for organisations and the way they operate and the people who work within and with them. As this discussion begins to draw to a close, the thoughts of a number of eminent academics and researchers, writing at the millennium, have been chosen to represent much of what is being said and to form the basis for speculation as to where organisations and those who work with them go from here.

The first of these articles is by Miles, Snow and Miles (2000). They start their article with a quotation from William E. Coyne, Senior Vice-President for Research and Development at 3M:

> Most modern companies now recognise that the best way to increase corporate earnings is through top-line growth, and the best route to top-line growth is through innovation.

The basic message of Miles *et al.* is that in the currently emerging era of continuous innovation, knowledge is the key asset whose exploitation will determine the success of many organisations. The issue which challenges them is, however, that they perceive no existing organisational model which is sufficiently worked out to ensure the facilitation of innovation. For example, they say (p. 301): 'Innovation cannot be managed hierarchically because it depends on knowledge being offered voluntarily rather than on command.' Furthermore, they maintain that approaches to facilitating innovation require investments that often appear to be unjustified within current organisational accounting systems.

Their argument is that models of organising which involve standardisation and, more recently, customisation, which have required, respectively, 'meta-capabilities' of co-ordination and delegation, are not longer sufficient for innovation to flourish. This is because organisations of the future need not just knowledge but knowledge generation and transfer, which in their turn require social interaction and exchange between organisational members. The logical outcome of this, they argue, is that *collaboration* is the key to innovation – what Miles *et al.* call the new 'meta-capability'. Acknowledging that collaboration is not entirely natural in many organisational cultures currently prevailing, they suggest three conditions for collaboration to happen:

- People need *time* to discuss ideas, reflect, listen and engage in a host of activities that might produce fresh ideas.
- They need to develop strong bonds of *trust* between each other – a willingness to expose one's views without the fear of being exploited and to probe more deeply for new insights and perspectives.
- People need a sense of *territory*, that is a 'stake' (marking one's place) in the outcomes of the collaborative process. These visible stakes might be: stock ownership, stock options, visible awards, collegial recognition and so on.

In organisational terms, they also maintain that the organisational model of the future will go beyond the functional, divisional, matrix and network organisations (such as those discussed in Chapter 3) and will involve alliances, spin-offs and federations – that is organisations operating more in virtual structures, with large degrees of self-management and self-directing teams.

Other writers have argued in similar ways to Miles *et al.* and many of them are discussed in Chapters 3 and 4. However, much of the tenor of the article by Miles *et al.* assumes a style of leadership which is participative, caring of followers and which recognises the role of everyone in the efforts to make any organisation successful. This is exemplified in Bennis's (2000) article: 'The end of leadership: Exemplary leadership is impossible without the full inclusion, initiatives and cooperation of followers' and in McGill and Slocum Jr's (1998) article: 'A *little* leadership please?' All these writers argue for the demise of 'top-down' leadership. Bennis (p. 73) says: 'The most urgent projects require the coordinated contributions of many talented people working together' and (p. 34): 'No change can occur without willing and committed followers.' He maintains that it is only in the solving of relatively simple technical problems that top-down leadership is effective. For the resolution of 'adaptive', complex, messy problems many people at all levels of the organisation must be involved and mobilised. A couple of further quotations (p. 76) will suffice to give the flavour of what Bennis has to say:

> Post-bureaucratic organisation requires a new kind of alliance between leaders and the led. Today's organisations are evolving into federations, networks, clusters, cross-functional teams, temporary systems, ad hoc tasks, lattices, modules, matrices – almost anything but pyramids with their obsolete TOPdown leadership.

> The new reality is that intellectual capital, brain power, knowhow, human imagination has supplanted capital as the critical success factor and leaders will have to learn an entirely new set of skills.

It is sufficient to note that McGill and Slocum Jr express their view of leadership in the title of their article 'A *little* leadership, please?' They argue for models of leadership which are 'non-positional, team-based, or empowering' (p. 40). It is not intended to go into the details of the full content of McGill and Slocum Jr's discussion here. It is certainly worth reading, however, in the hope of providing a counterbalance to the many articles lauding the 'hero' leader who, as it happens, is in most cases male and, in Western countries, white.

A paradox

A look back at the list of general trends for the future posed at the beginning of this chapter and a summary of the discussion so far paints a scenario as follows. On the one hand, there is a picture of people becoming more individualistic, independent, hedonistic, living for some of their adult lives alone, communicating increasingly through ICTs and with more choice in respect of the lifestyle they choose. This attitude to life and work is reinforced by the increase in 'non-standard' working which is frequently insecure and which does not engender organisational commitment. On the other hand, there are business 'philosophers' and academics and, to a much smaller extent, managers arguing for more organic, network and virtual organisations which require collaborative attitudes and behaviour on the part of their workforce, so that innovation – which is seen as essential for organisations to survive and prosper – can flourish. This implies a commitment to the principles of empowerment of subordinate staff.

However, in spite of the emphasis put on empowering employees to work in organic, network and virtual forms of organisations many large organisations continue to conform to hierarchical principles of structure and accountability as described in Chapter 3. The skills which managers need to be successful in this type of organisation are not those which comfortably agree with the principles of empowering subordinate levels of staff. Even if empowering abilities are developed, they are unlikely to be rewarded or acknowledged. Behaving in empowering ways does not support the culture and processes that make these managers successful. Many of the characteristics – such as showing determination, drive/energy, leading from the front, objective decision making and personal achievement – are not among the key empowering characteristics.

Chapters 4 and 8 discussed the concepts of the learning organisation and organisational learning. Schein (1999), in an article entitled 'Empowerment, coercive persuasion and organisational learning: do they connect?' notes how these concepts, together with those of 'generative' or double-loop learning, require employees to develop new thinking skills, new concepts and points of view and cognitively to redefine old categories and change standards of judgement. Such changes increase individuals' capacity to deal with situations in new ways and lay the basis for developing radically new skills.

By comparison with single-loop learning, which socialises individuals into specific attitudes, double-loop learning requires collaboration, but also a change in values and assumptions about how the world operates and what is good and what is bad. According to Schein, however, requiring individuals to learn to think and behave in these kinds of ways is essentially asking them to put themselves through transformational culture change – coming as they frequently have from organisational cultures suited more to traditional bureaucratic norms of command and control – not least, because these types of systems discourage creativity and innovation. He goes on to say (p. 7): 'But paradoxically, when we speak of "culture change" in organisations we are typically demanding levels of cognitive redefinition that can probably only be achieved by some version of coercive persuasion.' This is because these individuals are being asked to *disconfirm* what they have believed is *right* – what they have been used to doing for much of their organisational life.

This seems a worrying scenario if there is a belief, as Miles *et al.*, Bennis and others assert, in alternative, more satisfying and effective ways of running organisations. However, throughout this book, no one has argued that change is easy. The final section, therefore, draws together some threads in the hope that change can be seen as something which can and should be welcomed and which makes for an interesting life.

The multiple paths to change

In May 1996, the journal *Human Relations* brought out a special issue entitled 'Organizational change in corporate settings' which is recommended reading for anyone interested in investigating further different theories of change and their relationship to each other. What is interesting in the context of the present discussion is that all the articles, taken together, suggest there are many ways of understanding and managing change.

This is a view which has surfaced throughout the book and particular reference was made to it in Chapters 2 and 6 in the discussion of the work of Dunphy and Stace (1993) and Strebel (1996) who argue that different change contexts require different change policies and practices. In a later article, Stace (1996) refers to organisational contingencies and paths to change, concepts which chime with Strebel's advice on how to choose the right path to change, depending on the change context. Thus, for these scholars and others, provided the various contingent factors can be identified, *choosing* a path to change becomes uncontentious.

However, the idea of *choice* may not be what it seems. This is because contingency approaches to change assume, in the main, that change can be *planned*. However, as the discussion of Quinn's (1980) and Wilson's (1992) work in Chapter 2 shows, this is not always the case, as change emerges in ways that are frequently unexpected. In addition, even if one particular path has been chosen, a multitude of influences can arise to deflect both its end point and the means of getting there. What is more, the issue of planned change does not necessarily include the issue of whether change should progress incrementally or take place through more radical transformational means. Much depends on whether the world is seen as reasonably predictable, unpredictable or verging on chaos – in other words, whether the world is seen through the eyes of what Kirkbride, Durcan and Obeng (1994) term the modernist, sophisticated modernist or post-modernist views of change.

Briefly, a *modernist* view of the world would see change as incremental, evolutionary, constantly developing, following a linear path and worked out according to a known recipe about what should change and how. Thus modernists tend to believe in change models based on simple cause and effect: if the right levers are pulled in relation to desired outcomes, those outcomes should surely follow.

A *sophisticated modernist* view of the world would see change as transformational, revolutionary, periodic, following a circular path (i.e. 'moving in a complex and dynamic fashion from emerging strategy to deliberate strategy and back again' (Kirkbride *et al.*, p. 157)) and one where the end point can change as the change process unfolds. As a result, this view recognises that the world does not stand still for long, hence the requirement for an approach to change which, according to Mintzberg (1990), creates change in response to emerging strategy.

The *postmodernist* view of change is best summed up in the words of Kirkbride *et al.* (pp. 158–9):

> The post-modern world can … be seen as one characterised by randomness and chaos, by a lack of certainty, by a plethora of competing views and voices, by complex temporalities, and where organisations are unable to produce recipes for dealing with the unstable environment.

Others write similarly:

> In essence, the post-modernist approach rejects the notions of progress, linearity and regular patterning. Change can occur in any direction at any time, which itself could be conceived of in new ways such as 'spiral time'.
>
> (Burrell, 1992; Filicove and Filipec, 1986)

A cursory examination of some of today's organisations, and those in the future, will show that there is 'truth' in all these views of change – the 'trick' is to know when and where one or the other is current. For instance, in limited, constrained situations, a modernist view of change may be most appropriate and might loosely be linked to the hard systems model of change which implies transition rather than transformation and planned rather than emergent change.

The version of an OD model of change presented in the previous chapter is more congruent with a sophisticated modernist view of the world – provided the presence of continuous feedback loops is stressed and it is recognised that the vision and its associated change goals are not fixed – in the sense that the change process is never complete.

The postmodernist view of change does not easily attach itself to any recognisable model of change. What it does point towards, however, is a model of organisation which is organic, flexible, niche market oriented, where jobs are highly de-differentiated, de-demarcated and multi-skilled in a context of employment relationships based on subcontracting and networking (*see* Clegg, 1990 and the discussion of network and virtual organisations in Chapter 3). Change, in this context, could take on any number of faces and forms.

And so ...

Given what this chapter has said, successful change is more likely if the following happens. First, there is the need for continuous surveillance of the internal and external organisational environments as well as the temporal environment for, as pointed out in Chapter 1, time itself is a cause for change. Second, there is the need for change managers and facilitators to understand the characteristics of situations giving rise to change and be familiar with the different presenting characteristics so as not to think incremental change is appropriate when nothing but transformational change will do and vice versa. Finally, planning is all well and good, but success is more likely when plans remain flexible even to the extent of contemplating changes of vision, mission or purpose as time unfolds.

In summary, although change can be planned, it quite frequently simply emerges. Whether planned or emergent, it takes a number of different forms, each of which requires a different type of action. While there is no one best way to achieve successful organisational change, making efforts to understand the wide variety of change situations and to be familiar with the different characteristics of change itself will help organisations and their members negotiate appropriate paths to change and, therefore, face the future with some degree of confidence.

● ● ● ● To conclude ...

Change is about nothing if it is not about persistence. This means persisting in the face of an ultra-unstable environment; persisting in the face of systems which are built for stability rather than change; persisting in the face of plans which are out of date as soon as they are formed. It means applying the same principles to people as are applied to 'things' – that is, the knowledge that nothing is perfect. This means recognising that people will act in infuriating and annoying ways but that, when necessary, will bring the genius of their humanity to solve apparently insoluble problems. Change is not easy but it can be interesting. It is certainly worth the journey even if the place of arrival is surprising.

References

Adler, N. J. (1997), *International Dimensions of Organizational Behavior* (3rd edn), Cincinnati, OH, South Western College Publishing, ITP.

Bakshi, V. (1999), 'Financial products "must fit flexible work patterns" ', *Financial Times*, 10 February, p. 9.

Beer, M. and Nohria, N. (2000), 'Cracking the code of change', *Harvard Business Review*, May–June, pp. 133–41.

Bennett, R. (2000), 'Men outnumber women in working from home', *Financial Times*, 30 October.

Bennis, W. (2000), 'The end of leadership: exemplary leadership is impossible without full inclusion, initiatives, and cooperation of followers', *Organizational Dynamics*, pp. 71–80.

Brockner, J. (2000) 'Change: success in the detail', *Financial Times Mastering Management*, 30 October, pp.8–10.

Burdett, D. (1996), ' "Empowerment" defined', *Occupational Psychologist*, No. 28, April, pp. 33–4.

Burrell, G. (1992), 'Back to the future: time and organization', in Reed, M. and Hughes, M. (eds), *Rethinking Organization: New Directions in Organization Theory and Analysis*, London, Sage.

Clegg, S. R. (1990), *Modern Organization: Organization Studies in the Postmodern World*, London, Sage.

Cooper, C. (2001), 'Careers, work and life: ways of finding a better balance', *Financial Times Mastering Management*, 8 January, pp. 12–13.

Cummings, T. G. and Worley, C. G. (1993), *Organization Development and Change* (5th edn), St Paul, MN, West Publishing Company.

Daniels, J. D. and Radebaugh, L. H. (2001), *International Business: Environments and Operations* (9th edn), Upper Saddle River, NJ, Prentice Hall.

Department of Environment (1995) *Projections of Household in England to 2016*.

Dunphy, D. and Stace, D. (1993), 'The strategic management of corporate change', *Human Relations*, Vol. 46, No. 8, pp. 905–20.

Ekvall, G. (1991), 'The organizational culture of idea-management: a creative climate for the management of ideas', in Henry, J. and Walker, D. (eds), *Managing Innovation*, London, Sage.

ESRC (1998) *British Household Panel Survey*.

Filicove, B. and Filipec, J. (1986), 'Society and concepts of time', *International Social Sciences Journal*, Vol. 107, pp. 19–32.

Financial Times (2000), 'Women are still alien beings in certain parts of the City of London', *Financial Times*, 20 January.

French, W. L. and Bell, C. H. (1990), *Organization Development: Behavioral Science Interventions for Organization Improvement*, Englewood Cliffs, NJ, Prentice Hall.

Gersick, C. J. G. (1991), 'Revolutionary change theories: a multilevel exploration of the punctuated equilibrium paradigm', *Academy of Management Review*, Vol. 16, pp. 10–36.

Government Actuary's Department (1999), 'Marital status projections', *1996 Populations Projections*, Government Actuary's Department, New King's Beam House, 22 Upper Ground, London SE1 9RJ or http://www.gad.uk

Gracie, S. (1998), 'In the company of women', *Management Today*, June.

Gratton, L. and Pearson, J. (1993), 'Empowering leaders: are they being developed?' Occupational Psychology Conference, January.

Guildford, J. P. (1959), 'Traits in creativity', in Anderson, H. H. (ed.), *Creativity and its Cultivation*, New York, Wiley.

Harrison, R. (1970), 'Choosing the depth of organizational intervention', *Journal of Applied Behavioral Science*, Vol. 6, pp. 181–202.

Hayes, J. and Allison, C. W. (1994), 'Cognitive style and its relevance for management practice', *British Journal of Management*, Vol. 5, pp. 53–71.

Henry, J. (1991), 'Making sense of creativity', in Henry, J. (ed.), *Creative Management*, London, Sage.

Henry, J. (1994), Block 1, 'Perspective', in *Creative Management*, Milton Keynes, Open University.

Hofstede, G. (1980), *Culture's Consequences: International Differences in Work-related Values*, London and Beverly Hills, Sage.

Institute of Employment Research (1997/98) *1971–2006 – Review of the Economy and Employment*, University of Warwick.

Jaegar, A. M. (1986), 'Organization development and national culture: Where's the fit?' *Academy of Management Review*, Vol. 11, No. 1, pp. 178–90.

Kandola, B. (2001), 'The future of diversity', British Psychological Annual Conference, Glasgow, 28 March–1 April.

Keegan, W. J. (1989), 'International-multinational-global marketing: a typology', Chapter 1 in Keegan, W. J. (ed.), *Global Marketing Management* (4th edn), Englewood Cliffs, NJ, Prentice Hall.

Kehoe, L. (2000), 'Silicon power with added value', *Financial Times*, 8 November, p. 20.

Kirkbride, P. S., Durcan, J. and Obeng, E. D. A. (1994), 'Change in a chaotic world', *Journal of Strategic Change*, Vol. 3, pp. 151–63.

Kirton, M. (1976), 'Adaptors and innovators: a description and measure', *Journal of Applied Psychology*, Vol. 61, No. 5, pp. 622–9.

Kirton, M. (1984), 'Adaptors and innovators – why new initiatives get blocked', *Long Range Planning*, Vol. 17, No. 2, pp. 137–43.

Kluckhohn, J. P. and Strodtbeck, F. L. (1961), *Variations in Value Orientations*, Evanston, IL, Row, Peterson.

Kuratko, D. F. (1995), 'Developing entrepreneurship within organizations is today's challenge',

Entrepreneurship, Innovation and Change, Vol. 4, No. 2, pp. 99–104.

Laughlin, R. C. (1991), 'Environmental disturbances and organizational transitions and transformations: some alternative models', *Organization Studies*, Vol. 12, No. 2, pp. 209–32.

Laurent, R. C. (1991), 'Environmental disturbances and organizational transitions and transformations: some alternative models', *Organization Studies*, Vol. 12, No. 2, pp. 209–32.

Leiba, S. and Hardy, C. (1994), 'Employee empowerment: a seductive misnomer?' in Hardy, C. (ed.), *Managing Strategic Action: Mobilizing Change: Concepts, Readings and Cases*, London, Sage.

McAleer, N. (1991), 'The roots of inspiratiton', in Henry, J. (ed.), *Creative Management*, London, Sage.

McGill, M. E. and Slocum, Jr J. W. (1998), 'A *little* leadership, please?' *Organizational Dynamics*, Vol. 26, No. 3, pp. 39–49.

Maitland, A. (2000a) 'Women plan change of make-up in boardrooms: only 5 per cent of FTSE 100 directors are female, but campaigners seek to eliminate all-male culture', *Financial Times*, 7 November.

Maitland, A. (2000b) 'America's gender gap travels abroad', *Financial Times*, 20 October.

Majaro, S. (1988), *The Creative Gap*, London, Longman.

Miles, R. E., Snow, C. and Miles, G. (2000), 'The Future.org', *Long Range Planning*, 33, pp. 300–21.

Mintzberg, H. (1990), 'Strategy formation: schools of thought', in Frederickson, J. (ed.), *Perspectives on Strategic Management*, New York, Harper Business, pp. 105–235.

Parker, B. (1998), *Globalization and Business Practice Managing Across Boundaries*, London, Sage.

Quinn, J. B. (1980), 'Managing strategic change', *Sloan Management Review*, Vol. 21, No. 4, pp. 3–20.

Rajagopalan, N. and Rasheed, A. M. A. (1995), 'Incremental models of policy formulation and non-incremental changes: critical review and synthesis', *British Journal of Management*, Vol. 6, No. 4, pp. 289–302.

Ridderstrale, J. (2000), 'Business moves beyond bureaucracy', *Financial Times Mastering Management*, 6 November, pp. 14–15.

Robbins, S. P. (1996), *Organizational Behavior: Concepts, Controversies, Applications*, Englewood Cliffs, NJ, Prentice Hall.

Robbins, S. P. (2001), *Organizational Behavior,* Upper Saddle River, NJ, Prentice Hall.

Sathe, V. (1988), 'From surface to deep corporate entrepreneurship', *Human Resource Management*, Winter, pp. 389–411.

Scase, R. (1999) *Britain towards 2010: The Changing Business Environment*, Department of Trade and Industry, August.

Schein, E. (1999), 'Empowerment, coercive persuasion and organizational learning: do they connect?' *The Learning Organization*, Vol. 6, No. 4, pp. 1–11.

Skills and Enterprise Executive (2000), *Labour Market & Skills Trends 2000*, Department for Education and Employment, SEN 373, Crown Copyright.

Skills and Enterprise Executive (2001), 'Get a life, get a work life balance', Department for Education and Employment, SEN 399, Crown Copyright.

Smith, B. (1995), 'Not in front of the children: the realities of "involvement" in managing change', *Organisations & People*, Vol. 2, No. 2, pp. 17–20.

Sparrow, P. R. (2000), 'New employee behaviours, work designs and forms of work organization. What is in store for the future of work?' *Journal of Managerial Psychology*, Vol. 15, No. 3, pp. 202–18.

Stace, D. (1996), 'Dominant ideologies, strategic change, and sustained performance', *Human Relations*, Vol. 49, No. 5, pp. 553–70.

Strebel, P. (1996), 'Choosing the right path', Mastering Management, Part 14, *Financial Times*.

Williams, H. (1996), *The Essence of Managing Groups and Teams*, Hemel Hempstead, Prentice Hall.

Wilson, D. (1992), *A Strategy of Change, Concepts and Controversies in the Management of Change*, London, Routledge.

Author index

(Please note that the page numbers in brackets indicate end of chapter reference pages)

Subject index